DEBATING T

Debating the Holocaust

A New Look at Both Sides

By Prof. Dr. Thomas Dalton

Castle Hill Publishers
P.O. Box 243, Uckfield, TN22 9AW, UK
March 2017

HOLOCAUST HANDBOOKS, Volume 32:
Thomas Dalton:
Debating the Holocaust: A New Look at Both Sides.
3rd, slightly corrected edition.
Uckfield, East Sussex: CASTLE HILL PUBLISHERS
PO Box 243, Uckfield, TN22 9AW, UK
March 2017

ISBN10: 1-59148-178-3 (print edition)
ISBN13: 978-1-59148-178-2 (print edition)
ISSN: 1529-7748

Published by CASTLE HILL PUBLISHERS
Manufactured worldwide

© 2009, 2015, 2017 by Thomas Dalton

Distribution:
Castle Hill Publishers, PO Box 243
Uckfield, TN22 9AW, UK
shop.codoh.com

Set in Times New Roman

www.HolocaustHandbooks.com

Cover Illustration: Left, top to bottom: John C. Ball, Friedrich P. Berg, Arthur R. Butz, Robert Faurisson, Jürgen Graf, David Irving, Carlo Mattogno, Germar Rudolf. Right, top to bottom: Wolfgang Benz, Christopher R. Browning, Martin J. Gilbert, Deborah E. Lipstadt, Raul Hilberg, Franciszek Piper, Michael B. Shermer, Robert J. van Pelt.

Table of Contents

	Page
Author's Preface to the Second Edition	9
Introduction	11
PART I SITUATING THE HOLOCAUST DEBATE	**19**
Chapter 1: The Great Debate	**21**
The Core of Revisionism	26
Four Myths	28
Who's Who in the Debate	33
And in the Other Corner	35
Chapter 2: Truth vs. Lies	**39**
The Traditional Story	40
"Shocking and Strange"	42
A Question of Evidence	46
The Nuremberg Trials	47
Chapter 3: On the Origin, and Future, of the 'Six Million'	**53**
Holocaust by Numbers	55
A Most Remarkable History	58
The Saga Continues	61
Revisionist Death Figures	65
World Jewish Population	67
Another Theory	71
Chapter 4: Breaking it Down: The Death Matrix	**73**
The Hilberg Matrix	74
Coming into Focus	79
Life (and Death) in the Ghettos	81
The Einsatzgruppen	87
PART II DEATH CAMPS IN FOCUS	**97**
Chapter 5: Chelmno and the Nazi Camp System	**99**
The Language of Mass Murder	100
The Missing Hitler Order	105
Gas Chambers Galore	107
Death Camp Chelmno	112
Further Issues	119
Disposing of the Bodies	120
A Chelmno Death Matrix	123
Traditionalist Replies	124

Page

Chapter 6: The Reinhardt Camps (Part 1): Belzec, Sobibor, Treblinka **127**
    Orthodoxy and Estimated Fatalities 128
    Camp Structure and Maps 131
    The Death Matrices 136

Chapter 7: The Reinhardt Camps (Part 2): The Diesel Story **143**
    Electrocution, Steam, Diesels, Chlorine....................................... 143
    The Diesel Story 145
    Gerstein, Reder, and the Diesel Exhaust 145
    More Problems with Gerstein... 148
    More Problems with Reder... 150
    Traditionalist Reply 152

Chapter 8: The Reinhardt Camps (Part 3): The Vanishing Bodies **155**
    Disposing of the Evidence.. 155
    Burying the Bodies 156
    Exhuming and Burning 157
    Traditionalist Replies 161
    Excavations (I)—Belzec... 163
    Excavations (II)—Sobibor 167
    Excavations (III)—Treblinka 169
    A Better Account.. 172
    Closing the Camps, Tracking the Deportees 174
    The End of the Line 176

Chapter 9: Majdanek **177**
    The Death Matrix 178
    The Seven Chambers of Majdanek 182

Chapter 10: Auschwitz **189**
    The Essentials of the Auschwitz Story—The Main Camp........... 189
    Birkenau—Alleged Extermination Camp 192
    Estimated Fatalities 197
    The Death Matrix 198
    Death Matrix (I): The Gas Chambers... 200
    Star Witnesses 203
    Gassing Capacity and 'Actual' Usage.. 204
    The Mechanics of Gassing 206
    No Holes?... 208
    "Fixing a Hole…" 213
    The Leuchter Report... 219
    Death Matrix (II): Body Disposal 221

	Page
Furnaces and Capacity	223
The Hungarian Operation	227
Air Photo Evidence	229
A Revisionist Auschwitz	240

PART III   THE FUTURE OF THE DEBATE 243

Chapter 11: "Storytellers Supreme" 245
    The Problem of the Witnesses 246
    Elie and Viktor 250
    From Bad to Worse 252
    Moving Ahead: A Revisionist Holocaust 256

Chapter 12: Hoax? Fraud? Conspiracy? 259
    A 'Jewish Conspiracy'? 261
    Covering All the Bases 264
    Media Dominance 266
    Dominance in Government 268
    Exploiting the Holocaust 276
    A New World Order 280

Epilogue 283

Bibliography 301
    Traditionalist Sources—Cited or for Further Reading 308
    Traditionalist Web Sites 312
    Revisionist Sources—Cited or for Further Reading 312
    Revisionist Web Sites 315

Author's Preface to the Second Edition

The first edition of this book, published in 2009, underwent three initial printings, each with slight textual and layout modifications. The final version, marked 'Third printing,' has sufficed for the past six years. But recent developments in the news, in world events and in the historiography of the Holocaust have necessitated a revised second edition of this book.

The general organization and chapter structure remain unchanged. The most significant revisions are as follows: Chapter 4 on the death matrix is now based on the 6 million overall death toll, rather than Raul Hilberg's estimate of 5.1 million. Correspondingly, working (orthodox) figures for five of the six death camps have also been significantly increased; Auschwitz remains largely unchanged. Also, the sections on the ghettos and on the Einsatzgruppen have been significantly expanded in order to give appropriate space to these two important aspects. Chapter 5 on Chelmno now includes reference to three important works on that camp that were not available for the first edition. The account of the Reinhardt excavations in Chapter 8 has been updated based on recent developments at those camps. Chapter 9 on Majdanek has been significantly modified to reflect the recent writings of current camp director Tomasz Kranz. In Chapter 11, the 'revisionist Holocaust' estimate has been increased from 516,000 to 570,000, though this reflects no fundamental shift in outlook. Many of the statistics and factual data in Chapter 12 have been updated. And the epilogue has been significantly expanded.

Importantly, however, the general conclusion is unchanged: the traditional Holocaust story is deeply flawed, and its advocates continue to resort to lies, deception and heavy-handed oppression to stifle open discussion. Only an impartial and unbiased investigation can get to the root of the present debate. Here, as before, the reader is invited to be his own judge.

Thomas Dalton
1 May 2015

Introduction

This is a book about the Holocaust and about two competing views of that event. On the one hand we have the traditional, orthodox view: the six million Jewish casualties, the gas chambers, the cremation furnaces and mass graves. We know about the death camps. We are told about incriminating documents, photographs and hard evidence. Countless books and films reiterate the conventional view. Historians can call on thousands of surviving witnesses to give us eyewitness accounts. Traditionalists have the weight of history on their side.

On the other hand, there is a small, renegade band of writers and researchers who refuse to accept large parts of this story. They explicitly challenge the conventional view of history. Researchers who do such work are generally known as *revisionists*. They seek to revise the orthodox account of some past event. Holocaust revisionists, however, are a special breed. They challenge not simply historians, but an entire infrastructure dedicated to maintaining and promoting the standard view. They present counter-evidence; they expose inconsistencies; they ask tough questions. And they are beginning to outline a new and different narrative.

Thus has emerged something of a debate—a debate of historic significance. This is no peripheral clash between two arcane schools of thought regarding some minutia of World War II. It is about history, of course, but it also speaks to fundamental issues of our time: freedom of speech and press, the operation of mass media, manipulation of public opinion, political and economic power structures and the coercive abilities of the State. It is an astonishingly rancorous and controversial debate with far-reaching implications.

Most of the public is only dimly aware of this debate, if at all. Nearly everyone knows that "six million Jews were killed by the Nazis," and that gas chambers were used in the killing. But few have any idea about the origins of this story, its rationale and its justification. Fewer still know of the serious questions that have been raised against the traditional view; if they have heard of them, it is in the context of "a few right-wing neo-Nazi anti-Semites" who are trying to attack the Jews by questioning the Holocaust.

And not more than a handful of individuals truly understand the depth of the revisionist attack on the mainstream view.

The fact that so few are aware of what may be called the "Great Holocaust Debate" is perhaps unsurprising. Much has been invested in the conventional story. Textbooks and encyclopedias have been written about it. Historians have staked their personal reputations on it. Politicians have passed laws defending it. And wealthy and powerful interest groups have good reasons to sustain it. In short, very few of those in positions of influence want to acknowledge any kind of legitimate debate. There is no incentive to publicize it and strong pressure to avoid it. Those in the public eye know that, should they broach this subject, they will suffer the consequences. Advertisers will drop out. Financial backers will disappear. They may be sued. They will lose access and perhaps their jobs. They will be shunned. They will be vilified. And it will all be legal.

Despite this overwhelming influence of orthodoxy, the many problems of the Holocaust story refuse to be suppressed. Time and time again, in small and often unexpected ways, cracks in the traditional view appear. A surprising admission, a foolish statement, a slip of the tongue, a blatant absurdity; and those 'troubling questions' arise once again. Today, more people than ever suspect that all is not well with the standard view of the Holocaust—hence the need for a book such as this.

* * *

The Great Debate is marked by a striking partisanship. The traditional story is defended primarily by survivors, Jewish writers and researchers, and those who suffered at the hands of Nazi Germany—in other words, by people with a self-interest in sustaining the dominant view of a genocidal Nazi regime and an innocent and victimized Jewish people. Of the thousands of books on the subject, the vast majority are by Jewish authors. The revisionist perspective, by contrast, is promoted by a very small number of people: primarily Germans, people of German origin, and those inclined to be pro-German or anti-Jewish—again, not an unbiased group.[1] Charges of "lies," "conspiracy" and "hoax" are frequently launched by both sides. This leaves the average person in a quandary: he is faced with partisan advocates on both sides, and rarely, if ever, gets a complete and balanced picture.

My goal is to remedy this shortcoming. I intend to present an objective, impartial look at this debate. I will discuss the latest and strongest arguments

---

[1] Of course there are other revisionists not among these groups. Prominent revisionist Germar Rudolf has argued that, proportionately, the French are the most represented group among revisionists.

on both sides, examine the replies and offer an unbiased assessment. This is a challenging task, to say the least, but I believe that I am reasonably well suited for it. Unlike the vast majority of writers on the Holocaust, I am not Jewish—either by religion or ethnicity; nor are any members of my family. I am not of German descent. No one in my immediate family suffered or died in World War II. I am neither Muslim nor Christian, so I have no religious bias. My background is as a scholar and academic, having taught humanities at a prominent American university for several years now. I have a long-standing interest in World War II and in the present conflict in the Middle East.

To anticipate my overall conclusions, let me make my stance clear at the outset. After considering all the evidence, I find that the revisionists have a very strong case. Their argumentation is solid, their sources are well-substantiated, and their research is of a high caliber. It is not ironclad, however, and where problems arise, I attempt to call them out. But overall, the bulk of their arguments point to one general conclusion: that the traditional Holocaust story is significantly flawed. Orthodox historians have largely failed to respond to the many challenges that they raise. Instead, they seem to prefer to cover up, slander or avoid engaging with revisionism. This fact alone strongly suggests that orthodoxy has nothing to say in reply.

In what follows, I attempt to be a fair judge of both sides in the Great Debate. Every judge must make determinations. I do the same. But the fact that I find in favor of the revisionists—at least for now—does not invalidate my objectivity. I came to this debate a true skeptic, and it is only by weight of evidence and argumentation that I am persuaded of the strength of the revisionist view. Conceivably this could change in the future. I remain open to new evidence and new arguments. I have done my best, here, to fairly weigh both sides. In the end, whether I have succeeded in offering an objective analysis of this debate will be for the reader to decide.

This book is targeted at the general educated reader, but it holds to a high standard of scholarship. In examining the writings of the two opposing sides, I have taken nothing for granted. To the greatest extent possible, I have verified all quotations, checked all calculations, and noted errors—though I must say that laudably high levels of scholarship are to be found on both sides. Throughout this book I have attempted to use commonly available sources, should the reader wish to confirm any statements or quotations I offer here.[2] I have concentrated on English-language sources; this has its

---

[2] Wherever possible, quotations include in-text citations. For example, (Hilberg 2003: 29) refers to page 29 of Hilberg's 2003 publication (*The Destruction of the European Jews*), which can be found in the bibliography at the back. Such citations both let the reader know the time frame of the quotation, and avoid an excessive multiplication of footnotes. The end objective, after all, is to clearly cite reliable and verifiable sources, and I think I have achieved this goal. And, unlike most books on the subject (of either side), I

drawbacks, but fortunately most of the important sources are available in English, and so the problem is not too great. Where relevant, I have cited essential non-English writings as well.

I have also shown a preference for hard-copy publications—books and journal articles—over Internet publications. Web-based material is always questionable. It can change from one day to another, and disappear the next. Such sources are typically less-well-researched, and often rely on other, equally unreliable Web-based sources for their arguments. On the other hand, there are certain obvious advantages. Much controversial material can be published *only* on the Web, and this point must be noted. Also, it is very convenient, for example, that several complete revisionist texts are available free online. (This very fact should mitigate the notion of a profit motive of the revisionists.) And the rise of online video services like YouTube, Vimeo, and Hulu allow access to audio-visual material that can have a greater impact than printed works. Thus, as appropriate, I have included relevant Web page information.

Finally, I use terminology indicating the provisional nature of claims about the Holocaust. My use of "alleged," "so-called," scare quotes, and similar devices is simply meant to indicate that I am withholding assent until the case is fully examined. I tend to be skeptical of most things told to me by those in positions of power and influence, and this subject is no different. I recommend that the reader do the same.

As for my occasional quips, jabs and weak attempts at humor, I can only say that this is not intended as insult or dismissal. I aim to take a sometimes plodding and tedious debate and make it interesting and readable; it is a topic of profound importance, after all. But when one makes outrageous claims or puts forth obvious nonsense, *and then expects to be taken seriously...* then a sarcastic jab may be entirely appropriate.

* * *

Some might question the relevance of this whole topic. They might point out that the event under discussion happened over 70 years ago, that most who experienced it are dead, and that the enmities of the war are long gone. America and the European nations are friends and at peace (with each other, at least!). Japan is an important trading partner and poses no military threat. So why bother with the Holocaust? What's the big deal? "Yes, the Jews suffered," some may say. "So just leave them alone. Let them have their ol' Holocaust."

---

have included a full and complete index and bibliography.

I think it does matter, and not only to those who have a vested interest. For several reasons: First, there is the straightforward question of history. Regardless of what one may think, the Holocaust was an event of major historical significance. As with any historical event, it is important to get the facts straight and to develop consistent and coherent views about what happened. To understand what did, or did not, happen is vital for understanding the world of the mid-20th century, and by extension, the world of today.

Second, we are not allowed to forget about it, even if we wanted to. Coverage of the Holocaust is standard fare in every school curriculum. Children the world over read *The Diary of Anne Frank*, *Number the Stars*, *Waiting for Anya*, and *Butterfly*. Students learn about the gas chambers and the six million, about the innumerable Nazi atrocities.[3] We see Holocaust miniseries on television, *Schindler's List* and documentaries like *Night and Fog*. We celebrate "Holocaust Education Week," and we acknowledge January 27 each year as the "International Day of Commemoration" of Holocaust victims, as declared by the UN in 2005.[4] School children collect 6 million pencils, or 6 million paperclips, or 6 million pennies.[5] We visit Holocaust museums. We take college courses from endowed chairs in Holocaust studies.

---

[3] For example, in February 2008, French President Nicolas Sarkozy proposed strengthening an existing mandate to teach the Holocaust; his idea was that "every fifth grader will have to learn the life story of one of the 11,000 [Jewish] French children killed by the Nazis in the Holocaust (*New York Times*, Feb 16)." The proposal was rejected by the Education Ministry five months later, but even so, one wonders what could have impelled Sarkozy to propose such a thing; perhaps his own Jewish ancestry had something to do with it (a grandfather was Jewish).
Not to be outdone, the British then proposed that "every secondary school [in the UK] is to get a Holocaust specialist to ensure that the subject is taught comprehensively and sensitively" (*Times Online*, 7 Nov 2008). Ten percent of these specialists will receive a master's degree in "Holocaust education." "The scheme is part of a wider Holocaust education project funded by the Government" and a national charity. The project will also "send two sixth-formers [ages 16 and 17] from every school to Auschwitz" each year. More recently, in late 2010 it was reported that Australia will include the Holocaust, for the first time ever, in their national education curriculum (JTA, Dec 19).

[4] In 2011, the United Nations agency UNESCO signed an agreement with Israel "to promote Holocaust education and combat its denial" (JTA, Mar 8). This, after passing a 2007 General Assembly resolution that "condemns without any reservation any denial of the Holocaust" (A/Res/61/255).

[5] On 20 September 2004, the AP reported on a middle school in Tennessee, where, back in 1998, "students hoped to collect 6 million paper clips—one to remember each person killed in the Holocaust." Thanks to global publicity, they ultimate collected some 30 million clips. In that same year *Paper Clips*, an "award-winning" Miramax documentary, was released. Regarding the pencils, a Texas junior high school issued a press release on 15 May 2007: "Six million pencils for Holocaust project." In May 2011, High Tech High School in Chula Vista, California, began a project to collect 6 million pennies. Not to be outdone, in September of that year a Canadian high school undertook to collect "13 million pennies, one for each person who died in the Nazi genocides, including six million Jews" (*Toronto Globe and Mail*, Sep 4).

This is not by accident. It is a deliberate plan, to make sure we "never forget." And if we can never forget, then we should at least get the story straight.

Third, there is the drama of the debate itself. It is unlike anything else—the name-calling, the suppression of ideas, the jailing of dissenters, the burning of books. It is a debate that can scarcely be mentioned in polite company. It is, in a real sense, one of the last taboos in Western civilization. But as we know, taboos never last. They are the product of a given era, of specific social and political forces. When those forces shift, as they inevitably do, the taboo is lifted. Now is perhaps such a time.

Fourth, we have the underlying issue of free speech. I take a radical position in support of free speech. Speech is an (almost) absolute right. There is virtually no topic that should be out of bounds. Barring only such obscure cases as an immediate threat to human life, no words or ideas should be beyond discussion. I support vigorous and open debate on every conceivable topic, the Holocaust included. Suppressing speech only drives thought and expression underground; it can only lead to unethical and reprehensible manipulation of the public's ability to think for itself, and perhaps even violent response to the suppression. Those in power always have reason to fear free speech—all the more reason to defend it.

Fifth is the monetary angle. Billions of dollars have been given as restitution to Israel, to individual survivors and to Jewish organizations. These are tax dollars, provided by the workers of the affected nations—primarily Germany and Switzerland, to date. Restitution claims have not ended, and will likely not end in the foreseeable future. As recently as 2008, the Belgian government agreed to pay $170 million to survivors, their families and the "Jewish community." This is rather astonishing, given that Belgium was a *victim* of the war, not an aggressor. (The official reason: Belgium "failed to resist hard enough" against Nazi deportation of Jews.) Germany, though, suffers a seemingly unending parade of reparation deals. In late 2014, they were compelled to establish a new $250 million fund "for child survivors"; this fund is intended "to recognize psychological and medical trauma caused during their deprived childhoods." Compensation money, arising directly from the conventional Holocaust story, in turn flows back to sustain it. Restitution money buys political clout, where—in the US at least—it ends up as campaign contributions and issue ads. It encourages lawmakers to legislate in support of Israel and against revisionism—and they do.

Sixth, the State of Israel itself was a direct result of the Holocaust. In November 1947, two and a half years after the end of the war in Europe, the UN General Assembly approved Resolution 181, calling for independent Arab and Jewish states in Palestine. Jewish leaders immediately began formation of a political infrastructure, and declared the establishment of the

State of Israel in May 1948. There were precursor events, of course. The Zionist push for a Jewish homeland began in the late 1800s, and the Balfour Declaration of 1917 promised "a national home for the Jewish people." The process was thus in motion several decades before the end of World War II, but the Holocaust was the last straw. This is widely acknowledged today. In 2009, Israeli ambassador to the US, Michael Oren, declared the Holocaust to be Israel's "raison d'être."[6] A 2012 survey found that fully 98% of Israelis consider it fairly or very important that a "guiding principle" for Israel is "to remember the Holocaust."[7] Hence, if the Holocaust is called into question, so is the legitimacy of the Jewish state.

Seventh, the mere existence of Israel has far-reaching consequences. Its creation sparked the ethnic cleansing of Palestinian Arabs, which led to several wars and ultimately to the present Israeli occupation of the West Bank and other Palestinian lands. This occupation in turn is a crucial factor in the global "war on terror," which is in reality a war on Islam. The influential group of people who promote and defend the Holocaust are by and large the same people who push for war against Muslims worldwide. The same ideology—militant right-wing Zionism—is a major factor in both. In the United States, this same Jewish lobby also coerces the government to send roughly $6 billion per year to Israel in the form of military and economic aid.

Eighth: If we can be misled—or fooled, or deceived, or lied to—about the Holocaust, what other events might we be misled about? The same social forces that could give rise to and sustain a deficient Holocaust story could produce countless other stories that might be exaggerated, embellished, distorted or falsified.

Finally, the Great Debate tells us something important about the power structure of Western nations. Revisionists challenge not only orthodoxy; they challenge the power of the State. The leading advocates of the conventional view are in positions of great influence. They are wealthy. They have many supporters and virtually unlimited resources. They are able to turn the power of the State, and public opinion, against revisionism. The revisionists, few in number and poor in means, have only ideas. But as the masked man once said, *ideas are bulletproof*. They have a power of their own, unmatched by money, military or government. Ideas can penetrate to the heart of truth. This is the promise of revisionism. Whether it succeeds, time will tell.

* * *

---

[6] *New Republic* (6 Oct 2009).
[7] *Ha'aretz* (30 Jan 2012).

To repeat, I attempt here to take an impartial look at this clash of views. My role here is not that of a revisionist. I am a bystander in this debate, observing and commenting on a collision of ideas. This book is not a book of revisionism. It is a book *about* revisionism, and about two competing views of the truth. It assesses the ability of each side to marshal evidence, and to create a clear and consistent picture of the past.

The revisionist view of events is so far from what has been portrayed that we may have a hard time comprehending its possibility. A colleague once told me that he would be no more shocked to find no Eiffel Tower in Paris than he would to learn that the revisionists were right. Yet we can scarcely avoid asking ourselves this question: *Is it really possible that the traditional Holocaust story is wrong*? And not merely a little wrong, but significantly and fundamentally flawed? This is for each reader to decide. My objective is not to impose an overall conclusion, but rather to illuminate and articulate the main points, and to comment on their validity. I expect the reader to take nothing I say for granted. He is invited to check my sources, verify my quotations, and check my math. Ultimately, the reader must decide.

In such a complex issue as this one, it is wise to avoid making hasty judgments. My own journey was rather long. The present work was, in a sense, 30 years in the making. For roughly the first 10 years of my adulthood, I fully accepted the orthodox view. After all, the consensus was nearly universal, and I had no good reason to question it. During the next 10 years, doubts began to creep in. I started hearing stories that sounded odd, little points of conflict or contradiction, and strange gaps in the conventional storyline. About 10 years ago, I decided to begin a serious inquiry into the topic. I tracked down dozens of books on both sides, and spent many long hours in careful research. The results of my investigation are presented below.

I sense a turning point in the debate. It seems to be moving out of the shadows and into the realm of serious and legitimate discourse. Revisionists have strong arguments in their favor, and, despite book burnings and jail terms, they are not going away. Traditionalists seem of late to have lost their momentum. Perhaps they have no more counterarguments. Perhaps they have tired of defending the conflicting stories of survivors and witnesses. Perhaps they have reached the limit of their ability to fashion a comprehensible picture of those tragic events of 70 years ago. The debate will surely reach a new resolution, and I suspect that the result will be something different than what we presume today.

PART I

SITUATING
THE HOLOCAUST DEBATE

Chapter 1: The Great Debate

There can be no denying the Holocaust of the mid-twentieth century: it was called World War II. Roughly 50 to 60 million people died worldwide—about 70 percent of whom were civilians.[8] They died from a variety of causes including guns, bombs, fire, disease, exposure, starvation, and chemical toxins. Within this greater Holocaust there existed many lesser holocausts: the Allied fire-bombings of Dresden, Hamburg, and Cologne; the killing of hundreds of thousands of German soldiers and civilians by the victorious Allies after the formal end of the war; the US nuclear attacks on Hiroshima and Nagasaki, which incinerated 170,000 women, children, and elderly; and the Jewish Holocaust of Nazi Germany. It is this last Holocaust which has been the topic of heated debate over the years. It is this Holocaust that I address in this book.

Of the millions who died in the war, about 10 percent, or six million, are claimed to have been Jews killed by the Nazi regime, both in Germany and in its occupied territories. This Jewish Holocaust—*the* Holocaust, many would say—has been the subject of intense study for 70 years now, ever since the postwar Nuremberg trials of 1945 and 1946. Thousands of books and articles have been written on it; numerous films describe it; countless news stories have covered it. According to some, it is the "most well-documented event in history."[9]

In order to properly examine the Holocaust, we first need to know what exactly it was. The basic outline of the conventional story has been mapped

---

[8] According to standard sources, about 17 million soldiers died on all sides: 7.5 million for the Soviet Union, 3.5 million for Germany, 1.3 million for Japan, and some 4.7 million for all other countries combined. Civilian deaths are hard to determine, but the estimated losses in just the Soviet Union (19 million) and China (10 million) were huge. If we add 6 million Jews and roughly 3–5 million civilians in all other countries, we arrive at a total close to 55 million.

[9] For example, Rabbi Abraham Cooper recently said this: "No crime in the annals of history has been as well documented as Nazi Germany's Final Solution, the state-sponsored genocide that systematically murdered 6 million European Jews" (*Huffington Post*, 17 May 2012). According to the US Holocaust Memorial Museum (USHMM) website, "The Holocaust is one of the most well-documented events in history" (article: "Holocaust Denial and Distortion").

out for several decades now, and there is today a rough consensus. Here is one "widely accepted definition":

> When historians talk about the "Holocaust," what they mean on the most general level is that about six million Jews were killed in an intentional and systematic fashion by the Nazis using a number of different means, including gas chambers. (Shermer and Grobman 2000: xv)

Here is another, from an official source—Michael Berenbaum, former director of the US Holocaust Memorial Museum in Washington, D.C.:

> [The Holocaust was] the systematic state-sponsored murder of 6 million Jews by the Nazis and their collaborators during World War 2. (1993: 1)

These definitions imply that three key components are essential to the orthodox view: (1) the killing of roughly six million Jews; (2) homicidal gas chambers; and (3) intentionality on the part of the Nazi leadership. Should we lack any one of these three, according to this view, we have a tragedy, perhaps—but something less than 'the Holocaust.'

The conventional story begins with the persecution of German Jews in the 1930s. It accelerates with the round-up of Jews under German control in early 1940. It becomes mass murder with the shootings in the Soviet Union in mid-1941. It ends with gas chambers, mass graves, and burned corpses—either in open pits or crematoria. This heinous act, it is claimed, was a singular pinnacle of human evil. "Adolf Hitler [was the] incarnation of absolute evil," according to famed survivor Elie Wiesel; indeed, he says, Nazi crimes against the Jews "have attained a quasi-ontological dimension."[10] For Bartov (2015: 11), the Holocaust is a "black hole of violence and depravity." The Auschwitz crematoria are "the most perverse, insidious, indeed utterly demonic circumstances in the entire Nazi genocidal apparatus"; they reside "in the lowest chambers of hell," and represent "the very essence of Nazism's bottomless evil" (*ibid*: 241).

There remain, however, many open issues and many unanswered questions. Revisionists make challenging and troubling claims, ones that threaten to overturn major aspects of the Holocaust story:

> ➢ Key witnesses to the Holocaust have either falsified or greatly exaggerated important aspects of their stories.
> ➢ The figure of 'six million' has little basis in fact. This number, which theoretically could only have been known after the war, actually traces back decades before.

---

[10] *Time* magazine (13 Apr 1998).

- Major death camps, like Belzec, Sobibor, Chelmno, and Treblinka, have vanished without a trace—as have most of their alleged victims. Such a thing is not possible.
- Both of the alleged means of gassing victims—cyanide gas (under the brand name Zyklon B) and carbon monoxide from diesel exhaust—are impractical, unworkable, and simply ridiculous.
- No 'Holocaust order' from Hitler exists; nor was there any budget or any plan. How, then, could the Nazis have pulled off their perfect crime?
- Wartime air photos do not substantiate the traditional account of events.
- Why are there, even today, so many survivors?

It seems that no two writers on the Holocaust have the same opinion on these matters.

As I outlined in the Introduction, the disputants in the Great Debate fall into two clearly defined groups: *traditionalists* and *revisionists*. Were this any other matter of historical dispute, the two camps would typically engage in cordial, lively, and fact-based argumentation. They might attend joint conferences, praise each other's ingenuity, share lunch, and even grant a deferential respect to one another. But not with the Holocaust. Here, none of the usual rules apply. A kind of argumentative chaos reigns. *Ad hominem* attacks fly. Absurd charges are issued; as Specter (2009: 4) sees it, "Holocaust deniers... are intensely destructive—even homicidal." Reputations are impugned, and basic intelligence is challenged.[11] Strategic confusion and targeted obfuscation are the norms.

For starters, consider the names of the two groups. Holocaust revisionists are often called 'Holocaust deniers' by mainstream writers. This appellation is both derogatory and, technically, almost meaningless. What does it mean to 'deny' the Holocaust? How much of the conventional view does one have to reject in order to be a 'denier'? Take the three pillars of the Holocaust story. What does it mean to "deny" the six-million figure? Is 'five million' denial? Unlikely, given that orthodox icon Raul Hilberg consistently argued for roughly that figure. Four million? No—early traditionalist Gerald Reitlinger claimed in 1953 that the death toll could be as low as 4.19 million. To my knowledge, no one has ever called him a Holocaust denier. One million? Five hundred thousand? We can see the problem here.

What about intentionality? Does this refer to Hitler alone? Or must it include the likes of Himmler, Goebbels, Eichmann, and Göring? And how are

---

[11] The *ad hominem* attack is, of course, a common and elementary logical fallacy. Traditionalists hold the clear lead in the name-calling sweepstakes, though certain of the revisionist activists are well known for this tactic. As might be expected, name-calling—on either side—is a fairly sure sign of a deficiency of arguments.

we to judge intention? Spoken and written words can be misleading; discerning one's intention has long been a notorious philosophical problem. Clearly there is no ready answer to these many questions. It seems that being a 'denier' is rather like being an 'anti-Semite'—essentially in the eye of the beholder.

Revisionists in turn often refer to their opponents as 'exterminationists'—as in, those who believe that the Nazis were on a quest to eliminate the Jewish people from the face of the Earth. Traditionalists reject not only this label, but any label at all; any group designation implies that they are simply one school of thought, to be held on equal footing with the revisionists. The notion of a competition between schools of thought is anathema to them. In their eyes, there is only one basic truth about the Holocaust, and they are its guardians.

Some traditionalists have demonstrated amazing levels of arrogance. A good example is Pièrre Vidal-Naquet (1992: xxiv):

> It should be understood once and for all that I am not answering the accusers, and that in no way am I entering into a dialogue with them. ... [T]he contribution of the "revisionists" to our knowledge may be compared to the correction, in a long text, of a few typographical errors. That does not justify a dialogue... [O]ne should not enter into debate *with* the "revisionists". ... I have nothing to reply to them and will not do so. Such is the price to be paid for intellectual coherence.

Deborah Lipstadt mimics this stubbornness: "I categorically decline" to debate them, she says (1993: xiii). Such a reluctance to engage in debate suggests, of course, a fear of losing. The leading revisionists rarely pass up an opportunity to debate; the leading traditionalists, to the best of my knowledge, have never accepted one.[12] In this sense, most traditionalists are themselves 'deniers'; they deny that there is anything to debate at all.

More seriously, we now have a situation where the power of the State has been brought to bear against revisionism. In 1982 two influential Jewish groups, the Institute of Jewish Affairs and the World Jewish Congress, created a plan to combat the growth of revisionist publications. They issued a report, "Making the Denial of the Holocaust a Crime in Law," calling for widespread legislation against revisionism. Israel passed such a law in 1986, and France and other countries followed in the 1990s. Today there are 17 countries that have enacted or expanded laws against Holocaust denial,[13] os-

---

[12] With perhaps two minor exceptions: Traditionalist Michael Shermer appeared on the *Phil Donahue* television talk show in 1994, along with revisionists Bradley Smith and David Cole. And in 1995, Shermer debated revisionist Mark Weber. Videos of both events are available online.

[13] The current list includes Austria, Belgium, the Czech Republic, France, Germany, Israel,

tensibly to combat racist hate crimes against Jews or other minorities. Penalties ranging from severe fines to imprisonment can now be levied against those who openly challenge the conventional Holocaust story. The presumption is that revisionist writings or speeches will inflame violent extremists, or will 'corrupt the youth' (Germany), or will somehow bring unacceptable pain to Jewish people or others sympathetic to their suffering. I am unaware of any cases in which revisionist writings have been shown to be a contributing factor to anti-Semitic violence—but perhaps this is beside the point.

In recent years, several prominent revisionists have been arrested for challenging the traditional Holocaust account. Ernst Zündel, a flamboyant publisher and promoter of right-wing literature in Canada, was arrested in February 2003 in Tennessee for violating United States immigration statutes. He was quickly deported to Canada and held in prison for two years as a "national security threat." In March 2005 Zündel was deported once again, this time to his native Germany—where he was charged with distributing hate literature, and with maintaining a US-based revisionist Web site. In February 2007 he was sentenced to five years in prison, the maximum allowable under current German law. He was freed in March 2010, having served three years.

Germar Rudolf, a one-time doctoral student in chemistry in Germany, published the influential revisionist works *Vorlesungen über Zeitgeschichte* ("Lectures on Contemporary History," 1993) and *Grundlagen zur Zeitgeschichte* ("Foundations of Contemporary History," 1994). In a throwback to the Middle Ages, his books were not only confiscated, they were burned. Tried in 1994/95, he was sentenced to fourteen months in prison. Rudolf eventually fled to the US but was arrested on immigration charges in late 2005 and deported back to Germany. In March 2007, the German legal system sentenced Rudolf to an additional prison term of two and a half years. He was released in July 2009.

Noted British writer and historian David Irving came slowly and hesitantly to revisionism, over a period of several years.[14] He had been sympathetic to the German side at least since his 1977 book *Hitler's War*, but did not start to seriously question the Holocaust until the mid-1980s. It was not

---

Liechtenstein, Lithuania, Luxembourg, Poland, Portugal, Romania, Spain, and Switzerland. The latest additions to this honor roll include Hungary (2010), and most recently, Greece and Russia (2014). It may strike one as odd that modern industrial nations like these, which claim to uphold the right of free speech and inquiry, could resort to the banning of certain books and ideas—especially today, 70 years after the event. And odd it is; I elaborate on this in Chapter 12.

[14] It is debatable whether or not Irving truly counts as a Holocaust revisionist; his position continually shifts on this issue. Traditionalists almost uniformly portray him as such, but he himself apparently denies it, and other revisionists are reluctant to include him among their number. For the purposes of this book, however, I will classify him as a soft revisionist.

so much his writings as his speeches and interviews that got Irving into trouble. In 1993 Lipstadt labeled him a denier and neo-Nazi sympathizer in her book *Denying the Holocaust*. Irving sued for libel, losing in 2000. He was then arrested in Austria in November 2005 for an act of 'denial' committed sixteen years earlier, back in 1989. A Viennese court sentenced him to three years in prison in February 2006, though he was granted early release in November of that year.

More recently we have cases such as that of German-Australian revisionist Dr. Frederick Töben, who served three months in jail for a denial-related penalty in August 2009. And in February 2015, French revisionist Vincent Reynouard was sentenced (again) to prison, this time for two years. His crime: posting on-line videos challenging the conventional Holocaust story. The local French court actually saw fit to double the sentence that was sought by the prosecution. 'Deniers' are evidently a dangerous lot; no leniency shall be shown.

Such attacks, in addition to significantly raising the stakes of the debate, have a stifling effect upon free speech and academic freedom generally. Many groups and individuals have strongly opposed such heavy-handed acts of state censorship, even though they may disagree with the revisionists. Notable intellectuals such as Noam Chomsky—himself no revisionist—have spoken out on their behalf. One must wonder: How serious a threat can these people be? Why are they able to draw the attention of national legislators around the world? Whom do they threaten? And perhaps most important— Are they on to something? Do they in fact have a case to make, that the Holocaust story is fundamentally deficient? The State does not attack those who argue for a flat Earth, or warn against some imminent alien invasion. Those who are irrational, or cannot make a coherent case, pose no threat, and thus are left alone. Apparently the 'deniers' are not in this category. This fact alone should make the average person wonder—Could they be right?

The Core of Revisionism

Unlike the traditionalist view, revisionism resists a general characterization. The alternate depiction of events that revisionism promises is only dimly outlined at present, and opinions are too disparate and too variable to form a truly cohesive view. Nonetheless, there are certain points of broad agreement among a majority of serious revisionists; these constitute a kind of core of revisionism today. Among the general points of agreement are the following:

- Hitler did indeed dislike the Jews, and strongly desired to rid Germany of them. This desire was shared by most of the top Nazi leadership. Their antipathy had three sources: (1) Jewish domination of major sectors of German finance and industry;[15] (2) the Jewish role in the treasonous November Revolution at the end of World War I;[16] and (3) the prominent Jewish role in Soviet Bolshevism, which was seen by most Germans as a mortal threat.[17]
- To achieve this end, the Nazis implemented various means, including evacuations, deportations, and forced resettlement. Their main objective was to remove the Jews, not kill them. Hence their primary goal was one of *ethnic cleansing, not genocide*. This is why no one has ever found a Hitler order to exterminate the Jews.
- Of course, many Jews would likely die in the process, but this was an unavoidable consequence.
- The Germans actively sought places to send the Jews. One option under consideration was to forcibly acquire the island of Madagascar from France, and to ship them there.[18]
- By mid-1941, due to speedy victories in the Soviet Union, large areas of territory came under German control, and hence a new option emerged—the Jews would be shipped to the East.
- By mid-1943, things were turning bad for the Germans. Shipments to the East were no longer viable, and furthermore all available manpower was needed to support the war effort. Thus deportations became subordinated to forced labor—hence the heavy reliance on Auschwitz, which was first and foremost a labor camp.

---

[15] Traditionalist researcher Sarah Gordon (1984: 8-15) gives a good account of this dominance: "The reader may be surprised to learn that Jews were never a large percentage of the total German population; at no time did they exceed 1.09 percent of the population during the years 1871 to 1933... [In spite of this, the Jews] were overrepresented in business, commerce, and public and private service... Within the fields of business and commerce, Jews... represented 25 percent of all individuals employed in retail business and handled 25 percent of total sales... ; they owned 41 percent of iron and scrap iron firms and 57 percent of other metal businesses.... Jews were [also] prominent in private banking under both Jewish and non-Jewish ownership or control. They were especially visible in private banking in Berlin, which in 1923 had 150 private (versus state) Jewish banks, as opposed to only 11 private non-Jewish banks...."
This trend held true as well in the academic and cultural spheres: "Jews were overrepresented among university professors and students between 1870 and 1933.... [A]lmost 19 percent of the instructors in Germany were of Jewish origin.... Jews were also highly active in the theater, the arts, film, and journalism. For example, in 1931, 50 percent of the 234 theater directors in Germany were Jewish, and in Berlin the number was 80 percent..."

[16] See Dalton (2014).

[17] See Dalton (2013).

[18] For a good account of this episode, see Mattogno and Graf (2010: 179-193).

- A major problem with deporting and interning large numbers of Jews was disease, especially typhus. Therefore a major effort was needed to kill the disease-bearing lice that clung to bodies and clothing. All Nazi camps were thus equipped to delouse and disinfest thousands of people.
- The primary means for killing lice was in 'gas chambers,' in which clothing, bedding, and personal items were exposed to hot air, steam, or cyanide gas. The gas chambers described by witnesses really did exist—but each one was built and operated as a disinfesting chamber, not as a homicidal gas chamber.
- The larger part of witness testimonies—both from former (Jewish) inmates and from captured Germans—consists of rumor, hearsay, exaggeration, or outright falsehood. This does not mean that entire testimonies are invalid, but only that specific claims must be verified by scientific methods before we should accept them. In particular, claims about huge casualty figures, mass burials and burnings, and murder with diesel exhaust are largely discredited.
- The total number of Jewish deaths at the hands of the Nazis—the 'six million' number—has been highly exaggerated. The actual death toll was perhaps 10 percent of this figure: on the order of 500,000.

Individual revisionists place emphasis on different aspects of the above account, but all would likely agree with all these points.

Four Myths

An inquiry into the Great Debate of Holocaust revisionism cannot even begin until a few prominent myths are dismissed. Four are of particular importance:

Myth #1: *Revisionists believe that the Holocaust 'never happened.'*
This is a common caricature of the revisionist position. It implies a belief that there were no widespread deaths of Jews, that they suffered no persecution, that there were no gas chambers of any kind, and perhaps even that no Jews actually died at the hands of the Nazis. Those traditionalists who make this claim are being disingenuous at best. They seem to want the reader to believe that revisionism is so far out of touch with reality, and so extreme in its views, that it can be safely disregarded.

No serious revisionist doubts that extensive killing of Jews occurred, numbering in the hundreds of thousands, at least. No serious revisionist doubts that a catastrophe 'happened' to the Jews—whether they call it a 'holocaust' or not is incidental. Revisionists *do* dispute that the number of deaths was anything like five or six million. All accept that gas chambers existed in most or all of the German concentration camps; but they dispute the *purpose* of those chambers. And revisionists dispute that any German camps were ever built and operated as 'extermination camps.'

In one sense, the very statement of this myth is loaded. As I explained earlier, the event called 'the Holocaust' requires intentionality, homicidal gas chambers, and some 6 million Jewish deaths. If any of these three points is found to be significantly in error, then technically, 'the Holocaust' did not happen. But this, of course, is not what our orthodox historians mean when they make this charge. In fact, they never actually explain *what* they mean when they invoke this myth. Hence any such statement, by either side, to the effect that the Holocaust 'never happened' is pure propaganda.[19]

Myth #2: *Photographs of corpses prove the Holocaust happened.*
We all have seen the gruesome pictures of bodies stacked up outside some crematorium, or unceremoniously dumped into pits. These are offered as proof of 'Nazi barbarity,' and of the slaughter of the Jews. Yet many things about such photos are misleading. For one, we do not know, or at least are not told, whose bodies those are. They could be Jews... or Polish internees, or Russian POWs, or German inmates. In fact little effort seems to have been made to actually identify, or autopsy, any of those bodies.

Second, those famous photos came from the camps liberated by the British and Americans—primarily Bergen-Belsen. The problem is that these were not extermination camps. From the 'real' extermination camps, we have no corpse photos at all.[20] This fact alone should give us reason to consider whether aspects of the traditional story might be suspect.

Third, there were rampant outbreaks of typhus and other diseases that claimed thousands of lives in all the camps; yet the photos are used to imply that these were gassing victims. And fourth, the photos show at most several hundred corpses. This is so far from 'six million' that the vaunted photographs are almost meaningless as 'proof' of the Holocaust.

---

[19] The continued invocation of this myth borders on the absurd. As a case in point, consider the 2005 BBC series "Auschwitz: The Nazis and the Final Solution." After five hours of airtime—and no discussion of revisionist challenges—they insert, at the very end, a statement by former SS officer Oskar Gröning. As an elderly man, Gröning now sees it as his task "to oppose Holocaust deniers who claim that Auschwitz never happened." He adds, "I have seen the crematoria. I have seen the burning pits. And I want you to believe me that these atrocities happened. I was there." Of course, no revisionist in his right mind denies the existence of crematoria, pits, or the Auschwitz camp. Hence Gröning's statement is meaningless—added for mere dramatic effect.

[20] With one possible exception: a disputed (dubious) photo of Auschwitz showing a couple dozen corpses, possibly being burned. See Chapter 10.

Myth #3: *The Holocaust was a 'hoax.'*
This idea rests in large part on the writings of Arthur Butz, above all his widely read book *The Hoax of the Twentieth Century* (1976/2015). Butz continues to hold to this notion today, as do a handful of other revisionists, such as Robert Faurisson and Fritz Berg.

I explore this whole idea in more detail in Chapter 12, but briefly, what is a hoax? The term derives from the pseudo-Latin phrase *hax pax max* used by Renaissance-era conjurers and magicians to impress their audience. This same phrase is the source of the more benign magical incantation 'hocus pocus.' A 'hocus pocus' refers to a fabrication intended to entertain and amuse, whereas a hoax came to mean a fabrication intended to *deceive*, in a malicious sense. Both refer to contrived circumstances, carefully arranged to achieve a desired effect.

Now, it certainly is possible that the Holocaust story—especially the mass murder in gas chambers, and the 'six million'—was a kind of deliberate fabrication to achieve a desired effect of deception. But to my knowledge, no revisionist has offered any specific evidence to support this contention. Without solid evidence of deliberate falsification of at least large parts of the Holocaust story, we are unjustified in calling it a hoax. Individual lies, exaggerations, even gross exaggerations, do not qualify as hoaxes. Therefore, in my opinion, the Holocaust was not a hoax.[21]

However, this obviously does not mean that the story is true! It may still be rife with falsehoods, lies, and assorted absurdities. But there are many other ways in which untrue depictions of events can come to be widely believed, some of which are relatively innocent. Lacking hard evidence, we should grant the benefit of the doubt. Revisionism should attack the story, not the motive.

Traditionalists in turn leap on this hoax label and use it to their advantage.[22] They take it to mean a kind of global conspiracy, a large-scale collective effort to deceive the general public. They say, "Those deniers actually believe that the Jews could pull off this monumental fraud! They actually think that thousands of historians, writers, journalists, government leaders—everyone, in fact, who supports the standard view—are in on the scam, all conspiring to assist the powerful Jews. How stupid can they be?" And there is some weight to this. You cannot claim massive fraud without a solid basis for it. If someone lies, call it a lie. If someone utters a blatant absurdity, call it absurd. Revisionists risk looking foolish, and only hurt their cause, by arguing for a hoax.

That said, there is a kernel of truth in this myth. It may be fair to say that certain parties took undeniably tragic events and made the most of them.

---

[21] Crowell (2011: 9, 23), for one revisionist, concurs.
[22] For a good recent example, see Perry and Schweitzer (2002: 208-211).

They assumed the worst possible outcome, the worst possible death tolls, and turned the worst rumors into 'truths.' It may have been something like a fish tale, in which one catches a trout but claims it was a shark. Now, a fish tale is not a hoax—presuming that one *actually went fishing*, and *actually caught something*. It is untruthful, deceitful, and perhaps even malicious, but not a hoax. The undeniably tragic deaths of many thousands, whose remains were utterly obliterated, can easily become 'millions.' A falsehood, an exaggeration, a fish tale—but not a hoax.

Unfortunately the situation goes from bad to worse. An exaggeration gets repeated over and over. It becomes the basis for trials, billions of dollars in reparations, imprisonments, even death sentences. Then it must be defended at all costs. We can well imagine how such a situation could come about, step by step, over the course of 70 years.

Myth #4: *Revisionists are right-wing neo-Nazi anti-Semites.*
Again, a classic ploy: impugn your opponent so that the reader will be inclined to dismiss him. Unfortunately this occurs repeatedly in almost every traditionalist book that even touches on revisionism. Other, related charges usually follow. Zimmerman (2000: 119), for example, writes, "Everyone who has studied this [revisionist] movement realizes that the ultimate goal of denial is the rehabilitation of Adolf Hitler and the Third Reich." Quite a claim! One wonders how Zimmerman knows such things, and what his evidence might be.

Are revisionists right-wing? Since being right-wing is no crime, their critics presumably mean *far* right, which, they imply, is an evil thing. Of course this is only evil from the perspective of the left, but more to the point, it implies that traditionalists are not themselves right-wing—often far from the truth! Hard-core traditionalists, by whom I mean the militant Zionists, are among the most right-wing activists around—as are the evangelical Christians, who typically are strong supporters of Israel and the standard Holocaust story. Portraying all revisionists as right-wing is clearly a case of the pot calling the kettle black.

When revisionist writings touch on political issues, they are most often neutral with respect to the political spectrum. More important, this point is irrelevant to the arguments at hand. Whether a given revisionist is right, left, or center has no bearing on his arguments or his critique. Rudolf (2004) has noted that "revisionism is neither left nor right." Anyone from any point on the spectrum may see the need to challenge the traditional view. Two of the more prominent early revisionists, Paul Rassinier and Roger Garaudy, were staunch leftists. Recently, left-leaning political activists have begun to raise questions about the Holocaust. If the traditionalists don't like what the revisionists are saying, then they must counter their arguments, not slander someone's character.

Are revisionists neo-Nazis? None of the major writers openly admits to being a National Socialist, and few seem to care much about burnishing Hitler's image. And, as with the right-wing accusation, even if a revisionist were openly National Socialist, or an open admirer of Hitler, it would be irrelevant to the arguments presented.

Are the revisionists anti-Semites? An anti-Semite is, technically, one who 'displays hostility or discrimination against Jews as a religious or ethnic group.' Thus it is either a form of racism or religious discrimination, against Jews *as a whole*. Yet, again, one finds no such attacks in any serious revisionist work. The academic revisionists are, on the whole, passably respectful of Jews. If they target an ideology, it is frequently Zionism. Not all Zionists are Jews, and not all Jews are Zionists; thus, an anti-Zionist stance is neither racial nor religious discrimination. In fact, it is Zionism that is more inclined toward racism, in its oppressive and discriminatory attitude toward Palestinians and Muslims in general. And it may even turn out that the traditionalists do more to foster anti-Semitism, if it happens that they are found to be promoting—and legally enforcing—an unjustifiable myth of Jewish suffering. One can only imagine the repercussions, if a large section of the public should come to believe that they have been lied to about the greatest crime in history.

Today, 'anti-Semitism' has become a largely meaningless epithet, deployed either to slander one's opponents—or to shut them up. It is used simply because one does not like what the other says, and has nothing more intelligent to offer.[23]

---

[23] A more recent definition was endorsed in an official US government report, *Contemporary Global Anti-Semitism* (US Department of State, 2008). "Anti-Semitism is a certain perception of Jews, which may be expressed as hatred toward Jews. Rhetorical and physical manifestations of anti-Semitism are directed toward Jewish or non-Jewish individuals and/or their property, toward Jewish community institutions and religious facilities." Specific forms of anti-Semitism include:
 – "Denying the fact, scope, mechanisms (e.g., gas chambers) or intentionality of the genocide of the Jewish people at the hands of National Socialist Germany and its supporters and accomplices during World War II (the Holocaust)."
 – "Accusing the Jews as a people, or Israel as a state, of inventing or exaggerating the Holocaust."
But again, one wonders what is meant by such words as 'denying' or 'exaggerating.' Such terms are so broad as to potentially include almost any criticism, questioning, or inquiry into the event. Hence my point that 'anti-Semitism' is so ill-defined as to be almost meaningless. Or worse: to be whatever those in power want it to be.

Who's Who in the Debate

I will close this first chapter with a quick look at the main players on each side of the debate. Consider first the orthodox historians. Here we have an immediate problem. There are literally thousands of books on the Holocaust, and hundreds of new ones appear each year. The sheer number of authors is astounding. Everyone, it seems, is in on the game. Publishers who are reticent to publish on other worthy topics readily snap up proposals for new Holocaust books. Apparently it is a good career move to write, and to publish, on the Holocaust.

In order to bring some structure to the chaos of names, I will focus on the leading figures past and present, and on those few who have elected to engage with revisionism. Let me begin with those now deceased, and then move on to the currently active writers.

Among the more important past authors are:

> Gerald Reitlinger (died 1978). His book *The Final Solution*, first published in 1953, was one of the earliest detailed studies. It covered all aspects of the Holocaust, from the Jewish perspective. But there was one small problem: Reitlinger counted far fewer than six million deaths. His estimated range—from 4.2 to 4.58 million—is the lowest of any major author. Today such figures would border on heresy, but in 1953 there was no such tension. Even in the later revisions to his book, he did not significantly alter his numbers. Perhaps unsurprisingly, Reitlinger is not often cited by traditionalists today.
> Lucy Dawidowicz (died 1990). Her major works included *The War against the Jews* (1975, 1986), and *The Holocaust and the Historians* (1981). She estimated a total of 5.9 million Jewish fatalities.
> Jean-Claude Pressac (d. 2003). A pharmacist by training, and one of the few non-Jews to challenge revisionism. Pressac's work *Auschwitz: Technique and Operation of the Gas Chambers* (1989) was a direct response to the writings of Faurisson. A very detailed study of the design and operation of the Auschwitz crematoria and gas chambers, this work raised as many questions as it answered. It is far from the "definitive refutation" of revisionism that was sought.
> Pièrre Vidal-Naquet (died 2006). Author of *Assassins of Memory* (1992—French original in 1987), an early attempt to refute revisionism. Almost useless for assessing the validity of revisionist arguments, since he addressed nothing in specifics. An arrogant and polemical response to revisionism.

- Raul Hilberg (died 2007). Until his death, Hilberg was considered the preeminent expert on the Holocaust. His primary work, *The Destruction of the European Jews*, first appeared in 1961. In 1985 the book was expanded to a three-volume set. A third edition came out in 2003, clocking in at nearly 1,400 pages. Like Reitlinger, Hilberg is notable for his low overall death toll; he consistently calculated 5.1 million victims, which has become the lower limit of the 'acceptable' range—though even this is rarely mentioned.
- Yisrael Gutman (died 2013). His *Denying the Holocaust* (1985) was one of the first books to tackle the revisionist arguments, although it has not had much of a lasting effect on the debate.

Among current researchers, we have:

- Yitzhak Arad. His 1987 book *Belzec, Sobibor, Treblinka* remains the standard source for those camps—a rather amazing fact, given that it is nearly 30 years old. Arad was a research director at the Israeli Holocaust center, Yad Vashem.
- Shelly Shapiro. She compiled an anthology of essays against revisionism, *Truth Prevails: Demolishing Holocaust Denial* (1990).
- Kenneth Stern. He wrote *Holocaust Denial* (1993), which is only a cursory response to the arguments.
- Deborah Lipstadt. Her *Denying the Holocaust* (1993) is perhaps the best-known anti-revisionist work. Unfortunately, very little of this book addresses the actual arguments—as the reader is invited to confirm. Lipstadt and her book became widely known after historian David Irving sued her for libel. She is a professor of theology at Emory University in Atlanta.
- Michael Shermer and Alex Grobman. Co-writers of *Denying History* (2000)—after Lipstadt, the next most popular anti-revisionist source.
- John Zimmerman. His book *Holocaust Denial* (2000) was the first to seriously address, in detail, revisionist arguments. It is a technical, academic work, and plays a prominent role in the debate. Zimmerman is an accountant at the University of Nevada, Las Vegas.
- Robert van Pelt. His hefty 2002 book *The Case for Auschwitz* arose from his expert testimony for Lipstadt at the Irving trial. He is a professor of architecture at Waterloo University, Canada, and actively lectures on the Holocaust.
- Ian Kershaw. British historian, now retired, and author of several important works, including *Hitler 1936-1945* (2000) and *Hitler, the Germans, and the Final Solution* (2008).

> Christopher Browning. An American historian, also retired. Author of *Ordinary Men* (1992), *The Path to Genocide* (1998), and *The Origins of the Final Solution* (2004).
> Richard Evans. Retired Cambridge historian and author of an important three-volume series, *The Third Reich at War* (2003-2008). Regarding the Holocaust debate, his major contribution was *Lying about Hitler* (2001), recounting his version of the Irving-Lipstadt trial.
> Peter Longerich. A German historian currently working at the University of London. His books *The Unwritten Order* (2003), *Holocaust* (2010), and *Heinrich Himmler* (2011) have been influential in sustaining the orthodox view. As the youngest of the major active writers, Longerich may be expected to be the standard-bearer for some time to come.

In addition to these individuals, we must also include the standard reference works: *Encyclopedia of the Holocaust* (1990; I. Gutman, ed.) and more recently *The Holocaust Encyclopedia* (2001; W. Laqueur, ed.). Finally, we have the leading research organizations, which would include the Israeli group Yad Vashem (www.yadvashem.org) and the US Holocaust Memorial Museum (www.ushmm.org).

Anti-revisionist forces have been notably quiet in the past decade. Just one new book has appeared,[24] and only a handful of journal articles. This is in marked contrast to the outpouring of books by revisionists in that same period—some two dozen in total. Of course, thousands of traditionalist books and articles have appeared in that time, but virtually none of these take on the revisionist challenge. Officially, revisionism is now 'unworthy' of response; unofficially, it's good policy to avoid a battle that you may well lose.

And in the Other Corner…

Early revisionism, as mentioned, was marked by as much polemics and inflammatory language as scholarship. Revisionists thus tend to fall into one

---

[24] The (unpublished) book—actually, a "white paper" available only as a PDF file online—is *Belzec, Sobibor, Treblinka: Holocaust Denial and Operation Reinhard* (Harrison *et al.*, 2011). This is a unique case, however. The five authors are all 'professional bloggers,' not affiliated with any university or research center, and generally lacking in any formal qualifications. They have, in fact, been denounced by their fellow traditionalists for their shoddy practices. But the work does offer a detailed response to many revisionist arguments. It has generated an even-more-detailed revisionist response, *The "Extermination Camps" of "Aktion Reinhardt": An Analysis and Refutation of Factitious "Evidence," Deceptions and Flawed Argumentation of the "Holocaust Controversies" Bloggers* (Mattogno *et al.*, 2013).

of two subgroups: *activists* and *academics*. Both groups are important, and both have their own roles to play. Both groups require fortitude and courage, though in different ways. Naturally, some individuals fall into both categories; Faurisson and Töben come to mind.

For our purposes, the second group is of chief interest. The activists make the news, and poke their finger in the public eye, but it is the academics that do the important groundwork to establish the basis for revisionist claims. Academic revisionists conduct careful, scientific examination of the circumstances of the Holocaust, and write high-quality articles and books on their critiques. They deserve to be taken seriously. Early academics would include such people as Franz Scheidl and Paul Rassinier, whose initial work dates from the 1950s. But things did not really start heating up until the mid-1970s. From then on we find a growing number of serious, dedicated works. The major revisionist academics include:

- Arthur Butz. His 1976 book *The Hoax of the Twentieth Century* marked the beginning of serious revisionism. The latest revised edition came out in 2015. A dense and challenging book, but useful for scholarly research. Butz has a PhD in engineering, and is currently a tenured associate professor at Northwestern University, near Chicago, Illinois.
- Paul Rassinier (died 1967). He further developed his ideas in the 1960s, which appeared in English translations as *Debunking the Genocide Myth* (1978) and *The Holocaust Story and the Lies of Ulysses* (1990, 2nd ed.).
- Robert Faurisson. In the late 1970s he published some notorious revisionist articles in the French newspaper *Le Monde*. Since then he has been a leading figure in the movement, at once an academic and a promoter. His magnum opus is the four-volume French work *Ecrits Révisionnistes (1974–1998)*. Faurisson is a retired professor of humanities from Lyon University.
- Wilhelm Stäglich (died 2006). A PhD and judge in Germany, he wrote *The Auschwitz Myth* in 1979 (English version 1986), causing an uproar.
- David Irving. A prominent historian and expert on the Third Reich. A borderline revisionist; the Holocaust is not really his area of expertise, but he seems to get drawn in time and again.
- Friedrich Berg. A specialist on the diesel exhaust issue. Berg is an engineer and has been a leading advocate of "scientific" revisionism, based on objective data and scientifically verifiable facts.
- Samuel Crowell. Pseudonym for an American professor of history. Though not a major figure in revisionism, Crowell is, along with

Faurisson, the most scholarly. His monograph *The Gas Chamber of Sherlock Holmes* (2011) is an excellent "literary analysis" of the many problems with the conventional account.
- Thomas Kues. A Swedish scholar and multi-linguist. Kues has written some 50 revisionist articles, with a focus on the so-called 'Reinhardt' camps: Belzec, Sobibor, and Treblinka.
- Germar Rudolf. As a scientist (chemistry), writer, lecturer and publisher, Rudolf is a leading figure in revisionism today. His *Dissecting the Holocaust* (2003, 2nd ed.) and *Lectures on the Holocaust* (2011, 2nd ed.) are essential reading for anyone serious about the subject.
- Jürgen Graf. A Swiss researcher, and author or co-author of several important writings, including books on the Treblinka, Sobibor, Majdanek and Stutthof camps. He also wrote a definitive critique of Raul Hilberg, *The Giant with Feet of Clay* (2015, 2nd ed.).
- Carlo Mattogno. An Italian researcher, Mattogno is the leading writer of serious academic works. He has published detailed texts on the gas chambers and crematories of Auschwitz, and written or co-written major works on all five of the other 'extermination camps.' Unquestionably the leading technical expert among revisionists today.

If the reader is unfamiliar with most of the above names, we should not be surprised. There has been a concerted effort to ensure that the leading revisionist scholars are never engaged, never cited, and never publicized. This is another clue that all is not as it seems in the Great Debate.

With this short background in place, we can now begin to take a serious look at the traditional Holocaust story, analyzing its strengths and weaknesses. Chapter 2 will recount this story and examine the troublesome nature of historical truth—troubles which are greatly magnified with the Holocaust.

Chapter 2: Truth vs. Lies

Any aspect of a major war offers myriad opportunities and reasons to alter, edit, distort, or create evidence. This is particularly true with the Holocaust. Virtually every person or organization connected with this event has a strong interest in a particular outcome. Each has particular strengths and weaknesses. Each comes to the situation with a particular worldview in place. Each is motivated by a variety of factors: benign self-interest, greed, justice, revenge, hatred, naïveté. Some motives are malevolent, others not. In general it is very difficult to accurately discern a person's reason for acting, and thus we should be very slow to impute negative motives to others. Furthermore, we must deal with many fundamental human failings. People make mistakes. Memories fail. Senses deceive. All these factors present us with great difficulties as we attempt to work out our particular notions of truth.

Historical events pose a unique problem. To state the obvious, events of the past are truly and absolutely gone forever. The many actions that occurred during World War II have vanished from existence. We must resign ourselves to the fact that we will never know, with certainty, the actual truth of things as they happened. The best we can do today is to examine the physical and documentary remains of history and construct a comprehensible narrative—an explanation, of sorts. In a very real sense, constructing history is our task here. There is no other choice.

Regarding the Holocaust, there is already one such narrative: the traditional view of the 6 million Jewish deaths, the gas chambers, the cremation furnaces. But perhaps even this simple statement of the conventional story is assuming too much. Many people today believe that the Nazis "gassed 6 million Jews," or "burned 6 million Jews in the furnaces of Auschwitz"—both claims wildly incongruous with even the traditional version. Thus there is some benefit, I think, in reexamining the essential details of the conventional story. This will give us a base to work from, and also allow a better understanding of the perspective of both parties in the Great Debate.

The Traditional Story

Let me begin with some basic facts. The standard definition of the Holocaust given in Chapter 1 included three essential elements: 6 million Jews killed, the use of gas chambers (among other means), and a program of systematic, intentional killing originating from the top of the Nazi hierarchy. For this definition I cited a source from the year 2000.

However, even in the short time since then we have begun to see a subtle but important shift in the conception of the Holocaust. A good example from just three years later is the *World Book Encyclopedia*, 2003 edition. This is a putatively neutral source, but the entry on the Holocaust was written by the same Michael Berenbaum whom I cited in Chapter 1. So we can expect a fairly straightforward recounting of the orthodox view—and no discussion of revisionist challenges. All subsequent quotes in the present chapter are from this entry.

Berenbaum's entry begins with a revised definition: the Holocaust "was the systematic, state-sponsored murder of Jews *and others* by the Nazis during World War II." The inclusion of "others" is noteworthy. This has two consequences: (1) it maintains a high overall death total, significantly above the number of Jews, and (2) it emphasizes that non-Jews were also victims, hence broadening the base of sympathy. It is not only Jews who should see the Nazis as evil; in a sense, we *all* are victims.

"By the end of the war, the Nazis had killed about 6 million Jewish men, women, and children—more than 2/3 of the Jews in Europe." Hence, a prewar European Jewish population of about 8 million. "Historians estimate that perhaps as many as 11 million people were killed, including the Jews"—thus about 5 million "others." Accordingly, the others constitute about 45 percent of the Holocaust, Jews 55 percent. Any balanced assessment of this event should, therefore, roughly match these proportions. Even a cursory glance at the literature, however, shows that this is not the case. Writings on non-Jewish Holocaust victims cannot comprise more than 1 percent of the total.

"Many of the Holocaust victims were killed in specially constructed gas chambers, and their bodies were then burned." The vagueness of "many" is, of course, one of the key points of contention. Burning of the bodies turns out to be critical, for two reasons. First, it is strikingly difficult to completely consume a human body with fire, as we will see. Second, the act of burning yields a sort of total elimination of the corpses—and hence the primary evidence of the crime. If the bodies were simply buried somewhere in mass graves, we would then have the opportunity to dig them up, count them, perform autopsies, and so on. But "burned" is—gone.

This systematic mass murder was planned, we are told, by the highest levels of the Nazi government:

> Sometime in early 1941, the Nazi leadership finalized the details of a policy decision labeled "The Final Solution of the Jewish Question." This policy called for the murder of every Jew… under German rule. … At the Wannsee Conference, held in Berlin in January 1942, Nazi leaders further systematized the killing.

Revisionists take issue with such a statement, as will be seen later. To anticipate the main point: nothing in the Wannsee record indicates that the Jews were to be *killed*. Corralled into ghettos, yes. Expelled, yes. But murdered, no.

Berenbaum continues, "The slaughter began with Germany's invasion of the Soviet Union in June 1941." Shooting was too slow, so "they began using sealed vans. The prisoners choked to death on exhaust fumes as the van traveled to a burial pit." The majority of the so-called gas vans were diesel trucks, which were supposedly modified as killing machines.[25] But there is an immediate problem here: diesel exhaust, under anything approaching normal operating conditions, contains too little carbon monoxide, and too much oxygen, to kill people in any reasonable time—more on this in Part II.

Systematic killing supposedly began only with the alleged extermination camps, built in 1941 and 1942. The common view is that dozens or even hundreds of these camps were used to exterminate the Jews, including such infamous ones as Dachau, Buchenwald and Bergen-Belsen. But this is not the case, as the experts readily admit. Of the many concentration and labor camps run by the Nazis, only six were alleged centers of extermination: **Chelmno**, **Belzec**, **Sobibor**, **Treblinka**, **Majdanek** and **Auschwitz**. It was in these camps *only* that the mass gassings and mass burnings supposedly occurred.[26]

The gas chambers are at the horrific center of the traditional view. Eyewitnesses have described specific individual events—in themselves nothing

---

[25] The makes, models and engine types of the first set of gas vans, which were spontaneous make-shift solutions, are uncertain. The second set of trucks, however, is said to have been properly planned and designed for their homicidal purpose and was purchased from the Austrian Saurer company. Saurer, a pioneer in diesel engines, produced exclusively diesel trucks. See Alvarez (2011) for details.

[26] Of course, thousands (revisionist view) or millions (orthodox view) of Jews died at other locations, and in other ways. In fact, according to most researchers, the six death camps only account for about 50 percent of total Jewish casualties. The other half were killed in open-air shootings, or died in ghettos or of general deprivation or illness. But it remains the case that the only (alleged) systematic, industrialized mass killing of Jews occurred in those six camps. Also, the so-called extermination camps are sometimes referred to as "death camps," though this can be misleading. Large numbers of deaths occurred at many camps, and all of these could reasonably be called "death camps." Here, though, I will follow common practice and treat the two terms as essentially synonymous.

criminal—that have been merged into a composite view of the alleged gassing process:

> As many as 2,000 prisoners were sent into the gas chambers at one time. SS personnel poured containers of poison gas down an opening. Within 20 to 30 minutes, the new arrivals were dead.

The "containers" refer to cans of Zyklon B, a form of hydrogen cyanide gas that was stored in small gypsum pellets and used as a fumigation gas for rodents and lice. According to the standard story, SS men dumped the pellets into the chambers, allowing the gas to evaporate and quickly kill those inside. The encyclopedia mentions "20–30 minutes," but some have testified, under oath, that death came within 5 minutes or less. Shortly thereafter, workers entered the chambers and extracted the dead bodies. This gassing activity produced a huge quantity of corpses, which, for practical, sanitary and evidentiary reasons, had to be completely disposed of: "[the SS] burned the bodies in crematoriums or open pits."

Of the six death camps, the largest and most notorious was Auschwitz. "[A]bout 1.25 million people were murdered there." Actually, most historians now quote a figure closer to 1.1 million, of whom the vast majority—around 1 million—were Jews.

"Shocking and Strange"

Regarding Auschwitz, a fact *not* mentioned is perhaps as important as the ones stated. For 45 years, it was an "established fact" that 4 million people died at Auschwitz. This was the figure that showed up in *Time* and *Newsweek*, in the *Encyclopedia Britannica* and countless school texts. A plaque engraved with this number stood for years in the camp. In 1979, Pope John Paul II knelt and prayed for "the 4 million victims of Auschwitz."

Then in 1990, the number changed virtually overnight. On July 17, the *Washington Times* reported:

> Poland has cut its estimate of the number of people killed by the Nazis in the Auschwitz death camp from 4 million to just over 1 million. ... Shevach Weiss, a death camp survivor and Labor Party member of the Israeli Parliament, expressed disbelief at the revised estimates, saying, "It sounds shocking and strange." ... The latest Polish research is based on studies of prisoners' personal numbers, transport documents and data about Jewish ghettos. (p. A11)

This sudden change from 4 million to 1 million is indeed "shocking and strange." It is an astonishing revision of the standard Holocaust story—suddenly there were 3 million fewer deaths than previously believed. Prior to

1990, then, the total casualty figure for the Holocaust must have been 14 million, since it is 11 million now. Oddly, though, such a number has never appeared in print, to my knowledge.

But the more surprising fact is this: The number of Jewish deaths—the 6 million—did not change. How can that be? Quite simple: Before 1990 we were told there were 1 million Jewish and 3 million non-Jewish deaths; after 1990, it was 1 million Jewish deaths and *100,000 non-Jews*.[27] The story now is that the Poles, not wanting to be left out of the victimhood sweepstakes, had claimed a far greater number of Polish (non-Jewish) victims. But they had done so without any justification. By 1990, the evidence had become overwhelming, and the '4 million' could no longer be sustained.

> The vast majority of the dead are now accepted to have been Jews, despite claims by the former Polish communist government that as many Poles perished in Hitler's largest concentration camp. The revised Polish figures support claims by Israeli researchers that Poland's former communist government exaggerated the number of victims by inflating the estimate of non-Jews who died. (*ibid.*)

"Exaggerated" is an understatement. The non-Jewish death toll at Auschwitz dropped from 3 million to 100,000. This is a reduction of 97 percent. We can only imagine the consequences if a comparable drop should ever occur in the Jewish toll.

On the face of it, this dramatic change was a stunning setback for traditionalism. And in a sense, it was. The total magnitude of the Holocaust is now less than it used to be, and hence so is its historical significance. But on the other hand, this reduction serves to strengthen the position of those who prefer to emphasize the Jewish aspect of the Holocaust. Before 1990, Jews were a minority of Auschwitz deaths—1 million out of 4 million (25 percent). Now they are 90 percent, or roughly 1 million out of 1.1 million. Auschwitz is now a truly Jewish phenomenon.

Even more surprising: *Before 1990, Jews were a minority of the Holocaust*—6 million deaths out of some 14 million total (43 percent). Now they are, as noted above, the majority: 6 out of 11 million (55 percent). Hence this change at Auschwitz, trumpeted by revisionists as a victory, actually consolidated Jewish claims on the Holocaust.

---

[27] One million Jewish deaths at Auschwitz have been claimed at least since 1961, with the initial publication of Raul Hilberg's work *The Destruction of the European Jews*. Reitlinger (1953) argued for even less, something approaching 800,000. But there has always been disagreement about this number. Laqueur (2001: 177) points out that before 1990, the Poles, who were promoting the 4 million figure, claimed that there were at least 2.5 million Jewish deaths. Few Western researchers accepted such a high number. But of course, victims always have an incentive to exaggerate casualty figures.

To wrap up this little detour: Where did the outlandish figure of 4 million come from in the first place? The *Washington Times* states:

> Shmuel Krakowski, head of research at Israel's *Yad Vashem* memorial for Jewish victims of the Holocaust, said the new Polish figures were correct. "The 4 million figure was let slip [at the Nuremberg trials] by Capt. Rudolf Höss, the death camp's Nazi commander. Some have bought it, but it was exaggerated." (*ibid.*)

First of all, Krakowski is simply wrong. Höss testified that *3 million* died at Auschwitz.[28] The 4-million figure in fact came from Soviet testimony, and was pure propaganda.[29] Second, what does "let slip" mean? Does Krakowski expect us to believe that Höss made some careless slip of the tongue—as if he let out the secret to someone's birthday surprise? Unlikely. And I must beg to differ, once again, with the term "exaggerated." Höss's figure of 3 million was triple that accepted today. That's not an exaggeration; that's pure fantasy. And if this number, arguably the single most important piece of Höss's testimony, is pure fantasy, how much of the rest should we believe?[30] But considering that Höss was likely tortured and coerced into making his so-called confession, the 3-million figure is not surprising. The Nuremberg trials were as much theater as they were legal proceedings—as I explain below.

The traditional Holocaust story ends with the dismantling and destruction of the death camps, Hitler's death by suicide, and Germany's surrender in May 1945. As the Allies progressively overran the concentration camps, their photos and other details reached the outside world. The camps held thousands of sick and emaciated people; huge piles of clothes, shoes, and personal belongings; and, in some cases, remnants of gas chambers and crematoria. Here then was "proof of Nazi savagery." Survivors told the horrific stories of things they heard and experienced: disease and hunger, humiliation and forced labor, the gas chambers, dead bodies, and pervasive fire and smoke from the burning of corpses. By all accounts it added up to only one thing: a deliberate scheme of mass murder.

Then came the Nuremberg tribunals of 1945 and 1946, and a series of ancillary trials in the following years. The accused Germans submitted written statements of confession, explaining their roles in the whole affair. Victims gave eyewitness testimony. Photos and documents were entered into the official record. In the end, most of the German leaders were executed,

---

[28] IMT (vol. 33), pp. 275-278. This is the Blue Series—see note 36 below.
[29] IMT (vol. 39), pp. 241, 261.
[30] Browning (2004: 544) observes that "the testimonies of especially Höss and to some extent Eichmann are confused, contradictory, self-serving, and not credible." Problems with Höss's testimony, and that of many other witnesses, are summarized in Appendix B.

and many of the lesser figures served lengthy prison terms. Once this was all over, it remained for the survivors to elaborate on their experiences, academics to research and document every conceivable aspect—and for the victims to seek, and receive, restitution. This process continues to this day. A monumental, expensive, and time-consuming Holocaust machine is in place, working day and night to ensure that we "never forget."

One immediate effect of the Holocaust was a surge in support for a Jewish homeland in Palestine. Since the late 1800s, the Jewish movement known as Zionism had pushed the international community to grant Jews land on which they could create a Jewish-only state. Various proposals were made, but the Zionists insisted upon the Biblical lands of Palestine. This might have worked, except that several hundred thousand Arabs were already living there. Jews, of course, had lived there as well for centuries, but in much smaller numbers. And they had not been a ruling power in that region for over 2,000 years.[31] Even as late as World War I, they constituted just 10 percent of the population. Yet they demanded their own state.

In 1917 the British, about to obtain colonial rule over the area, decided to support the idea of a Jewish "homeland" in Palestine. Caught in a stalemate in World War I, the British badly needed American aid. But the Americans were rightly reluctant to enter a foreign war. The best option for the British was to mobilize the American Jewish lobby to sway Woodrow Wilson, and thus to draw in the US. And the only card they had to play was Palestine. Thus Britain made a "contract with Jewry," promising Palestine to the Zionists in exchange for bringing America into the war; this was the famous Balfour Declaration. As we know, the plan was a success.[32]

Jewish immigration increased, but it met with Arab resistance. In 1947, in the shadow of the Holocaust, the matter went to the UN. The General Assembly—not the Security Council—agreed to a partition plan in November, and shortly thereafter the purging of native Palestinians from the land began. Nearly 800,000 Palestinians were bribed, coerced, or driven off their land in order to make way for the new Jewish state, a state deemed necessary and appropriate in light of the Holocaust. This conflict has only intensified and broadened in the intervening 70 years. Zionism and the existence of the state of Israel are thus closely related to the current Holocaust debate.

---

[31] The last Jewish rule ended in 63 BC, when the Roman Empire incorporated Palestine.
[32] For details see Dalton (2013).

A Question of Evidence

Before getting into the details of the arguments, it is worth examining how, and from whom, we have come to know the traditional story. This matter is closely related to the general *question of evidence*. For the Holocaust, as for almost any crime, there exist four general categories of evidence:

1) **Eyewitness accounts**, from surviving victims;
2) **Statements of confession or innocence**, from alleged perpetrators;[33]
3) **Documentation**, relating to the crime (including photographs); and
4) **Material evidence**—bodies, murder weapons, physical structures, etc.

These four categories can be split in half. The first two, being subjective, rely on an individual's perception and memory. They are subject to either willful or inadvertent manipulation. They are at the whim of the personal motives of the individual: fear, hatred, desire for revenge, desire for fame, eagerness to exonerate or gain leniency for oneself, and so on. And they can change over time; a statement made shortly after the war may differ substantially from one made years later.

The second two, being objective and physical, can be measured, tested, and analyzed. They are not subject to individual whim, though they do admit of varying degrees of interpretation. Like all physical things, these objective pieces of evidence do change over time, but very slowly. They change only with the gradual aging that all objects experience—unless of course they have been counterfeited, tampered with or deliberately destroyed, which is always a concern.

Consequently, in both the court of law and the court of science, the latter two categories generally have priority over the former two. Particularly so when the personal statements involve either the accused or the plaintiffs, neither of whom is unbiased. Necessarily, such statements are of questionable value. Consider this: If you suddenly came across a fistfight between two people, and after it was over wanted to know what happened, you could ask each of the two combatants for their view—but you probably would not get the straight story from either one. If you ask Jewish death camp survivors for their view, and German guards or camp officials for theirs, you will probably not get the straight story. This is no surprise. Of course, the best testimony is that of a neutral third party, an innocent bystander, who can objectively observe events with no equity in the outcome. Unfortunately such individuals are very rare here. We are, for practical purposes, stuck with biased and partial statements as our subjective evidence.

---

[33] Supplemental testimony is also often sought by neutral parties and by subject-matter experts. I address these later, as appropriate.

This raises an important point in the Great Debate. Traditionalists rely more heavily on the first two (subjective) categories of evidence. They point to dozens of survivor witness statements and testimonies, and to the postwar confessions of the leading Nazis, to make their case. This is not to say that they ignore the physical evidence, but it is generally less supportive of their arguments, and hence is usually de-emphasized. The revisionists, on the other hand, rely more heavily on physical evidence and the physical conditions at the camps. They examine the ruined remains of buildings, analyze photographs, assess wartime documentation, and perform calculations based on scientific information. Not that the revisionists ignore personal statements—but they use them differently. Whereas traditionalists tend to look for consistency and commonality in witness statements to construct a possible picture of events, revisionists look for inconsistency and implausibility, in order to undermine witness credibility. And of course they promote the views of witnesses who support their case. Both tactics are familiar to any good trial lawyer.

The net effect is that the traditionalists are on relatively shaky ground. Revisionists who stick to objective evidence and scientific analysis have the firmer footing. This is one reason why the debate has become so interesting.

The Nuremberg Trials

With the Holocaust, our primary sources of information include the above categories of evidence that were created or documented during or immediately after the war. A large portion of this evidence—at least regarding the first three categories—was compiled for the famous Nuremberg war crimes trials. These were a series of 13 separate trials spread out over five years (1945–1949).

The most important of these was the first, which ran from November 1945 to October 1946. It was administered by a group called the *International Military Tribunal* (IMT), and presided over by an eight-judge panel—two each from the four victor nations: US, United Kingdom, Soviet Union and France. The Americans ran the show. Twenty-two leading German officials were tried, including Göring, Hess,[34] Speer and Bormann. Nineteen were convicted, 12 executed.

---

[34] Just to avoid potential confusion: Rudolf Hess, the Nazi party deputy leader and personal secretary to Hitler, is not to be confused with Rudolf Höss, the former Auschwitz commander. Höss was central to the Holocaust, Hess irrelevant. Regarding pronunciation, 'Hess' rhymes with 'yes,' whereas the vowel in 'Höss' sounds like the vowel in English words like 'fir.' To add to the confusion: 'Höss' is also spelled 'Hoess' and even 'Höß.'

The remaining twelve trials were conducted by the Americans alone, involving nearly 200 lesser defendants. In spite of what some think, the emphasis of the trials was not on the Holocaust; in the thousands of pages of documents and testimony, Jews play a very minor role.[35] The primary goal was to establish that Germany was the cause of the war, and hence to duly punish its leaders. Other concerns, such as prosecuting war crimes and crimes against humanity, followed as a consequence.

The proceedings of these trials, especially the first one, form the core of our primary evidence.[36] Additional valuable testimony comes from the hundreds of post-Nuremberg trials and from statements made outside of court proceedings, primarily in the form of books or memoirs. Memoirs published soon after the war are often useful, but the later they were published, the lower their value. We find new "eyewitness accounts" and "confessions" appearing in print decades after the end of the war, and even to the present day; for the most part these have little evidentiary value.

The US team which instigated the entire trial process was heavily weighted with Jewish-Americans—so much so that a leading American prosecutor, Thomas Dodd, felt compelled to remark on this fact in a series of personal letters. They appear in his book *Letters from Nuremberg* (2007), edited by his son, the former US Senator Christopher Dodd. As the younger

---

[35] According to Dodd (2007: 37), "In the millions of words in the [Nuremberg] transcript, a relatively small percentage is devoted to Hitler's grotesque measures against the Jews." Even Elie Wiesel was struck by this fact: "I am not sure why the Jewish tragedy did not play the major role it should have. … The more I read about it, the less I understand" (ibid.).

[36] Unfortunately, the various formats under which they were published are confusing and difficult to track down. Three versions are particularly important:
1. The IMT proceedings are most fully documented in the massive 42-volume work titled *The Trial of German Major War Criminals*, published by the IMT in 1947; this work is also referred to as the Blue Series. This series includes the main pieces of evidence against the highest-ranking German officials, and thus is central for the Holocaust. The full set of these volumes is quite rare; even many major research universities do not have it. Fortunately it can be found at the online database Hein Online. The first 22 volumes are available online as part of Yale University's Avalon project.
2. The remaining 12 trials are documented in the 15-volume set *Trials of War Criminals before the Nuremberg Military Tribunals*, published by the US Government Printing Office (1951–1952)—a.k.a. the Green Series.
3. Finally, there is the 10-volume work *Nazi Conspiracy and Aggression* (US Department of State, 1946). This set, also called the Red Series, contains English translations of many of the German documents included in the full 42-volume IMT set. Also available on the Yale Web site.

To add to the confusion, the UK government published two further sets:
4. A condensed British version of the IMT trial, published under the same name as the US version, except in 23 volumes; and
5. A British version of the 12 post-IMT trials, published as *Law Reports of Trials of War Criminals* (14 volumes).

These last two sets are rarely cited in recent literature.

Dodd first recalls, "the United States was the key force behind the trial and had provided most of the funding for it" (p. 35). To cover for American control, a British jurist was appointed as presiding judge.

In a letter of 20 September 1945, Thomas Dodd explains his concerns about Jewish dominance:

> The staff continues to grow every day. [Jewish-American] Col. Kaplan is now here, as a mate, I assume, for [Jewish-American] Commander Kaplan. [Jewish-American] Dr. Newman has arrived and I do not know how many more. It is all a silly business—but "silly" really isn't the right word. One would expect that some of these people would have sense enough to put an end to this kind of a parade. ... [Y]ou will understand when I tell you that this staff is about 75% Jewish. (p. 135)

Dodd clearly felt that this undermined the integrity of the trials:

> [T]he Jews should stay away from this trial—for their own sake. For—mark this well—the charge "a war for the Jews" is still being made, and in the post-war years it will be made again and again. The too-large percentage of Jewish men and women here will be cited as proof of this charge. Sometimes it seems that the Jews will never learn about these things. They seem intent on bringing new difficulties down on their own heads. I do not like to write about this matter... but I am disturbed about it. They are pushing and crowding and competing with each other, and with everyone else. They will try the case I guess... (pp. 135f.)

Revenge and compensation thus seem to have been the prime motives, rather than truth or justice. How else to explain a staff that is three-quarters Jewish, from a nation in which they were less than a 2 percent minority? In light of this, the shortcomings of Nuremberg are not surprising.[37]

I do not have the space here to recount the many problems with what the chief justice of the US Supreme Court, Harlan Stone, called a "high-grade lynching party in Nuremberg" (Mason 1956: 716). But a few points are in order. To begin with, we called them 'trials' but they were unlike any normal legal proceedings. In a real trial, there are three main parties involved: the accused, the plaintiff, and the impartial judge/jury. The judge and jury assume a neutral stance, hear evidence from both sides, allow cross-examination, and make impartial decisions regarding guilt, innocence, and punishment. All these were seriously deficient at Nuremberg. They were *victor trials*, conducted by the winning side, anxious to punish the losers, to portray them as barbaric madmen, and to justify the Allies' own actions that resulted in mass civilian casualties—actions which might well have been declared

---

[37] For a more detailed account of Jewish involvement in the trial, see Weber (1992).

criminal had *they* lost the war. It was predetermined that the Germans were guilty, that they committed mass murder, and that no act of retribution could be too harsh.

This is not simply my opinion. It is confirmed by those who were there at the time. For example, consider the comments of one American judge, Charles Wennerstrum, who presided over the "Hostages Trial," which was the seventh of the 12 later trials. Wennerstrum stated the obvious: "The victor in any war is not the best judge of the war crime guilt." The original Nuremberg trial was "devoted to whitewashing the allies and placing sole blame for World War II upon Germany." Trial proceedings were fundamentally biased. "The prosecution has failed to maintain objectivity aloof from vindictiveness, aloof from personal ambitions for convictions… The entire atmosphere is unwholesome," added Wennerstrum. Most troubling was the use of highly questionable testimony by captive Germans:

> [A]bhorrent to the American sense of justice is the prosecution's reliance upon self-incriminating statements made by the defendants while prisoners for more than 2½ years, and repeated interrogation without presence of counsel.

Today such testimony would be inadmissible in court; back then, it was par for the course. Upon packing up to return to America, Wennerstrum remarked, "If I had known seven months ago what I know today, I would never have come."[38]

And it wasn't only the Americans. In 2012 it was revealed that the British extensively tortured captive Germans in order to extract "confessions." Ian Cobain's book *Cruel Britannia* describes a facility known as the "London Cage," through which thousands of Germans passed—to be beaten, sleep-deprived, tortured, and in some cases murdered. As noted above, the most disturbing aspect was "when interrogators switched from extracting military intelligence to securing convictions for war crimes."

Normally such illegal tactics would be resolved by appeal to a higher court. But this was not the case at Nuremberg. The IMT was literally beyond the rule of law. It was absolutely sovereign, holding total authority over the proceedings. It set its own rules. Decisions were absolute. Appeal was impossible.

Normal legal trials are bound by rules of evidence; that is, valid evidence must be presented in support of key accusations, evidence that can be challenged and potentially excluded. But not the IMT. Consider Article 19:

> The Tribunal shall not be bound by technical rules of evidence. It shall adopt and apply to the greatest possible extent expeditious and non-

---

[38] *Chicago Daily Tribune* (23 Feb 1948, p. 1).

technical procedure, and shall admit any evidence which it deems to have probative value. (IMT, vol. 1: 15)

In other words, testimony did not have to be confirmed with material or forensic evidence. The IMT could accept virtually any statement as fact: opinion, hearsay, rumor, inference, belief. Furthermore, any facts that it chose to take as "common knowledge," no matter how they were obtained or how improbable they were, required no proof or evidence at all. This is known as "judicial notice."

Article 21: The Tribunal shall not require proof of facts of common knowledge, but shall take judicial notice thereof. (IMT, vol. 1: 15)

Once the court has taken judicial notice of something, it stands as an established fact. If the defendant should happen to disagree, he has no recourse. If the court "judicially notices" the standard Holocaust story, or the 6-million death figure, then it becomes unquestionable in the courtroom. This was true in 1947, and it is still true today. Modern courts, particularly in Europe, will "judicially notice" that 6 million Jews died at the hands of the Nazis. Consequently, anyone charged with Holocaust denial cannot even challenge this point in his own defense. And if his lawyer raises the issue, he or she will in turn be charged with 'denial'! The situation borders on the macabre.

Of particular concern were the means by which the IMT prosecutors were able to draw out so-called confessions from the German defendants. One revisionist describes it as a process of

threats of all kinds, or psychological torture, of non-stop interrogation and of confiscation of property of defendants as well as of coerced witnesses. Intimidation, imprisonment, legal prosecution and other means of coercion were applied to witnesses for the defense; distorted affidavits, documents, and synchronized translations; arbitrary refusal to hear evidence, confiscation of documents, and the refusal to grant the defense access to documents; as well as to the systematic obstruction of the defense by the prosecution... (Köhler 2003: 99f.)

Some affidavits, or legal confessions, were drafted by the Allied prosecutors and given to the witnesses to sign. They were then entered into the official record. Imagine how this might go: An imprisoned German officer, completely at the mercy of his captors, gets beaten and abused until he decides to 'talk.' He babbles some half-coherent words which are written down and 'clarified' by some American scribe. A statement is typed up, handed to the defendant, and told to sign—with a vague promise of leniency. Many who cooperated, and were deemed sufficiently safe, were freed or given light sentences; others were found guilty anyway and duly executed. This is obviously a recipe for bogus testimony, and may well explain the outrageous claims made by Höss, Mauthausen camp Commandant Franz Ziereis and others. At the very least it casts a large shadow of doubt over every German confessional statement in the proceedings.

Beyond the many volumes of court proceedings, we have, as mentioned, statements made outside the trial setting, both by Germans and survivors. In addition to the documents logged at Nuremberg, there were thousands of others that were retained by the Allies; of special interest are those acquired from Auschwitz and Majdanek. This has added some twists to the whole situation. Auschwitz, for example, was seized by the Soviets, who then held nearly all confiscated documents under lock and key until the late 1980s. The release of these has had mixed results, with both parties claiming additional victories and confirmation of theories.

In all of this, one kind of evidence is notably lacking: *material evidence*. This fact is perhaps the most shocking to contemplate. One would assume that, after 70 years, researchers have accumulated a veritable mountain of hard physical evidence in support of the conventional account. But this is not the case. In fact, quite the opposite. For example, a large proportion of the victims' bodies, we are told, were buried before they were exhumed and burned. And yet we cannot find evidence of these huge mass graves. Nearly all of the 6 million corpses were ultimately incinerated—and yet, apart from the Auschwitz crematoria, we cannot begin to explain how all those bodies were burned. Nor have we found more than an infinitesimal fraction of the tons of ash that would have been produced. Entire camps have all but vanished—notably, Belzec, Sobibor, and Treblinka. And the entire bureaucratic mechanism of the Holocaust has also disappeared—despite the fact that thousands of functionaries would have to have been involved with the process. We have no budget, no plan, no logistics, no Hitler order—nothing to suggest that the deliberate murder of millions took place.

In short, hard physical pieces of evidence of the alleged crime—bodies, ash, fire pits, mass graves, buildings, incriminating documents—are astonishingly absent. Either the Germans pulled off a near-miraculous erasure of virtually every trace of evidence, or the conventional view must change.

We can now begin to examine in detail the key elements of the Great Debate. I start with a look at the infamous number '6 million' and its surprising history.

Chapter 3: On the Origin, and Future, of the 'Six Million'

> *"The round figure of 6 million admits of no serious doubt…"*
> —*Holocaust Encyclopedia* (2001: 139)

The Holocaust was, above all, a crime of mass murder. This fact leads us to consider certain basic questions: How many people were killed? When, where, and how did they die? And, where are their remains? This chapter will tackle the first of these questions; the latter are addressed in Part II.

Traditionalism has straightforward answers to these questions. Five to six million Jews died. They were killed in all parts of the theater of war, and over several years, but primarily during 1941–1944, and primarily in the concentration camps and in various open-air shooting massacres. The remains have all but vanished.

Revisionists are not satisfied with this story. They want specifics, details and a clear and logical account of events. They want evidence. They want to know how, *technically*, it was possible to kill some 6 million people—fully half of these in the six death camps—and most over a period of just four years. This is a reasonable and logical demand. Yet traditionalists don't see it that way. They see this as an imposition, an intrusion, an unwelcome foray into difficult and troublesome ground—even as a personal insult. They take the basics of the story as a matter of faith, not to be questioned.

This is, in fact, exactly what was stated in the French paper *Le Monde*, in a 1979 response to Robert Faurisson by 34 leading French historians and intellectuals. At the conclusion of their essay, they wrote:

> It must not be asked how, *technically*, such a mass murder was possible. It was technically possible because it happened. This is the required point of departure for any historical inquiry on this subject.[39]

---

[39] *Le Monde* (21 Feb 1979, p. 23): "*Il ne faut pas se demander comment, techniquement, un tel meurtre de masse a été possible. Il a été possible techniquement puisqu'il a eu lieu. Tel est le point de départ obligé de toute enquête historique sur ce sujet.*"

Now this is a truly astonishing statement. We are being told that we cannot question an event of history, or how it happened. We cannot ask if or how it was possible; *it was possible because it happened.* This astounding bit of anti-rationalism recalls the medieval thinking of St. Anselm, who, in his attempt to comprehend God, said, "rather than seeking to understand so that I can believe, I believe so that I can understand."[40] Rather than trying to understand the Holocaust rationally so that we can justify our belief, we are told by the traditionalists that we must simply believe—we must have *faith*—and only then can we grasp "the truth."

Let's turn, then, to the single most important statistic of this event: the '6 million.' The matter of the total number of Jewish Holocaust victims seems straightforward, but there are difficulties in even posing such a question. In particular, we need to understand a few of the complexities involved with such basic terms as *Jewish*, *Holocaust*, and *victim*.

Jewishness is determined both by religion and ethnicity, which makes for confusion. The Germans employed an ethnic or racial model for the qualification, and so relied extensively on lineage in making determinations. Most ethnic Jews are also religious, but many are not; and a minority of religious Jews are of various other ethnicities. The Nazis were primarily concerned with the ethnic Jews, whether religious or secular. Orthodox Judaism is matrilineal: if you are born of a Jewish mother, you are Jewish. According to this definition there are no mixed offspring; you are either 100 percent, or not at all. The Nazis, on the other hand, classified people by mixed ancestry—full Jewish, one-half, one-quarter, etc. If we are counting Jewish fatalities, then it is unclear how to tally those of mixed ancestry.

We have already defined the Holocaust, but an important issue in the current context is its duration. Some would say it started on *Kristallnacht*— 9 November 1938, the night of the attacks on Jewish synagogues and businesses. Others would pick out the 1939 German invasion of Poland, which is the traditional start of World War II. Some cite the attack on the Soviet Union in mid-1941, when (according to orthodoxy) the mass killing of Jews first began. Yet others might point to the Wannsee Conference of January 1942, at which time the Nazis supposedly formalized their mass-murder plans. And those who would prefer the highest death toll may go all the way back to early 1933, when Hitler assumed power. There is no real consensus, then, on when the Holocaust began; this adds a further difficulty to our calculus.

The third term, 'victim,' is the most ambiguous. For those interested in high death rates, any Jew who died, for nearly any reason, anywhere in Eu-

---

[40] Anselm, *Proslogion* (ca. 1080 AD), Chapter 1.

rope, during the entire time of Hitler's rule (1933–1945) counts as a Holocaust victim. By this method, one can easily reach a figure of 6 million or more. In fact, the number becomes almost arbitrary at this point.

And then we have the distinction between 'died' and 'killed.' Most think that the Nazis killed 6 million, that is, deliberately murdered them in gas chambers, in mass executions, and by other means. But of course, Jews died all throughout the Nazi period of a variety of causes: old age, disease, illness, injury, suicide, homicide. In fact, in any sufficiently large group of people, about 1 percent die of various causes each year. If, as Berenbaum suggested, there were 8 million Jews in Europe prior to Hitler, then this group would experience some 80,000 deaths annually. Over the 5½ years of war in Europe, roughly 440,000 Jews would have died—if the Nazis had completely ignored them. If we count the time since the rise of Hitler, nearly 1 million would have died.[41]

How shall we count these 'natural' deaths? Surely they are not part of "the Holocaust," since they would have died anyway. Surely we should subtract 1 million or so deaths from our nominal total of 6 million, if we want an accurate accounting. But traditionalists do not see it this way. Any Jew who died, for any reason, counts as a 'victim.'

Holocaust by Numbers

So, how many Holocaust victims were there? We have already seen one official figure: 11 million, of whom 6 million were Jews. Others count only the Jews. But even Jewish deaths cover a wide range. For example, taking the highest estimates for just the six extermination camps (Auschwitz, Treblinka, Majdanek, Belzec, Sobibor, and Chelmno), we get a number in excess of 14 million—an absolute absurdity. As I will demonstrate, getting all the numbers to add up can be quite a challenge.

But let me be clear: Since the end of the war, most leading traditionalists have argued for a Jewish death toll in the range of 5 to 6 million. The lower end of this range is marked by Hilberg's 5.1 million, and by Wolfgang Benz's (1991: 17) "minimum" of 5.29 million. By far, however, the majority of writers accept a number approaching the upper limit of 6 million. This is the number that appears everywhere the Holocaust is discussed. According to traditionalism, it is almost sacrosanct. As Robinson (1976: 281) says, "there can be no doubt as to the accuracy of the estimated figure of some six million victims." The *Holocaust Encyclopedia* informs us that this number "admits of no serious doubt." In the Introduction, I mentioned various school

---

[41] Doubtless many Jews today who claim to have relatives who "died during the Holocaust" refer to people who were simply natural fatalities.

projects to collect 6 million pencils, pennies, or paper clips. This notorious figure has become a virtual obsession for many. In 2013, a book was published containing only the single word "Jew"—printed 6 million times.[42]

From a revisionist standpoint, the '6 million' has two major problems. First, we are never presented with a detailed breakdown of this number. By general consensus, Jewish deaths fall into three categories: *camps*, *ghettos*, and *shootings*. Therefore, it should be a simple matter to state clearly how many Jews died in each category, and when, such that the numbers add up to 6 million. This is such an elementary bit of analysis for a number that "admits of no serious doubt" that one would expect it to show up repeatedly and consistently in every scholarly inquiry. In fact it shows up—almost nowhere. The leading websites of USHMM and Yad Vashem do not have it. Encyclopedias do not have it. None of the leading traditionalists discusses it. Hence another clue that something is awry with "the most well-documented event in history."[43]

The second problem arises with this question: *How soon, reasonably speaking, would it have been possible to determine the total number of Jewish deaths?* This seemingly innocent question, all by itself, threatens to unravel the central thread of the Holocaust.

Recall a few facts of history. The Germans surrendered in May 1945. Europe was in chaos, and Germany in ruins. Literally millions of displaced persons and other refugees had been scattered to the winds. Any attempt to survey the war dead of any ethnicity would have been out of the question. One would have had to locate all the mass killing sites, examine forensic evidence at thousands of locations, exhume mass graves, and scour all concentration camps—including the six so-called death camps—for concrete and quantifiable evidence of mass murder. The process would have taken months under ideal circumstances, and more likely several years. But this is not what happened.

The first Nuremberg trial ran from November 1945 to October 1946, and one could perhaps surmise that it was in the course of the trial investigation that this number appeared. And indeed, the '6-million' figure was there. Its first appearance came at the very start of the trial, in the testimony of Wilhelm Höttl (or Hoettl). Recalling the words of Eichmann, Höttl testified that around 4 million Jews died in the concentration camps, and another 2 million

---

[42] See Chernofsky (2013). The book comes in at 1,250 pages.
[43] In fact the *only* slight exception I have found is in Stackelberg and Winkle (2002: 330). But they provide neither detail nor analysis: "Approximately 3 million victims of the Holocaust died in the six extermination camps in the east. Another 1½ million fell victim to the Einsatzgruppen and other [mass shooting] units... Perhaps as many as another 1½ million died of deprivation, disease, or abuse in the ghettos of eastern Europe, concentration camps, and the literally hundreds of labor camps run by the SS..." It hardly inspires confidence. I will take up this issue in Chapter 4.

in other ways.⁴⁴ A second appearance came in March 1946, when British prosecutor Maxwell Fyfe was interrogating Hermann Göring; Maxwell Fyfe cited Höttl's earlier testimony of 4 million plus another two.⁴⁵ A third occurrence came with a prosecutor's statement of 30 September 1946: "Adolf Eichmann… has estimated that the policy pursued resulted in the killing of 6,000,000 Jews, of which 4,000,000 were killed in the extermination institutions."⁴⁶ Thus the figure became codified at Nuremberg and has never relinquished its grip.

But the interesting question is this: When did the famous number *first* appear? Surprisingly, it was in circulation well before Nuremberg. In September of 1945, the *New York Times* reported this: "Loss of six million Jews during the war has made extremists of all Zionists…" (2 Sep)—as if it were common knowledge at that point. And in fact, it was. A month earlier they reported that "six million [Jews] have perished at the hands of the Nazis" (5 Aug). One month before that, on July 17, Jewish activist Abba Kovner gave a speech in Italy lamenting "the loss of six millions"; "we saw how the six million faced the great test… before their deaths," he exclaimed.⁴⁷

But this is only the beginning of the story. David Irving recounts an incident from June 1945 in which lead American prosecutor Robert H. Jackson was departing for Europe and the trials:

> A few days before leaving for London, Jackson [had] his first meeting with several powerful Jewish organizations who had already made quite clear to him they wanted a hand in running the trial… [T]hree leading lawyers, Judge Nathan Perlman, Dr. Jacob Robinson, and Dr. Alexander Kohanski, came to exert pressure… "How great were these [Jewish] losses?" inquired Jackson, seeking a figure to use at the coming trial. "Six million," responded Dr. Robinson, and indicated that the figure included Jews in all Nazi-occupied lands "from the Channel to Stalingrad." (1996: 61f.)

Jackson was rightly skeptical about this number; he noted in his diary, "I was particularly interested in knowing the source and reliability of his estimate as I know no authentic data on it." Robinson's reply—that it was an extrapolation from known prewar population statistics—was, in Irving's words, "somewhere between a hopeful estimate and an educated guess." In fact, it was far less than that.

The Germans surrendered on May 7. But just six days later, Lord Wright, chairman of the UN War Crimes Commission, could state this: "It has been

---
⁴⁴ IMT (vol. 31: 86). Himmler was reportedly disappointed, believing that the number "must be more than 6 million."
⁴⁵ IMT (vol. 9: 611).
⁴⁶ IMT (vol. 22: 496).
⁴⁷ See Kovner (1945/1976: 673, 680).

calculated that in all about six million Jews were deliberately slaughtered [in gas chambers] and other ways" (NYT, 13 May, p. SM4). How could Lord Wright have been so confident of this number, less than a week after the war? Who "calculated" this figure? And what evidence did they have?

But the war was indeed over, and it was at least theoretically possible to have such a figure. But that could not have been the case five months earlier. And yet in January 1945, the NYT was able to headline a story: "6,000,000 Jews Dead" (8 Jan, p. 17). The source of this number was "exiled economist" Jacob Lestchinsky; how he came to this determination, they did not say.

These are only the first steps of our inquiry into the history of the most famous number. This entire matter constitutes a fascinating subtext to the larger Holocaust story.

A Most Remarkable History

Consider for a moment the following scenario. Suppose someone were reading an account of Jewish persecution, and they came across the following quotations from the *New York Times*:

- "Appeal for aid for Jews: American Committee tells of Suffering Due to War. The American Jewish Relief Committee called a conference... to consider the plight of more than 6,000,000 Jews who live within the war zone."
- "In the world today there are about 13,000,000 Jews, of whom more than 6,000,000 are in the very heart of the war zone; Jews whose lives are at stake and who today are subjected to every manner of sorrow and suffering."
- The belligerent government in Europe "has only one aim in view, to exterminate the Jewish race."
- The head of a Jewish aid society "declared that even the wrongs of the Belgians could not be compared to the outrages heaped upon the Polish Jews. 'Nearly six million Jews are ruined, in the greatest moral and material misery... And the world is silent.'"
- "Six millions of Jews are living in lands where they are oppressed, exploited, crushed, and robbed of every inalienable human right."
- An appeal for an aid fund "to alleviate the suffering of Jews in the European war zones... [whose] suffering is unparalleled in history. ... [W]omen, children, and babies must be saved if the Jewish race is to survive the terrible holocaust..."
- "6,000,000 Jews need Help."

Naturally we would assume this was an account of World War II, perhaps in the later stages of that tragic conflict. But we would be wrong. In fact the above quotations were published... *during World War One*. Incredible as it may seem, all of these passages are dated between December 1914 and October 1918—virtually the entire duration of WWI.[48] 'Six million suffering Jews,' 'holocaust,' 'extermination': these were well established themes of the First World War, three decades before that other World War.

As one might guess at this point, these were not the first such references. Perhaps the earliest published connection dates all the way back to 1850. The newspaper *Christian Spectator* (16 Jan, p. 496) printed a short article on "Spiritual statistics of the world." They list the global population as 1 billion, of which "6,000,000 are Jews." Two decades later, the NYT reported similarly: "there are now living about 6,000,000 Israelites, nearly one half of whom live in Europe" (12 Sep 1869, p. 8).[49] One may speculate that it was around this time that the number '6 million' came to represent 'all the Jews.' Henceforth, whenever 'all the Jews' were under threat, the standard figure came up.

Just a few years later, there were already signs of trouble. The NYT reported in 1872 on the "persecution of Jews in Roumania" (23 Mar, p. 4). Gentile mobs were attacking them, and it appeared that "the blood-thirsty assailants would stop short of nothing but Jewish extermination"—an early precursor of claims of German extermination that would come some 70 years hence.

Or perhaps just eight years hence. In 1880 we read a striking report on "pleas for German Jews" (20 Dec, p. 2). The article examines a speech by German philosopher Eugen Dühring, and his "effrontery to demand the extermination of the entire [Jewish] race, in the name of humanity." The writer then speaks of petitions, before the German parliament, whose purpose is "extermination—the annihilation of the Jewish race."

The first mention of 6 million suffering Jews comes already in 1889. In a short article, the NYT (10 Feb, p. 14) asks "How many Jews are there?" The low estimate of "the ubiquitous race" is 6,000,000. "With the exception of half a million," it adds, "they are all in a state of political bondage." Two years later, in 1891, we read about the sorry state of "Russia's population of

---

[48] Specifically: (2 Dec 1914, p. 12), (14 Jan 1915, p. 3), (15 Apr 1915, p. 4), (28 Feb 1916, p. 8), (22 Jan 1917, p. 6), (24 Sep 1917, p. 20), and (18 Oct 1918, p. 12)—respectively. Unless otherwise stated, all remaining quotations in this chapter are from the *New York Times*.

[49] Interestingly, they provide some detail by country. Russia is #1, with 1.3 million Jews, or 22% of the world total. Germany is high on the list, with a total of 446,000 Jews (7.4%).

5,000,000 to 6,000,000 Jews," and of "the fact that about six millions persecuted and miserable wretches" still cling to their religion, against all odds.[50] The Russian government had been engaged in running conflicts with its Jewish population for several years, beginning when a few Jewish extremists managed to assassinate Czar Alexander II in 1881. Thus began a multi-year string of stories about the "6 million suffering Jews of Russia."

Such stories would prove useful to the nascent Zionist movement, which had only recently come into being. Its mission was—and is—to encourage world Jewry to settle in Palestine. The early Zionists were eager to play up Jewish suffering in order to promote mass emigration from Europe. Referring to the Jews of Russia, noted activist Stephen Wise said this in 1900: "There are 6,000,000 living, bleeding, suffering arguments in favor of Zionism" (11 Jun, p. 7). In 1901, the *Chicago Daily Tribune* reported on the "hopeless condition" of the "six million Jews in Russia" (22 Dec, p. 13).

A 1903 article is of particular interest. A pogrom in Kishinev in April of that year resulted in 47 deaths. The NYT dubbed this "a massacre," and reported a statement by the *Jewish Chronicle*: "We say it [the Russian government] is steeped to the eyes in the guilt of this holocaust. ... [The Jews are seen as] a perilous pest which must be slowly annihilated, [and Russians] will think themselves justified in accelerating the process of extermination..." (16 May, p. 1). All this is a remarkable anticipation of events to follow in Nazi Germany.

Periodic and often minor anti-Jewish actions were always portrayed in the most dramatic terms. The NYT despaired over "our 6,000,000 cringing brothers in Russia" (23 Mar 1905, p. 7). Later that year came a polemic against a Russian leader who "caused 6,000,000 Jewish families to be expelled" (1 Nov, p. 2)—which is impossible, incidentally, since that would have involved some 25 million Jews. In 1906 we read of "startling reports of the condition and future of Russia's 6,000,000 Jews"; it is a "horrifying picture" of "renewed massacres" and "systematic and murderous extermination" (25 Mar, p. SM6). At this point, one is tempted to ask, What is it about the Jews, such that they are subject to repeated threats of "extermination"?

In 1910, we find "Russian Jews in sad plight," and we are saddened over "the systematic, relentless, quiet grinding down of a people of more than 6,000,000 souls" (11 Apr, p. 18). In 1911 the NYT reported that "the 6,000,000 Jews of Russia are singled out for systematic oppression and for persecution by due process of law" (31 Oct, p. 5). Once again, we find '6 million'; 'systematic'; 'extermination'—a clear trend is forming. And yet things got worse still:

---

[50] The article goes on to quote a writer, E. Lanin, as observing that the Jews "remain steadfastly faithful to a religion that cause their life to be changed into a fiery furnace ..." Little could they have known how prophetic that imagery would be, some fifty years later.

That Russia is pursuing a definite anti-Jewish policy, that the condition of the Jews in Russia is worse now than it ever was before will be gathered from the following extracts... [T]he restrictive laws now in existence... intensif[y] the oppression of the Jews, and by which it is making the 6,000,000 Jews a people economically exhausted—a people without any rights at all. (10 Dec, p. SM8)

Soon thereafter, World War I began. The reader is invited to review the passages cited above. By late 1918 the war was nearing its end. After years of dire reports about the endangered Hebrew race, did we have 6 million Jewish fatalities? No. Somehow they all managed to survive. Instead of attending their funerals, we were then called upon to aid their recovery: "Six million souls will need help to resume normal life when war is ended," writes the NYT (18 Oct, p. 12).

The Saga Continues

One might have thought that this would have been the end of the stories of the 6 million. Sadly, no. The famed number simply shifted to a new region. In September of 1919, we find that it is now the *Ukrainian* and *Polish* Jews who are subject to misery: "6,000,000 are in peril" (8 Sep, p. 6). We are further horrified to read that "the population of 6,000,000 souls in Ukrania and in Poland... are going to be completely exterminated." Naturally, this is "the paramount issue of the present day."

By this time, other periodicals were playing up the infamous number. As an example, we have this notable piece from the journal *American Hebrew*:

> From across the sea six million men and women call to us for help, and eight hundred thousand little children cry for bread. ... In this catastrophe, when six million human beings are being whirled toward the grave by a cruel and relentless fate... Six million men and women are dying from lack of the necessaries of life... In this threatened *holocaust* of human life... (31 Oct 1919, p. 582).

Thereafter followed a string of similar reports, all in the NYT:

- "unbelievable poverty, starvation and disease [for] about 6,000,000 souls, or half the Jewish population of the earth" (12 Nov 1919, p. 7).
- "typhus menaced 6,000,000 Jews of Europe" (12 Apr 1920, p. 16).
- "hunger, cold rags, desolation, disease, death—six million human beings without food, shelter, clothing" (2 May 1920, p. E1).
- A new fund "for Jewish war sufferers in Central and Eastern Europe, where six millions face horrifying conditions of famine, disease, and death" (7 May 1920, p 11).

> "Russia's 6,000,000 Jews are facing extermination by massacre"— again! (20 Jul 1921, p. 2).

By late 1922, a new threat loomed on the horizon. A 33-year-old German was the up-and-coming head of a new political party: the NSDAP, or Nazi Party. And this young man was allegedly receiving financial aid from a famous American industrialist. The story prompted this headline: "Berlin hears Ford is backing Hitler" (20 Dec, p. 2). Hitler's party is described as "nationalist and anti-Semitic"; he allegedly gave speeches "inciting his audience to kill Jews and Socialists." A much more ominous report came a couple months later, when we read that "a part of the program of Herr Hitler... is the extermination of the Jews" (8 Feb 1923, p. 3). Though by this time, "extermination" of the Jews was old news indeed.

For the next few years, the '6 million' fell into disuse. But it was reawakened when Hitler assumed power in January 1933. The NYT reported on a "Hitler protest" vote by some local New York government officials. Rabbi Stephen Wise issued an appeal: "We in America have taken the lead in a battle for the preservation of German Jewry," adding that his group "is now active in relief and reconstruction work in Eastern Europe where 6,000,000 Jews are involved" (29 Mar, p. 9).

Three years later, we read in the *London Times* of "6,000,000 unwanted unfortunate" Jews, and of "these 6,000,000 people without a future" (26 Nov 1936, p. 15). On that same day, the NYT reported on a speech by British Zionist Chaim Weizmann, who "dwelt first on the tragedy of at least 6,000,000 'superfluous' Jews in Poland, Germany, Austria." In early 1937, we hear that "five to six million Jews in Europe are facing expulsion or direst poverty" (26 Feb, p. 12). These reports inaugurated a spate of references to '6 million' that carry us right into the war years.

In 1938, the NYT ran an article headlined "Persecuted Jews Seen on Increase" (9 Jan, p. 12). "6,000,000 victims noted," they said—referring to a combined total in Germany, Poland, and Romania. One could hardly have a blunter anticipation of the tragedy to come.

The very next month we hear about "a depressing picture of 6,000,000 Jews in Central Europe, deprived of protection or economic opportunities, slowly dying of starvation, all hope gone..." (23 Feb, p. 23). By May, it was the "rising tide of anti-Semitism in Europe today which has deprived more than 6,000,000 Jews and non-Aryans of a birthright" (2 May, p. 18). Later that year, the *London Times* printed an account of the "treatment of German Jews"; "the problem now involved some 6,000,000 Jews," they wrote (22 Nov, p. 11). Bear in mind: the start of World War II was still nearly a year away.

Into early 1939, the *London Times* continued to report on Weizmann's view that "the fate of 6,000,000 people was in the balance" (14 Feb, p. 9). War began in September of that year, and anti-Nazi propaganda accelerated. In mid-1940, the NYT quoted Nahum Goldmann: "Six million Jews are doomed to destruction if the victory of the Nazis should be final" (25 Jun, p. 4). This was still at least one full year before Hitler allegedly decided to begin his program of Jewish mass murder—according to our experts. How could Goldmann have known what was to come?

By early 1942, the Americans were in, and it was truly a world war. The Germans had begun their program of ethnic cleansing, and were accelerating the movement of people. In the NYT we read that Heinrich Himmler "has uprooted approximately 6,000,000 human beings" and shipped them into occupied Poland, "where they necessarily starve and freeze to death and die of disease" (18 Jan, p. SM10). By mid-1942, the situation was looking grim. It was "a vast slaughterhouse for Jews" in Europe; one million were reported dead, and the remainder of the "6,000,000 to 7,000,000" at risk (30 Jun, p. 7). By December the Jewish death toll was reported as 2 million, representing one third of the 6,000,000 "in Hitler's domain." It was, said the NYT, "a holocaust without parallel" (13 Dec, p. 21).

The sad tale continued throughout the war years:

➢ Hitler intends "the extermination of some 6,000,000 [Jewish] persons in the territories over which [his] rule has been extended" (*London Times*, 25 Jan 1943).
➢ "Save doomed Jews," says Rabbi Hertz; the world "has done very little to secure even the freedom to live for 6,000,000 of their Jewish fellow men" (2 Mar, p. 1).
➢ Two million are dead, "and the four million left to kill are being killed, according to plan" (10 Mar, p. 12).
➢ "Five and a half million Jews in Europe are reported to have been put to death" (10 May 1944, p. 5)—still one full year before the end of the European conflict.
➢ And again later: "Dr. A. Leon Kubowitzki... reported that 5,500,000 Jews had been killed in Nazi controlled countries" (27 Nov, p. 14).

Premature references to '6 million' were not limited to the NYT or the *London Times*. Hilberg (2003: 1302) explains, in a footnote, that "the same number [of 6 million] was given in June 1944 by a Jewish emissary, Joel Brand, who had been sent out by Eichmann from Hungary for ransom negotiations with the Allies..." And just the month before, in May 1944, Zionist activist Rabbi Dov Weissmandel wrote:

[H]eads of government and radio must announce what was done to our people in the slaughter houses of Belzec, Malkinia [Treblinka],

Sobibor, and Auschwitz. Till now six times a million Jews from Europe and Russia have been destroyed. (in Dawidowicz 1976: 327)

This, fully one year before the end of the war.

It thus appears that the figure of 6 million represents a sort of constant in Jewish suffering, irrespective of circumstances. It seems to possess a kind of magical symbolism, and hence becomes a sacred icon of Jewish persecution. In fact the number 'six' itself is highly significant within Judaism. The Jewish star is six-sided. The world was created in six days, according to the Jewish (Old Testament) Bible; man himself appeared on the sixth day. The number is furthermore associated with Jewish enslavement, suffering, and death. In the Book of Exodus (21:2) we read that a Hebrew slave is allowed to be kept for only six years. The same book records that "600,000 men" left Egypt during the Exodus (12:37). And Roman historian Tacitus—likely drawing from Jewish sources—reports that 600,000 Jews were besieged, and presumably killed, during the revolt of 70 AD (*Histories* V.13).

But there is a yet more remarkable claim. Rabbi Benjamin Blech (2004: 214f.) cites a passage in Leviticus (25:10): "It shall be a jubilee for you, when each of you shall return to his property and each of you shall return to his family." The original Hebrew word for the phrase "you shall return" (ובשח) was apparently incorrect. It left out the 'vav' (ו). Furthermore each Hebrew letter, and word, corresponds to a number; 'vav' is six. The 'number' of the misspelled original word is 708. Hence Blech concludes that the Jews were fated to return in a year ending in 708—but missing 'vav,' or 'six.' Sure enough—the year of the Jewish 'return' to Palestine was 1948, or 5708 in the Hebrew calendar. Blech writes: "We did return, lacking 6— an all-important 6 million of our people who perished during the Holocaust." With God himself behind the sacred number, the revisionists don't stand a chance.

Thus we see that the '6 million' has an amazing history. What shall we conclude from this? First, I trust it is clear that this extended legacy, by itself, does not *prove* that 6 million did not die in a Nazi Holocaust. Further, it does *not prove* a conspiracy, a hoax, or anything of the sort. But it does beg an explanation. It is highly unlikely, to say the least, that all those '6 millions' throughout history were true and accurate figures. By inference, the same doubt holds for the Holocaust.

More likely is the fact that '6' came to represent the Jewish people, and that 600,000, or later 6,000,000, came to represent 'all the Jews.' Like the term 'holocaust' itself, the '6 million' was obviously well established many years before the rise of the Nazis or the onset of World War II. As such, the figure likely stands as a purely symbolic number rather than as literal truth.

Revisionist Death Figures

The strange and improbable history of the '6 million' causes many revisionists to suspect that something is not quite right. I think we can say that, in all likelihood, reference to this number is mere symbolism in place of factual truth.

So a fair question at this point: How many Jewish deaths do the *revisionists* claim?

I will provide more details later, but they might begin by pointing to the official Israeli Holocaust agency, Yad Vashem. This institution tracks all known Holocaust victims—Jews only, of course. On their Web page they maintain an online database of victims. Six million? No. Today, 70 years after the fact, they have "an estimated 4.3 million" names (as of 2014). This is striking, especially for a people known for rigorous and accurate record-keeping throughout the centuries. After seven decades, they are still nearly two million names short.

But there are many inherent problems with such a database: (1) Anyone can enter virtually any name, fictional or otherwise. Evidence is not required, and Yad Vashem seems to have no ability to verify entries. (2) One finds many duplicate, or near-duplicate, names. Small misspellings can lead to multiple entries. (3) Separated families might well have entered each other's names, if they were never reunited. (4) Anyone missing, for any reason, may well be assumed to have been killed, when in fact their whereabouts are simply unknown. (5) Name changes often occurred after Jews relocated to other countries, making them hard to track, hence missing, hence presumed dead. (6) The database does not distinguish natural deaths from those killed. (7) It does not distinguish those killed by the Nazis from those killed by, say, the Russians—or the western Allies.

And there is considerable irony in this Yad Vashem figure; anyone else claiming to know of 'only' 4.3 million victims would surely be considered a despicable revisionist. Of course, Yad Vashem still holds to the sacred 6 million; they are just working on the remaining names. In any case, revisionists can point to this as a kind of ceiling figure or upper limit—the actual death total, they can say, must be less than 4.3 million.

Next, we have the important demographic study originally done by Walter Sanning in 1983—*The Dissolution of Eastern European Jewry* (3rd edition 1990). His detailed investigation of census records and immigration statistics confirms, first of all, that in the early 1930s about 6 million Jews lived in the areas of Europe that would come under Nazi influence. By 1939 this had dropped to 5 million. Over the next two years, massive emigration, primarily out of Poland, dropped this figure to below 3 million. Thus at the nominal start of the Holocaust in 1941 there were only about 2.7 million

Jews in the German sphere of influence. Of these, some 1.4 million were identified as survivors (by Jewish census groups),[51] leaving about 1.3 million missing—though not necessarily dead. This is Sanning's theoretical maximum death toll. Many of these likely survived as well or died of non-homicidal causes. Hence Sanning's estimate of the actual death toll attributable to Nazi actions is lower still: about 300,000.

A survivor number of roughly 1.4 million is deceiving, however. In 1997, some fifty years after the war, the so-called *Spanic Report* stated that there were between 834,000 and 960,000 living survivors.[52] This range was largely confirmed in 2000 in the *Ukeles Report*.[53] Clearly it is impossible for there to have been 1.4 million survivors in 1945, and then still almost 1 million after fifty years.

An interesting development occurred in 2003, with a study by Israeli professor and demographics expert Sergio DellaPergola. He used a revised counting method, and a revised definition of 'survivor':

> [The term 'survivor' refers to all living Jews] who at least for a brief period of time were submitted in their locations to a regime of duress and/or limitation of their full civil rights... whether by a Nazi foreign occupying power or by a local authority associated with the Nazis' endeavor—or had to flee elsewhere in order to avoid falling under the above-mentioned situations.

We notice, first of all, that this is a remarkably generous definition; any Jew suffering any degree of "duress," for even a "brief period of time," was a Holocaust victim—and if he lived, a survivor. Second, by this definition, DellaPergola determines that the actual number of survivors in 2003 is 1,092,000—a 21 percent increase over the mean value from 1997.[54] Hence by simply redefining things he was able to show a dramatic increase, rather than, as one would expect, a rapid decrease. Of course there is a limit to such chicanery. At some point the number must go to zero. Already by 2010, Jewish periodicals were admitting that the figure was down to 520,000.[55] It will be interesting to track this figure over the coming years.

---

[51] The NYT reported figures of 1.2 million survivors (11 Feb 1945), and later a range of 1 to 1.5 million (17 Feb).
[52] Spanic, A., *et al.*, "Shoah Survivors and Their Number Today."
[53] Ukeles, J. "A Plan for Allocating Successor Organization Resources," Report of the Planning Committee, Conference on Jewish Material Claims Against Germany.
[54] This was the third most generous definition, out of four considered by DellaPergola. The fourth included, literally, *every Jew alive on earth during the war*, since the Nazis' alleged intent was "to destroy all Jews worldwide." Every Jew who survived the war years is thereby a survivor. A move to that definition would boost the 2003 survivor figure to 3.4 million.
[55] JTA (6 Dec 2010).

Projecting back 70 years, any living population today would have been roughly five times as numerous back then. Thus the total number of survivors in 1945, using DellaPergola's definition, must actually have been about 5 million.

The question then is: How many Jews lived under the influence of the Nazi regime? Weber (2001) argues that the figure could be as low as 5.2 million, or as high as 8 million. This would leave a total number of unaccounted persons in the range of 200,000 to 3 million. And again, these would count as missing, not necessarily dead. And even if all were dead, it does not distinguish Nazi-induced deaths from all other categories.

Irving has written: "I have always argued that the original Holocaust figures are probably exaggerated by a factor of ten..."[56] Thus we can assume he holds to a figure of 500,000 to 600,000, though he does not make a detailed argument for such an estimate.

Preeminent revisionist Germar Rudolf has no definite answer to this question of total Jewish deaths. However, when pressed to give a probable estimate, he says, "I think that something like half a million would come close" (2011: 45). Thus we can construct a rough consensus among revisionists: a total Jewish death toll, at the hands of the Nazis, of 300,000 to 600,000 persons. I provide more details on this in Chapter 11.

This of course is a dramatic reduction, down to just 5 or 10 percent of the official figure. And this would bring Jewish losses down to 1 percent or less of the total World War II fatalities. Assuredly, this represents tremendous loss of human life, and leaves many grieving families and survivors. But it would make the Jewish Holocaust all but insignificant in the larger tragedy of that war.

Most important, this new, smaller range of deaths demands a wholesale reconstruction of the conventional account of the killings. Revisionists thus need to provide some basic details. They must give a rough breakdown of the deaths, *by cause* and *by year*, that is generally plausible given what we know about the death camps and other Nazi actions. In Part II of this book, I address these matters directly.

World Jewish Population

Jewish losses are typically calculated by the traditionalists—and occasionally by their opponents—via exhaustive, but not entirely verifiable, analyses of each individual country's losses. Though useful in some ways, this technique has the feel of a giant shell game. One tries to count moving bodies as

---

[56] Quoted from his brief comments on Meyer (2002); posted at <www.fpp.co.uk/Auschwitz/Osteuropa/Fritjof_Meyer2.html>

they are shipped from ghetto to camp, camp to camp, and country to country. It is a recipe for confusion. Opportunities are rife for over-counting, double-counting, and miscounting.

The same is true for calculations of pre- and postwar Jewish populations in specific countries. People moved amongst multiple countries for varying periods of time, occasionally changing names in the process. Many Jews were not citizens of their countries of residence, making them extremely difficult to track. And national borders changed, compounding the difficulties. To the uninitiated observer, the mathematical gyrations can be truly bewildering and inconclusive.

Thus a good argument can be made that only by examining the *global* Jewish population, before and after the war, can one arrive at a moderately reliable confirmation of total deaths. Even a basic analysis of population figures is enlightening.

Let me start with the most-reliable and least-contentious numbers: those since the end of the war. Table 1 shows world Jewish population at six intervals since 1948.[57]

Table 1: World Jewish Population	
YEAR	POPULATION
1948	11,500,000
1955	11,800,000
1970	12,630,000
1980	12,840,000
1990	12,870,000
2000	13,191,500

These numbers are plotted in Chart 1. These numbers are widely accepted by all sides. They indicate a slow, steady growth since the war, at a rate of about 0.3 percent per year. This is just one-sixth of the global population growth rate—about 1.8 percent per year—over that same period. The Jewish population is one of the slowest growing of any major ethnicity.

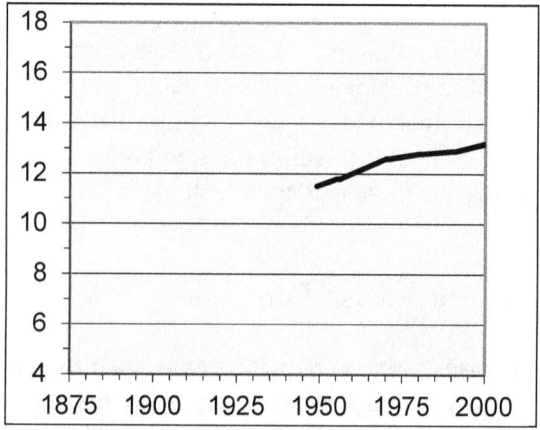

Chart 1: World Jewish Population, in millions, since 1948, actual.

---

[57] Data are from the Israeli Central Bureau of Statistics—accessed via www.jewishvirtuallibrary.org.

Now, going backward in time from the end point of 1948, we should ask ourselves this question: Based on the conventional Holocaust story, what should this plot look like? The answer is quite straightforward: a loss of 6 million from roughly 1940 to 1945—which would look like a spike upward to about 17.5 million just before that—preceded by continuation of the slow but steady growth, comparable to what we have seen since 1948. In other words the expected plot would be as shown in Chart 2.

But this is not in fact what we find. If we look at the period from the late 1800s to 1900, we can compare the expected numbers to actual ones that were reported in those years. Above I cited two such reports from the *New York Times*: in both 1869 and 1889 the global total is estimated at 6 million. For two additional data points we can refer to the 1900 and 1910 editions of the *World Almanac*, which give figures of 7.2 million and 8.2 million, respectively. When overlaid upon the previous plot we can see the discrepancy—see Chart 3.

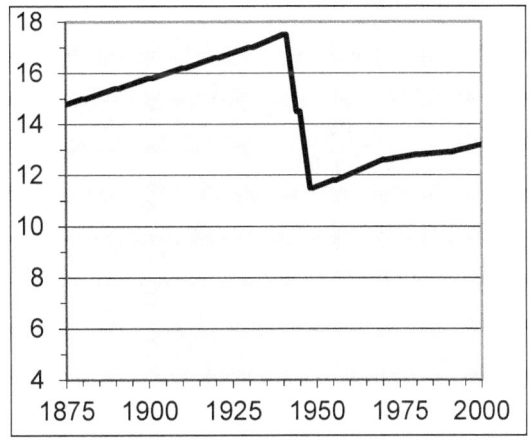

Chart 2: World Jewish Population, in millions, from 1875, assuming the loss of 6 million during World War II.

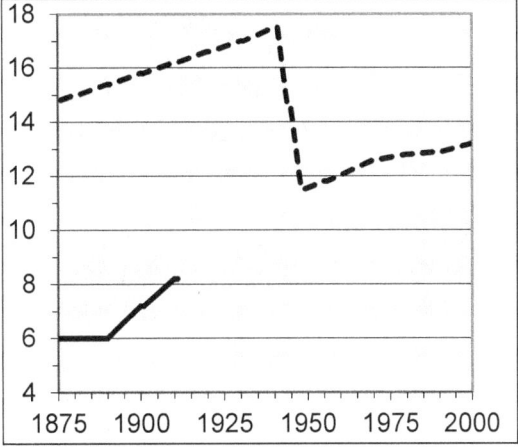

Chart 3: As Chart 2 (dotted), plus actual World Jewish Population until 1910.

Table 2: World Jewish Population

YEAR	POPULATION
1882	7,800,000
1900	10,600,000
1914	13,500,000
1922	14,400,000
1925	14,800,000
1939	16,728,000

Those four data points are clearly far below the 'expected' numbers; this is the first indication of a problem. But they do indicate a slow and steady growth—of about 0.5 percent per year, on average.

Given these early data points, one can readily see the problem for the traditionalists. In order to fill the gap between the late 1800s (of around 6 to 7 million) and the necessary prewar figure of 17 to 18 million (in order to show the 6-million loss), they would have to claim a dramatic, unprecedented population growth in the intervening period. And in fact, this is precisely what they have done. The Israeli Bureau of Statistics currently claims the following numbers, shown in Table 2. These figures are plotted in Chart 4.

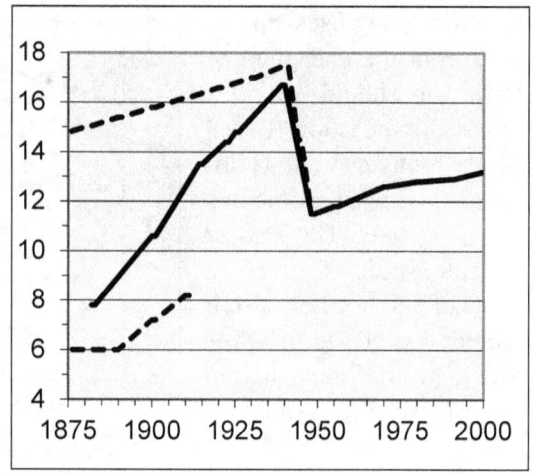

Chart 4: As Chart 3 (dotted), plus necessary (and claimed) pre-WWII World Jewish Population growth to reach claimed pre-Holocaust population.

We immediately notice a few points. First, they start about 2 million higher than reported in the late 1800s. Second, they fall a bit short of the necessary 6-million drop. But thirdly, they indicate an extremely high growth rate—on the order of 1.4 percent per year, almost *double* the global rate at that time (0.8 percent), and *nearly five times* the Jewish growth rate since the war. This is especially problematic, given the *Times* reports, cited above, in which Jews were:

- "all in a state of political bondage" (1889)
- facing "renewed massacres" and "systematic extermination" (1906)
- "economically exhausted" (1911)
- "subjected to every manner of suffering and sorrow" (1915)
- "reduced to unbelievable poverty" (1919)
- facing "horrifying conditions of famine, disease and death" (1920)
- facing a global "war of extinction" (1932)
- "slowly dying of starvation, all hope gone" (1938)

These are not exactly the conditions under which one would expect a booming population. At best we would expect a flat trend, if not a precipitous decline. And in fact Gordon (1984: 8) observes that, in the period 1870-1933, "the rate of natural increase among Jews was extremely low compared to that of the German population." Something is clearly not right with the prewar figures.

As further evidence, consider the recent "population boom" in the UK. In 2009 it was reported that Britain's population grew at a rate of 0.7 percent per year, the highest in nearly 50 years.[58] But this figure was inflated by immigrants, who accounted for about one-third of the growth. For the Jews there could be no 'immigrants.' Their growth had to be completely 'natural,' that is, surplus births over deaths. To maintain a natural growth rate of 1.4 percent annually over six decades and in the worst of conditions is virtually impossible. The contrast with their postwar growth rate of just 0.3 percent is stark.

Yet more confirmation that the alleged 1.4 percent figure is wrong comes from recent projections of growth in adherents to Judaism. Between 50 and 60 percent of Jews consider themselves religious, and their growth rate certainly exceeds that of secular Jews, owing to larger families. In April 2015, Pew Research estimated that the global population of religious Jews would increase from 13.86 million in 2010 to 16.09 million in 2050.[59] This corresponds to 0.37 percent growth annually. Factoring in a lower secular rate, and we again get a global figure of around 0.3 percent per year. Thus from 1950 to 2050—an entire century—global Jewish population has (or will) grow by less than half a percent per year. And yet we are expected to believe that from 1880 to 1940 their population grew at an explosive 1.4 percent rate. We may be excused if we find this implausible.

Another Theory

Looking back at Chart 3, the revisionists see a different possibility; see the solid line in Chart 5. The early data points seem to grow quite naturally to a level very near that reported after the war. Allowing for normal growth, and a loss of about half a million during the war, this is the picture revisionists paint. They then ask: Which scenario is more realistic and more likely? (Compare the solid lines in Charts 4 and 5.)

The answer seems clear, and the revisionists would

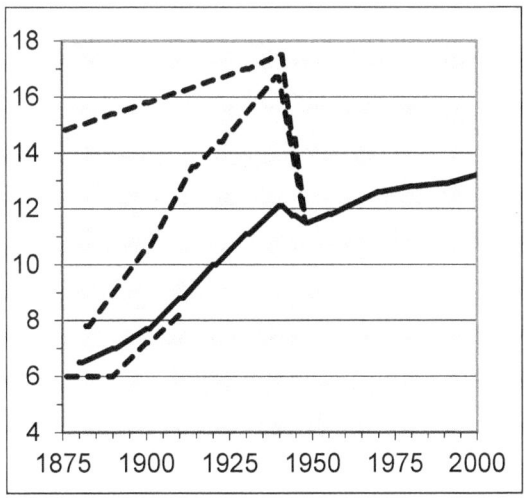

Chart 5: As per Chart 4 (dotted), plus World Jewish Population development according to the revisionist theory.

---

[58] BBC News: "Population growth at 47-year high" (27 Aug 2009).
[59] "The Future of World Religions," Pew Research Center (2 Apr 2015).

have a compelling case strictly on the basis of global population alone, except for some discrepant statistics that were published between 1900 and the start of the war. These numbers seem to confirm the traditionalist claim of a dramatic population boom. For example, they can cite the following reports (Table 3).

Table 3: World Jewish Population, as reported (1915–1941)

YEAR	POPULATION	SOURCE
1915	13 million	NYT (14 Jan, p. 3)
1917	12 million	NYT (21 May, p. 5)
1918	9–12 million	NYT (18 Oct, p. 12)
1919	12 million	NYT (12 Nov, p. 7)
1920	15 million	World Almanac
1926	14.9 million	NYT (9 Apr 1936, p. 19)
1933	14 million	Daily Express
1936	16 million	NYT (9 Apr 1936, p. 19)
1941	15 million	NYT (7 Jun, p. 5)

So we notice that these 'as-reported' numbers are generally lower than claimed, though not nearly as low as the revisionist proposal. And they do follow the same general rapid growth pattern that the traditionalists claim. Might these not, then, largely confirm the standard account?

I think not, simply because of the large improbabilities involved. Consider just the likelihood that the global Jewish population jumped from 7.2 million in 1900 (*World Almanac*) to 13 million in 1915 (NYT). This would imply an unbelievable 4 percent annual growth. Even the lower end of the range given in 1918 (9–12 million) would mean a highly unlikely 1.2 percent growth per year.

So where did these unrealistically high numbers come from? In virtually every case they were self-reported by Jewish agencies. And we must recall that the push for Zionism accelerated after 1900, as did the global clout of the Jewish lobby. Both these reasons might compel Jewish statisticians to inflate global population numbers, or at least work from the highest possible projections. It is thus not hard to imagine that the reported numbers after 1900 could be significantly overestimated. Zionists and lobbyists were caught in a bind: they wanted both high population numbers *and* dramatic reports of Jewish deprivation, suffering, and death. Depending on the circumstances, they played one card or the other, and no one bothered to point out that the two were mutually incompatible.

My conclusion, therefore, is that both the 'as reported' numbers and the Israeli Bureau of Statistics figures are likely 30 to 40 percent overestimates for the years 1900 to 1940. The revisionist estimates (Chart 5) are probably closer to the truth.

Chapter 4: Breaking It Down: The Death Matrix

The traditional account of Jewish deaths is a clear case of missing the forest for the trees. In order to begin to understand and justify any death total, we should be able to answer the most basic questions about it: *How many* died*?* By what general *cause?* And over what *time?* I don't mean in great detail—just the most basic breakdown of any proposal. *Give us the numbers that add up to 6 million.*

The casual reader would probably presume that such a thing has been done many times, in many different places, by many different Holocaust researchers—all reaching a similar conclusion. But he would be wrong. Most sources simply offer no breakdown at all. Neither "Holocaust" entries in *World Book* nor *Encyclopedia Britannica* provide numbers that add up to 6 million. It's not on the Wikipedia entry. And you will not find it in the online encyclopedias at USHMM or Yad Vashem. Most individual researchers avoid this as well, preferring to dive into great detail on camp deportations, or on death figures for a certain mass shooting. We find generic quotations from survivors, or an in-depth analysis of a given death camp. But virtually nothing on the big picture.

Occasionally a source will give rough figures that imply 6 million, but not in a way that allows any meaningful analysis. One example is an article from *The Australian* (14 Feb 2009). The reporter, Peter Wilson, castigates revisionist sympathizer Lady Michèle Renouf for pressing this very point. At the end of his lengthy article he offers the following elaboration: "Experts say up to 3.4 million were killed at the [six] main death camps" (followed by numbers for each), and "at least 1.5 million more were killed by mobile SS death squads." "The rest"—evidently, the remaining 1.1 million—were killed "in various other ways." Wilson is clearly satisfied with this refutation of Renouf, but the skeptical reader is left with many questions.

Other sources will list a breakdown of Jewish deaths by country of origin, with a total that approaches 6 million. But as I discussed in the previous chapter, these numbers are highly speculative and offer many opportunities for error. Most importantly, they explain neither how nor when the people are alleged to have been killed—presuming, that is, that they were in fact murdered.

Obviously I cannot have read all of the thousands of books on the Holocaust, but in my research I have found almost nothing addressing the most basic questions, the ones that might allow a coherent understanding of the deaths.

The Hilberg Matrix

With one small exception: Raul Hilberg. Hilberg (2003) alone takes the smallest step, a mere baby step, toward clarifying the situation. Out of three volumes and more than 1,300 pages, he offers us, at the very end, with no further explanation or justification, in Appendix B ("Statistics of Jewish Dead"), two tables: "Deaths by Cause," and "Deaths by Year"—reproduced here as Tables 4 and 5.

Table 4: Hilberg Estimates "Death by Cause"		
GHETTOIZATION AND GENERAL PRIVATION		
German-controlled ghettos		over 600,000
Theresienstadt and non-ghetto privation		100,000
Transnistria colonies		100,000
	Total:	over 800,000
OPEN-AIR SHOOTINGS		
Einsatzgruppen, mobile operations, etc.		1,400,000
CAMPS		
German death camps		up to 2,600,000
Concentration/labor camps		over 150,000
Romanian camps		100,000
Croatian and other		under 50,000
	Total:	up to 2,900,000
	TOTAL DEATHS:	5,100,000

Table 5: Hilberg Estimates "Death by Year"	
1933-1940	under 100,000
1941	1,100,000
1942	2,600,000
1943	600,000
1944	600,000
1945	over 100,000
TOTAL:	5,100,000

I find it illuminating that Hilberg, the one person moving tentatively in the right direction, also offered the lowest death total of any major traditionalist—5.1 million. And to his credit he held to this number for over forty years, since the release of his first edition in 1961. It is almost as if he could see that the '6 million' was untenable as soon as the first small steps were taken to dissect that number.

Again, it is unfortunate that Hilberg does not give the reader any indication of how he obtained these numbers.[60] If the calculations are hidden somewhere in his 1,300 pages, I was not able to find them.

The next obvious step, then, is to combine the two tables. We would like to know, for each of the three main causal categories (ghetto/privation, shootings, camps), how many died in each of the years. In other words we would like to complete the following table:

	Pre-1941	1941	1942	1943	1944	1945
Ghettos	?	?	?	?	?	?
Shootings	?	?	?	?	?	?
Camps	?	?	?	?	?	?

such that the 'totals by cause' add up, and the 'totals by year' add up. However, even this apparently trivial task is not so easy. Lacking details from Hilberg, we must infer values that are reasonable—given the traditionalist account—and yet still add up to, or close to, his totals. It ends up being something of a mathematical puzzle. I encourage the reader to give it a try. After spending some time at this, I can understand Hilberg's reluctance.

Nonetheless, the figures given in Table 6 below seem to be reasonable, while still roughly matching Hilberg's totals (numbers are in thousands).

Table 6: The Hilberg Death Matrix (in Thousands)

	Pre-1941	1941	1942	1943	1944	1945	TOTALS
Ghettos	50	300	300	50	30	30	760
Shootings	50	600	600	100	25	30	1,405
Camps	0	200	1,750	400	660	20	3,030
TOTALS	100	1,100	2,650	550	715	80	5,195

I emphasize that these are neither Hilberg's nor any other traditionalist's data—precisely because they offer no such detail at all. This is simply my attempt, based on general claims about those three categories, to match Hilberg's overall numbers.

---

[60] There is a small bit of added detail, only on the death camps, in Hilberg's Table 9-8 (pp. 958f.). And a footnote at the end of the table cites three or four sources for some of his numbers—such as the Höfle report for the precise Belzec figure. But these do not begin to supply the needed detail or justification.

Such analysis I call, for lack of a better euphemism, a *death matrix*. It lays out the details of deaths by cause and over time. It is essential for understanding the progression of events in the Holocaust. And it turns out to be very useful in portraying the strengths and weaknesses of the conventional view.

The Hilberg matrix is insufficient, however, because it only accounts for some 5 million deaths. We don't believe Hilberg; we believe in the 6 million. We don't trumpet Hilberg; we trumpet the 6 million. As long as orthodoxy maintains the 6 million, we are obligated to try to analyze that larger figure. Thus we need to construct something comparable: a '6-million death matrix.' We can then expand the data, hoping to get a clearer picture of what is being alleged.

Our efforts, though, are immediately frustrated; no one gives us a high-level breakdown of the 6 million comparable to that of Hilberg. One possible starting point is the six death camps. But which figures shall we use? Let's consult the two leading research organizations: USHMM and Yad Vashem. Unfortunately their numbers disagree—for every camp. The figures that they list on their respective Web sites are shown in Chart 6.

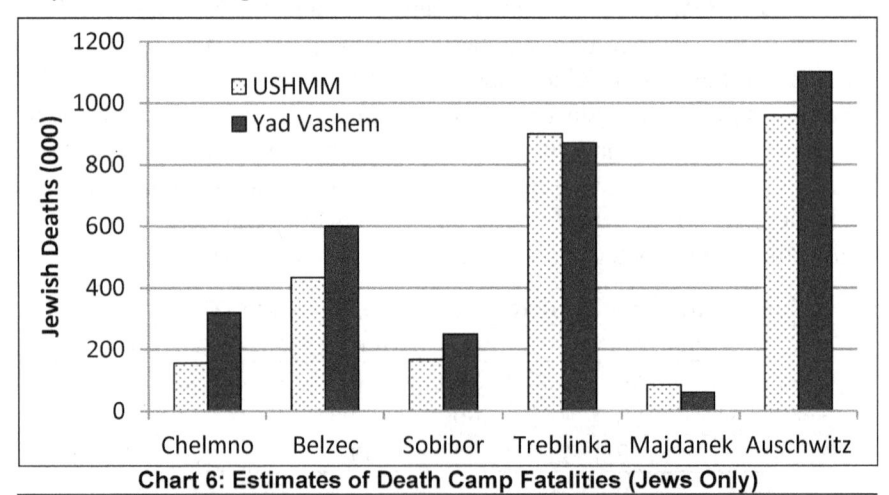

Chart 6: Estimates of Death Camp Fatalities (Jews Only)

It is perhaps surprising that we find such divergence in numbers. And the situation only gets worse when we consult other camp experts. In later chapters I will show the wide range of figures for each camp; the variation is astonishing.

In the meantime, we need to select target numbers for each camp. I propose taking a rough average of USHMM and Yad Vashem. This would yield the following numbers:

Table 7: Average Death Camp Death-Toll Figures	
Majdanek	75,000
Sobibor	225,000
Chelmno	250,000
Belzec	550,000
Treblinka	900,000
Auschwitz	1,000,000
TOTAL:	3,000,000

These figures meet our provisional needs. They roughly approximate the conventional view, and they reach the proposed total of 3 million—one half of the Holocaust.

This, then, is half the story. But we also have the other categories of deaths. Apart from the above six, there were many other camps in which lesser numbers of Jews died—in the hundreds of thousands, we are told. And Hilberg's totals for ghettos and shootings will have to be scaled up, if we are to reach the 6 million. Therefore we may plausibly propose the following:

Table 8: Author's Proposed Death-Toll Figures	
6 death camps:	3.0 million
Other camps:	0.4 million
Ghettos:	1.0 million
Shootings:	1.6 million
TOTAL:	6.0 million

Again, these figures seem reasonably close to traditionalist claims, and most importantly, they sum up to the requisite total.

Now we can begin to construct a new, high-level death matrix. Working from these round figures, and anticipating details to follow, I propose the numbers shown in Table 9.

Table 9: '6-Million' Death Matrix (in Thousands)						
	Pre-1941	1941	1942	1943	1944	1945	TOTALS
Ghettos	70	360	420	80	50	20	1,000
Shootings	40	450	900	175	20	15	1,600
Camps	10	135	2,065	490	650	50	3,400
TOTALS	120	945	3,385	745	720	85	6,000

These will serve as our working estimates of the numbers that must be true, on the conventional view, if we are to sustain the overall total of 6 million. Again, I do not claim absolute precision here. Surely some of these figures need adjustment. But for every number that goes up, another must go down; this is elementary math. I am open to improvement here. Hence my offer:

Table 10: Jewish Death Totals, by Year and by Cause – 1933-1945 (in Thousands)

	1933-1940	J	F	M	A	M	J	J	A	S	O	N	D	Total 1941
Ghetto / privation:	70	10	20	30	30	30	30	35	35	35	35	35	35	360
Shootings:	40	2	2	2	4	5	45	60	65	85	55	60	65	450
Camps (total):	10	9	10	11	11	11	12	12	12	12	12	10	13	135
6 Death Camps (see below)	0												5	5
Other camps	10	9	10	11	11	11	12	12	12	12	12	10	8	130
	120													**945**
Death Camps:														
Chelmno													5	5
Belzec														0
Sobibor														0
Treblinka														0
Majdanek														0
Auschwitz														0

	J	F	M	A	M	J	J	A	S	O	N	D	Total 1942
Ghetto / privation:	35	35	35	35	35	35	35	35	45	45	25	15	420
Shootings:	85	70	70	50	40	30	40	60	195	120	105	35	900
Camps (total):	40	29	127	118	90	83	285	363	339	296	199	92	2,060
6 Death Camps (see below)	28	17	115	106	77	69	271	350	326	283	187	82	1,910
Other camps	12	12	12	12	13	14	14	13	13	13	12	10	150
													3,380
Death Camps:													
Chelmno	5	26	13	55	21	27	9	16	45	33			245
Belzec				50	50	15	25	55	145	90	60	10	550
Sobibor					25	25	25	0	0	9	9	8	110
Treblinka								175	135	165	185	100	800
Majdanek										4	4	4	15
Auschwitz		2	4		10	10	10	25	25	25	24	20	190

	J	F	M	A	M	J	J	A	S	O	N	D	Total 1943
Ghetto / privation:	10	5	15	15	15	15	15	4	3	2	2	2	80
Shootings:	25	20	15	15	15	15	15	15	10	10	10	5	175
Camps (total):	76	67	39	45	45	39	38	37	21	35	17	17	495
6 Death Camps (see below)	74	65	37	42	42	36	35	34	19	33	15	15	465
Other camps	2	2	2	3	3	3	3	3	2	2	2	2	30
													750
Death Camps:													
Chelmno													0
Belzec													0
Sobibor	10	11	12	12	14	14	14	14					115
Treblinka													100
Majdanek	4	4	4	4	5	5	5	4	4	4	18		60
Auschwitz	20	20	6	16	18	17	16	16	15	15	15	15	190

	J	F	M	A	M	J	J	A	S	O	N	D	Total 1944	Total 1945	Total
Ghetto / privation:	4	6	6	6	6	5	5	4	2	1	1	1	50	20	1,000
Shootings:	2	2	2	2	2	2	2	2	1	1	1	1	20	15	1,600
Camps (total):	18	19	21	24	113	213	108	71	45	10	6	2	650	50	3,400
6 Death Camps (see below)	16	17	19	21	110	210	105	68	42	8	4	0	620	0	3,000
Other camps	2	2	2	3	3	3	3	3	3	2	2	2	30	50	400
													720	**85**	**6,000**
Death Camps:															
Chelmno													0	0	250
Belzec													0	0	550
Sobibor													0	0	225
Treblinka													0	0	900
Majdanek													0	0	75
Auschwitz	16	17	19	21	110	210	105	68	42	8	4		620	0	1,000

If any orthodox researcher would like to propose better numbers, and to justify them, I will gladly comply.

Coming into Focus

Now we need to take one last important step. In order to get the clearest view possible, we need to expand these numbers into *monthly* statistics—see Table 10. Then the big picture comes into focus, and we are better able to assess the plausibility of the overall picture. Monthly figures are necessarily conjectural, since we lack such detailed evidence. However, something like what is shown in Table 10 must be correct in order to reach the yearly totals—and consequently the 6 million.

Also, I include here the monthly estimates for each of the six death camps. Due to their importance, we need to overlay their numbers with the larger Holocaust. The breakdown that I propose here is based on numerous sources, some of which I will explain later. Surely these figures need revising. This is only a first approximation. Again, I invite those with more expertise to correct them, and give us a more accurate picture of events.

To better envision what is transpiring, I include two further graphs: Chart 7 shows the monthly deaths, in thousands, tracked over time, and Chart 8 the running total of all deaths, cumulating in the 6 million.

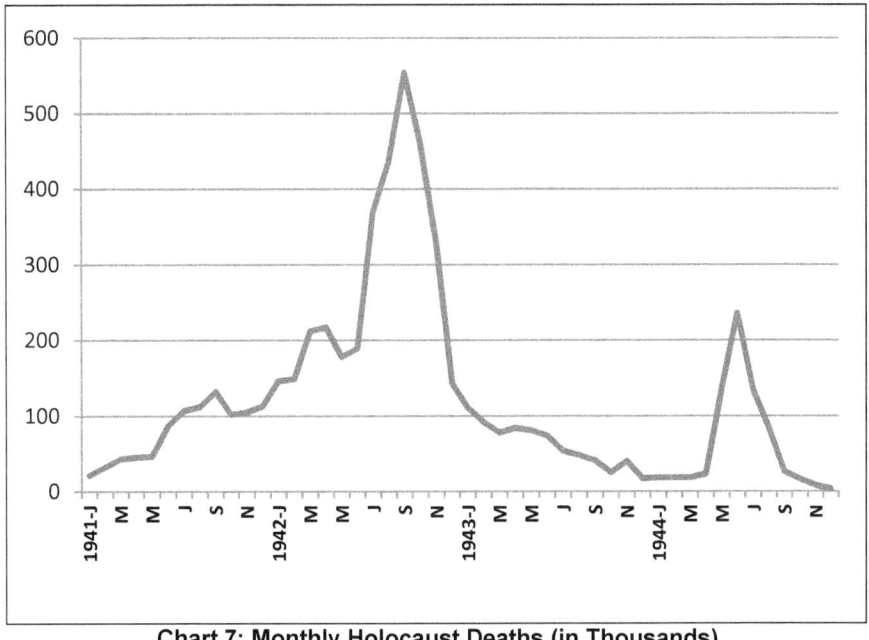

Chart 7: Monthly Holocaust Deaths (in Thousands)

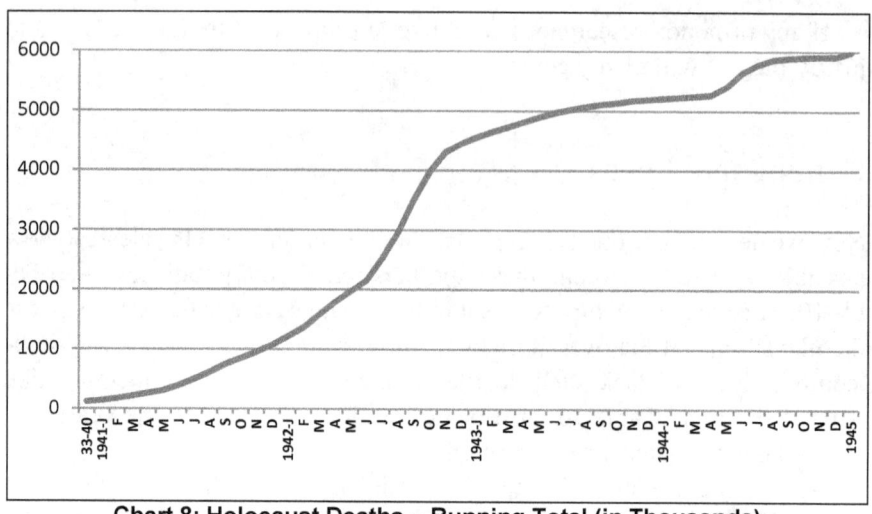

Chart 8: Holocaust Deaths – Running Total (in Thousands)

This, then, is the 'master plan' for the Holocaust. All numbers are out in the open, everything is clear and concise, everything adds up. Such detail may seem excessive, but it turns out to be critical in allowing us to assess the 6-million total, and the specifics of each death camp. If we hope to pass judgment in the Great Debate, we need to know exactly what we are talking about.

In fact even this much detail, as basic as it is, goes well beyond anything readily found in the massive corpus of traditional literature. A few researchers, like Arad (1987) and Czech (1990), have laid out death statistics over time, but only for individual camps, and without integrating these data into a larger picture of events. The vast majority of writers do not even begin to address the topic this way. I can only speculate why this is so. Two possible reasons come to mind. First, the details necessary to confirm such numbers are lacking, thus putting the reconciliation of such calculations beyond the ability of the researchers—in which case, though, how can they justify the 6 million, not to mention their claim about the "most well-documented event in history"? The alternative possibility is that they do not *want* to do this, because it will bring into harsh relief the deficiencies of the standard view.

To be fair, revisionists also fall short when it comes to articulating their view in this kind of detail. But the violation is not nearly as severe. Traditionalists are the ones who claim to know the truth of what happened; it is they who bear the burden of proof, of demonstrating a clear picture of events. Revisionists need only show that the proposal put forth by the other side is implausible. They *should* create an alternative, but they have no burden to do so.

And in fact the revisionists are beginning to sketch out an alternative. Their overall death figure is about 10 percent of the orthodox view, and thus by simply reducing the standard numbers proportionately we have something of a start toward a complete revisionist picture. In some cases they can do better than that, as I will explain in the chapters to follow.

Life (and Death) in the Ghettos

To give one indication of the situation faced by anyone seeking the truth, consider the roughly 1 million ghetto deaths. First, a little context. Ghettos were generally small sections of cities that were designated as Jewish-only areas. They began to be formed in early 1940, and most were established by the end of 1941—more than 1,000 in total, so we are told. There were some two dozen very large ghettos, but the vast majority were quite small, holding less than 1,000 people. From early 1943, they began to be dismantled; hence the average ghetto life was about two years.

Contrary to popular belief, ghettos were not prisons. Many were completely open, and Jews could come and go as they pleased—they were only required to live and do business there. Oftentimes the ghetto was marked only by a sign. Clearly they were never intended as a means of mass killing. Longerich evidently agrees:

> The establishment of the ghettos was carried out so haphazardly and slowly that it would be wrong to see it as a systematic policy ultimately aimed at the physical annihilation of the Jews (2010: 166).

Ghettos were, however, the logical first step in a program of exclusion, removal, and expulsion. If the Nazis indeed wished to ethnically cleanse the Reich, and later also other areas under their control, they would have begun by rounding up Jews, confining them to specified areas, and then methodically transporting them out. And this is precisely what happened. For example, the two largest ghettos—Lodz (200,000 Jews) and Warsaw (400,000-590,000)[61]—were established in February and November 1940, respectively. Jews were confined there until new areas opened in the East, upon which time the deportations commenced.

In the above death matrix I have assumed a total ghetto casualty figure of 1 million. Is this correct? If we were to check our standard sources, what would we find? Nothing. The reader is invited to look for this number; it will be a long search. It does not appear in either older sources or newer, in print or online. Friedman's (1954) early detailed study, for example, lists no death figures at all, either for individual ghettos or as a whole. More recent sources

---

[61] The high estimate of Warsaw is found in Longerich (167). The next largest ghettos, according to Corni (2003: 195), were Lvov (103,000), Minsk (100,000), Bialystok (50,000), Kaunas/Kovno (42,000), Czestochowa (40,000), Lublin (36,000) and Radom (32,000).

are little better. Corni's (2003) chapter on "Life and Death" in the ghettos gives a scattering of mortality statistics, but nothing comprehensive. He provides detailed—down to the individual—monthly deaths for the two largest ghettos (Warsaw and Lodz), but only for 10 and 18 months, respectively (pp. 205f.). And he draws no overall conclusions from these. He closes the chapter by citing the Nazi statistician Richard Korherr, who allegedly claimed that 760,000 Polish Jews died in ghettos through December 1942 (p. 218)—though this total is clearly marked by Korherr as the sum of "emigration, excess mortality, and evacuation."

In his so-called definitive Holocaust study, Longerich (2010: 167) allots just one vague sentence to the ghetto deaths. Citing Hilberg, he writes that "the total of Polish Jews killed prior to and during the period of ghettoization before the violent ghetto clearances began was approximately 500,000." Only Polish Jews? What about the many ghettos in other countries? And what does "prior" mean? And why exclude the "violent clearances"? And for that matter, what was the basis for Hilberg's figure—the man who could find only 5.1 million deaths overall? Longerich does not explain.

Or consider Dean (2010). He provides exactly the kind of concise summary that should include an overall death figure, and yet we find only two mortality numbers, both for the Warsaw ghetto. Perhaps appropriately, one of the newest dedicated studies, by Michman (2011), has no death statistics at all.

Online sources are equally deficient. Wikipedia ("Jewish Ghettos in German-occupied Poland"), for example, provides a nice list of 272 Polish ghettos, including "number of Jews confined" (maximum? average? final?), but no death statistics, nor even references to any. It does list the presumed destination of the ghetto residents; virtually all went to one of the six extermination camps, directly or indirectly. These will be examined shortly. The USHMM website ("Ghettos") gives no numbers, and states only that "the Germans and their auxiliaries either shot ghetto residents in mass graves located nearby, or deported them, usually by train, to killing centers where they were murdered." How many mass graves? Where are they? Have they been examined? No answers. Yad Vashem says simply, "Many Jews died in the ghettos."[62]

We must keep in mind how simple our request is. The essential equation is this: Jews went into the ghettos; some died there; the remainder was shipped out. More explicitly:

(# Jews died in ghettos) = (# Jews entering ghettos) − (# Jews deported out)

---

[62] Yadvashem.org, Holocaust Resource Center, "Ghetto".

This again is elementary logic. And yet it seems to exceed the grasp of our traditional historians. Why can't we get even rough estimates of this basic equation?

Since it is evidently too taxing a demand to request overall death statistics, let's make it easier. Let's look at the largest and most examined ghetto: Warsaw. Here we theoretically know everything, and in great detail. As early as 1954 Friedman could write, "The bibliography of publications on the Warsaw ghetto is so extensive that it is impossible to enumerate even the more important studies" (p. 79, n 76). How much more detailed is our knowledge today—over 60 years later?

So, we ask our question: *How many Jews died in the Warsaw ghetto?* Once again, we come away empty-handed. No sources provide even a plausible estimate of this essential number.

In fact, our experts cannot even clearly answer the simpler question: How many Jews were *in* the Warsaw ghetto? Friedman (1954: 79) says 420,000 to 500,000. Corni (2003: 195) says 400,000. Dean (2010: 342) says "some 450,000." Longerich (2010: 167) says 410,000 to 590,000. Quite a range! If we don't know how many people we have to start with, we certainly can't answer the follow-up questions regarding deaths and deportations. And if we can't answer those questions, well, our entire picture of the Holocaust is up in the air.

All is not lost, however. Unlike the hundreds of other ghettos, we do have some partial death statistics for Warsaw. Corni (2003: 206), for example, gives us a table with monthly death figures, running from January 1941 to June 1942; these average 3,853 per month. But why stop there? The ghetto existed for another full year. Can we extrapolate this monthly figure for the entire duration? This would imply some 120,000 total deaths. If not, why not?

If so, how do we reconcile this number with the following facts presented by the USHMM?

- "83,000 [ghetto] Jews died of starvation and disease" between 1940 and mid-1942;
- Between July and September 1942, "the Germans deported about 265,000 Jews from Warsaw to Treblinka";
- Upon closing the ghetto in mid-May 1943, 42,000 were deported to three camps, 7,000 died fighting, and another 7,000 were shipped to Treblinka;
- 11,500 Warsaw Jews survived in the city until it was captured by the Soviets in 1945.[63]

---

[63] www.ushmm.org, encyclopedia entry for "Warsaw." The reader is invited to review this entry, and to try to determine the overall death toll for this ghetto.

For all that, no overall death number—for the most well-known and thoroughly studied ghetto of them all. Instead, they force the reader to make inferences. If, for example, 83,000 died between November 1940 and (say) June 1942, this implies an average of about 4,400 per month—which is not the same as the 3,853 per month that Corni proposes, incidentally. At the USHMM rate, and given that the camp ran for one more year, we should expect another (12 × 4,400 =) 52,800 deaths. Combined with the 7,000 killed during fighting, this yields a total of 142,000 deaths. Is this correct? We don't know. Why don't they tell us?

For that matter, what was Corni's source for his numbers? He cites an obscure, undated (presumed 1960) German text, *Faschismus—Getto—Massenmord*. This in turn is a translation from an even more obscure, also undated (presumed 1957) Polish source. Page 138 of this text has one table with the numbers used by Corni. But even here there are problems. There is no accompanying explanation at all—no elaboration, no context, nothing. Also, the entry for December 1941 is 43,239—a ridiculously high figure, and obviously incorrect, and thus Corni uses the number from the accompanying chart (4,366). But if there are such gross and blatant errors, how can we trust any of the numbers?

One reason for the reluctance to establish an overall death toll may be the obvious lack of evidence—that is, absence of victims' bodies. Based on Corni's data, the Warsaw ghetto yielded nearly 130 corpses per day, on average, for two or more years. What did they do with the bodies? They could not bury them, since they were in the middle of a large city. They had neither crematoria nor wood to build pyres. So—what happened to the bodies? And are there any remains that we might examine today in order to confirm things?

Unsurprisingly, none of our ghetto experts addresses this thorny issue. At best we find mere passing comments in other sources. For example, in a 1942 article in the NYT we read that the Warsaw Jews "have no means for funerals, so the dead are put into the street, where they are collected by the police" (7 Jan, p. 8).[64] If the police collected the bodies—4,000 or 5,000 per month—what did they do with them? Bury them? If so, where? Did they even count them? More unanswered questions.

Without such answers, we cannot really trust any information here. For all we know, the actual numbers could have been quite low. If there were 400,000 Jews in the Warsaw ghetto, this would imply 4,000 natural deaths per year, or about 11 per day. With this low number, we can well understand how the bodies may have disappeared without a trace. But Corni and others tell us that some 130 Jews died every day—ten times the natural rate. The

---

[64] The same article, incidentally, claims that 300 per day were dying, mostly due to typhus—the very disease that the Germans were trying so hard to forestall.

NYT said 300 per day, or 30 times the natural rate. These are much harder to explain.

Or maybe it was much worse than we presume. In one striking 1943 report in the NYT, we read that "approximately 10,000 people are killed daily in Warsaw alone by different means; the cruelest and most inhuman instruments, which only the black satanic spirit of Hitlerism can invent, are employed" (7 Feb, p. SM16). Think of it—10,000 per day! In a ghetto area of barely over one square mile! Perhaps the reporter, the "noted novelist" Sholem Asch, was guilty of a bit of poetic license. When we are dealing in fiction, anything goes.

It must be kept in mind how simple an analysis we are seeking. The main points could be addressed in a single paragraph. Here's how it might go:

> The Warsaw ghetto held 350,000 Jews at its opening, a number that peaked at 450,000 in mid-1942 and declined to 80,000 when it was closed in May 1943. Overall, 500,000 Jews passed through the ghetto. Of these, 40,000 died in the ghetto of natural causes, and 10,000 were shot there by the Nazis. The 50,000 bodies were dumped into three mass graves in a nearby forest, which were exhumed and studied in 19xx. The remaining 450,000 people were eventually transported out of the ghetto—300,000 to Treblinka, 100,000 to Majdanek, and 50,000 to other concentration camps.

That's it—very simple, very concise, and everything adds up. Of course these numbers are purely fictitious. We look to our experts to supply actual statistics. But answers are not forthcoming. And if the well-known Warsaw ghetto holds such mysteries, we can only imagine the sad state of the overall ghetto picture.

In the end, we are left with an empty sack. We must account, somehow, for roughly 1 million deaths in the ghettos. Yet we have no useful data on even the largest and best-studied ones. Furthermore, we must always keep in mind the natural death rate. If, say, 3 million Jews were confined to our "1,000 ghettos," we then would expect some 30,000 deaths per year—or nearly 100 per day—due strictly to natural causes. One hundred deaths per day, spread over several countries and some 1,000 different locations, could easily vanish amidst a major war. But more to the point, this would yield only some 100,000 deaths in total—a mere 10 percent of the claimed figure.

By confining the Jews, the Nazis certainly contributed to infectious diseases, malnourishment, and other maladies, and thus must be held responsible for those 'excess' deaths, along with any isolated shootings or other direct actions they committed. But we have no idea how many such deaths occurred.

Let's summarize our problem here. The ghetto system ran essentially for three years: 1941-1943. Over this time period, we are told, some 1 million ghetto deaths occurred; hence almost 28,000 per month, on average, or about 925 per day. Every day, somewhere in the system, 925 bodies were either buried or burned. Somewhere, in total, are the remains of 1 million people. Or so we are told.

And yet we have no record of any such bodies whatsoever—no mass graves, no crematoria, no open-air pyres, no 'dumping in the river' stories—*nothing*. Not even the natural deaths are accounted for, which causes us to suspect that the total number of interned Jews was perhaps much smaller than claimed. And if we can't find the victims, how can we hope to understand the Holocaust?

These are relevant questions that revisionists ask. Lacking good answers, they conclude that perhaps far fewer deaths actually occurred. Perhaps the Warsaw ghetto saw only a couple of hundred, rather than thousand, deaths per month. This, at least, would be easier to explain. But then the total deaths in the ghetto would amount to something on the order of 10,000, rather than 100,000 (or more).

And then consider this easily overlooked fact: Even on the standard view, well over 1,000,000 Jews were transported out of the ghettos at some point—most to death camps, it is claimed. But clearly, *these cannot count as "ghetto" deaths, since they are later to be counted as "extermination camp" deaths*. Here is another opportunity ripe for double-counting. But without the most basic details, such as given above, we simply don't know how the deaths are being counted. This is not too much to ask, surely, for "the most well-documented event in history."

Let me close this section with one more proposal. I would suggest that the ghettos experienced deaths at roughly *triple* the natural rate—in other words, about 3 percent per year. Table 11 lists the twelve largest ghettos (according to Corni), accounting for perhaps one third of the total ghetto population. It also includes their size, duration, and total casualties at the assumed 3 percent annual rate.

Table 11: Ghetto Population Data

GHETTO	COUNTRY	TOTAL POP.	MONTHS IN OPERATION	TOTAL DEATHS (@ 3%)
Warsaw	Poland	400,000	22	22,000
Lodz	Poland	162,000	54	21,870
Lvov	Ukraine	103,000	24	6,180
Minsk	USSR	100,000	27	6,750
Bialystok	Poland	50,000	28	3,500
Kaunas/Kovno	Lithuania	42,000	35	3,675
Czestochowa	Poland	40,000	18	1,800
Lublin	Poland	36,000	12	1,080
Radom	Poland	32,000	16	1,280
Kielce	Poland	27,000	13	878
Krakow	Poland	24,000	23	1,380
Vilnius	Lithuania	20,000	25	1,250
	Totals:	**1,036,000**		**71,643**

As we can see, this gives a total of about 72,000 deaths. Of this, we will say that one-third represents the natural deaths (1 percent annual), and the other two-thirds represent Nazi-induced "Holocaust" deaths; this latter figure comes to about 48,000. If we then extrapolate this figure to the other ghettos, they contribute an estimated (2 × 48,000 =) 96,000 deaths. Overall then, we get a total death count of (48,000 + 96,000 =) 144,000 ghetto deaths, which I will round up to 145,000. This will serve as our revisionist estimate.

The Einsatzgruppen

We find a recurrence of our ghetto problems in the second major death category: *open-air shootings*. This event was dominated by the work of the roving Einsatzgruppen, or mobile military squads, whose objective, allegedly, was to round up and kill Soviet Jews. In my conventional assumptions, I have taken a total figure of 1.6 million Jewish deaths by shooting.

Again, some context is helpful. Germany attacked the Soviet Union in June 1941, rapidly capturing large amounts of land. As the main army advanced eastward, there arose a constant danger of attacks by insurgents from the rear. The Germans therefore established the Einsatzgruppen—"mission groups"—to protect the soldiers. They were organized into four main units (A, B, C, D), consisting of around 3,000 men,[65] supplemented by a fifth "special-purpose" group. These were supported in their mission by police battalions, SS brigades (referred to as HSSPL), and perhaps one or two other groups. In addition to their main role, these groups were also allegedly given

---
[65] Per Longerich (2010: 185).

"authority to murder members of the intelligentsia, the clergy, and the nobility, as well as Jews and the mentally ill"[66]—a formidable task.

The killing method was straightforward: shooting at close range, with bodies dumped in pits. There are some vague reports about the use of "six gas vans," but details are so murky that we can conclude nothing about them.[67] The Einsatzgruppen and affiliates were responsible for a large majority of the shootings of Jews, on the standard view, but there seems to be little agreement on the actual number. A variety of recent figures is given in Table 12.

Table 12: Recent Einsatzgruppen Death-Toll Estimates	
DEATHS	SOURCE
1 million (over)	USHMM (2015: Web)
1.25 million	Yad Vashem (2015: Web)
1.3 million	Headland (1992: 106); Hilberg (2003)
1.4 million	Pohl (2008: 57)
1.5 million	Desbois (2008)
1.7 million	Snyder (2009)
2 million	Sturdy Colls (2015: 20)

With such variety in orthodox estimates, it is little wonder that we have such a hard time making sense of things.

As always, we must focus on the big picture here. If we allow that most of the shootings occurred over some 18 months—June 1941 to December 1942—this means that the four Einsatzgruppen and their auxiliary groups collectively managed to kill, on average, almost 65,000 Jews per month—or around 2,200 per day. More impressively, they managed to bury the bodies at the same rate; more on this shortly.

To get a grasp of this scale of killing, we need more detail; we need an Einsatzgruppen death matrix. Longerich and most others fail to do this. For them, it is sufficient to cite a string of alleged individual events—450 shot here, 2,400 shot there, etc.—and leave it at that. Such statistics, of course, tell us little about what actually happened and when. And more importantly, they fall far short of 1 million or more.

Of recent researchers, only Headland (1992) attempts to provide real details. Citing Nazi reports, he calculates totals for each of the main Einsatzgruppen and the SS brigades (nothing for police battalions or others) through December 1942. His figures are as follows (p. 105):

---

[66] Longerich (2010: 144).
[67] See Longerich (2010: 279). Hilberg wisely ignores all discussion of these Einsatzgruppen gas vans.

Table 13: Einsatzgruppen Death Toll Numbers by "Gruppe" (per Headland)	
Gruppe A	364,000
Gruppe B	134,000
Gruppe C	118,000
Gruppe D	92,000
HSSPL	445,000
Total	1,153,000

But there are immediate problems, as he recognizes. First, these are, allegedly, *all* victims—Jews and non-Jews alike. Traditionalists assume that Jews were the large majority, perhaps 90%, though this could be drastically erroneous. Also, the HSSPL number is "certainly only part of their operations" (p. 106); such indeterminateness is a common ploy, and it leaves open the possibility of arbitrarily high ultimate figures.

But there are more fundamental problems. "It is not easy," admits Headland (p. 92), "to obtain a clear picture of any distinct features" of the Einsatzgruppen reports; "the irregularity of the reporting frustrates us at every turn." He continues:

> There is also evidence to suggest that some Einsatzkommando and Einsatzgruppen leaders deliberately exaggerated the numbers of persons shot for their own self-aggrandizement... If these exaggerations existed, there is no way to determine by how much and where the numbers were embellished. (pp. 97-102)

It gets worse:

> The impossibility of determining an exact total becomes even more obvious when one examines closely the numbers given in the tables... Anything approaching a final total for the entire period of the war cannot be realized.

Pohl (2008: 57) concurs; he says, with typical understatement, "The number of Jewish deaths in Ukraine... can only be determined with great difficulty." But wait—this is part of the "most well-documented event in history." Why is this huge portion of the Holocaust such a mystery?

Headland states that "it is unlikely that historians will ever get beyond educated estimates as to the number of persons killed in the eastern territories..." (p. 106). "We may conclude," he says on faith, "that the estimate of Raul Hilberg that over 1,300,000 Jews were killed in the east by the Einsatzgruppen and other SS agencies and collaborators is probably as close to a true figure as we are likely to find." What he means is this: 'Hilberg is famous, and thus we should just accept his number—despite its lack of substantiation—because we have no basis for anything better, and something of that size is needed to even begin to approach the 6 million.' It hardly inspires confidence.

Be that as it may, we are obliged to attempt to construct a death matrix for open-air shootings based on the data at hand—one that reaches the nominal total of 1.6 million. For the sake of calculation, let's assume that the Headland numbers (above—through 1942) are all Jews. Then we will assume that the numbers rise slowly throughout 1943, getting to the required Einsatzgruppen total of 1.3 million; their actions were almost certainly complete by this time. On top of this we must add in another 300,000 non-Einsatzgruppen shootings in order to reach the requisite overall figure of 1.6 million. These are the numbers shown in the master chart (Table 10).

Under these assumptions, the daily killing rate was very high: an *average* of over 1,000 shootings per day, for the four-year period 1941 through 1944. However, during three spectacular months—September to November 1942—it shot up to nearly 4,000 per day, thanks to some ferocious killing by the SS brigades.[68] Monthly killings for the primary Einsatzgruppen period (June 1941 to December 1943) are shown in Chart 9.

But there is an elephant in this room as well, one that Headland, Hilberg, Longerich and all the others studiously avoid: the absence of bodies.

Consider the three-month shooting peak of September through November 1942. We will set aside the myriad difficulties of hunting down, rounding up, and shooting an average of 4,000 people per day—for 120 straight days. Let's assume this was done. Each day, the five groups have a total of some 4,000 dead bodies on their hands. Now what? The obvious answer is to bury them—in crude, deep, mass graves. In such a grave one can pack at most six to eight bodies per cubic meter.[69] Consequently, the daily toll of 4,000 killings required a space of around 600 cubic meters—a hole that is, for example, 10 m × 12 m × 5 m deep.[70] In other words, a new, very large hole, every day, for 120 straight days. Even an 'off' day of only 1,000 shootings would require a hole of size 5 m × 6 m (15 × 18 ft), and 5 m deep, to accommodate the bodies.

What about a 'bad' day? The single worst alleged massacre was at Babi Yar, Ukraine. On 29 September 1941, Einsatzgruppe C supposedly slaughtered 33,771 Jews in one day. To accommodate these bodies, they would

---

[68] The main contributor during this period was HSSPL leader Hans Prützmann; according to traditionalists, his group single-handedly managed to shoot 363,000 Jews in this four-month period. See Longerich (2010: 353) or Headland (1992: 104f.). For a revisionist view, see Mattogno *et al.* (2013: 419).

[69] Though even this is a stretch. Imagine a cube-shaped, open-top wooden box, measuring one meter (3 feet 3 inches) on each side. Now imagine six or eight random people—short and tall, skinny and fat—trying to cram themselves into that box.

[70] In English units, roughly 30 ft × 36 ft in area, and 15 ft deep. Of course, if the killings were divided amongst the groups, so would the burial task.

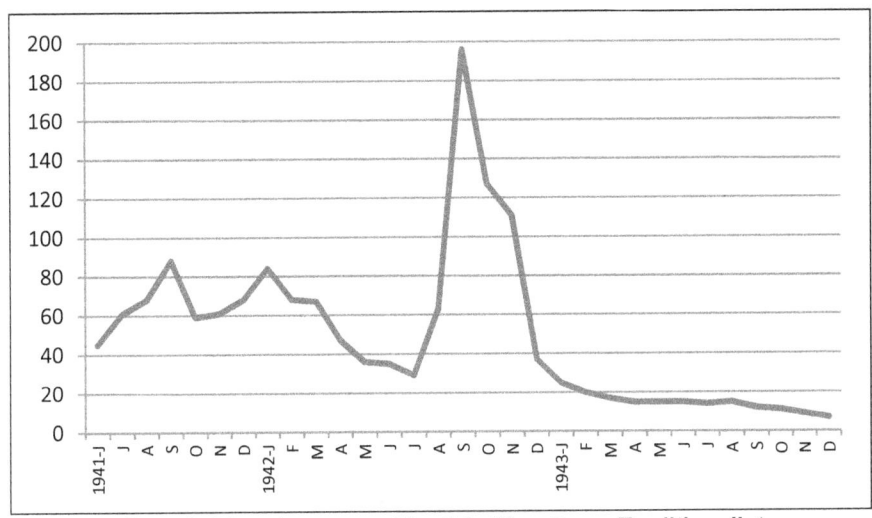

Chart 9: Einsatzgruppen Monthly Shootings, Traditionalist (in Thousands)

have had to dig a colossal trench 10 m wide by 100 m long, and 5 m deep. This alone would have been a major construction effort—all for a single day's killing.

So, revisionists raise some obvious questions: Who was doing all that digging? Every day, year round, for two and a half years? Even in ice and snow? Did each team have a diesel excavator with them? And further: Where are all those holes? If 1.3 million Jews were shot and buried, it would have required, for example, 1,000 such holes, each containing an average of 1,300 bodies. Or maybe it was 2,000 holes with an average of 650—and so on. This gives an idea of the magnitude of the problem.

And then the decisive questions: How many of these holes have we found? And how many bodies were in them?

Traditionalists have their answers at the ready. By the end of 1942, the Nazis allegedly realized that they had made a huge mistake. So many mass graves, with so many bodies, left a vast amount of incriminating evidence. (Why they would have worried about this, we are never told.) Therefore they initiated "Aktion 1005"—a plan to destroy the evidence of their mass shootings. Longerich (2010: 410) explains: "In June 1943 the commandos began to open the mass graves in the occupied Soviet territories, first in the Ukraine, then in White Russia, and finally in the Baltic states." These teams were "extraordinarily thorough," he says:

> The mass graves were opened up, the corpses were burned on piles of wood or steel grilles, then the ashes were examined for valuable objects, gold teeth above all, before the bones were ground and the ashes scattered or buried. Then all other traces that could have indicated the

places of execution were removed, and the murder scene dug over and planted.

Well, that settles that.

Longerich evidently has a low opinion of his readership. Are we supposed to accept this outlandish and impossible story at face value? Over 1 million corpses, buried in over 1,000 mass graves, spread over hundreds of thousands of square miles, were located, exhumed, and burned to ash on large campfires. The subsequent tons of ash—human plus wood—were sifted for teeth, bones, and other "valuables." The bones were ground up (how?), and the whole mess was then "scattered" or buried, such that not a trace remains. The killers also engaged in a bit of landscaping work at the end, just to make sure.

This is a ludicrous story, but it is conveniently ludicrous. It attempts to explain away the gaping hole—the fact that we have found no evidence even approximating the 1.3 million supposed victims. Indeed, by a sort of perverse logic, the absence of bodies *confirms* the traditionalist view: 'Of course there are no bodies; that was part of the plan.'

Even if the Nazis had attempted such a thing, there are substantial problems here:

1. Were they so stupid as to not think of this problem at the outset? And yet so brilliant as to, later on, effect the total elimination of evidence?
2. Merely finding all the mass graves again, after one or two years, would have been a major task in itself. The Nazis obviously had no GPS systems or satellites. They would have required an extensive and extremely detailed set of hand-drawn maps and written descriptions. Why do we have no evidence of such things?
3. Digging up hundreds of thousands of rotting corpses would have been a messy, awkward, and revolting job under the best of conditions—and impossible during frozen winter months.
4. The amount of wood required to burn decayed, rotting corpses would have been astronomical. Note: the Nazis weren't merely 'cooking' the bodies, they were *burning them to ash*. To do this on an open-air fire requires an immense amount of fuel, something like 160 kg (350 pounds) of wood per body, at minimum.[71] A modest, 1,000-person grave would thus demand at least 160,000 kg (175 tons) of firewood. And the fire would have failed in the case of cold, rain, wind, or other adverse conditions.
5. On what basis can our experts claim that the Einsatzgruppen used "steel grilles"? Do they have any record of these? Any remaining examples, any photographs—anything?

---

[71] Details to follow in subsequent chapters.

6. The ash would have been overwhelming. Each body, plus the wood to burn it, would produce about 9 kg (20 pounds) of ash; 1,000 bodies yields 20,000 pounds, or 10 tons of ash. Can we imagine the Germans "sifting" through mountains of ash, in the cold and rain, pulling out teeth and bones—each tooth individually inspected for gold, each bone tossed into the "grinder" pile?
7. Grinding hard material such as bone requires large, power-driven machinery. Do we have any evidence that such machines existed, and were towed all over Eastern Europe?
8. Buried ash remains as ash for years, decades, even centuries. If they buried the ash, it is still there. Why have we not found it?
9. Disturbed earth, as in the huge grave pits, cannot simply be erased. Merely filling them in with dirt does not do the job, nor does "digging over and planting." Modern technology can easily detect such disturbances, even from the air. Why have we not found these huge pits?

The problems compound—to an embarrassing degree. One wonders about the thinking process and motivation of researchers like Longerich. Do they understand these problems but choose not to discuss them? If so, they are profoundly deceiving their readers. Do they not understand the problems at all? Then they are hardly competent to discuss the matter. Either way, it is disastrous for them.

The question at this point is: Why has no one sought these many mass graves, or looked for other direct evidence of the Einsatzgruppen crimes?[72] As it turns out, one man has: a Catholic priest, father Patrick Desbois. His efforts culminated in a recent book, *The Holocaust by Bullets* (2008). Desbois tracked down hundreds of witnesses to the shootings and was—allegedly—able to find hundreds of mass graves across Ukraine. In the Foreword to the book, USHMM research director Paul Shapiro is effusive; Desbois has succeeded in "lifting the veil" on this murky aspect of the Holocaust. Consequently we "now know the whole truth in all of its frightening detail," thanks to "a magical marriage of the evidence." Desbois has not only "found the mass graves," but he has "added astonishing ballistic and forensic findings as well." An important outcome of this work is that it "will help to combat Holocaust denial."

This book, then, should be expected to answer our basic questions about the Einsatzgruppen killings: the death statistics, grave sizes and locations, killing dates, and so on, leading conclusively to a total figure (he claims) of

---

[72] Another complicating factor: there are countless mass graves in Ukraine due to Stalin's reign of terror during the years 1937-1941. Any such graves discovered were naturally attributed to Nazi actions. Occasionally, however, the truth emerges. For example, a brief 1989 NYT story (25 March) revealed that a Ukrainian mass grave, holding up to 300,000 bodies and long attributed to Nazi mass murder, was really due to Stalin.

1.5 million. Our hopes are high; not only is the book praised by the experts at the USHMM, but it won the 2008 National Jewish Book Award in the "Holocaust" category.

But once again we are disappointed. The book is striking for its near-total lack of specifics. Numbers like "800 eyewitnesses" and "800 mass extermination sites" come from press reports on Desbois, but appear nowhere in the book itself. We read numerous reports of relatively small killings—a few dozen or hundreds. But this is no surprise. No one denies that the Germans rounded up and killed many thousands of people. And with good reason: they were facing daily attacks from partisans, many of whom were Jewish, and the function of the Einsatzgruppen was to suppress resistance and protect the troops.[73]

But even the killing of some hundreds or thousands is a very long way from one million. The largest shootings cited by Desbois are: 10,000 in Rawa-Ruska (p. 29); "more than 8,000" (p. 66); 10,000 in the countryside (p. 98); 40,000 killed alongside the Bug river (p. 225, note 5); and the largest single incident, "more than 90,000 people" ("most Jews") in the forest of Lisinitchi. Altogether, roughly 140,000 Jews—about 10 percent of his claimed total, assuming these are true and accurate.

Oddly, Desbois offers no discussion of the single most notorious Einsatzgruppen massacre, at Babi Yar—mentioned above. It is not as if we don't know the general location. There are a number of memorials in the area today, but no one, to date, has found any of the mass graves. This would have been an ideal place to start, but Desbois passes it right over.

Regarding the many mass graves found, we are given only vague descriptions. One such grave, in Rawa-Ruska, allegedly held 1,200 Jews. There are "10 or more pits" in Busk, which later turn out to be 17 (p. 176). Numerous locations or small villages are claimed to have graves "just over there," or "in the middle of the village," or "in the nearby forest," but we are given no specifics, no details, nothing tangible. Desbois asks one witness to show him a particular burial pit; the reply: "I could show you [only] roughly where it is because the ditch has been filled in since then" (p. 79). The largest grave finding, by far, was at Lisinitchi. Here he encounters 57 mass graves, but again we are given no details whatsoever; no map, no sizes, no photos, no sketches, no analysis.

At last, we read that an excavation of sorts was carried out, at Busk. The 17 graves were opened over the course of three weeks, but out of respect for Jewish law, only the top layer of bodies could be uncovered.[74] Desbois's

---

[73] Similar actions are conducted by all modern militaries, including most recently during the US presence in Iraq and Afghanistan.

[74] With Jewish law prohibiting full and scientific excavations, we have little hope of discovering the truth.

analysis is, unfortunately, all but nonexistent. We learn nothing at all from this excavation—no grave size or depth, corpse or bone count, time and cause of death, identity of victims and perpetrators, nothing. A helicopter was hired to take aerial photos of the graves (p. 178)—but they were evidently unworthy of reproduction here, despite a lengthy insert of full-color photographs of aggrieved villagers. Desbois completed the excavation process by covering the graves over in tarmac, to ensure that they were undisturbed—by future truth-seekers, perhaps. All in all, his "excavation" is a farce.

Then we have the other bit of "astonishing" evidence: spent cartridges from German pistols. The main find was in the village of Khvativ, where a pit containing 300 cartridges was uncovered. In Desbois's simplistic reasoning, "300 cartridges, 300 bullets, 300 people executed here" (p. 53). To call this "proof of genocide," as he does, is beyond comprehension.

Some other strange aspects of the book: a witness recalls a "cremation oven" (p. 38); the widespread use of local children in the mass killings (p. 82); the use of "hemp and sunflowers" to burn the corpses (p. 67); the use of three young girls to walk barefoot on the corpses, in the pits, to pack them in more tightly (p. 84); and numerous reports of pits "moving for three days" after the graves were filled in. Such reports strain credibility, to say the least.

In the end, there is a great irony here: Desbois's work appears to better support the *revisionist* account of events than the traditional view. He found a few large mass graves of perhaps 1,500 bodies or so, a number of medium-sized graves containing around 100 bodies, and a large number of smaller ones holding a few dozen. Thus we may reasonably conclude—lacking further details—that his "800 mass graves" averaged about 100 bodies each, yielding a total figure approaching 80,000. This is completely consistent with the revisionist position, which argues that the actual death figures are about 10 percent of the claimed values—which, in this case, means something in the range of 100,000 to 150,000.

So once again we are frustrated and disappointed in our attempt to marshal firm, analytical evidence for these alleged monstrous crimes. The numbers do not add up, nothing is quantified, and no attempt is made to understand, scientifically, the specifics of the crimes. Other recent sources offer little help. Works like Rhodes (2002) or Langerbein (2004) give the usual totals, and discuss in great detail numerous isolated shootings, but fail to give any breakdown of figures, over time, that would plausibly reach the desired figures. Nor do they discuss the near complete absence of physical evidence: graves, bones, ashes, bullet casings, pyres, and so on.

Traditionalists, then, seem to be wholly unjustified in their claims of 1 million, or 1.5 million, shooting deaths. A more rational explanation is this: that the Einsatzgruppen and affiliated groups shot far fewer people, and far fewer Jews, than is claimed. No one doubts that they did kill many people, perhaps thousands, of all varieties. There was a war going on, after all. No one doubts that the bodies were frequently and unceremoniously dumped in pits. But to have killed well over 1 million Jews, buried them all, dug them all up a year or two later, burned them all to ash on wood fires, sifted through all the ash, and then hidden the ashes—this is impossible. The fact that we have evidence of no more than a fraction of this story is telling. On this matter, our traditional historians are either grossly incompetent or blatantly deceptive.

We now have some idea of the many problems with the ghetto and shooting deaths, which combined must account for around 2.6 million fatalities, or nearly half of the Holocaust. All these problems recur, in a more explicit manner, in the infamous death camps. It is to this topic that I now turn.

PART II

DEATH CAMPS IN FOCUS

Chapter 5: Chelmno and the Nazi Camp System

Concentration camps have been an aspect of war for well over a century. The Soviets developed and implemented their gulag system in the 1930s and 1940s. The British employed similar camps during the Boer War in the early twentieth century. The Americans used them in the Civil War and World War II, and today maintain an extralegal concentration camp at Guantanamo Bay, Cuba. Concentration camps are defined as temporary or provisional prisons that house criminals, enemies, and other undesirables, as well as implement forced labor. They furthermore usually detain people without trial or due process. Such camps are typically beyond the reach of civil law.

The Nazi camp system began in 1933 with the establishment of Dachau, near Munich. By the peak of the war, some 27 primary facilities were operational (following Orth [2009: 183]). These may be divided into three groups. First, the 21 'normal' camps, where no mass killings occurred:

- Arbeitsdorf
- Bergen-Belsen
- Buchenwald
- Dachau
- Flossenbürg
- Gross-Rosen
- Herzogenbusch
- Hinzert
- Kauen
- Mauthausen
- Mittelbau
- Natzweiler
- Neuengamme
- Plaszow
- Ravensbrück
- Riga
- Sachsenhausen
- Stutthof
- Vaivara
- Warsaw
- Wewelsburg

Then we have the two so-called hybrid camps, where both forced labor and mass murder allegedly occurred:

- Auschwitz
- Majdanek (aka Lublin)

I note here that the Auschwitz facility included three components: the main camp (Auschwitz-I, or *Stammlager*), nearby Birkenau (Auschwitz-II), and the industrial plant Monowitz (Auschwitz-III).[75] Roughly 98 percent of all the alleged Auschwitz killings occurred at Birkenau.

---

[75] Sometimes Auschwitz-III also refers to all other labor satellite camps, of which there were 44, all told; see http://en.wikipedia.org/wiki/List_of_subcamps_of_Auschwitz.

Finally, the four "pure extermination" camps, which only existed, on the orthodox view, for killing:

- Chelmno (aka Kulmhof)
- Belzec
- Sobibor
- Treblinka

Jürgen Graf argues that these last four should not be classified as concentration camps at all. As he says,

> There are very few surviving documents relating to these four camps, and there is no material evidence at all. There is not the slightest proof that any program of mass extermination was carried out in these camps at all; all the allegations made in this regard are based solely on unreliable "eyewitness" testimony. (2003: 286)

Rather, Graf's view is that they were strictly transit camps, serving as way stations in the deportation network. Jews would be sent to those camps to be disinfested, temporarily detained, and then shipped on to points further east. Those who died in transit would be buried, and perhaps cremated. I will consider the evidence for this argument in subsequent chapters.

Each main camp had several smaller auxiliary camps; there were hundreds of these in total. Though Jews were undoubtedly interned in them, and many died there, the auxiliary camps played little overall role in the Holocaust. I will therefore pass them over. But we do need to examine the connection between the camp system and the Nazi plan for the Jews.

The Language of Mass Murder

According to the conventional view, systematic mass killing of Jews began in the summer of 1941.[76] At this point, of the six death camps, only the original Auschwitz facility (Auschwitz I) was in existence—but it had not yet been used for mass murder. The other five were not functional until late 1941 or early/mid-1942.

The orthodox view claims that the program of Jewish extermination originated at the very top of the Nazi hierarchy, with Hitler himself. This is a key pillar of the conventional Holocaust story. As the "embodiment of evil," it is essential that Hitler be seen as personally responsible. After all, he had spoken out strongly against the Jews at least since his book *Mein Kampf*, dating from the mid-1920s. He clearly wanted the Jews out of Germany, and

---

[76] There had been sporadic killing before then, of course. And not inconsequential: on the conventional view, some 330,000 Jews had already been killed by mid-1941 (see the master chart in Chapter 4). But this was not "systematic"—or so we are told.

achieving this was a top priority. The debate is whether Hitler wanted them *expelled*, or *killed*.

Traditionalists often point to his famous Reichstag speech of January 1939, eight months prior to the outbreak of war in Europe. Hitler said:

> If the international Jewish financiers in and outside Europe should succeed in plunging the nations once more into a world war, then the result will not be the Bolshevization of the earth, and thus the victory of Jewry, but the annihilation [*Vernichtung*] of the Jewish race in Europe!

It sounds bad, of course. But there are at least two problematic aspects of this allegedly revealing speech. First, Hitler's annual Reichstag speeches were the equivalent of a State of the Union address by an American president. Each one was a major event. Each was fully public, broadcast throughout Germany and reported across the world. In fact, nearly the entire speech—including the infamous "annihilation" remark—was published in the *New York Times* (31 Jan, p. 7) the very next day.[77] Thus we have to ask this question: How likely is it that Hitler had just revealed to the world his "secret plan" for the destruction of the Jews? This is absurd, of course. Clearly he meant something else by the remark. And this is our second issue: the true meaning of what Hitler said.

At this point we need to delve into some details of the German language. The word that Hitler used was *Vernichtung*—typically translated into English as 'annihilation,' 'destruction,' or 'extermination.' But it is not so simple. The root of this word is *nichts*, 'nothing.' In verb form, *vernichten* means 'to bring to nothing.' This, in fact, is the same meaning as 'destruction'; to destroy is literally to deconstruct or 'unbuild' something.

To destroy or deconstruct a people, or an organization, does not demand the killing of the persons in question. It simply means to eliminate their effective power as a collective group. Such usage is common in politics, even today. In September 2014, president Barack Obama told the world that he intended to "degrade and ultimately destroy ISIS" (the Islamic State). Clearly he did not mean that he was planning to kill every member of ISIS. But he did intend to take violent action against them, and assuredly some would die. (Interestingly, Obama went on to describe ISIS as a "cancer" that requires "eradication"—precisely the kind of talk that Hitler was so vilified for.) Strange how history repeats itself.

Not uncoincidently, the same ambiguity that exists for *Vernichtung* is found in the English 'extermination.' This latter word derives from the Latin *ex+terminare*, meaning 'out of (*ex*) boundary (*terminus*).' In other words, to exterminate something is to drive it out, beyond the border, and thus to rid

---

[77] Strangely, the remark drew no comment in the NYT.

oneself of it—by any means. It does not demand the killing of the thing in question. This is as true in English as it is in German. Webster's confirms this, defining extermination as "to get rid of completely," or "to effect the destruction or abolition of." And this is exactly what the revisionists claim Hitler wanted: to push the Jews to the East, into the Soviet Union, beyond the borders of the Reich. Thus it is clear that Hitler was revealing his plan, not for mass murder, but for the potential ethnic cleansing of the Reich—*if* the Jews brought another world war upon Germany.

Unsurprisingly, two years later, in his January 1941 Reichstag speech, Hitler repeated the warning: "If Jewry drives the world into a general war, the role Jewry plays in Europe will be over!" (*das Judentum damit seine Rolle in Europa ausgespielt haben wird*.) This, perhaps, was less ominous but more explicit: Jews will no longer function as a cohesive group in Europe, if a global war breaks out. And in fact it would, later that year. The Jews would indeed be 'destroyed,' *vernichtet*.

All this points to another infamous word that Hitler and others often used regarding the Jews: *ausrotten*. This word derives from *aus+rotten*, meaning literally to 'root out' or 'uproot.' And indeed, the Oxford English-German dictionary translates the phrase 'root out' to *ausrotten*. It is functionally a synonym of *vernichten*.

Conversely, the dictionary translates *ausrotten* as both 'exterminate' and 'eradicate.' We have already examined the former. What about 'eradicate'? This word derives from the Latin *e(x)+radix*, meaning 'to pull up by the roots'—hence 'to root out' or 'to totally remove.' Clearly one could 'root out' the Jews, for example, without killing any of them. And again this seems to be what Hitler actually intended: that he wanted the Jews uprooted (eradicated) and driven out (exterminated). These meanings are combined in the term *ausrotten*. If this were to happen in Germany, the Jewish presence there would be destroyed—not the Jews themselves, but their presence and their economic role in German life. As with *vernichten*, nothing in this entails the killing of people.

We get further evidence of this relatively benign meaning of the German terms from the NYT itself. In March 1933 they reported on a speech by Rabbi Schulman, in which he decried Hitler's "economic persecution [that] aims at the extermination of the Jewish people" (13 Mar, p. 15). The following month, we again read of the Nazis' "deliberately calculated [plan] to accomplish the economic extermination of the Jews" (6 Apr, p. 10). Such reports were correct; they drew upon Hitler's harsh but nonlethal use of the words *ausrotten* and *vernichten*. But already by June of 1933, the NYT began to drop the economic piece of the picture. Hence we read, simply, that "Hitler's program is one of extermination" (29 Jun, p. 4). And in August, the ominous final message is clear: "600,000 [German Jews] are facing certain extermination" (16 Aug, p. 11). Thus we can see the rapid evolution from a plan of economic dismantling and removal (reality) to a distorted vision implying outright murder (fiction). None of this, of course, was explained to the reading public.

Yet more evidence comes from the extensive diary of Joseph Goebbels. Between May 1937 and the end of the war he made 123 entries on Jews and the Jewish question.[78] In describing Nazi policy toward them, the most-commonly used words—apart from *vernichten* and *ausrotten*—are *evakuieren* (to evacuate), *abgeschoben/abschieben* (to expel or deport), *aus... heraus* (to move out), and *liquidieren* (to liquidate, to get rid of). Notably absent are graphic and explicit words such as *töten* (to kill), *ermorden* (to murder), *erschiessen* (to shoot), and *vergasen* (to gas).

And it is not only the individual words; the entire context of his passages on the Jews involves nothing but extended discussion of their removal, deportation, evacuation and the like. Would Goebbels lie to himself, or use code words or euphemisms in his own private diary? Obviously not. When he said "evacuation" or "deportation," that's clearly what he meant. Nor did he mean deportation to any homicidal gas chambers; such things are never mentioned in his lengthy writings.[79] Nazi intention was clear: the Jews would be packed up and shipped out, to the East, to the newly captured areas of western Russia, and there they would be dumped.

Finally, let's look at the private talk of Hitler himself. From 1941 through late 1944, he conducted long evening sessions with friends and party intimates. These discussions—monologues, actually—have been published as *Hitler's Table Talk* (see Hitler 2000). Among a wide range of topics, he makes some 16 references to Jews and the Jewish question, over a period of about three years.[80] Every one of these passages refers, in the German original, to evacuation and removal; not one refers to killing, gassing or mass murder. For example:

> ➢ "If any people has the right to proceed to evacuations, it is we... We consider it a maximum of brutality to have liberated our country from 600,000 Jews. And yet we have accepted... the evacuation of our own compatriots!"[81] (8-11 Aug 1941—six months before the first so-called extermination camp was opened.)

---

[78] For a full account of all the diary entries see Dalton (2010).
[79] Again, he would have had no reason to avoid mention of gas chambers in his private diary. Yet they are totally absent—as is reference to Auschwitz, Treblinka, and the other so-called death camps.
[80] Hardly the "obsession" with Jews that has been portrayed.
[81] Hitler is referring to the evacuation of 800,000 Germans from East Prussia during WWI, having been driven out by the advancing Russians.

- "The Jew, that destroyer [of culture], we shall drive out (*setzen wir ganz hinaus*)" (17 Oct 1941).
- "I prophesied to Jewry that, in the event of war's proving inevitable, the Jew would disappear from Europe (*aus Europa verschwinden*)... Let nobody tell me that, all the same, we can't send them to the [Russian] morass!" (25 Oct 1941).
- "This sniveling in which some of the [German] bourgeois are indulging nowadays, on the pretext that the Jews have to clear out (*auswandern müssten*) of Germany, is typical of these holier-than-thou's. Did they weep when, every year, hundreds of thousands of Germans had to emigrate… ?" (19 Nov 1941).
- "One must act radically. When one pulls out a tooth, one does it with a single tug, and the pain quickly goes away. The Jew must clear out of Europe (*Der Jude muss aus Europa heraus*)… For my part, I restrict myself to telling them they must go away (*Ich sage nur, er muss weg*)… But if they refuse to go voluntarily, I see no other solution but extermination (*Ausrottung*)." (25 Jan 1942).
- "The Jews must pack up, disappear from Europe (*Der Jude muss aus Europa hinaus*)!" (27 Jan 1942).
- "[The Jew] bears in mind that, if his victims suddenly became aware of [the damage he causes to society], all Jews would be exterminated (*erschlagen werden*).[82] But this time, the Jews will disappear from Europe (*aus Europa verschwinden*)." (3 Feb 1942).
- "We shall regain our health only by eliminating (*eliminieren*) the Jew." (22 Feb 1942).
- "Until Jewry… is exterminated (*ausrottet*), we shall not have accomplished our task." (30 Aug 1942).
- "I have already cleared the Jews out of Vienna (*Der Juden habe Ich aus Wien schon heraus*)…" (25 Jun 1943).

Hitler obviously had no reason to hold back his language when speaking amongst such close colleagues. If he had truly wanted to kill the Jews, he would have said so—more than once, and in no uncertain terms. Instead we find not one instance of such talk. Perhaps this is why so few of our traditional historians cite these monologues of Hitler; such passages are hard to explain, on the standard view.

The lesson here is clear. Simplistic translations are highly misleading, as are all the alleged implicit references to mass murder. One must seek out the original German text, find the words that Hitler, Goebbels, and others actually used, and put them into proper context. Our traditional historians never bother to do this; it seems not to serve their larger purposes.

---

[82] Literally, 'beaten down' or 'beaten to death.'

The Missing Hitler Order

The debate over the meaning of these terms could be resolved if we had a definitive order from Hitler authorizing the mass murder of the Jews. As it happens, nothing like this exists. As Rudolf (2003a: 34) explains, "not a single bureaucratic document exists dealing with the summary extermination of Jews, specifically no order signed by Hitler which states the like." And again: "to this very day no document has been found, which orders the mass murder of Jews... In fact, not even a bureaucratic trace of such an order or directive exists" (Rudolf 2011: 146). Irving (1978: xvii) observes that "there was not the slightest written evidence" of a Hitler order. Perhaps somewhere in the massive diary of Goebbels? No. As Irving (1996: 388) again remarks, "Nowhere do the diary's 75,000 pages refer to an explicit order by Hitler for the murder of the Jews."

Lest we doubt the revisionists, we have this statement by a conventional historian: "No document survives bearing an extermination order signed by Hitler, nor any document attesting to the existence of such a written order" (Burrin 1989/1994: 20). His explanation: "In all likelihood, the orders were verbal ones." Charles Sydnor effectively surrendered this point, stating that the overall structure of Hitler's Reich "made written instructions to murder the Jews of Europe unnecessary"[83]—a convenient explanation. More recently, Kershaw (2008: 96) has offered perhaps the definitive statement on the issue:

> [By the early 1990s] the archives of the former eastern bloc started to divulge their secrets. Predictably, a written order by Hitler for the 'Final Solution' was not found. The presumption that a single, explicit written order had ever been given had long been dismissed by most historians. Nothing now changed that supposition.

And yet... Hitler *must* have ordered it. How to explain this? Traditionalists tie themselves up into knots trying to make sense of this situation. Hilberg is a case in point. Originally, he spoke of *two* Hitler orders, without supplying any specifics (1961: 177). When it became clear that no such orders existed, Hilberg retreated to a bizarre view, namely, that the Nazis acted via some kind of magic telepathy. In 1983 he said:

> What began in 1941 was a process of destruction not planned in advance, not organized centrally by any agency. There was no blueprint and there was no budget for destructive measures. They were taken step by step, one step at a time. Thus came about not so much a plan

---

[83] Cited in Zimmerman (2000: 146).

> being carried out, but an incredible meeting of minds, a consensus mind reading by a far-flung bureaucracy.[84]

"Incredible" indeed. As Faurisson has said, if it is incredible, why should we believe it? Truly, it seems unbelievable that such a program as the mass murder of 6 million people could be carried out with no written order, no budget, no plan—and yet be perfectly executed, to the point of eliminating every material trace of the crime. Even as late as 2003, Hilberg was still fumbling around for an explanation:

> The process of destruction… did not, however, proceed from a basic plan. … The destruction process was a step-by-step operation, and the administrator could seldom see more than one step ahead. … In the final analysis, the destruction of the Jews was not so much a product of laws and commands as it was a matter of spirit, of shared comprehension, of consonance and synchronization. (2003: 50-52)

Kershaw attempts to account for the lack of the critical order by citing Hans Mommsen. On his view, "the key to the emergence of the Final Solution was to be found… in improvised bureaucratic initiatives whose dynamic prompted a process of 'cumulative radicalization' in the fragmented decision structures of decision-making in the Third Reich" (2008: 94)—a statement scarcely more coherent than Hilberg's.

Most recently, Bartov (2015: 7) laments that "when and how the decision was made… has haunted scholars for decades." The problem, of course, is that "no specific order by Hitler to carry out the 'final solution' was ever found, most probably because he never issued one in the first place." The only alternative is that Hitler "preferred oral instructions." And yet this is hard to reconcile with the idea that the Holocaust was a "vast undertaking," one that involved "hundreds of thousands of officials at all ranks" (8). Could anyone, even Hitler, actually put into motion a monumental bureaucratic initiative like this, with a mere wink and a nod?

The lack of an explicit order by Hitler has three important implications. First, as mentioned, this undermines one of the three main pillars of the conventional story. Second, Hitler becomes less culpable in the killings—which now appear more as renegade actions by underlings rather than part of a systematic, strategic genocide. And third, because of the absence of systematic execution, it seems more likely that fewer actual killings may have occurred, thus strengthening the revisionist case. The targeted murder of 6 million people, more than half of these in just two years, could only have happened with a clear and consistent top-down plan. Lacking this, the death toll was likely much less.

---

[84] *New York Newsday* (23 February 1983; Part II, p. 3).

Finally, it is worth pointing out that, in one sense, the whole issue of intention is incidental. Even if Hitler intended outright mass murder, and even if he issued a written order, intention is not actuality. Intending to kill six million people is a different matter than having the functional means of doing so, which is different yet again from having physically carried it out. It is far from clear that the Nazis had the functional means of killing that many people in the manners described, or that they in fact were able to do it—even granting the intention.

Gas Chambers Galore

Nearly every main camp, and many of the smaller ones, had gas chambers—though this is not as ominous as it sounds. The problem was this: thousands of people, often poor, living in close quarters under harsh and unsanitary conditions. Diseases were rampant. Typhoid fever, dysentery, and even malaria all caused great misery. The chief problem, though, was *typhus*. Historically, typhus has had disastrous consequences in Europe. Anywhere people massed together under marginal living conditions, the disease took a huge toll.

This was especially true under conditions of war. As far back as the Peloponnesian War (430 BC), the city of Athens was hit by an epidemic that killed about one-third of the population.[85] Napoléon's forces, which were devastated in Russia in 1812, experienced an 80-percent death rate due to typhus and related diseases. One hundred years later Russia itself was wracked by epidemic; between 1919 and 1922 it had some 10 million cases of typhus, with an estimated 3 million deaths. Poland was also affected at this time, particularly the Jewish population, among whom the disease was especially prevalent.[86]

Typhus is easily transmitted by lice. In order to prevent a catastrophic epidemic in the camps, one which could spread to the local population, it was necessary to regularly disinfest the people and their belongings. The most effective lice killer of the day was hydrogen cyanide gas (hydrocyanic

---

[85] There has been some debate about the exact disease that caused the plague of Athens, but recent investigation has named typhus as the culprit. See "Scholars point to Pericles' killer," *Baltimore Sun* (30 Jan 1999).

[86] See Berg (1988). He argues that the Eastern European Jews in particular seem to have had a religious aversion to bathing, which obviously compounded the problem. Also, Crowell (2011: 31) explains that, during the interwar period (circa 1916–1920), many disinfestation gas chambers were built in Poland, including by the Americans—and at Auschwitz, no less. ("The American effort included the establishment of several disinfection stations, including one at Auschwitz.") These chambers also used cyanide gas.

acid, or HCN), concentrated into small gypsum pellets, under the brand name Zyklon B.

The Nazi government was greatly concerned about the introduction of typhus into their midst as they advanced to the east. Thus a standard part of every camp's routine was (a) to cut off everyone's hair; (b) shower or bathe them with soap; and (c) treat clothing, bedding and other items to a lengthy exposure, in a sealed room or gas chamber, with Zyklon B. These were absolutely necessary actions to save inmates' lives, protect camp personnel, and forestall a wider outbreak.

The gas chambers could be as small as a cubicle of a few cubic meters in size, or large enough to enclose an entire freight train car.[87] Often they were the size of a small room, with tight-fitting doors and windows. Typical examples can be found even today at the Auschwitz, Majdanek, Dachau and Stutthof camps. The use of these gas chambers and the toxic Zyklon B was so widespread that literally millions of people were impacted—for the better. Berg (1986: 90) cites a 1944 German article: "During the war, the clothing and equipment of approximately 25 million people have already been fumigated with hydrocyanic acid [Zyklon]." The same article mentions that about 650 Zyklon gas chambers were in use or near completion. There were other methods of killing lice, namely with hot air or steam; but these were generally more expensive and less effective.[88]

Apart from the typhus-oriented Zyklon chambers, there was another kind of alleged gas chamber, one which operated with carbon monoxide (CO). This toxic gas plays a key but little-known role in the Holocaust story. If proven, it would greatly strengthen the traditionalist view because carbon monoxide has no ability to eliminate lice or to protect against germs; it is only lethal to people (or other mammals). As I will show in detail, of all the alleged gassing deaths of Jews, *roughly two-thirds were due to carbon monoxide, and only one-third to Zyklon B*. Yet it is the Zyklon that gets all the

---

[87] See Berg (1988, 2008). As he emphasizes most strenuously, railroad car gassing would have been a near-ideal way to mass murder Jews. They were already on the trains, and the delousing tunnels were functional and well established. After a gassing, the train would have simply had to pull away and travel to a disposal site. As an added benefit, the natural draft of the moving train—and the open cattle cars that held the bodies—would obviate any need for time-consuming and dangerous ventilation schemes. It is hard to believe that the Nazis wouldn't have adopted this method immediately, if in fact they were committed to a mass murder scheme—which again suggests there was no such intention.

[88] In fact the Germans had developed an all-new high-tech approach to killing lice, based on microwave radiation—also referred to as VHF or ultra-shortwave. They piloted the device in Majdanek in 1943, and installed a permanent facility at Auschwitz in June 1944. It should be emphasized that it was the concentration camps that benefited from this advance first, even before German soldiers and civilians. For a good account see Nowak and Rademacher (2003: 312-323).

attention—perhaps because of the serious problems associated with murder by CO.

All six of the so-called death camps operated primarily with gas chambers, according to the standard view. Chelmno is addressed below, and the others are covered individually in the chapters to follow. The 21 normal concentration camps were not sites of mass murder, but seven of these are alleged to have had functioning homicidal gas chambers anyway. (Nearly all had *delousing* gas chambers.) These seven camps warrant a brief mention, if only because some people are under the impression that they were part of the so-called Final Solution.

- **Sachsenhausen.** Laqueur (2001: 238) writes that a homicidal Zyklon gas chamber was built there in March 1943, but was used "on special occasions only." It was utilized sporadically for some two years, over which time "several thousand" were killed; percentage of Jews unknown. And today? Only a floor of a small, 2 meter × 3 meter room. According to Rudolf (2011: 66-69), the gas chamber building was demolished by East German police in 1952. He contends that the Soviets concocted a story that an ordinary delousing chamber was a homicidal chamber, and then via their surrogates in East Germany, destroyed the evidence.[89]
- **Mauthausen** (today, Austria). Laqueur claims that a basement Zyklon gas chamber was built in late 1941 and operated until May 1945. The death toll is said to have been some 3,500 to 4,000 people, with an unknown percentage Jews. Also, mobile "gas vans" were allegedly used to kill people via exhaust gas. These vans supposedly shuttled between Mauthausen and a satellite camp, Gusen. The gas vans are problematic in themselves—see discussion below. The gas-chamber building is still intact today.
- **Neuengamme.** Only two mass gassings allegedly occurred there, with a total of 484 victims. Both supposedly used Zyklon. No remaining physical evidence of gas chamber exists today.
- **Natzweiler** (today, France). The subcamp Struthof was allegedly the site of "experimental" gassings which killed 130 people, mostly Jews.
- **Stutthof** (today, Poland). This camp had a "converted" delousing chamber that operated in 1944 and is said to have killed over 1,000 people, most of them Jews. Remaining physical evidence: one small building, 3 meter × 5 meter.

---

[89] Actually, it was worse than that. It appears that the Soviets in fact *fabricated* a homicidal chamber in 1945 after they liberated Sachsenhausen. Evidently worried that the ruse would someday be exposed, they then destroyed their own chamber, the original delousing chamber(s), and all ancillary evidence. See Friedrich Jansson (2014).

> **Ravensbrück.** A Zyklon chamber, said to hold 150 people, was deployed to kill some 2,300 people, mostly women. (Ravensbrück was designated as a women's camp.) Remaining physical evidence: a memorial plaque.

The seventh camp is Dachau; this one deserves a more extended discussion. According to Laqueur, the Germans built a chamber there in March 1942 but apparently never bothered to use it: "it is difficult to... say with certainty whether the Dachau chamber was ever used for its designated purpose." The chamber exists today, in the building designated as Barrack X. It is a large room, about 40 square meters in area, sufficient for gassing some 400 people, on the standard view. Tourists are regularly paraded through it as yet more evidence of "Nazi barbarity."

In the immediate aftermath of the war, no doubt existed that this was a homicidal chamber. An early US Army report referred to "a systematic policy of extermination" at the camp (Perry 2000: 14f.). It also mentioned "fake shower heads... from which gas was then released." At Nuremberg, the so-called Chavez Report changed the story; now the gas emanated from vents in the floor. In May 1945 it changed again. The *New York Times* reported on "a gas chamber at Dachau disguised as a bathhouse." Along the top of the room were rows of "perforated pipes" through which the gas was introduced (9 May, p. 17). Later that year they wrote that "Jews had been 'ruthlessly wiped out' by hanging and firing squad and gas chambers at Dachau" (21 Oct, p. 11).

Questions about the veracity of such reports soon arose. In 1954, American military attorney Stephen Pinter published a short article in a German periodical, claiming to have visited Dachau and several other western camps without finding evidence of homicidal gas chambers. A few years later, he reiterated this view in a short letter to a Catholic magazine:

> I was in Dachau for 17 months after the war, as a US War Department Attorney, and can state that there was no gas chamber at Dachau. What was shown to visitors and sightseers there and erroneously described as a gas chamber was a crematory. Nor was there a gas chamber in any of the other concentration camps in Germany.[90]

By all appearances, the American military modified the existing barrack once they gained control of the facility, to create a "homicidal gas chamber" from what was, originally, an ordinary shower room. The ceiling seems to have been substantially lowered. New, heavy-duty, vault-like doors were installed. And two "Zyklon chutes"—small metal fixtures mounted in the outside wall—seem to have been mortared in place after original construction of the building. Thus we have some evidence, at least, that the American

---

[90] *Our Sunday Visitor* (14 June 1959, p. 15).

military committed fraud at Dachau, in order to further the gas-chamber story and perhaps to justify their own atrocities there and elsewhere.

Today, as the USHMM admits, "there is no credible evidence that the gas chamber in Barrack X was used to murder human beings." A sign at the camp now says, cleverly, "this was the center of potential mass murder." Of course—any room, in any building, is a site of "potential mass murder." A separate sign admits that the room "was not used for mass murder." Appropriately, leading traditionalists like Hilberg (2003) and Longerich (2010) avoid all mention of gas chambers there.[91]

We can draw three important conclusions from these seven camps. (1) The alleged total gassing death toll is low—some 10 or 20 thousand, maximum. As tragic as these deaths might be, they are inconsequential compared to overall war losses, or to the 'six million.' (2) The percentage of Jews is unknown. (3) There is a striking lack of evidence, suggesting that some or all of these claims are either exaggerated or outright false. We now know that, categorically, there was no large-scale mass murder at any of these camps. Other infamous camps, such as Bergen-Belsen and Buchenwald, are not today claimed by *any* traditionalist to have ever had homicidal gas chambers. But many people, even today, have a different impression. During the Nuremberg trials, both the British and the French claimed to know of mass gassings at Dachau, Buchenwald, Mauthausen, and Sachsenhausen—all of which is now acknowledged to be untrue.[92]

The case of Bergen-Belsen is particularly instructive. This camp was the source of some of the most horrendous photos of dead bodies—huge piles of corpses found by the British. But as far as we can tell, the vast majority of these people were victims of typhus, not murder. Today even a staunch anti-revisionist like Zimmerman can say, flat-out, "Bergen-Belsen did not have gas chambers" (2000: 107). And yet many have claimed that prisoners, especially Jews, were gassed there. Dimont (1962: 383) wrote that Jews were "herded and stored until shipped to the gas chambers of Treblinka, Belsen, Majdanek..." In 1985, *Time* magazine referred to Belsen as a "gigantic death camp"; it was, they said, "one of some 100 camps created to effect... the extermination of the Jewish people."[93] (Wrong.)

The Belsen myth persists even up to the present day. A 2008 story in the British newspaper *Independent* referred to Britain's "gruesome discoveries at Bergen-Belsen in 1945, where piles of skeletal corpses lay amid the

---

[91] See Dalton (2011) for several recent photographs and an elaboration.
[92] IMT (vol. 19: 434; vol. 37: 148). See also Rudolf (2011: 63-70).
[93] *Time* (29 April 1985, p. 21). They also refer to the "4 million" killed at Auschwitz—also wrong.

camp's death ovens and gas chambers..."[94] "Death ovens" and "gas chambers" at Belsen? It is unbelievable that allegedly responsible journalists would use such language today. One wonders: Does no one fact-check Holocaust stories anymore?

Finally, we have the eyewitnesses. Israeli athlete Shaul Ladany claimed, in a 1972 article, to have been imprisoned in Belsen as a youth. "I actually went into the gas chamber but was reprieved. God knows why." Today we realize that this was a flat-out lie. Jewish survivor Robert Spitz recalled his stay there in a 1981 book. He described showering there, in a *real* shower, in 1945, after which he recalls: "What I didn't know then was that there were other showers in the same building where gas came out instead of water" (1981: 197). Completely untrue and likely a product of the many rumors that circulated in the camps. As recently as 1993, the Montreal *Gazette* reported on survivor Moshe Peer, who, he claimed, had been gassed at Belsen no fewer than six times—and survived:

> As an 11-year-old boy held captive at the Bergen-Belsen concentration camp during WWII, Moshe Peer was sent to the gas chambers at least six times. Each time he survived, watching with horror as many of the women and children gassed with him collapsed and died. To this day, Peer doesn't know how he was able to survive. "Maybe children resist better, I don't know." (5 Aug 1993, p. G7)

Again, totally untrue. People like Ladany, Spitz and Peer give survivors a bad name. It makes one wonder how much untruth is in other allegedly firsthand accounts.

On to the heart of the Holocaust: the six "death camps." I begin with perhaps the least well-known of the six camps, Chelmno.

Death Camp Chelmno

There are good reasons for Chelmno's obscurity. As Graf (2003: 286) says, "Of Chelmno, we know next to nothing." Mattogno (2011b: 7) concurs: "Documentation about it is almost nonexistent." There are few physical remains, no unambiguous photographs,[95] and only scant mention by witnesses. Yet somehow it features in the corpus as the site of up to 10 percent or more of all death camp fatalities.

---

[94] *Independent* (5 May 2008).
[95] There is a single photo purporting to show victims disembarking at Chelmno; see Berenbaum (1993: 84). The citation is only "Jewish Historical Institute, Warsaw." No information is given on the photographer, the date, or any specifics of the people or location. A photo of an alleged Chelmno gas van is shown on Wikipedia ("Chelmno").

Unsurprisingly, the death estimates for this camp vary widely. Table 14 gives some idea of the range—all traditionalist sources:

Table 14: Chelmno: Death Estimates (Jews only)

Deaths	Source
360,000	Gilbert (1981: 329)
350,000 (up to)	Laqueur (2001: 231)
320,000	Yad Vashem (2015: Web)
275,000 (approx.)	Krakowski (2009: 225)
250,000	Goldberg (2004)
215,000	Benz (1991: 495)
156,000 (over)	USHMM (2015: Web)
152,000 (over)	Montague (2012: 188)
150,000 (over)	Hilberg (2003: 1320)
150,000	van Pelt (2002: 80)
85,000 (under)	Pressac (2000)

Recall that I have adopted a median figure of 250,000, for purposes of assessing the overall Holocaust.

Chelmno wasn't even a fixed camp per se, but rather more of a processing station and, separately, a burial ground. Victims arrived by truck at the small village of Chelmno on the Ner River, 60 km northwest of Lodz, Poland. There they found a large country manor—variously called a "mansion," "palace," "Schloss," or "castle," depending on the source—where they disembarked.[96] A map of the Chelmno village, with the location of the 'palace,' is shown in Illustration 1 (after Krakowski). Note that it is directly in the center of the village—a church across the street, residential houses all around: an odd location for a death camp.

Upon arrival, the Jews were then told they would be shipped further on to the East, to labor camps. Instead, claim the historians, they were herded down a ramp into waiting vans—vehicles that were modified to gas them. Hence the Chelmno murder weapon: *gas vans*.[97]

Once done, the van would head out to the "forest camp," a plot of land some 5 km from the village—see Illustration 2 (after Montague). Here the bodies would be unceremoniously buried in large mass graves. Later, for obscure reasons, the Germans decided to exhume the bodies and burn them—details to follow below.

Chelmno was such a mystery that, for decades, virtually no detailed studies existed. The best one could hope for was a short encyclopedia entry or references to obscure foreign-language documents. The only revisionist

---

[96] This building was demolished by the Germans in April 1943. Only portions of the foundation remain today.
[97] For a detailed revisionist study of these vehicles, see Alvarez (2011).

treatments were two short pieces by Weckert (2003a, 2003b). Just in the past few years have we seen lengthy, dedicated works appear. To date we have three such books: two orthodox accounts, by Krakowski (2009) and Montague (2012), and one revisionist analysis by Mattogno (2011).

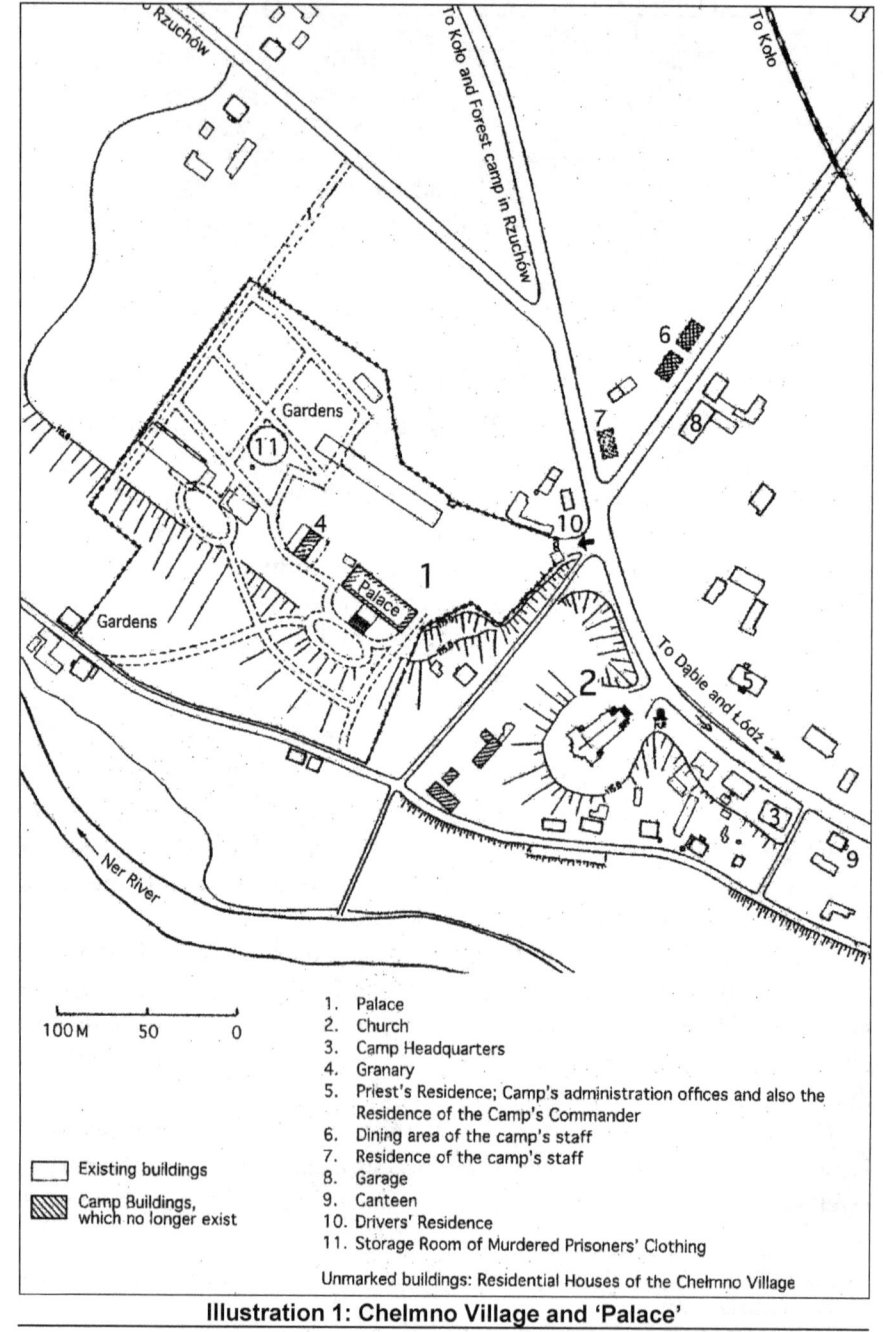

1. Palace
2. Church
3. Camp Headquarters
4. Granary
5. Priest's Residence; Camp's administration offices and also the Residence of the Camp's Commander
6. Dining area of the camp's staff
7. Residence of the camp's staff
8. Garage
9. Canteen
10. Drivers' Residence
11. Storage Room of Murdered Prisoners' Clothing

Unmarked buildings: Residential Houses of the Chełmno Village

Illustration 1: Chelmno Village and 'Palace'

Our best source of information on any camp is wartime documentation, but unfortunately, as Mattogno emphasizes, this is virtually nonexistent. The traditionalist Montague (2012: 2) agrees; he laments the "little physical evidence" remaining, the "absence of camp records and other relevant Nazi documents," and the fact that "[camp] photographs remain tragically lost to history." Current accounts of the camp are based almost entirely on unreliable witness testimony given in various postwar trials, and on a scattering of data derived from incomplete excavations.

Let's try to reconstruct the origins of the camp. As the first in existence, Chelmno was supposedly the 'experimental' death camp, the one that would establish the process for the others to come. It was in the summer of 1941, following early successes against the Soviets, that the Germans began to devise their Final Solution for the Jews—mass murder, on the standard view, or evacuation to the East, according to revisionists. Presumably acting on (missing) orders from Hitler, Himmler surveyed his technical experts for the best way to kill masses of people. Based on their experiences to date, they

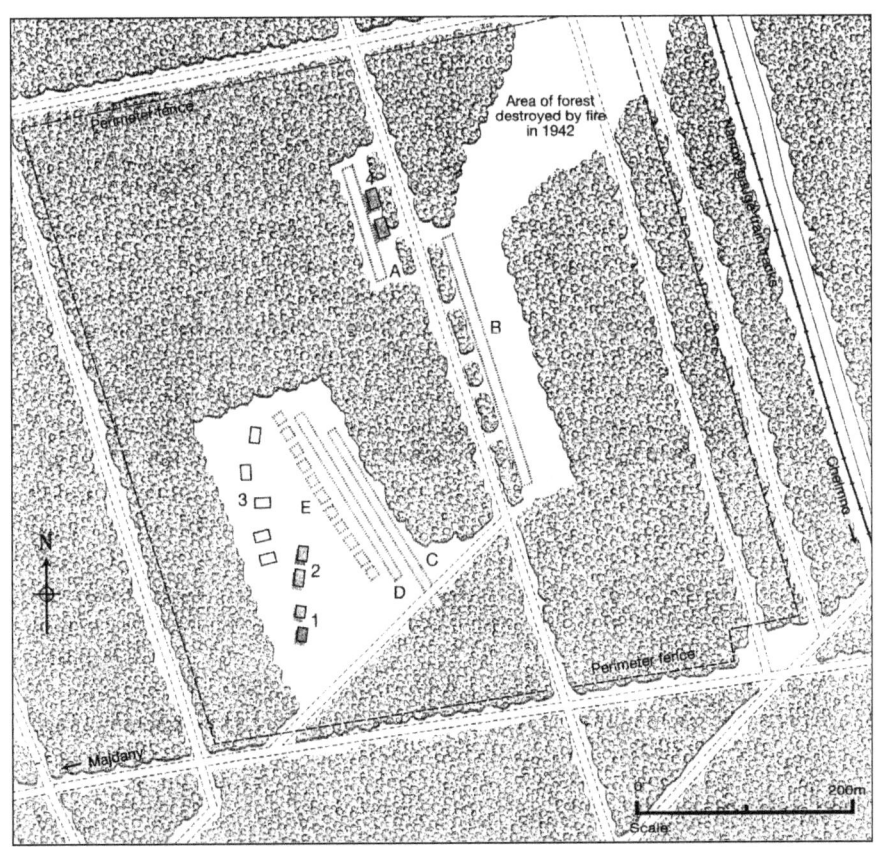

Illustration 2: Chelmno Forest Camp (mass graves A, B, C, D, E)

knew that shooting and ghetto confinement would not work. One of Himmler's men, Ernst Grawitz, allegedly proposed using "a fast acting, highly volatile gas."[98] As Mattogno demonstrates, they had many alternatives, including the highly toxic phosgene and diphosgene gasses. Even the vaunted Zyklon was considered only moderately toxic among those studied. The least-toxic gas on the list was carbon monoxide. And yet the Nazis inexplicably elected to use carbon monoxide in their prototype death camp.

The Germans had two ready sources of carbon monoxide. One was compressed gas, transported in large metal cylinders. The other was exhaust gas produced by motor vehicles. Compressed gas was expensive to produce and awkward to transport, but engines were everywhere. Every car and every truck automatically produced carbon-monoxide exhaust—for free. The choice was obvious.

But which type of engine to use? The Germans had three alternatives at that time. One was a standard gasoline engine, which put out CO gas at concentrations between 1 and 6%. This is sufficient to do the job; CO is generally fatal within 30 minutes at levels above 1%.

A second option, though, was much better: producer- or wood-gas generators. These devices burned wood or coke/coal in a small stove in order to *create* CO gas, which was then used as fuel in the engine. Producer-gas generators were very efficient at producing high-concentration carbon monoxide—typically in the range of 18-35%. At these levels, anyone exposed to this gas would die very quickly.[99]

But the Nazis, we are told, passed over these two options, preferring instead their third alternative: a diesel engine. As it happens, and unbeknownst to nearly all witnesses and historians, diesels produce very little carbon monoxide—only about 0.1% for most of their operating range.[100] The average person could breathe 0.1% CO for one full hour, and experience little more than a severe headache or mild nausea. Incredibly, then, after choosing the *least-toxic* gas, the Germans inexplicably chose the *least-effective means* of producing that gas. We may be excused if we are skeptical of this alleged scheme.[101]

---

[98] Cited in Mattogno (2011b: 21).

[99] Though hazardous, such devices were well-known to the Germans, who mass-produced them; some 500,000 were in use throughout the Reich. And obviously a producer-gas homicidal chamber would have been a potential fire hazard—given that high levels of CO are flammable—but the Germans would have had no problem engineering such a system, if they desired.

[100] Diesels have long been used in mines, submarines, and other confined spaces for precisely this reason. Granted, as I will explain shortly, they can be 'detuned' to produce somewhat more of the gas, but this severely impairs the drivability of the engine; and the same engine that killed the Jews also drove them away, as we are told. And in any case, why detune a diesel when you have plenty of producer gas generators available?

[101] For a detailed examination of the many problems with diesel exhaust as a murder

The non-toxicity of diesel exhaust is confirmed in the medical literature. Rudolf (2011: 228) notes that there are only two known instances in which a diesel was implicated in someone's death. The first, from 1998, involved an 83-year-old man who was exposed to diesel exhaust. A subsequent investigation showed, however, that he died from a soot-induced heart attack, not CO poisoning.

The second case dates from 2008. Research conducted by Griffin *et al.* (2008) resulted in a report titled "Diesel fumes *do* kill." Concerned that "an extensive [10-year] literature review produced no scientifically reported cases of fatal CO poisoning attributed to diesel fuel exhaust," the authors set out to find—or produce—at least one such case. And they succeeded: Thanks to their lobbying efforts, a single case of a 52-year-old male with chronic health problems, who died in the cab of his heavy truck, was recertified as CO intoxication due to motor-vehicle exhaust. Thus, despite the authors' clear intentions, this report seems to support the revisionist position. Given the wide range of possible failure modes that could result in elevated CO output—mistuned engines, over-rich fuel, blocked air intakes, overloaded engines—it is striking that we now have on record only a single instance of death from diesel exhaust.

It must be admitted that, under extreme conditions, it is possible to rig a diesel to put out more than 0.1% CO content. It has long been known that certain engines will emit up to 6% CO for very high fuel-air ratios.[102] This requires full throttle—and hence a heavy engine load—and an altered system to either inject too much fuel, or allow too little air. But it would take the equivalent of an overloaded truck with a severely maladjusted engine, going up a very steep hill, for 20 or 30 minutes, for this to happen. Sitting at idle, even "revving the engine" (Montague 2012: 206), would not begin to approach this condition.

Berg (2003: 456) describes a 1957 experiment in which a diesel air intake was deliberately reduced about as far as possible—to 2.5% of normal size—in order to test exhaust toxicity on live mammals. But even this only yielded a 0.22% CO content. Evidence suggests that humans could survive for an hour or more at this rate. And this study further shows just how hard it is to produce elevated CO levels from diesel exhaust.

In fact there is one very important case study suggesting that it takes a far higher CO concentration to bring about death than is commonly assumed. Flanagan *et al.* (1978) report on a suicide case with gasoline (not diesel) engine exhaust, which at idle contains about 5.5% CO. The victim ran a hose from the exhaust pipe into his closed vehicle, causing the interior CO content to rise almost linearly from zero to nearly 5% in 20 minutes. He furthermore

---

weapon, see Berg (2003) or Rudolf (2011: 224-233).
[102] See, for example, Holtz and Elliott (1941).

tape-recorded his suicide, and based on breathing and coughing sounds, doctors were able to track symptoms with rising CO levels. Due to the small cabin space, the CO reached the "fatal" 1% level within just four minutes. At 10 minutes it reached 2.5% and the victim was still alive, taking six breaths per minute. At 13 minutes (3.7%) he was near comatose, but still alive and still breathing. Not until the 20-minute mark, at nearly 5% CO content, did the tape go silent. To replicate such an event with a *diesel* gas van, in *half the time*, would be virtually impossible.

Thus we see that there are myriad problems with diesel exhaust as a murder weapon, particularly in a moving vehicle. And yet these seem to cause no concern to our traditionalists, who continue to insist on the diesel gas van story. In the authoritative Oxford study, for example, Karen Orth (2010: 370) writes, "Chelmno and the Reinhard camps [i.e. Belzec, Sobibor, and Treblinka] killed with carbon monoxide gas generated by diesel truck motors..." When so much time and effort have been invested in one version of a story, it is difficult to change.[103]

But let's continue our standard account. Having settled on diesel engines, the Germans then needed to select an appropriate vehicle. According to witnesses, the gassing vans were modified versions of commercial trucks, ones built in the style of furniture or moving vans. As Montague sees it, there were four such vehicles in total at Chelmno: two smaller Opel Blitz vans and two larger Saurer trucks.[104] Each had a large "hermetically sealed" cabin in the rear,[105] separated from the driver's cab. The small vans could hold 25 to 30 people, and the larger 50 to 70. The vehicles were retrofitted with flexible exhaust pipes that could easily be redirected to a hole in the floor of the rear cabin. Exhaust gas, on this view, would pour into the cabin, quickly killing all inside—within 10 minutes, as we are told. The dead bodies could then be conveniently trucked away for disposal at the forest camp.

The mere fact that the Germans bypassed more-deadly gases, and then opted to use a diesel engine to kill with CO, is sufficient for a rational investigator to dismiss the entire gas-van story. But there are other problems with it. For example, it is physically impossible to pump exhaust gas into a "hermetically sealed" cabin. Either the engine will stall, or the cabin will be blown apart. It would have needed a complex system of pressure valves to let out the air as the exhaust gas came pouring in. But no one has ever described such a scheme. If we had an actual gas van at our disposal, we could

---

[103] One exception is the German writer Achim Trunk, though he wrote in the context of the Reinhardt camps, not the gas vans. See my discussion in Chapter 7.
[104] As Alvarez (2011) points out, however, this is a contradictory claim; the Opel Blitz used only gasoline engines.
[105] Montague (2012: 201).

easily answer such questions; unfortunately, not one has survived. (More problems of 'vanishing evidence.')

Furthermore, we have a much more-plausible explanation for the wartime accounts of such vehicles. Trucks running on producer-gas systems were in fact called *Gaswagen*, or 'gas vans.' Additionally, the Germans had specially outfitted vans for use with Zyklon to delouse clothing and personal items; these too were called 'gas vans.' But when word got around of the (true) existence of gas vans, combined with the (true) fact that people were dying and being buried or cremated, and at the same time friends and family members were being shipped out of ghettos, never to be seen again, we can imagine how stories of homicidal gassings in vans could emerge.

How do our two traditionalists handle these issues? On the critical question of diesel versus gasoline engines, and the subsequent production of deadly CO gas, both Krakowski and Montague are completely silent. The word 'diesel' appears not once in Krakowski's book. Montague never specifies the engine type, nor informs the reader of the critical difference. Late in the book he allots one paragraph to "the question of the type of gasoline these vehicles used" (p. 208), but then neglects to answer the question. It is clear that he uses the term 'gasoline' as a generic for engine fuel, failing to make the crucial distinction between ordinary gasoline (petrol) and diesel fuel.

Perhaps, says the critic, they really were *gasoline* engines. As I noted above, the smaller Opel Blitz vans did indeed run on gasoline—in contrast to the Saurers, which ran only on diesel. But according to the official story, it was the larger Saurers that formed the basis for the expanded second phase of gassing in vans; and these definitely could not have been gasoline. And any use of gasoline engines is contradicted by a string of witnesses and experts who insist on diesels.

Further Issues

As I stated, Chelmno is largely a mystery camp. How, then, do we know anything about it? The traditionalist case rests heavily on just two letters: one by SS chemist Becker (dated 16 May 1942), and the other a memo (dated 5 June 1942) to SS department head Rauff. The former is quite explicit about the homicidal purpose of the vans—so much so that Weckert (2003a) and Alvarez (2011) have declared it an outright forgery, both on content and style. The latter memo speaks in oblique terms about the "subjects" and the "load," and how, in just six months, "97,000 have been processed, using three vans" (97,000 *what*?). And there are again numerous indications of forgery, including Rauff's signature. Of all the anti-revisionists only Zimmerman attempts to refute Weckert, in two footnotes (2000: 356-359)—with questionable success. The average reader has little ability to assess either case here.

Finally, the gas vans are alleged to have also played a role in the Einsatzgruppen killings. As we saw in Chapter 4, they are claimed to have killed some 1.3 million Jews. Most of them were shot, but according to some accounts, a large portion—up to one quarter—died in mobile gas vans. If so, then the gas vans were key players in the Holocaust:

> In all, approximately 700,000 persons were murdered in the vans—roughly half on occupied Soviet soil and the remainder at the Chelmno extermination camp. (*Holocaust Encyclopedia*, 2001: 231)

If this is true, gas vans with diesel engines must have been a *very* efficient means for killing. And yet all the evidence is to the contrary.

Disposing of the Bodies

Killing at Chelmno allegedly began in late 1941 and continued on for some ten months. For most of this time, the Germans took the bodies to the forest camp and dumped them into long, narrow mass graves (Illustration 2). After eight months or so, someone apparently decided that there was too much incriminating evidence in the ground. Thus the plan changed: The bodies would be dug up and burned to ash.

According to Montague (2012: 115f.), the Germans initially built four crude crematoria in the forest camp. These "did not work very well," and so two newer, more efficient ones were constructed—evidently displacing the old ones. These latter two contained "tall chimneys" that "belched smoke." This in itself is quite odd: the top-secret Nazi program to destroy the Jewish people is now betrayed by vast amounts of smoke emanating from an otherwise nondescript forest location.

Apparently, though, the new crematoria worked—but we can only imagine the many difficulties with digging up, transporting, and burning thousands of rotting, disintegrating corpses. Be that as it may, over a period of about eight weeks the Nazis managed to burn not only the previously buried bodies but also the new ones generated by the still on-going gassings. In total, we are told, they burned 250,000 bodies in eight weeks—an average of 4,460 bodies per day.

To say that this strains credibility is an understatement. Even the large and "highly efficient" Auschwitz crematoria, under absurdly high assumptions, could not burn more than 2,000 per day; and by more-reasonable assumptions, only some 350 to 400 per day.[106] So how could two experimental crematoria in the middle of a Polish forest handle an average of 2,200 each per day, every day, for nearly 60 straight days?

But there are yet more problems. The Chelmno crematoria used wood for fuel. Montague quotes a camp guard's wife:

> Two crematoria were built. ... The bodies were arranged in layers in these ovens. Between each layer of bodies was a layer of wood. Gasoline was poured over the pile of bodies and wood when the corpses were to be burned in the fire. (p. 116)

The amount of wood required to fully burn a human body is not inconsiderable. As shown in Appendix A, one needs about 160 kilograms (350 pounds) of wood per body to fully incinerate it. This is a rough estimate, since the amount of wood needed per corpse varies with the number of bodies to be burned, condition of the corpses, environmental conditions, and so on. Small pyres, of less than 10 bodies, have very high wood requirements. Pyres of individual bodies, as are performed in Hindu cremation ceremonies, require between 250 and 550 kg of wood, and burn from four to six hours.[107] If the Germans were burning several hundred at once, the efficiency increases to the point where they would have needed only some 150 or 160 kg per body. But this is still a substantial amount of fuel.

Thus 250,000 corpses would have required a mind-boggling 40 million kilograms (44,000 tons) of wood. Putting this in perspective, the Eiffel tower weighs about 7,300 tons. Thus the Germans would have required nearly six Eiffel towers' worth of wood to fully consume those bodies. If locally supplied, the entire area would have been deforested. If trucked in, there would have been a document trail and witnesses. Yet we have no record of such huge amounts of wood moving into, or being processed at Chelmno.[108]

Dead bodies do not burn to nothing; they leave plenty of *ash*, and so does the wood. The combined human and wood ash amounts to about 9 kilograms

---

[106] According to Mattogno's assumptions. See Table 28 in Chapter 10.

[107] In a 2013 article on the climate impact of funeral pyres, it was stated that "the typical pyre is constructed of 550 kg of wood and a few kilograms of biological and synthetic materials... Once the corpse is placed on the pyre, the burning takes four to six hours" ("A burning question," *Environment and Energy News*, 29 Oct). During the 2015 earthquake in Nepal, so many had died that wood was running short; even in those conditions, "250 kg of wood [is] needed for each cremation" ("Nepal earthquake: First glimpse of devastation," *Independent* (UK), 27 Apr).

[108] Montague (118) mentions that "a crew was formed to cut wood and transport it to the vicinity of the crematoria," but he provides neither the source of this information nor any usable details.

per body.[109] For 250,000 bodies, the ash pile would have been monumental: roughly 2.2 million kg in total, or about 42 tons per day.

What did they do with all this ash? As Montague (118) explains, it was initially "simply buried in pits four meters deep and eight to ten meters wide. Later [it] was sprinkled around the area of the forest floor." This method would work for a small amount of ash, but it is utterly impracticable for anything like 40 tons daily.

But even this was not the end of problems for the beleaguered crew at Chelmno. Even the most-efficient wood-fired crematoria cannot incinerate hard body material, such as bones or teeth. Therefore the huge piles of ash had to be sifted through, every day. The hard remnants then had to be further processed in a "bone grinder." Montague (117) admits as much: "After the corpses were burned, small bone fragments remained. These too had to be disposed of. It was decided to crush the bone fragments into powder. A bone grinder was required for this purpose." Incredibly, according to Montague, the Germans turned to none other than Chaim Rutkowski, head of the Jewish Council in the Lodz ghetto! As luck would have it, he was fresh out of grinders; the Germans thus had to resort to other means to acquire one.

Confirmation of these fantastic stories should theoretically exist in the mass graves. On the conventional view, something like 170,000 bodies were buried before the exhumations began. We know where the graves are; in fact, there is a victim memorial there today. Montague discusses the graves in detail, and supplies a helpful map (Illustration 2). Today we see evidence of three long (circa 200m), thin (8m) disturbances, one smaller disturbance of some 60m in length, and about a dozen isolated pits. In total, these could indeed have held the requisite number of bodies. And if the ash was buried, as Montague claims, it will still be there today; as I noted before, ash survives as ash for centuries.

Surely, then, orthodox researchers have conducted detailed examinations of the graves and ash, confirming the standard view—true? Not quite. As Mattogno explains (pp. 95-105), there have been four excavations of the Chelmno mass-grave sites: in 1945, 1951, 1986, and 2003. The first three were so poorly conducted that nothing conclusive can be determined. The 1986 examination, for example, found "a huge amount of crushed human

---

[109] As shown in Appendix A, a corpse reduces down to about five percent of the initial mass in case of complete combustion, leaving behind only incombustible ashes. This is a minimum figure, which could surely not be attained in open air cremations where some charred remains must be expected. Five percent is therefore a conservative estimate. Wood ash is harder to estimate, since it varies by type of wood, dryness of wood, humidity, temperature, and burning configuration and time. Revisionist estimates range from 0.33 percent (Neumaier; complete combustion) to 8 percent (Mattogno 2004c; incomplete combustion), by mass. For my calculations, I use an intermediate figure of 4 percent.

bones" at the presumed location of the corpse-burning site, but we are given no measureable details. Four bags of sample earth were analyzed, of which only "a few percent" consisted of bone fragments or ash (p. 97). The latest investigation in 2003 produced, once again, no objective, quantifiable data. Whatever is in those pits today, it evidently does not support the orthodox view, or else we surely would have heard about it in great detail. Perhaps these are the reasons why both Krakowski and Montague completely ignore the question of excavations.

A Chelmno Death Matrix

Montague provides one additional helpful bit of information. In his Epilogue he supplies daily deportation figures for the entire operational period. But we have two concerns with this data. First, as usual, he simply assumes that all deportees were subsequently killed; on the revisionist thesis, of course, they were *actually deported* to locations further east. Second, his numbers are too low; they reach only 172,000 in total. Thus we must scale them up in order to attain the desired 250,000.

This allows us to construct a provisional death matrix for the camp. I include monthly death statistics as well as monthly burial or burning numbers—see Table 15.

Table 15: Death Matrix for Chelmno (in Thousands, except last row)

	1941	1942												Total
	D	J	F	M	A	M	J	J	A	S	O	N	D	
Gassing (Gas Vans):	5	26	13	55	21	27	9	16	45	33				250
Body Disposal:														
Buried:	5	26	13	55	21	27	9	16						172
Exhumed & burned:									86	86				172
Direct, gas vans to burn:									45	33				78
Total burnings:									131	119				250
bodies burned/day:									4,367	3,967				

As we can see, the peak month for gassings was March 1942, during which some 55,000 Jews are alleged to have been killed. If true, this would imply that more than 1,800 were killed per day, on average. And this was achieved using only three or four gas vans, according to Montague. If the two smaller held 30 each, and the two larger 60 each, then one full load would kill 180 Jews. It would thus have required 10 full loads each day, every day, for that month. The Chelmno team was busy indeed.

As a final point of mention, I have chosen to overlook data by Montague and others suggesting that there was a short second phase of killing at Chelmno in the summer of 1944. This event is even less well-attested than the main phase, and in any case only amounts to some 5,000 to 7,000 persons—inconsequential in the larger picture.

To summarize revisionists' primary concerns:

1. *No documentary evidence of the camp itself.* Apart from the two dubious letters mentioned above, we have no bureaucratic trail, no drawings, no map, no photographs, no construction papers, no work orders—nothing.
2. *No quantifiable excavations.* Despite four attempts over 70 years, we have no analyzable data on the alleged mass graves, nor any evidence of the vast quantity of ash that would have been produced.
3. *The use of carbon monoxide from diesel gas vans.* At best this is an awkward, impractical and illogical method of killing people. Far better options existed. It would never have been employed by the evil geniuses that the Nazis were said to be.
4. *Huge wood requirements.* About 730 tons per day, and nearly 44,000 tons in total.
5. *Huge amounts of ash produced.* Some 42 tons per day—which must have been carefully sifted for bones and teeth, before being made to vanish.
6. *Smoke signals.* No way to hide massive amounts of smoke from burning corpses, for two full months.

Traditionalist Replies

Almost nonexistent. The two recent dedicated works by Montague and Krakowski fail to address any of these important issues. Perhaps for good reason, our general-purpose Holocaust experts have evidently decided to simply ignore the camp. Longerich (2010) gives just passing mention on seven or eight scattered pages. The anthology by Bartov (2015) cannot even muster this much. Those who specialize in confronting revisionism likewise have little to say. The one person most expected to address this, Zimmerman, provides barely half a dozen references. Except for the diesel exhaust, not a word is offered to answer or explain the other revisionist concerns.[110]

To the critical diesel-CO problem, Zimmerman devotes all of one footnote (pp. 355f.), which covers not only the gas vans but all the other 'diesel' camps as well—some 2.5 million deaths in total, on the standard view. The upshot of his counterargument: (a) they might have been gasoline engines; and (b) even if not, diesels can still be rigged to put out toxic levels of CO

---

[110] As noted above, Trunk (in Morsch 2011) addresses the diesel question, but only for the Reinhardt camps. He has nothing to add to the discussion on Chelmno.

"without any problem." It is, he says, a "trivial process." This is a vast overstatement. It may be theoretically possible, under extreme conditions that could not be long maintained, but it would make no sense to do so when far better alternatives existed—better even than gasoline engines.

My conclusion: The 'mystery camp' remains largely mysterious. The traditional death toll—some 250,000, by my reckoning—is unsustainable. Conventional sources on Chelmno never explain how they arrived at their numbers, and there exists no forensic or material evidence to justify anything close to this number. The vans, the bodies, the fuel and the ash have all but vanished, as has all documentary and photographic evidence. And the alleged gassing method is quite frankly absurd.

Furthermore, we can easily understand how stories of homicidal gas vans came to exist. Real but non-lethal gas vans were in use at this time. Many Jews did in fact get sent through the Chelmno station, on their way out of the Lodz ghetto—"never to be seen again." Doubtless many of them died *en route*. Likely some of the bodies were taken to Chelmno to be disposed of. Perhaps some were buried and others burned on crude pyres or 'crematoria.' But the evidence suggests that this number was much smaller than 250,000—perhaps a few thousand at most. Revisionists apparently have no specific counterproposal for the number of deaths. Mattogno (2011b) declines to offer a figure. I will take 2,000 as a nominal estimate, until further projections become available.

As to the gas vans themselves, it's not clear if the revisionists are absolutely denying their existence, or simply the scale of killing with them. Surely it was possible that some renegade killing occurred, perhaps even in a vehicle or two that were rigged to kill with exhaust gas, as crude and inefficient as that would be. It would seem prudent to accept the possibility that there was at least some occurrence, somewhere, of killings in vans. Again, this could be another kernel of truth behind the larger fish story.

Chapter 6: The Reinhardt Camps (Part 1): Belzec, Sobibor, Treblinka

> *"The* [Reinhardt] *camps were built under primitive conditions. ... Their temporary and primitive character... was due to the fact that no budget was allocated for their construction;* [camp architects] *were forced to improvise and economize."*
> —Tomasz Kranz (2003: 221)

In early 1942 a conference of Nazi leaders was held in a suburb of Berlin called Wannsee. According to existing German documents and meeting minutes, the objective of the gathering was to initiate a program of evacuation of the Jews out of the Reich, or at least to corral them into designated Jewish ghettos where they would be isolated from the general public. There was no explicit talk of mass killings, even though the meeting was highly confidential and restricted to ranking Nazi officers. Even so, traditionalism has it that the Wannsee Conference was a kind of kick-off of the extermination of the Jews. The Website of the USHMM claims that the purpose of the meeting was

> to discuss and coordinate the implementation of what they called the "Final Solution of the Jewish Question"… Despite the euphemisms which appeared in the protocols of the meeting, the aim of the Wannsee Conference was clear to its participants: to further the coordination of a policy aimed at the physical annihilation of the European Jews.

Orthodox historians believe that all discussions, even those at the highest and most confidential levels, operated under a kind of code language in which 'deportation' or 'evacuation' meant murder. There is no proof—nor even a hint—that such a code ever existed, or any explanation of how it would have been implemented by the "hundreds of thousands" of functionaries at all levels of government. Yet this is the sole explanation given to account for the utter lack of incriminating language.

It was decided at Wannsee to begin evacuations with the Jews of the 'General Government' (*Generalgouvernement*), a large area of central Poland that included Warsaw, Krakow, and Lublin. In total, some 2.3 million Jews lived there. The process of seizing Jewish property and eventually cleansing the General Government via forced deportations was called Operation Reinhardt. The focus was to be on three new camps—Belzec, Sobibor and Treblinka—that would serve, on the revisionist view, as collection points and gateways to areas further east: the newly captured Soviet territories. Thus, revisionism sees these camps exclusively as *transit camps*—as way stations in the ethnic cleansing of the Reich and Poland.

As a consequence of the Reinhardt organizational structure, the three camps had many characteristics in common, and thus are frequently examined together. I will do the same in the following three chapters. Stories about the camps share many of the same problems and many of the same contradictions. And all three came to a surprisingly similar end.

Orthodoxy and Estimated Fatalities

Regarding competing views of the Reinhardt events, we are fortunate to have dedicated texts on both sides of the debate. The orthodox case, even to this day, is based largely on a single work: Arad's 1987 book *Belzec, Sobibor, Treblinka*. This is the standard academic source for these camps. Additionally, a small number of other books dedicated to each camp supplement Arad's basic picture:

Belzec:
- A. Kola: *Belzec* (2000)

Sobibor:
- T. Blatt: *Sobibor: The Forgotten Revolt* (1996).
- J. Schelvis: *Sobibor: A History of a Nazi Death Camp* (2006).

Treblinka:
- G. Sereny: *Into That Darkness* (1974).
- A. Donat: *Death Camp Treblinka* (1979).
- C. Webb, M. Chocholaty: *The Treblinka Death Camp* (2014).

Overall the picture is strikingly sparse—only some half-dozen academic English-language books, in total, over the past four decades, to address the three camps that are such key elements of the Holocaust. A few relevant journal articles have appeared as well, and I will cite those as necessary.

To be clear, I emphasize that these handful of books are only a minuscule fraction of the total orthodox output. There have been hundreds of other books that mention these camps or refer to them in some way. There have also been a comparable number of journal articles and news stories. But all these others draw heavily upon the sources listed above.

On the revisionist side, we have recent dedicated works on all three camps:

- C. Mattogno: *Belzec* (2011).
- J. Graf, T. Kues, and C. Mattogno: *Sobibor* (2010).
- C. Mattogno and J. Graf: *Treblinka* (2010).

The above works will serve as my primary sources.

Like Chelmno, the Reinhardt camps are said to have existed purely for extermination. There were no releases and no transfers; every person sent there, we are told, died there.[111] And like the Chelmno Saurer vans, their gas chambers operated strictly on the exhaust of diesel engines (although there is disagreement regarding the Sobibor camp, as will be discussed later). Given the many problems with mass murder via diesel exhaust, this story has immediate concerns—and all the greater, given the far higher death toll.

As before, there is a very wide range of death estimates for all the camps. Tables 16-18 give some idea of the disparity among orthodox historians.

I remind the reader of the assumed figures that I am using, in order to sustain the total of 6 million:

- Belzec: 550,000
- Sobibor: 225,000
- Treblinka: 900,000

In each case these are roughly median figures among conventional estimates. Traditionalists should have no dispute with these numbers.

The wide range of death estimates raises an immediate concern for revisionists. It's not so much the sheer numerical variation—although this is also of concern—but more that the estimates have little basis in fact. For example, at Belzec early postwar death tolls of 3 million and 1.8 million were quickly dismissed, and in 1947 a Polish commission set the number at 600,000: "this figure... passed into official historiography and is almost unanimously accepted even today, although it is based on an absolutely arbitrary method of computation" (Mattogno 2011: 47).

In essence, the commission estimated the number of train transports, number of cars per train, and number of people per car—and then added it all up. There was no documentation to support their estimates, and witnesses

---

[111] However, this is not true. Mattogno documents several instances of movements out of the camps.

directly contradicted their assumptions. Finally, and importantly, all numbers were of people *deported* to Belzec. It was a pure assumption that every person sent to Belzec died there. Recent excavations have yielded remains of only some tens of thousands of people—see below. Hence the 600,000 indeed seems to be an arbitrary number.

Only recently has a new document come to light. British decoders intercepted many German radio transmissions during the war, and one of these listed a number of 434,508 for Belzec as of end of 1942—reproduced in Mattogno (2011: 127). This single document is the source of the USHMM number—again, assuming that 100 percent of deportees were killed. In fact it tells us nothing about actual deaths. Deportation figures unsupported by forensic data provide little basis from which to estimate death statistics.

Totals for Sobibor presumably followed similar reasoning, but we lack a detailed accounting of how those numbers evolved. Arad (1987: 390) can only come up with deportation statistics for about 100,000 people—less than half his total. Schelvis (2007: 198) supplies figures adding up to 170,000, which is still far short of most estimates.

Regarding Treblinka, Soviet propagandists trumpeted a 3-million figure as early as 1944—see discussion in Chapter 8 on excavations. The witness Samuel Rajzman testified that 2,775,000 people were deported to Treblinka, and presumed all killed. In December 1945 a Polish judge, Zdzislaw Lukaszkiewicz, performed a simple set of calculations, arriving, "without

Death Estimates (Jews only) for:

Table 16: Belzec

DEATHS	SOURCE
<1,000,000	Tregenza (2000: 242)
800,555	O'Neil (1999: 104)
600,000	Yad Vashem (2015: Web)
550,000	van Pelt (2002: 6)
434,000	USHMM (2015: Web)
< 150,000	Pressac (2000)

Table 17: Sobibor

DEATHS	SOURCE
350,000	Bauer, in Zimmerman (2000: 106)
300,000	Bem and Mazurek (2012: 129)
250,000	Yad Vashem (2015: Web)
200,000	van Pelt (2002: 80)
170,000	Schelvis (2007: 198)
>167,000	USHMM (2015: Web)
>150,000	Hilberg (2003: 1320)
< 35,000	Pressac (2000)

Table 18: Treblinka

DEATHS	SOURCE
3,000,000	The Black Book (1946: 407)
<1,200,000	Noakes and Pridham (1995: 1156)
1,074,000	Auerbach (in Donat 1979: 53)
974,000	Golczewski (in Benz 1991: 495)
950,000	Browning (2010: 137)
< 925,000	USHMM (2015: Web)
< 885,000	Webb and Chocholaty (2014: 193)
870,000	Yad Vashem (2015: Web)
< 800,000	Hilberg (2003: 1320)
780,863	Snyder (2009)
750,000	van Pelt (2002: 80)
< 250,000	Pressac (2000)

any exaggeration," at 781,000 victims.[112] In 1946, Rachel Auerbach performed a similar calculation, arriving at 1,074,000—also presumably without any exaggeration. Mattogno describes several further such attempts, all variations on the same theme. All contain critical but unverified assumptions, together with the key assumption that every deportee was murdered. There has been no attempt by traditionalists to determine what was physically possible, or what the material evidence—or lack thereof—might suggest.

Camp Structure and Maps

Belzec was the first of the camps to become operational, in March 1942. At 75,000 square meters (18 acres) it was the smallest of the three—half the size of Treblinka, and one-quarter that of Sobibor. Sobibor allegedly began gassings shortly after Belzec, in April 1942. Treblinka opened a few months later, in July.

The design and operation of the three camps shared several common features, according to the traditionalists:

- All were square or rectangular in layout.
- All opened with three gas chambers, and expanded later on—Belzec and Sobibor to six, Treblinka to thirteen.
- All were on railroad lines.
- All had at least two distinct zones: an entry or reception zone, and an "extermination area." These were connected by a narrow pathway called "the tube."
- As noted, all allegedly murdered their victims with carbon monoxide in the form of diesel-engine exhaust.
- All initially buried their victims, but then later (at different dates) exhumed the bodies and burned them on crude steel-grate pyres made from old railroad rails.

The following are layout plans of the three camps, as assumed by Arad—see Illustrations 3-5. For death camps, they were surprisingly well outfitted.

---

[112] Lukaszkiewicz calculated one train transport to Treblinka per day, for 135 days (from August to December 1942), and then one per week for the next four months—151 transports in total. Each is assumed to have had 50 cars, each car 100 deportees. Thus: 151 × 5,000 = 755,000. Finally he adds in 26,000 more people for August 1943. See Mattogno and Graf (2010: 96-98).

A striking fact: *None of the three camps had a crematorium.* Unfortunate, since this would have made the task of burning the bodies much cleaner and much more efficient. Surely a crematorium would have been standard equipment for any true extermination camp. Surely the Nazis would have learned their lesson from their 'experimental death camp' Chelmno. Camps without crematoria suggest that they were never really designed for mass killing in the first place, but rather for the purpose of temporary holding—just what

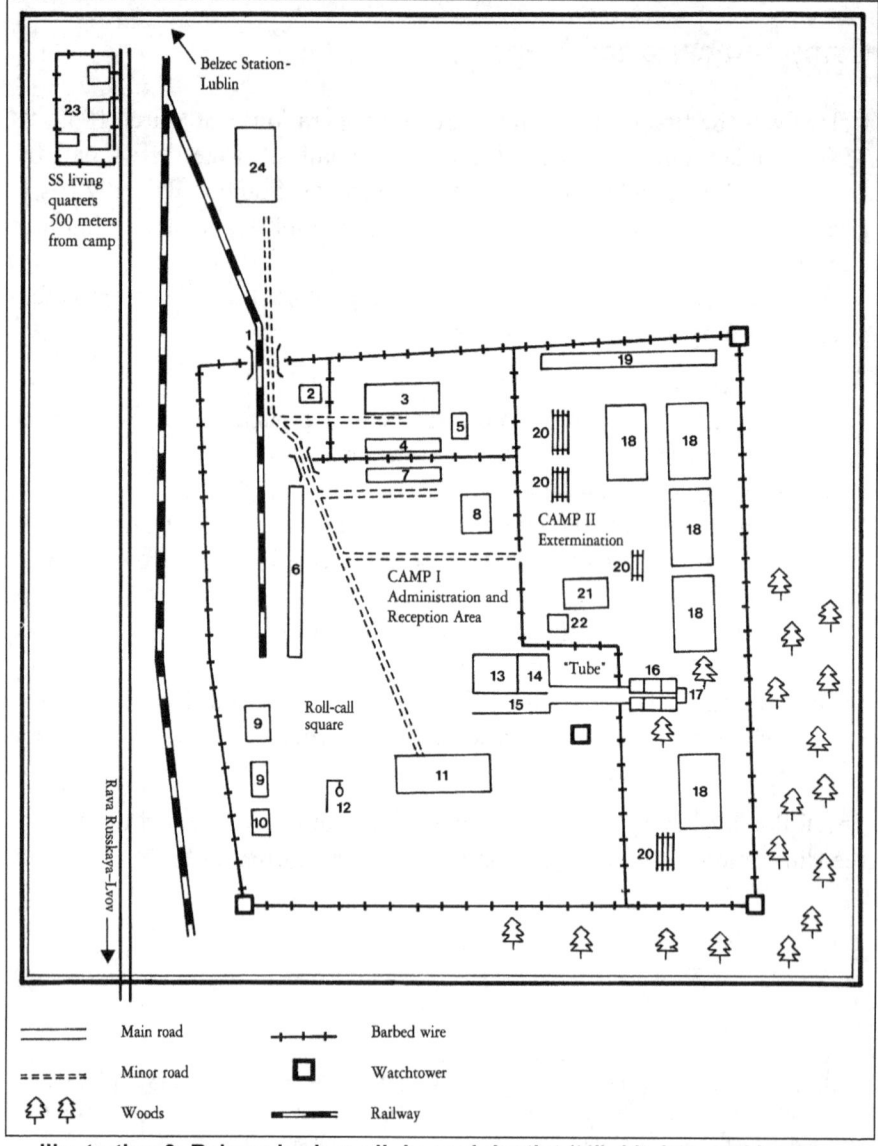

Illustration 3: <u>Belzec</u>: barber, clinic, and dentist ('4'), kitchen and laundry ('10'), garage ('7'), tailor and shoemaker ('8'). Taken from Arad (1990d: 296)

THOMAS DALTON · DEBATING THE HOLOCAUST 133

one would expect for a transit camp. And pit burials and open-air burning on crude pyres are clearly small-scale makeshift procedures—just what one would expect for sporadic disposal of a small number of dead bodies.

The tube of each camp plays a prominent role in witness stories. This dreaded pathway was described by many as the means by which family and friends disappeared forever. On the standard view, victims arrived in the entry zone, were forced to undress, given haircuts, and sent naked down the

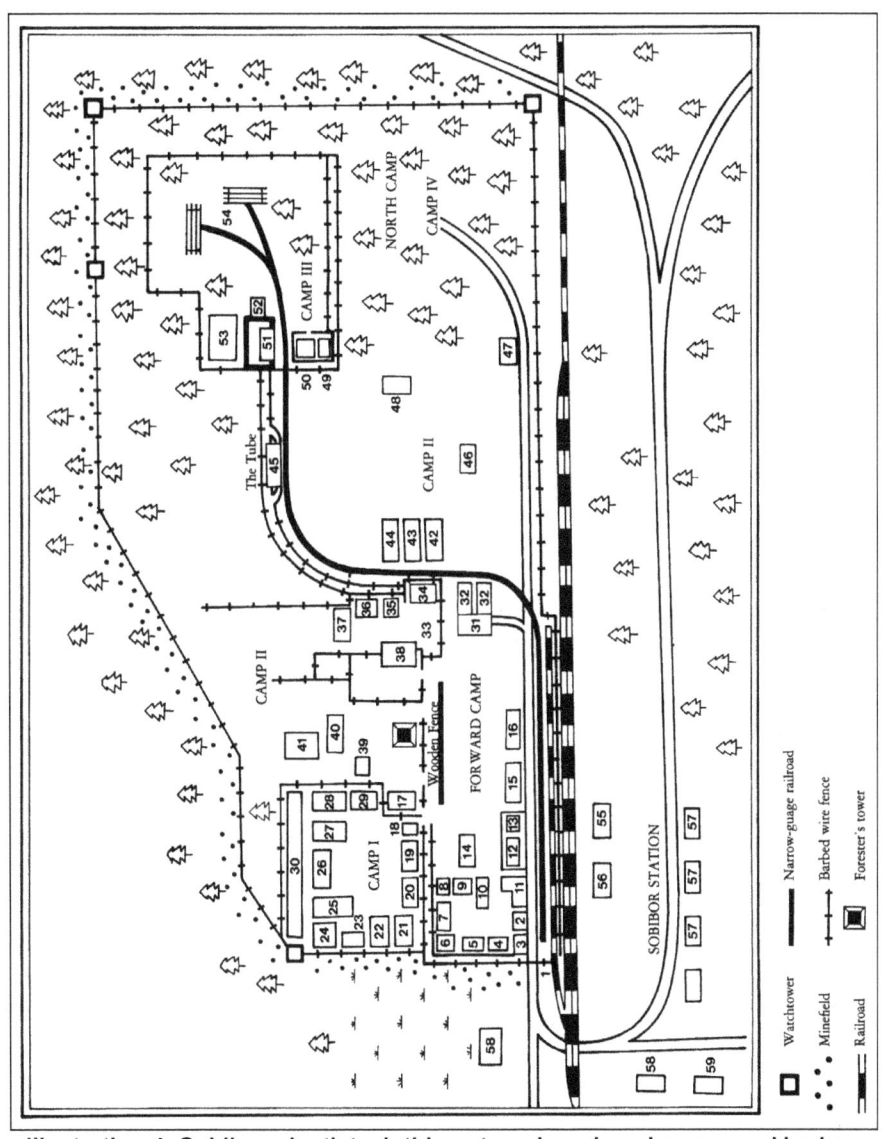

Illustration 4: Sobibor: dentist, clothing store, laundry, showers and barbershop, bakery, tailor shop, carpenter, smith, painter's shop, shoemaker, stable and barns, ironing room, garden, chapel. Taken from Arad (1990d: 294)

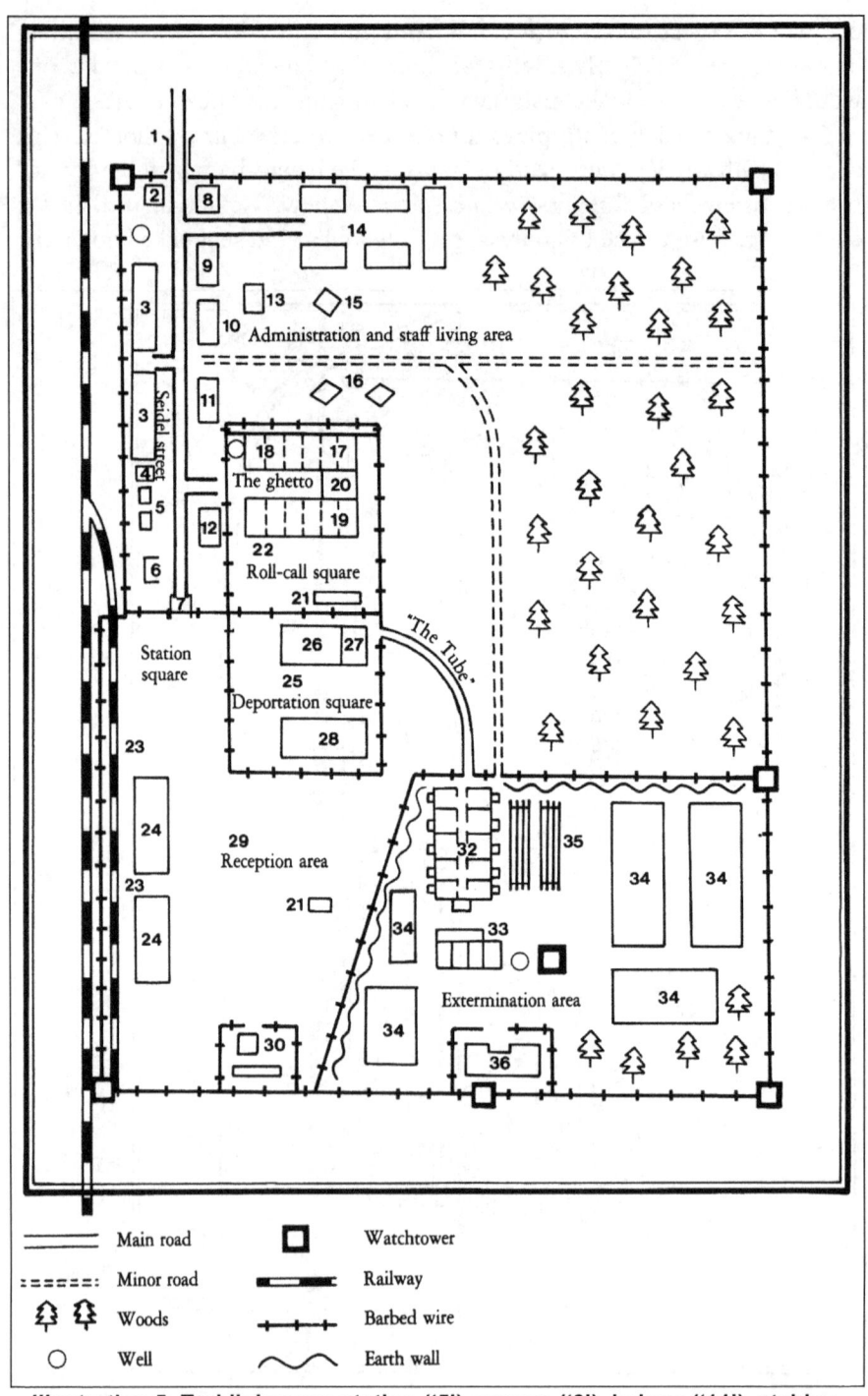

Illustration 5: Treblinka: gas station ('5'), garage ('6'), bakery ('11'), stables, chicken coop, pig pen ('16'), kitchen ('18'), locksmith and blacksmith ('20'), and even *a zoo* ('15'). Taken from Arad (1990d: 298)

tube to their deaths in the gas chambers. It was a fiendishly efficient production line of death.

In fact, this whole procedure has another, entirely benign explanation. It corresponds exactly to an ideal delousing facility. The incoming, possibly infested inmates would arrive at the camp in the 'dirty' zone. They would be registered or at least screened, sorted by gender, have their hair cut—a hygienic measure, to eliminate lice in the hair—disrobed, and then passed naked through a gateway or tube into a shower area. Their clothes would be deloused, either in gas chambers with real Zyklon gas, or with steam or hot air, and then returned to the owners in the 'clean' zone. Once clean, they would have had absolutely no contact with the dirty zone. After short-term holding, clean inmates would be transferred on to the next designated location or camp.

We can imagine how this must have appeared to the typical frightened, fatigued, possibly sick inmate. Friends and family are separated from him. They are taken away, sent down the tube, perhaps never to be seen again—vanished, gone, 'exterminated.' In the chaos of mass movement of people, the Nazis presumably had little concern about keeping families, especially Jewish families, together. The main objective was to ship them east, most to forced-labor camps. And the last thing the Germans wanted in their labor camps was a local typhus epidemic.

Graf and Mattogno (2012: 182) describe the situation quite well:

> [S]ince the selected inmates who were transferred elsewhere [via the tube] did actually disappear from the camp, those who remained behind became convinced that their departed comrades had been murdered. This conviction was strengthened by the fact that before leaving the camp, the selected inmates went through showers and delousing… This procedure left the remaining inmates with one powerful impression: their fellow prisoners had been sent to where the gas chambers were; they had not returned; *consequently*, they had been gassed.

This whole process of chaotic disinfestation was familiar to the Eastern European Jews for decades prior to World War II. It seems to have naturally led to concerns about being killed. One notable instance, from 1893, was recorded by a Jewish woman, Mary Antin; she gives an account of a procedure in Germany that is strikingly similar to the tales told by camp survivors.[113] It is perhaps unsurprising, then, that a comparable event, occurring amidst the chaos of war, could elicit a similar response in the 1940s.

---

[113] "In a great and lonely field, opposite a solitary house within a large yard, our train pulled up at last, and the conductor commanded the passengers to make haste and get out. [...] [The conductor] hurried us into the one large room that made up the house, and then into the yard. Here a great many men and women, dressed in white, received us, the women

On top of this, there were the very real deaths from disease, sickness, and exhaustion. Some were dead on arrival at the camp. Others died on site. To be sure, some were executed. All these dead bodies had to be processed in a rapid and sanitary manner. At first, mass burials would have been the most convenient method, but the increasing body count, and threats to ground water—corpses can quickly contaminate a camp well—demanded a cremation effort. So it would have made sense, at some point, to stop burials and initiate open-air burnings—provided the overall body count was small enough to be manageable. Revisionists accept all these events, but propose a vastly smaller number of bodies, as I will explain.

The Death Matrices

Tables 19-21 are proposed death matrices for each of the three camps. For Belzec and Treblinka, I have used Arad's (1987) transport data with appropriate adjustments to achieve the necessary totals. For Sobibor, I have drawn from a variety of standard sources. Again, I do not claim that these are absolutely correct. I only claim that *something* like these figures must be true, on the orthodox view, if the '6 million' is to be maintained.

Some immediate points can be drawn from these matrices. First, for Belzec: According to Laqueur (2001: 179) the Belzec chambers had the combined capacity to kill 15,000 people per day. This can be calculated as

---

attending the women and girls of the passengers, and the men the others. This was another scene of bewildering confusion, parents losing their children, and little ones crying; baggage being thrown together in one corner of the yard, heedless of contents, which suffered in consequence; those white-clad Germans shouting commands, always accompanied with 'Quick! Quick!'—the confused passengers obeying all orders like meek children, only questioning now and then what was to be done with them. And no wonder if in some minds stories arose of people being captured by robbers, murderers, and the like. Here we had been taken to a lonely place where only that house was to be seen; our things were taken away, our friends separated from us; a man came to inspect us, as if to ascertain our full value; strange-looking people driving us about like dumb animals, helpless and unresisting; children we could not see crying in a way that suggested terrible things; ourselves driven into a little room where a great kettle was boiling on a little stove; our clothes taken off, our bodies rubbed with a slippery substance that could be any bad thing; a shower of warm water let down on us without warning; again driven together to another little room where we sit, wrapped in woolen blankets till large, coarse bags are brought in, their contents turned out, and we see only a cloud of steam, and hear a woman's voice to dress ourselves, —'Quick! Quick!'—or else we'll miss—something we cannot hear. We are forced to pick out our clothes from among the others, with the steam blinding us; we choke, cough, entreat the women to give us time; they persist, 'Quick! Quick! Or you'll miss the train!' Oh, so we really won't be murdered! They are only making us ready for the continuing of our journey, cleaning us of all suspicions of dangerous illness. Thank God!" From the book *The Promised Land* (1985). Originally published as *From Plotzk to Boston* (1912).

follows. The floor area of each chamber is estimated, based not on drawings, documents, or photographs but simply on witness statements—arriving at a figure of 20 square meters. Next it is assumed that a fully packed chamber could hold up to 10 people per square meter—that is, about one person for every square foot[114]—and hence 200 people per chamber. In its latter phase, the camp had six chambers. Six chambers could thus gas up to 1,200 people at a time. Each gassing, Laqueur says, took 20 to 30 minutes. Allowing 30 minutes to load, and one hour to unpack the dead bodies, we can figure a two-hour cycle. Therefore, working nonstop round the clock, Laqueur assumes it is possible to perform 12 or more gassing cycles per day. Truly a fearsome capability.

If we look at the daily gassings actually claimed, however, we see a striking contrast. Peak fatalities occurred in August 1942, with a total 145,000 deaths or about 4,800 per day. So the 'capacity' of 15,000 per day was never approached, even in the busiest month. A more typical month allegedly gassed about 50,000 people, or some 1,650 per day—around 10 percent of 'capacity.'

This fact makes a mockery of the claim that the Germans needed to double their number of chambers, from three to six, in July 1942. The original three could have handled the whole killing load easily, with no more than 4 or 5 gassing cycles per day.[115] Thus we see a common problem with traditionalist accounts of gas chambers: they frequently cite huge capacity figures as a kind of evidence of the monstrous evil of the camps, when, even on their own accounts, such figures were rarely if ever attained. Even with the horrendous fatalities claimed, the Nazis built about 10 times as much gassing capacity at Belzec as they actually needed. That was poor planning on their part, to be sure.

---

[114] Here's an exercise to try: Draw a square on the floor, 1 meter × 1 meter (about 3 feet 3 inches on a side). Find ten typical people, including several children, and ask them to all stand together in that square. This gives some idea of the conditions in a fully packed chamber. Certainly this is theoretically possible, especially under contrived circumstances, such as five thin women each with an infant. But it would be extremely difficult to achieve with a random mix of people on a long-term basis.
Then consider the findings of the Düsseldorf court in the 1964 Treblinka trial. They accepted as realistic figures of 350 people in a 16-square-meter chamber—or 22 people per square meter.
As a final test, see whether you can fit 28 people into that same square. This number, amazingly enough, is seriously promoted by some supporters of the orthodox view. See Provan (1991) or Muehlenkamp (2006).

[115] The original three chambers were 32 square meters each, or about 100 square meters total. Thus one full gassing could handle 1,000 people. Four or five gassings—that is, 4,000 to 5,000 persons per day—could have easily handled the necessary capacity. Incidentally, the 15,000 daily capacity was a figure also cited by the SS officer Kurt Gerstein (see Arad 1987: 101)—except he claims to actually have witnessed this. Gerstein's statement has a number of problems, as we will see.

Table 19: Death Matrix for Belzec (in Thousands where indicated)

	1942											Total 1942	1943				Total
	M	A	M	J	J	A	S	O	N	D			J	F	M	A	
Gassing (in 000):	50	50	15	25	55	145	90	60	50	10		550					550
# of gas chambers:	3	3	3	3	6	6	6	6	6	6							
gassings/day (total):	1,667	1,667	500	833	1,833	4,833	3,000	2,000	1,667	333							
gassings/day/chamber:	556	556	167	278	306	806	500	333	278	56							
Body Disposal:																	
Buried (in 000):	50	50	15	25	55	145	90	60	50	10							
Exhumed & burned (in 000):										110			110	110	110	110	550
Total burnings (in 000):										110			110	110	110	110	550
bodies burned/day:										3,667			3,667	3,667	3,667	3,667	

Table 20: Death Matrix for Treblinka (in Thousands where indicated)

	1942											Total 1942	1943						Total 1943	Total
	J	A	S	O	N	D							J	F	M	A	M	J		
Gassing (in 000):	175	135	165	185	100	40						800	40	30	15	10	5		100	900
# of gas chambers:	3	3	3	10	10	10							10	10	10	10	10			
gassings/day (total):	5,833	4,500	5,500	6,167	3,333	1,333							1,333	1,000	500	333	167			
gassings/day/chamber:	1,944	1,500	1,833	617	133	133							133	100	50	33	17			
Body Disposal:																				
Buried (in 000):	175	135	165	185	100	40						800	40	30	15					
Exhumed & burned (in 000):																215	220	225		
Direct, gas ch. to burn:																10	5			
Total burnings (in 000):																225	225	225	225	900
bodies burned/day:																7,500	7,500	7,500		

Table 21: Death Matrix for Sobibor (in Thousands where indicated)

				1942						Total 1942					1943					Total 1943	Total
	A	M	J	J	A	S	O	N	D		J	F	M	A	M	J	J	A	S		
Gassing (in 000):	25	25	25	0	0	9	9	9	8	110	10	11	12	12	14	14	14	14	14	115	225
# of gas chambers:	3	3	3	3	3	3	6	6	6		6	6	6	6	6	6	6	6	6		
gassings/day (total):	833	833	833			300	300	300	267		333	367	400	400	467	467	467	467	467		
gassings/day/chamber:	278	278	278			100	50	50	40		56	61	67	78	78	78	78	78	78		
Body Disposal:																					
Buried (in 000):	25	25	25			9															
Exhumed & burned (in 000):							28	28	28												
Direct, gas ch. to burn (in 000):							9	9	8		10	11	12	12	14	14	14	14	14		
Total burnings (in 000):							37	37	36		**10**	**11**	**12**	**12**	**14**	**14**	**14**	**14**	**14**		
bodies burned/day:							1,233	1,233	1,200		333	367	400	400	467	467	467	467	467		

The Sobibor gassings were, relatively speaking, small potatoes. After the busy first three months, total gassings were never more than a few hundred per day, on average. The camp was also unusual in that only a small percentage of the total fatalities were buried before cremations commenced. 'Only' some 85,000 bodies were allegedly buried, after which all remaining victims went directly from gas chambers to pyres.

In this camp we see an even greater mismatch in 'capacity' versus 'actual.' Sobibor's original three (smallish) chambers could handle about 5,800 per day, and yet those busy first months averaged about 830 actuals per day—around 14 percent of capacity. So what did the Germans do? *They doubled the number of chambers*: to six, in October 1942. And they did this even as their arrivals were *cut in half.* Thus, by early 1943, the camp was utilizing a mere 3 percent of its capacity. This, of course, makes no sense at all. Clearly something is wrong with the standard account.

But consider now Treblinka. In many ways, this camp had the worst problems of them all. The camp began operation in July 1942, in a big way: some 175,000 Jews gassed that first month alone, on the traditional view. The first four months saw an astonishing 660,000 gassings—an average of nearly *5,500 per day*, for a solid 120 days. This was the deadliest extended pace ever achieved, at any camp, throughout the entire war.

How does Treblinka's gassing capacity stack up? The camp was originally built with three small (16 sq m) chambers, sufficient to gas some 5,800 per day, the same as Sobibor. As it happens, this is nearly a perfect match to the 'actuals.' But once again, something strange happens. The camp adds ten new double-size chambers, even as the number of arrivals drops precipitously. By early 1943, camp capacity was up to 38,000 per day, but arrivals had fallen to under 1,000 per day. Now they were running, once again, under 3 percent of capacity.

But the absurdity really comes to the fore when we look at the whole picture. Recall that the three Reinhardt camps were allegedly operating under a common plan and common leadership. Surely there was careful coordination of all camp activities. And yet the three camps, taken in total, had a truly incredible gassing capacity. From October 1942 on, the combined capacity was something like *65,000 people per day.* Or 1.9 million per month. Or 23 million per year. Using only diesel exhaust. And all this not counting Auschwitz! The ridiculousness of such a system speaks for itself. And yet our orthodox historians seriously expect us to believe that the Nazis designed, built, and operated precisely such a system.

At the rates claimed, all three Reinhardt camps were rapidly accumulating bodies. Inexplicably, no one in the Nazi hierarchy seemed to have a plan regarding how to handle the growing mountain of corpses. Initially the camps did the only thing they could: dig pits and bury them—the same tactic used at Chelmno. But that camp figured out, already by August 1942, that burials were bad policy; hence they commenced burning. Clearly, this lesson would have immediately been relayed to the Reinhardt camps. In August 1942 the message should have gone out: *Stop burying your bodies, just burn them.* And yet Sobibor continued burying their corpses for two more months. Belzec, four more months. And Treblinka soldiered on for a full eight more months, burying hundreds of thousands of bodies in the process. All this is inexplicable, if the Germans were the master organizers that we are told.

With this overview in place, we are now well-situated to look in more detail at the specifics of camp operation—namely, the actual gassing process, and the ultimate disposal of bodies. These are the subjects of the two chapters to follow.

Chapter 7: The Reinhardt Camps (Part 2): The Diesel Story

Electrocution, Steam, Diesels, Chlorine...

The current orthodox view is almost unanimous that Jews were killed at the Reinhardt camps in carbon monoxide gas chambers, supplied by diesel engines. But this was not always the story. Early on a whole variety of means were mentioned, most of them absolutely fanciful and beyond belief. Over time the more bizarre means faded away, leaving diesel exhaust as the official story.

During the years 1942–1946, the dominant account of murder at Belzec was of mass killings by electrocution on large "metal plates" submerged in water. In some versions the killings took place in "electrically charged vats." These reports are examined by Mattogno (2011: 11-22); today they are all completely discredited.

At Treblinka, early contemporary reports came in the middle of the camp's operational life, and reported not diesel exhaust but rather *steam*. The most important of these reports was published 15 November 1942 by the Jewish resistance movement of the Warsaw ghetto. It refers to chambers into which "water-steam" is piped: "The hot steam comes in to the chambers through pipes installed there... While this machinery of death is in action, the doors and valves are hermetically closed" (in Mattogno and Graf 2010: 54). Apparently the steam acted quickly: "15 minutes later the execution is complete" (p. 56).[116] The *New York Times* reported this same account in mid-1943.[117] And a 1944 report by Rabbi Silberschein refers to gas chambers that

---

[116] Of course, this is the same report that said "2,000,000 murdered Jews, or the greater part of Polish Jewry, are already buried in the area of Treblinka..." (p. 57). We must bear in mind that the revisionists reject *all* such accounts of mass murder, not only the diesel exhaust stories. Furthermore, we note that even such an authoritative figure as Arad has seriously misrepresented this 15 November 1942 account. His discussion on pages 354f. totally omits any mention of steam, preferring instead to talk simply of the "gas chambers"—as if it is understood what kind of gas it was. And of course, no mention of the "2,000,000" victims already as of November 1942, when the official tally shows only 500,000 at that point.

[117] 8 August 1943 (p. 11).

operated "under the influence of the water vapor" (p. 61). All this with little questioning about the dubiousness of steam as a weapon of mass murder. As Reitlinger admitted, in his understated way, "It is difficult to see how people could be exterminated with steam" (1968: 149).

But it is not difficult to see that this was in fact a part of the delousing process. Real steam chambers were used for a time to kill lice on linen and clothing. But these were small cubicles, far too small for mass murder. And of course, hot showers for humans also "steam," though not fatally. So one can imagine that word of Nazi steam chambers, combined with actual hot showers and people disappearing after being cleaned, could lead to talk of murder by steam.

From 1944 through the end of 1945, various other conflicting witness accounts emerged about Treblinka, citing a variety of killing methods: steam, evacuation of air, chlorine gas, "Cyklon gas," as well as engine exhaust. The decisive switch to exhaust gas—not yet diesel—came from a 1944 report by Jankiel Wiernik. He allegedly spent an entire year in Treblinka, which was an unbelievably long time for a death camp. Wiernik spoke simply of "a motor taken from a dismantled Soviet tank." During the gassing procedure "the motor turned on and connected with the inflow pipes, and, within 25 minutes at the most, all lay stretched out dead…"[118]

Likewise at Belzec, the shift to engine exhaust came, in this case, from just two witnesses. In fact virtually the entire Belzec gassing story rests on just these two witnesses:

> Two sources provide detailed accounts of the gassings in Belzec: the testimony of Rudolf Reder, the only prisoner who escaped from Belzec and survived, and that of Kurt Gerstein, an SS officer who visited the camp… (*Holocaust Encyclopedia*, 2001: 232).

Gerstein claimed to have visited both Belzec and Treblinka in August 1942. Reder was one of a handful of Jewish escapees (the others died), and the only to testify at length in front of the Polish Central Commission for Investigation of German Crimes in 1946.[119] Unfortunately for traditionalists, both witnesses have now been largely discredited—as I will explain shortly.

---

[118] Citation from Mattogno and Graf (2010: 71). This is the same Wiernik who spoke of 500 persons in a 25-square-meter chamber, an impossible 20 people per square meter. And 1,200 people in a 50-square-meter chamber, an even more impossible 24 per square meter. And of airtight chambers in which people had to "suffer for hours" when the motor didn't work—when they surely would have suffocated within 30 minutes.

[119] Another Belzec witness, Chaim Hirszman, had "joined the new communist militia in Stalinist Poland tasked with the crushing of Polish underground, torture, makeshift executions, and mass deportation to Siberia of over 50,000 political undesirables. Hirszman was shot in March 1946 […] in the course of an anti-communist insurrection against the new reign of terror, before he was able to give a full account of his camp experience." (http://en.wikipedia.org/wiki/Rudolf_Reder)

Notably, Gerstein explicitly referred to the engine as a diesel, whereas Reder was adamant that it was fueled by gasoline. This is a significant issue, as we know. It is interesting that Gerstein's version won out in the long run, even though Reder's made more sense!

The Diesel Story

As we all know, Zyklon B, or cyanide gas, attracts nearly all the attention when discussion comes around to "Nazi gassings." And yet far more people—about twice as many—were allegedly killed not with Zyklon but with carbon monoxide. This is one of those little-known, little-discussed, but problematic issues for traditionalism. In the first edition (1961) of his *Destruction of the European Jews*, Hilberg made this (almost) clear in a table summarizing the camps and their killing method(s) (p. 572). A clearer, more up-to-date version appears in the anti-revisionist book by Shermer and Grobman (2000: 128):

Table 22: Methods of Gassing, by Camp		
CAMP	NUMBER KILLED	KILLING METHOD(S)
Auschwitz-Birkenau	1,100,000	Zyklon B
Treblinka	900,000	Carbon monoxide
Belzec	600,000	Carbon monoxide
Sobibor	250,000	Carbon monoxide
Chelmno	152,000	Carbon monoxide
Majdanek	60,000	Zyklon B and carbon monoxide

Thus nearly 2 million Jews were allegedly killed by carbon monoxide, versus some 1 million with Zyklon. If we add the 350,000 supposedly killed by the Einsatzgruppen with gas vans in Soviet territory, the CO total rises to about 2.2 million—over 35 percent of total Holocaust deaths. Therefore the whole issue of mass CO gassings is vital to the conventional story.

Gerstein, Reder, and the Diesel Exhaust

The final move to diesel exhaust in the Reinhardt camps came out of Gerstein's infamous report on Belzec and Treblinka. Gerstein's report on diesels, combined with Wiernik's on engine exhaust, formed the basis for a 1947 Treblinka report by Elias (Eliyahu) Rosenberg, which referred to "exhaust fumes of a single diesel engine" (in Mattogno and Graf 2010: 75). In this way diesel exhaust came to form the core of present-day historiography of that camp; Treblinka was henceforth officially "diesel." Gerstein also won out over Reder at Belzec; Sobibor came along for the ride.

Thus all three camps are today considered, officially, diesel-gassing camps. Yad Vashem's Website (2015) says this: "At each of the three [Reinhardt] camps, hundreds of thousands of Jews were murdered by exhaust gas from diesel engines." On the USHMM page we read: "In 1942, systematic mass killing in stationary gas chambers (with carbon monoxide gas generated by diesel engines) began at Belzec, Sobibor, and Treblinka."

Gerstein signed his report while imprisoned and awaiting trial after the war. He died in a French prison in 1945, allegedly by suicide, but under highly suspicious circumstances. For this reason, and because of the many patent absurdities in his report, revisionists strongly suspect he was tortured into signing. The statement is excerpted in Arad (1987), but with a number of strategic omissions. It is fully reprinted in Appendix A of Butz (2015). For years Arad obviously considered it significant; he called it "one of the first and most important documents" on the gassings, and deemed it overall "reliable" (1987: 102). Interestingly, he then soured on Gerstein just three years later. His Belzec entry in Gutman's 1990 encyclopedia has not a single mention of this star witness; only Reder is discussed.

Gerstein stated that Odilo Globocnik, leader of the Reinhardt operation, sent him to "improve the service in our gas chambers, which function on diesel engine exhaust" (in Arad 1987: 101). At Belzec, Gerstein was present at a gassing. Jews were packed into four chambers, "750 persons" per chamber. Each chamber, recall, was only 20 square meters in area.[120] This would mean a density of 38 people per square meter—an absolute impossibility. (Refer to Appendix A of the present book.) Gerstein was either badly mistaken, lying, or coerced into admitting to an impossibility.

There were technical problems with the diesel engine. He waited "50 minutes, 70 minutes, and [still] the diesel did not start. ... After 2 hours and 49 minutes—the stopwatch recorded it all—the diesel started. ... After 32 minutes [more], all were dead..." Mattogno has pointed out the obvious—that people cannot be packed into an enclosed room for hours and still live.[121] A fully loaded, 10 people-per-square-meter chamber will lead to death by asphyxiation within about 30 minutes.[122] *In fact, this would have been a far*

---

[120] In his statement Gerstein mentioned an area of 25 square meters, but I am using the generally accepted figure here.

[121] See Mattogno and Graf (2010: 133f.).

[122] In an enclosed space, death comes quickly once oxygen is consumed and carbon dioxide levels reach 10 percent. A somewhat excited person, standing still, will produce about 0.3 liters (0.0003 m^3) of CO_2 per minute. The original Belzec chambers were allegedly 4 × 8 m, and could hold at most 320 people. Assuming a 2-m high room, the chamber volume was 64 m^3. One person's body takes up about 0.1 m^3 (3.5 ft^3) of space, so 320 people would take 32 m^3, or half the volume of the room. This leaves 64 − 32 = 32 m^3 of air. The 320 people, breathing heavily, produce 320 × 0.3 = 96 liters (.096 m^3) of CO_2 per minute, which is equal to 0.3 percent of the available air. So each passing minute raises CO_2 by another 0.3 percent. The room would hit 10 percent in 30 minutes, and all would

better way to kill people—by sheer suffocation. No need for carbon monoxide, diesel engines, or dangerous Zyklon. Less expense, less work, no chemical traces left behind. Surely the SS would have preferred this option if they were determined to kill masses of people.

Nonetheless, the diesel story became entrenched at all three camps. Hilberg (2003: 959) cites Gerstein, and also observes, "Belzec is reported to have been equipped with a diesel motor; Treblinka is said to have had one from the start..." (p. 936)—evidently accepting both as true. Later he says, "In the much smaller camp of Belzec the diesel engine was located in a shack..." (p. 1028). The *Holocaust Encyclopedia* (2001) describes the procedure: "The chamber was sealed, the diesel engine was started, and carbon monoxide gas was pumped into the chamber" (p. 231). A witness, SS Sergeant Schluch, said, "For the gassings an engine was started up... [J]udging from the sound, it was a medium-sized diesel engine" (in Mattogno 2011: 68).

Of the three camps, only Sobibor is still in some dispute as to the engine type. This is important because, as we have seen, diesel exhaust is very low in CO content for virtually its entire operating range, whereas gasoline-engine exhaust is sufficiently high to cause death. In fact, the *only* explicit statement on behalf of gasoline at Sobibor is testimony by SS technician Erich Fuchs. He describes his visit there to set up the chambers:

> We unloaded the motor. It was a heavy Russian gasoline engine (presumably a tank or tractor motor) at least 200 horsepower (V-motor, 8 cylinder, water cooled). We installed the engine on a concrete foundation and set up the connection between the exhaust and the tube.[123]

He goes on to describe an experimental gassing of 30 or 40 Jewish women: "I fixed the motor on a definite speed... About ten minutes later the thirty to forty women were dead."

Some problems with Fuchs's statement: First, it is counterintuitive that the Germans would use a Russian tank or tractor engine when they had their own high-quality engines. A foreign machine would have been difficult to operate and hard to repair—bad qualities for the key element in your mass-extermination scheme. Second, many Russian tanks of that era were in fact powered by diesel engines, not gasoline. Third, ten minutes is an extremely short time to cause death, given a lightly packed chamber with lots of fresh air to be displaced. But we must keep in mind that Fuchs gave his statement while on trial in 1963 for Nazi-era crimes; perhaps uncoincidently, he got off with a very light sentence (4 years for complicity in 79,000 murders).

---

very quickly be dead.
[123] Arad (1987: 31); Graf *et al.* (2010: 257f.).

But overall, the consensus is clearly toward diesel at all three camps. Mattogno and Graf (2010: 43) cite the German edition of the *Encyclopedia of the Holocaust*: "Belzec, Sobibor, and Treblinka were built within the framework of the Operation Reinhardt... These extermination camps used carbon monoxide gas, which was produced by diesel engines." Noted traditionalist Léon Poliakov cited the Gerstein diesel statement in his 1971 book *Harvest of Hate*; immediately following which he wrote:

> There is little to add to this description, which holds good for Treblinka and Sobibor [as well as Belzec]. The latter installations were constructed in almost the very same way, and also used the exhaust carbon monoxide gases from Diesel motors as the death agent. (p. 196)

And as I noted earlier, the current (2015) editions of the online encyclopedias at both Yad Vashem and USHMM explicitly refer to diesels. Other sources simply do not specify the engine type, as if it were irrelevant; more likely they do not want to raise this troublesome issue.

More Problems with Gerstein

The decisive Gerstein report, which specifically names diesels as the gas source, contains an important bit of information that contradicts not only itself but also gasoline engines, and in fact any source of carbon monoxide whatsoever: the dead bodies pulled out of the gas chamber are *blue*. The problem is that people who die from CO poisoning are distinctly *red* or *pink*, not blue.[124] Gerstein said, "The bodies are thrown out, blue, wet with sweat and urine..." (in Butz 2015: 327). This line was notably excluded by Arad, but he does include a similar comment from a secondary witness, the SS doctor Pfannenstiel: "The corpses were not exceptional. Some of the faces were blue" (p. 104). Arad also cites testimony by Schluch: "The corpses were besmirched with mud and urine or with spit. I could see that the lips

---

[124] The red or pink coloration is not inevitable. It depends on the precise circumstances, the individual reaction to the gas, and so on. But it would have been an obvious characteristic of a large number of bodies, given the alleged volume of gassings. Griffin *et al.* (2008: 1208) summarizes a review of 94 cases of CO poisoning, stating that only "30% of all reviewed cases did not show classic cherry red discoloration." Therefore, 70 percent did. This could not have been overlooked by the witnesses.
This point is further underscored by a widespread practice in the American meat industry—namely, the treating of meat with carbon monoxide in order to maintain the "fresh pink or red" appearance. This little-known process, banned in Europe and Canada, was debated in the US Congress in 2007.
Provan (2004) attempts to show that CO poisoning can sometimes produce blue or cyan coloration on bodies. But these rare cases result from long, slow poisoning at low CO concentrations—completely unlike the alleged rapid gassing in the Nazi chambers.

and tips of the noses were a bluish color" (p. 71). Thus we have at least three witnesses implicitly refuting the CO story. And none recalls seeing red or pink corpses.

We have reports of blue-colored victims at Treblinka as well. The eyewitness Rachel Auerbach recalled: "The bodies were naked; some of them were white, others were blue and bloated" (in Mattogno and Graf 2010: 24)—nothing about CO poisoning would cause "bloating," incidentally. Another unnamed eyewitness reports second-hand that "the corpses have a bluish color" (p. 49). And noted Treblinka survivor Chil Rajchman claimed that "[the corpses from the gas chamber] had completely black faces, as if they had been burnt, and their bellies were bloated and colored blue."[125] This is triply absurd: neither blackening, bloating, nor blue coloration is associated with any aspect of gassing. Blue corpses make for dramatic testimony, but unfortunately for traditionalism, they severely undermine one of its key claims.

Based on the impossible density and duration of the gassing, and blue coloration of victims, Gerstein's detailed account of the Belzec gassing cannot be correct. But that's not the only problem with his statement:

- He describes incredible piles of clothes at Treblinka. He saw "veritable mountains of clothing and underwear, about 35–40 meters high" (in Arad 1987: 102). This is a pile some 120 feet in height, equal to an 8- or 10-story building.
- The Belzec mass grave pits, located next to the gas chambers, are impossibly large: "The bodies were thrown into large ditches of about 100 × 20 × 12 meters" (in Butz 2015: 327; this sentence deleted by Arad). These have been definitively disproved by recent excavations at Belzec—see Chapter 8.
- Gerstein's estimate of total deaths at Belzec and Treblinka is ridiculous: "At Belcek [sic] and Treblinka nobody bothered to take anything approaching an exact count of the persons killed. ... Actually, about 25,000,000 persons were killed..." (in Butz 2015: 328; this claim deleted by Arad). Compare to my assumed total for the two camps of 1.4 million.

Arad (pp. 102f.) makes passing reference to Gerstein's "exaggerations," but still deems him "reliable"—until he ignores him altogether three years later. Mainstream historian Michael Tregenza, an expert on Belzec, has likewise abandoned him:

> Based on the current state of our research, we must also designate Gerstein's material on Belzec as questionable, even belonging to the

---

[125] In Kues (2010). Kues discusses a range of absurdities in Rajchman's narrative.

realm of fantasy in some places. ... [his account, along with Reder's], regarding the Belzec camp must be considered to be unreliable. (2000; cited in Rudolf 2011: 372)

To his credit, Hilberg has essentially ignored Gerstein's statement from the start. From the 1961 first edition of his book through 2003, he allots only one brief paragraph to it. Yad Vashem has no mention of it at all. Of the contemporary traditionalists, only Zimmerman seems to want to continue breathing life into the report. He argues (2000: 103) that because Gerstein told three others about his experiences, prior to his capture, and that we can apparently confirm that he told them, that therefore he is "credible." A postwar written account by one of these three, the Swedish official Baron von Otter, "confirms Gerstein's revelations." Yet Zimmerman seems to be alone in this conclusion.

More Problems with Reder

With Gerstein out, traditionalism is left with Reder as the chief Belzec witness. Arad admits precisely this point:

[O]nly one [Jew] escaped to tell the gruesome tale—Rudolf Reder, who spent four months in the camp... Apart from this one source, information on Belzec had been difficult to come by, compared with evidence on the other extermination camps. (1990a: 179)

Reder, however, is not without his problems as well. First of all we notice that he was supposedly in the camp for four months; again, a very long time for an "extermination" camp. Especially so, considering that he was over sixty years of age at the time—not much use as a laborer, which would have been the only reason for keeping someone alive.

But there are bigger issues. In his Nuremberg testimony Reder claimed that 3 million people died at Belzec (see below). This is by far the highest figure ever given—compare to the chart at the beginning of Chapter 6—and roughly five to ten times higher than the mainstream historians. Arad (1987) quotes Reder several times, but never mentions his "estimate."

Reder describes the gas chambers and engine exhaust, and specifically cites the source as a gasoline engine (see Mattogno 2004b: 40). He also notes that some kind of pipe ran from the engine to the chamber, but that after a gassing, he recalled no exhaust smoke or odor. However, Reder explicitly observed that the gasoline-engine exhaust "was evacuated from the engine directly into the open air, and not into the chamber" (in Mattogno 2011: 38). This is shocking, considering that it was precisely this exhaust gas that was supposed to do the killing. And then, what was the point of the engine at all?

Ironic—the one viable witness claiming that it was a gasoline engine, and he refutes the whole story by stating that the toxic gas was vented away![126]

Reder also testified on the mass graves at Belzec. As cited in Mattogno (p. 74), he stated:

> A [single] grave was 100 m long and 25 m wide. A single grave contained about 100,000 persons. In November 1942 there were 30 graves, i.e. 3 million corpses.

In follow-up testimony he added that all 30 graves were identical, and all dug to a depth of 15 m, or 46 feet. This is astoundingly deep, especially considering that the water table lies just 5 meters down. So either the Germans were pumping a lot of water, or he was way off the mark. Furthermore, the total area of the graves would have been 30 × (100 × 25) = 75,000 square meters—almost exactly equal to the entire area of the camp. Unlikely, to say the least. But there is no need to speculate; thanks to recent excavations—discussed in the next chapter—we now know that Reder's description was completely false.

Again, it is revealing to see how other traditionalists treat Reder. Hilberg, in some 1,300 pages, gives him a total of one single footnote (p. 1037). Zimmerman (2000) has no mention of him at all. Neither do Longerich (2010) or Bartov (2015). So the other pillar seems to have fallen. Perhaps for this reason, traditionalists have little more to say about Belzec, period. If it were not for the notable excavations performed in the late 1990s, it would have completely dropped out of sight.

To summarize: There are fundamental difficulties in committing mass murder with diesel exhaust. Hence the number one problem revisionists have with the Reinhardt camps: *Murder by carbon monoxide from diesel exhaust is awkward at best, and ridiculous at worst.* A stationary diesel engine is almost impossible to adjust to produce more than a minuscule amount of CO. It also, incidentally, puts out a reasonably high oxygen content, sufficient to keep people alive unless the engine approaches full load. And exhaust gas cannot be pumped into a "hermetically sealed" room without an elaborate circulation scheme—of which we have no evidence at all. The whole story simply does not add up.

---

[126] The fact that there was a diesel engine running in some adjacent shack is not at all ominous. Every camp required engine-powered generators to supply dependable electricity. These would have run almost continuously—hence we can understand one possible source of the rumors of "continuous gassing."

Traditionalist Reply

We are by now unsurprised that the diesel topic is almost completely avoided by every anti-revisionist writer. One struggles in vain to find reference to "carbon monoxide" or "diesel engine exhaust" for any of the three camps. This is a strong implicit admission that traditionalism has no reply to Berg and the revisionists. For example, van Pelt (2002: 23) just touches on the issue in passing, enough to call Berg's conclusion about the diesel story "rubbish," but he quickly moves on. In van Pelt's defense, he is writing about Auschwitz, and since there were no CO gas chambers there, he has no need to address them. So he may legitimately bypass the issue, as may the other Auschwitz specialists.

But the others have no excuse. Stern (1993), Lipstadt (1993), Shermer and Grobman (2000), and Perry and Schweitzer (2002) utterly ignore the whole topic. They apparently have no viable defense.[127]

Only Zimmerman attempts to save the day—but not very much. As mentioned in Chapter 5, he devotes all of one paragraph to the subject (2000: 176f.), and one lengthy, but late-added, footnote (pp. 355f.). In the main text he simply says, "it is possible that other types of engines were also used," meaning gasoline engines or producer-gas generators. But he cites no sources or evidence—evidently forgetting (or ignoring) the fact that the eyewitness Reder spoke explicitly of a gasoline engine (though with exhaust vented into open air). And he also apparently forgot—or ignored—the fact that blue corpses rule out any kind of carbon monoxide poisoning.

In the footnote Zimmerman again argues that the engines could have been gasoline, and that the witnesses might have merely been mistaken about the engine type. His one tangible piece of evidence is a citation of a wartime engineering study (Holtz and Elliott 1941; misdated by Zimmerman as 1943) on diesel exhaust, which he says shows that diesels can in fact put out toxic levels of CO under certain extreme conditions. But this much is known and admitted. The question is, whether it would have made sense to attempt to run a foreign-made diesel at some extreme conditions, for months on end, simply in order to produce a gas that could be much more easily generated—with, for example, a producer-gas system.

Recently, the 'anti-denial' bloggers have attempted to address this issue. After admitting that "it is simply not feasible to use diesel engines for gassings… when one has access to petrol engines," Romanov (2006) claims that

---

[127] One exception is the German writer Achim Trunk. In his essay "Lethal Gasses" (in Morsch et al, eds. 2011) he admits that it would have been technically infeasible to kill masses of people with a diesel engine. In his opinion, it is "more likely" that the Germans used gasoline engines. But this is contradicted by both historiography and the lack of red or pink corpses. For a longer discussion of Trunk's essay, see Mattogno (2014: 24-37) or Alvarez (2011: 26-28).

the diesel issue is "irrelevant" because, in his view, anyone who claimed that the gassing engine was a diesel was simply mistaken. He argues that the "most knowledgeable" witnesses mentioned gasoline, but he can cite only *two*: Fuchs (for Sobibor only), and Reder, who said the exhaust gas was sent into the open air! And Romanov ignores the entire producer-gas argument, which is much more effective, cheaper, and simpler even than gasoline. He ignores as well the "blue-corpse" claims, which argue against *any* CO poisoning scheme. His argument is entirely unconvincing.

Finally: If the case for gasoline is so compelling, why don't we hear this from the leading Holocaust researchers? Hilberg, Laqueur, Arad, Yad Vashem, USHMM, *et al.* have continued to speak of diesel engines. Zimmerman and the bloggers should convince their fellow traditionalists before taking on revisionism.

Chapter 8: The Reinhardt Camps (Part 3): The Vanishing Bodies

If one were serious about confirming the stories of mass murder at the camps, the obvious first step would be to look for evidence on the grounds of the camps. Witnesses are very clear regarding where and how people were killed, and where their bodies were disposed of. And true enough, some excavation has been attempted at each of the Reinhardt camps. The big questions: What do they show? And which story do they support?

Disposing of the Evidence

Before examining the excavations, let's complete the story of how the Nazis disposed of those hundreds of thousands of bodies at the three camps. Just as the camp structures and alleged gassing routines were similar, so too were the disposal methods. All three camps shared the same problems—problems that were not inconsiderable.

We recall from the death matrices that each camp followed a common pattern: burying bodies for several months, and then exhuming and burning the remains on crude open-air pyres (not crematoria). It may be useful to keep in mind the key dates for each camp. Table 23 lists the dates at which each camp began operation, began burnings, and then ceased operation.

Table 23: Key Dates for Reinhardt Camps			
CAMP	OPEN	BURNINGS	CLOSED
Belzec	Mar 1942	Dec 1942	Apr 1943
Sobibor	Apr 1942	Oct 1942	Sep 1943
Treblinka	Jul 1942	Apr 1943	Jul 1943

All three camps share similar issues, so let me take Belzec as an example. Recall the numbers from our Belzec death matrix (Table 19). On the conventional view, the Nazis murdered 550,000 Jews there over a period of about ten months, during which time all bodies were buried. Then at the very end of the killing phase, word came down to exhume and burn the corpses.

And they were given a strict timeline: five months in which to complete the grisly task.

Evidently the Germans succeeded in this monumental task without difficulty—at least according to Arad. He explains the burning procedure concisely:

> A special installation was put to serve as a crematorium, made out of iron rails used for railways. Bones that resisted the flames were crushed, and these remains, together with the ashes, were buried in the ditches [i.e. mass graves] from which the corpses had been removed. (1990a: 178)

This simple story is rife with difficulties.

Burying the Bodies

Let's examine separately the burial and burning phases. Dead bodies, however acquired, must be disposed of quickly and safely. As noted, the most immediate and easiest option is to bury them in mass graves. But this has at least three drawbacks: (1) dead bodies can, over time, occupy a large amount of space; (2) they can quickly contaminate ground water, making wells unusable; and (3) they can be dug up in the future and used as incriminating evidence against those who buried them. Burial works best for small numbers of bodies, or as a temporary measure. But according to orthodoxy, the Germans, knowing full well the magnitude of their task, nonetheless spent months digging huge holes in the ground to bury their ever-growing quantity of corpses.

As I stated previously, one can reasonably pack only some six to eight bodies per cubic meter of grave space.[128] Assuming a median figure of seven per cubic meter, we can easily calculate the requirements of each camp. At Belzec, the 550,000 bodies would require roughly 78,000 cubic meters. Needless to say, this is an extremely large space. If we assume a typical, large, trench-like mass grave of size 5 m × 100 m, and 4 m deep, it would have required no less than 40 such graves to hold all the bodies.

As we recall, Belzec was not a large camp. The total surface area of those 40 mass graves would amount to 20,000 square meters, about one-third of the entire camp area—clearly impossible. And yet all eyewitnesses place the mass graves directly within camp boundaries. So where did the Germans put the bodies?

---

[128] Assuming a typical mix of average bodies. Obviously one could pack infant bodies more densely than this.

Sobibor was less of an issue. There the Nazis had only some 85,000 bodies to bury, which would have taken up a mere 12,000 cubic meters of space, or about six large mass graves.

Treblinka, by contrast, had huge problems. At this camp the entire death toll of 900,000 was reached before burnings began, and thus all 900,000 were allegedly buried on site. By my calculations, this would have required 128,000 cubic meters—about 4.5 million cubic feet—of grave space, or an incredible 64 large, trench-like mass graves.

Do we have any direct evidence of such large mass graves at Treblinka? Actually, yes. One witness, Elias Rosenberg, claims to have known the precise measurements of a Treblinka grave: 120 × 15 × 6 m deep.[129] This is an astoundingly large grave, in fact. The volume of such a pit is 10,800 cubic meters, and hence able to hold about 75,000 bodies—or 1/12th of the total. Thus the Nazis would have needed 12 graves of those monstrous dimensions to contain the victims.

On the other hand, what do our maps tell us? Recall that Arad supplied detailed layouts of all three camps—see Illustrations 3-5. In each case he identified the mass graves by location and approximate size: at Belzec ('18'), Sobibor ('54'), and Treblinka ('34'). In no case do the dimensions shown on these diagrams begin to approach the necessary size or number of graves—unless they were 50 or 100 m deep, which is an outright impossibility.

Exhuming and Burning

As the killing phases came to an end, camp commanders were evidently ordered, in turn, to halt burials, exhume already buried bodies, and cremate all corpses. As noted above, this decision was made at Sobibor in October 1942; at Belzec in December 1942; and at Treblinka in April 1943. This timing in itself raises another troubling issue for traditionalism: had the extermination of the Jews been centrally planned and coordinated, surely the Germans would have implemented a *single decision date* for something as crucial as burning away the evidence. The fact that these dates were spread over six months—or eight months, if we include the Chelmno decision in August 1942—suggests local, ad hoc decisions; and correspondingly, no centrally planned extermination at all.

Despite the 'successful' crematoria built in the Chelmno woods, the Reinhardt camps evidently found this solution impractical. Instead, the bodies were burned on impromptu and entirely amateurish metal pyres or grids, made from old railroad rails. Each structure would have required five or six rails of considerable length, spaced about ½ meter apart. The grids would

---

[129] Cited in Mattogno and Graf (2010: 138).

have had to be raised a meter or two above the ground to allow space for wood and for airflow. Descriptions of the alleged pyres vary, but we can assume a nominal length of some 30 m, or about 100 feet.

Now, it must be acknowledged that burning thousands of damp, decaying bodies on an open-air grid would have been an extremely difficult, cumbersome, and time-consuming process. The bodies would have needed to be stacked like cordwood, in layers, in an attempt to burn enough at once. Laying bodies crosswise on the rails, one can place about four bodies per meter of length. Thus a single layer on a 30m-long pyre could have held 120 bodies.

To maximize the burning, the bodies would have had to be stacked to a height of five or six layers. Assuming a corpse layer height of about 30 cm (1 foot), five layers of bodies—600 or so in total—would have formed a stack some 1.5 m (4.5 feet) high. Any higher than this and the bodies would threaten to topple over, in a smoldering and burning mess.

A question: How many such pyres would have been required at each camp? For Sobibor, no problem. At its peak the camp incinerated around 1200 bodies per day (see death matrix), which could have been achieved with two or three such pyres. Belzec was a bigger concern. For five straight winter months, five such pyres per day, every day, would have been consumed—come wind, rain, or snow. Treblinka, though, would have been a veritable conflagration. For four solid months, *over 10 pyres per day*, every day, would have been required.

And these were not the least of their problems. When we try to understand how the Germans set about to burn large numbers of bodies on metal pyres, using wood for fuel, we see that all the Reinhardt camps had very specific, very serious problems.

1. <u>Pyres are very inefficient</u>. Bodies will only burn once (a) all water is driven out, and (b) the remaining mass is heated to the burning point, at least 500 degrees Celsius. In a pyre with a fixed platform—i.e. the rails—a large portion of the heat from below is lost into the air. Furthermore, as the wood below burns down, even greater losses occur because the heat is farther from the bodies. These problems are solved by a crematorium, which maintains high heat in a small, enclosed space. The Germans knew this, but inexplicably opted for a crude open fire.
2. <u>Huge amounts of wood are required</u>. Under normal conditions, the Nazis would have needed roughly 160 kg (350 pounds) of wood per body to fully incinerate it.[130] If we accept the traditional picture, the figures for the Reinhardt camps are astounding:

---

[130] The anti-denial bloggers contest this figure, as I explain below.

- Belzec: 590,000 kg (675 tons) per day. In total, 88 million kg (100,000 tons).
- Sobibor: 197,000 kg (225 tons) per day (peak). In total, 36 million kg (41,000 tons).
- Treblinka: 1.2 million kg (1,400 tons) per day. In total, 144 million kg (164,000 tons).

As with Chelmno, these are unbelievably large amounts. Sobibor camp would have required the equivalent of six Eiffel Towers' worth of wood; Belzec, 14 Eiffel Towers; and Treblinka, 22 Eiffel Towers. In no case do we have any record or witness statement of any such huge amounts of wood entering the camp, being stored, or being prepared for the pyres. If the wood had been collected nearby, hundreds of acres of land would have been deforested; if it had been shipped in by train, there would have been numerous records of wood deliveries. There is no evidence for either occurrence.[131]

3. <u>Can't burn all layers at once.</u> The bulk of the heat would have impacted only the bottom layer of bodies; upper layers, in the cool air away from the flames below, would have taken much longer to dry out and burn up.
4. <u>Can't stack bodies very high.</u> Rotting corpses are not like neat hardwood logs; they would have made a terrible mess if anyone attempted to stack them too high. Five or perhaps six layers would have been the absolute most at any one time—about 600 or 700 bodies. Thus we can dismiss claims of burning thousands at once.
5. <u>Can't burn bodies fast enough.</u> Stacked wood, under a fixed grill, does not burn very fast. (Think how long a campfire burns when a few large logs are put on it.) A single 3 × 30 m pyre can only burn about 7,200 kg (16,000 pounds) of wood per hour. A 600-body pyre would require 96,000 kg of wood, thus taking about 13 hours just for the wood to burn. And this does not include set-up time, cool-down, or ash-sifting and disposal.
6. <u>Smoke signals.</u> Burning rotted corpses would have inevitably produced billowing clouds of smoke, every day, for months on end. This 'smoke signal' would have been visible for miles—bad policy for a death camp. Locals would have quickly figured things out, if they

---

[131] One finds only sporadic reference to wood brought into the camps. For example, Arad (1987: 171) cites testimony of a Sobibor driver: "I used to bring foodstuffs to the camp and also wood for cremating the killed..." The amount was evidently underwhelming. And Schelvis (2006: 111) simply states that "the cremation of the exhumed bodies... required huge quantities of wood, but plenty could be found in the neighboring forest." Plenty, that is, for hundreds or maybe even thousands of corpses, but certainly not hundreds of thousands. But once again, without specifics we have no way to judge the quantities involved.

hadn't known already. Allied planes flying overhead could have seen it, and perhaps photographed it—though we have not a single photograph of anything like this.

7. <u>Huge amounts of ash produced</u>. Combined wood and corpse ash amounts to about 9 kg (19 pounds) per body. The total amounts of ash, under orthodox assumptions, are impressive:
   - <u>Belzec</u>: 33,000 kg (73,000 lbs.) per day. In total, 5 million kg (5,700 tons).
   - <u>Sobibor</u>: 11,000 kg (24,000 lbs.) per day (peak). In total, 2 million kg (2,300 tons).
   - <u>Treblinka</u>: 68,000 kg (148,000 lbs.) per day. In total, 8.1 million kg (9,200 tons).

   Furthermore, as noted in Chapter 5, the burning of bodies leaves behind a large amount of unburned bones and teeth. So all this ash, every day, would have had to be sifted for bones and teeth, which would then have had to be ground to dust. And we do have reports that at least some such grinding was attempted. Arad (1987: 171) quotes a former Sobibor inmate: "The bones were crushed into ashes with hammers..." Arad describes the same process for the other two camps. But the problems would be staggering. Just consider the problem of the teeth. Imagine this, for example: How long would it take to find and smash 10 or 20 million teeth—"with hammers"? If not sifted out, they must still be there, in the ground, waiting to be discovered.

8. <u>Large amount of burial space for the ash</u>. Then the whole mass of ash would have had to be disposed of. Was it hauled away? Dumped in the river? Spread over some farmers' fields? No—as I quoted Arad earlier, "the ashes... were buried in the ditches from which the corpses had been removed." Now, it must be admitted that this would be an incredibly idiotic thing to do: to murder hundreds of thousands of people, burn their bodies, and then bury the ashes in the very place they were murdered. Hidden in plain sight, as they say.

As the weight of the ash was monumental, so too was its volume. Each cubic meter will hold about 375 kg (825 lbs.) of combined wood/corpse ash. Clearly the space was available; no matter how many bodies they had, ash space requirements are obviously less than that of unburned bodies. Even so, the total volume of ash at each camp is remarkable:

- <u>Belzec</u>: 13,000 cubic meters
- <u>Sobibor</u>: 5,300 cubic meters
- <u>Treblinka</u>: 21,600 cubic meters

This ash should be an easy target to find—if it is there.

Traditionalist Replies

How do the traditionalists respond to these issues? Essentially by ignoring them. None of the published anti-revisionists address any of these pressing concerns. Van Pelt, Hilberg, Longerich, Evans, and Lipstadt all offer no response. They naively assume that everything simply happened as described: pits dug, bodies buried, corpses burned to ash... all with no problems. Granted, these issues are more scientific than historical, and our experts may need to call in help. But then, why have they not done so?

Only the bloggers Harrison *et al.* (2011) have attempted to respond. Theirs is an impressively detailed reply, and I will spare the reader the minutiae; the work is available online, for those so inclined. Functioning simultaneously as amateur historians and amateur scientists, this quintuplet of writers does their best to produce academic-looking work. Apart from Harrison, group members lack advanced degrees, and hold no teaching or research positions. They have published nothing with established printing houses—despite the on-going eagerness for Holocaust works. And yet they fashion themselves as the premier defenders of orthodoxy, at least with respect to the Reinhardt camps.[132] If true, we can expect the professional historians to begin copiously citing their work; to date, though, this has not happened.

In sum, their reply to the above concerns is this: *The Jews were miniature people.* They were all very short, and they were emaciated. A large percentage—upwards of two-thirds or more—were children, they claim. These tiny people took up very little space in the gas chambers, and their bodies took very little space in mass graves. When burned, they burned quickly, leaving very little ash. This seems to be the answer to all problems.

In an unpublished paper, Charles Provan (1991) attempted to prove that extremely high body densities were in fact possible. He claimed to have built a box with a floor area equal to three square feet—21" × 21", or 0.28 square meters—and 1.5 m (almost 5 feet) high. In this box he was able to pack eight "people"—attaining an equivalent density of 19 bodies per cubic meter. But this is deceiving. In fact he packed in: three short adults (5'7", 5'6", and 4'10"), four children under age 8, and one baby doll (representing an infant). Provan's experiment succeeds only if the Jewish victims were at least 63 percent young children. Obviously this could have occurred on a limited, selective basis, but long-term, over hundreds of thousands of people, it is a highly dubious claim.

But even this study was insufficient for the bloggers, who argue for higher densities still. Indeed, they claim (2011: 418) that one could pack an

---

[132] As I noted in Chapter 1, this work drew a lengthy revisionist reply: Mattogno *et al.* (2013).

astounding 20 Jewish bodies per cubic meter. Or perhaps even more: at one point (p. 421) they imply that up to *25 bodies* could fit in each cubic meter—25 infants, maybe; 25 adults, never.

Since the Jews were miniature people, the bloggers claim, their bodies decayed quickly, leaving less mass to be burned away to nothing. In order to estimate wood and ash conditions, we need an idea of how much wood it takes to cremate a given unit of organic flesh; in other words, what is the nominally required "wood-to-flesh" ratio? Revisionist estimates run from 3.5-to-1 up to 10-to-1 or more. On their view the complete burning, down to ash, of a 45 kg (100 lbs.) corpse, for example, would take at least 158 kg (350 lbs.) of wood[133]—and perhaps much more, under adverse conditions. Such a figure is confirmed by ceremonial burnings of the deceased in Hindu culture, in which as much as 400 kg of wood is needed to fully consume a body.

The bloggers think it much easier to burn rotting flesh. After running through some analytical gyrations, they determine (2011: 468) that the ratio is an amazing 0.56-to-1. In other words, they actually assert that a 45 kg corpse could be completely consumed by only 25 kg of wood. This is an astonishing claim, frankly. To be taken seriously, the bloggers would have to conduct careful scientific experiments under controlled conditions in order to prove such a claim. This is something their fellow traditionalists could easily do, given their vast surplus of financial resources to draw from. It should be no problem for them to acquire, say, 1,000 dead hogs, bury them for six months, construct a Reinhardt-like pyre, exhume the corpses, and then burn the hogs to pure ash—using only a 0.56-to-1 wood-to-flesh ratio. They could then gather up the remains, sift for bones and teeth, manually pound them to dust, and measure the results. That could put the whole matter to rest. Until this happens, their figures remain pure speculation.

Again, I emphasize that all this comes only from the bloggers. The official, published literature is utterly vacant. Search the anti-revisionist books for substantial reference to these issues, and you will find: Lipstadt—nothing. Shermer and Grobman—nothing. Perry and Schweitzer—nothing. Stern—nothing. Van Pelt has only this to say:

> The evidence for the [extermination] role of Treblinka, Belzec, and Sobibor... is much less abundant [than for Auschwitz]. There are very few eyewitnesses, no confessions that can compare to that given by Hoess, no significant remains, and few archival sources. (2002: 5)

---

[133] Recently, Köchel (2015) has suggested that it may take 135 kg of dry hardwood to consume one body. Green wood would require roughly double this figure. His estimate is based on actual animal incinerations in 2001. With dry wood and ideal burning conditions, Köchel's ratio would be 3.0-to-1. But since these conditions were likely rare for the Germans, his study largely confirms Mattogno's and Graf's estimate.

Zimmerman should have ridden to the rescue here. Instead he offers only passing mention on a dozen separate pages, referring to notoriously unreliable witness testimony—see Appendix B for a summary of witness claims. Belzec and Sobibor are virtually devoid of reliable witnesses. Treblinka has more names, but they offer little help. Zimmerman cites the following in his defense:

- Willenberg (but no details)
- Zabecki ("never actually in Treblinka"; witnessed only "transports"; memoirs never translated into English—evidently not very informative)
- Stangl (camp commandant; "never denied" his crimes; no further details)
- Franz (2nd in command; "cannot say how many Jews in total were gassed")
- Mentz ("Gunman of Treblinka"; stated [erroneously] that there were 5 or 6 gas chambers)
- Mattes, or "Matthes" (SS sergeant; stated "300 people could enter each gas chamber")
- Horn (SS guard; testified at Demjanjuk trial; no details)

This is essentially the sum total of witness testimony that Zimmerman presents, for as important a camp as Treblinka. And we must bear in mind: witness testimony is *the pivotal element* in the case for mass murder.

Also casting a negative light are the witnesses ignored by Zimmerman because they claim ludicrous things, or give us outright lies or obvious hyperbole. Samuel (Shmuel) Rajzman and Jankiel Wiernik are two prominent examples of Treblinka witnesses who made outrageous statements, and hence are conveniently overlooked.

Excavations (I)—Belzec

Most of these contentious issues could be quickly resolved if authorities simply excavated the camps. Various options exist. They could literally dig up the grave areas and see what is there; this would be the best alternative, but thanks to Jewish law forbidding "desecration" of the dead, this is not allowed. The second-best choice is to dig core samples at regular intervals; this in fact was done, as I explain below. The third option, and least desirable, is to use some modern remote-sensing technology such as a nonintrusive ground-penetrating radar.

Consider Belzec. As it happens, two excavations have been conducted there since the war. The first was a Polish investigation in 1945. This group dug nine large holes, up to 10 m wide and up to 8 m deep. Their findings: Sand mixed with intermittent human ash, along with scattered bones. No firm conclusions can be drawn, but from the wording—"some charred remains," "part of a human body," "a human skull," "two shinbones and a rib," "one partially burnt specimen," etc.—it suggests something on the order of hundreds of bodies, and certainly not hundreds of thousands.[134]

Evidently this sufficed for some 50 years. Then in the late 1990s a radical step was taken: an official agency of the Polish government decided to perform truly scientific excavations at the Belzec site, for the first time, with the hope of confirming the mass graves. And find mass graves they did—33 in all. A report was written and published by the lead researcher, Andrzej Kola (2000). Two interim reports were published by one of the team, Robin O'Neil (1998; 1999). News headlines appeared, touting the "new secrets" revealed at Belzec. Zimmerman was obviously impressed; he mentions the news no less than three times (pp. 19, 134, 234), though without offering any details.

Mattogno too was impressed, but for entirely different reasons. He argues that this survey shows the *opposite* of the intended result, and strengthens the revisionist case considerably.

Following a systematic, grid-like pattern, Kola's team sank 2,227 holes, pulling out core samples. Of these, 236 showed evidence of mass graves. From these isolated samples, spaced at least 5 m (17 ft) apart, Kola attempts to sketch the outlines of 33 quasi-distinct burial pits—see Illustration 6.

The graves have an average surface area of about 180 square meters, or almost 6,000 square meters in total—less than 10 percent of the camp. The total volume is about 21,000 cubic meters. Thus, both in area and volume the total grave space is far less than that required—in fact, the volume is only about one-quarter of the necessary space. Kola's "33 mass graves" could actually hold about 147,000 bodies, if filled to the brim. But even if they did, *what happened to the other 400,000 bodies?*

Kola's map points to another issue. The irregular shape and layout of the graves suggests something other than an orderly, SS-planned burial site. It is haphazard, ad hoc, unplanned—precisely what one might expect if there had been no grand strategy of extermination. Furthermore, these graves are utterly inconsistent with Arad's map, shown in Chapter 6. His layout, therefore, is seriously in error—along with perhaps other aspects of his account.

Furthermore, according to the traditional story, the graves should contain primarily the burnt remains of the victims, some 550,000 in total. But it would not be unreasonable to find a small number of unburned corpses as well.

---

[134] Report cited in Mattogno (2011: 79).

[Illustration with legend:]

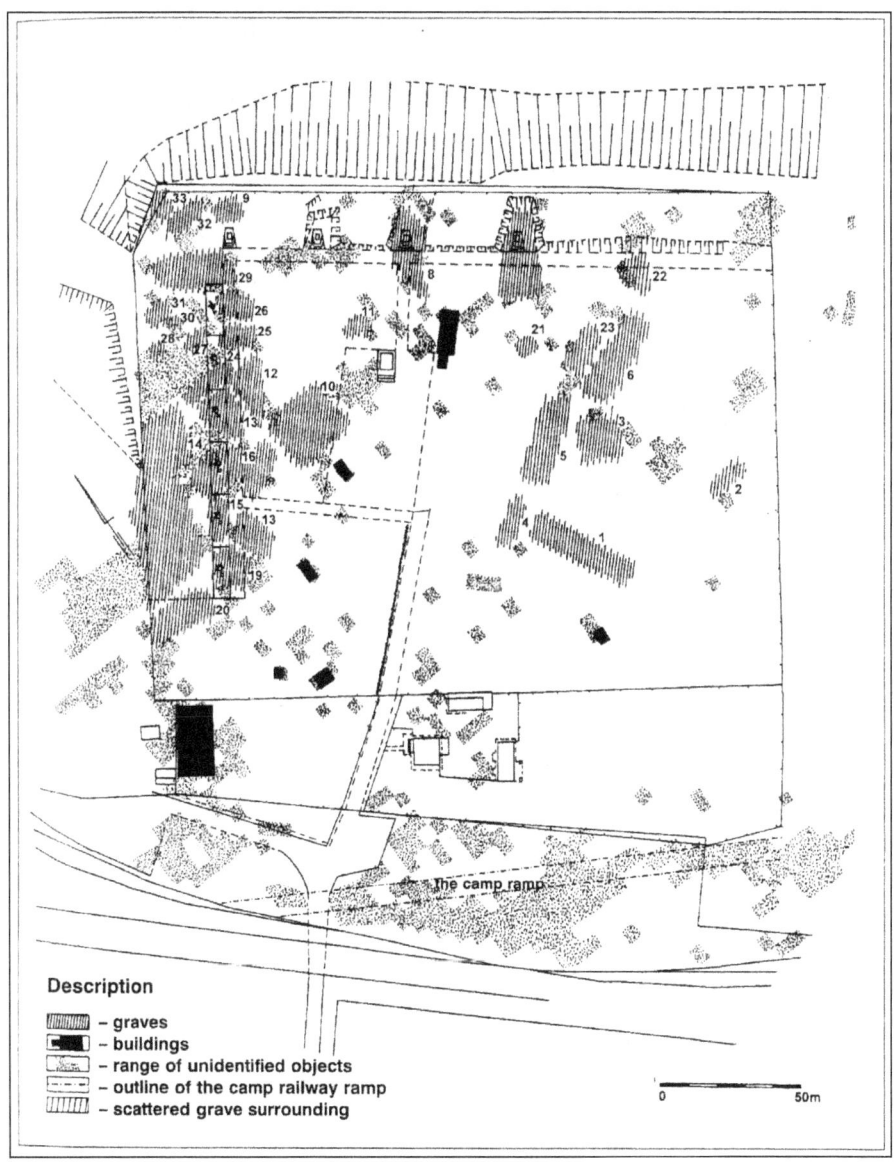

Description
- graves
- buildings
- range of unidentified objects
- outline of the camp railway ramp
- scattered grave surrounding

Illustration 6: Belzec Mass Graves, per Kola.

Of the 236 samples showing evidence of human remains, most were in the form of human ash. Kola published details on the most significant 137—though with a highly ambiguous and cryptic pictorial analysis. Of these, only six bore traces of unburned corpses. The thickness of the corpse layer was always less than one meter—out of a total depth of 5 m—and always at the bottom of the graves. One meter of thickness corresponds to perhaps three or four bodies, so if each of the six positive samples cut through this many, Kola has found, technically, no more than some two dozen unburned corpses. Surely there are more than these in total under the camp, but lacking a full-scale excavation, we will not know.

And what did someone like O'Neil conclude from this? His 1998 article, at which time only two graves with corpses had been found, makes a bold prediction: "How many [unburned] bodies remain in these two graves is difficult to establish. To be sure, there are many thousands" (p. 54). How O'Neil jumps from positive evidence of only two dozen bodies to "thousands" is left unexplained. Tregenza (2000: 258) is more specific, but no more justified: "on the order of at least 15,000." By comparison Mattogno (2011: 79) concludes: "the most probable interpretation is that the graves contained at most several hundred [unburned] corpses." But, as noted, a small number of unburned bodies is consistent with the conventional account of things. Thus one wonders why O'Neil and Tregenza felt compelled to infer vast figures when in fact they were unnecessary.

Of the ashes themselves, they seem to be far short of the required amount. The ash that Kola found was not pure, but mixed with sand—often more than 50 percent. And more than half of his relevant samples had only a very thin sand/ash layer, sometimes almost down to nothing. Kola's analysis is so poor that it is difficult to come to clear conclusions, but Mattogno (p. 87) determines that these data are "absolutely incompatible" with any mass incineration.

The Polish surveyors at Belzec were not only looking for bodies; they were hoping to confirm the existence of the gas chambers themselves. In fact, two sets of gas chambers: the original three (March–June 1942), and the later six (July–December)—each in its own building. The former was of wood on a concrete foundation, and the latter was explicitly described as a brick-and-concrete structure, which certainly would have left an unmistakable mark.

But the team found no evidence of any gas-chamber buildings. O'Neil wrote in 1998, halfway through the work, "We found no trace of the gassing barracks dating from either the first or second phase of the camp's construction" (p. 55). By the time of the final report, Kola claimed to have found evidence for the second, larger gassing facility—except that the structure he found was all wood, not concrete. Rather than rejecting his gas-chamber hypothesis, Kola surprisingly rejected all standard accounts of a brick-and-concrete building as erroneous. And in fact the only reason he decided that this structure was a gas chamber in the first place was simply because it was in the "right location"—hardly conclusive proof.

In the end, the Belzec excavations led to highly mixed results. Yes, there were many bodies buried there, most after being burned. But (a) both sides of the debate agree that many people died there, people who must have been burned or buried, and (b) the total mass of remains is much smaller than the traditionalists would have us believe. Based on the excavation data, Mattogno (p. 91) concludes that "it is possible to infer, from what has been discussed above, an order of magnitude of several thousands, perhaps even some tens of thousands" of deaths. But certainly not *hundreds* of thousands.

What should thus have been a triumphal moment for traditionalism quickly evaporated. Kola's Belzec report was released in 2000, and yet it garnered very little discussion in the orthodox literature. The 2001 *Holocaust Encyclopedia* gives the excavations no mention at all, nor do the 2015 online encyclopedias of either USHMM or Yad Vashem. Van Pelt (2002: 12) grants it all of one sentence, misleadingly mentioning the "enormous mass graves" found. Hilberg (2003) completely ignores it, as do Longerich (2010) and Bartov (2015).

Kola's report seems to have faded into obscurity—in more ways than one. His book is virtually unobtainable. Major research libraries do not have it. It is not on Amazon.com. Even the publisher, the US Holocaust Memorial Museum, can't get it for you. This is very odd, given its early status as the definitive proof of mass murder at Belzec. We can be sure that, if the book really were so conclusive, it would be readily available everywhere. Sometimes the smallest clues betray the largest truths.

Excavations (II)—Sobibor

Here we have a similar story to that of Belzec, though with lesser numbers. Nearly 85,000 bodies were buried there between April and October 1942, at which time exhumations and burnings commenced. A variety of excavation activity has occurred at Sobibor since 2000; Bem and Mazurek (2012) provide a concise overview. They identify three specific phases of digging.

(1) Once finished at Belzec, Kola moved on to Sobibor. During 2000 and 2001, his team bored 3,805 core samples, spread over nine hectares (about 23 acres). Among other objectives, write Bem and Mazurek (p. 98), Kola "hoped to pinpoint the location of the gas chambers." Upon completion, Kola claimed to have found seven mass graves and five building structure remains (Objects "A"-"E"). All of the mass graves contained skeletal remains—that is, unburned bodies—which argues *against* the bury-exhumeburn thesis. Total volume of the six main graves was estimated at around 14,700 cubic meters, sufficient to hold the required 85,000 bodies. But as Graf *et al.* (2010: 123) point out, simply because they were large enough "does not mean that [that many] corpses *were* buried in them." Furthermore, due to random and uncontrolled diggings at the site after the war, there is a "high probability" that the graves were originally "considerably smaller"

than at present. In any case, data from the core samples did not result in any determination of numbers of victims.

Regarding the building remains, one large structure—Object E—was hinted at by Kola to be the gas chamber; unfortunately, he says, "it is impossible to give a simple answer [to this question]." Graf *et al.* (pp. 159f.) explain why: (a) witnesses said the gas chamber building was brick, and yet Kola's structure was all wood; (b) at the presumed location of the diesel gassing engine, Kola found only spent ammunition casings; and (c) the huge size of the object—some 80-100 meters in length—was never mentioned by any witnesses.

The problems here for traditionalism are significant, to say the least. Notably, Kola's report has never been translated into English or any western language.

(2) In the second phase, in 2004, Bem and colleagues hoped to find both the gas chambers and the 'tube' or path—also called the *Schlauch* or *Himmelfahrtstrasse*—that led to the chambers. Pursuing the thesis that Object E was the gas-chamber building, they found a small rectangular space "that was tentatively interpreted as the room for the combustion engine [not "diesel"?] producing the exhaust fumes that were pumped into the gas chambers" (p. 105). Regarding the Tube, their investigation "had not produced the expected results," meaning, they found nothing.

(3) The third phase, running from 2007 to the present, was guided by Israeli archeologist Yoram Haimi. Continuing previous efforts, Haimi's team too sought the chambers and the tube. Regarding the all-important chambers, hopes invested in Object E turned out to be in vain: "we can, with a high degree of certainty, state that Object E is not the remains of the gas chambers" (p. 113). Its purpose and function thus remain unknown, and the search for the chambers goes on.

Regarding the Tube, Haimi and team found a long pattern of parallel postholes. "This pattern of two rows... are interpreted as being the remains of the final section of the *Himmelfahrtstrasse*, which should have led to the gas chambers" (p. 126). Unfortunately for the team, this pattern leads to what is now a large—roughly 30m × 30m—asphalt-paved memorial space; excavating there would mean tearing up the sacred memorial site.

Compounding the difficulties, it was announced in early 2014 that the Poles would build a new visitor's center and a nearly mile-long "memorial wall"; this would have the effect of ending, or at least severely inhibiting, further exploration in those areas.[135] I note also that the focus seems to have moved completely away from the mass graves and their contents. Evidently

---

[135] "At Sobibor: Building in the heart of a death camp." Posted at www.timesofisrael.com (8 Mar 2014).

this was not a productive area of research, as it was not yielding "the expected results."

But Haimi and his team are optimistic. As reported in the above news story, they await permission to excavate under the asphalt paving. "Under this square—almost the size of a soccer field—they expect to find remnants of the gas chambers."

And find them they did—perhaps. In September 2014, news media reported that the long-sought Sobibor chambers had been found. The German periodical *Der Spiegel* wrote that Haimi and Mazurek "uncovered the remains of the gas chambers of Sobibor."[136] Though in fact we find that the freshly dug-up foundations and walls are merely the "suspected" remnants of "four gas chambers." This in itself is odd, given that orthodoxy has long proclaimed three, or six, chambers. Near the end of the news article we discover that "the archaeologists still don't have final proof that these are the gas-chamber foundations." Surely, though, we won't have to wait long.

Meanwhile, dispute about the number of Sobibor victims goes on. A footnote[137] in the 2012 Bem and Mazurek report states that "the Germans committed 300,000 murders here"—a figure that significantly exceeds not only my presumed figure of 225,000, but also that of both the USHMM and Yad Vashem. On the other hand, skeptical revisionists such as Graf, Mattogno, and Kues say this: "It must be stressed that this is only a rough estimate, but we find it probable that the number of Sobibor victims is in the vicinity of 10,000 dead" (2010: 169). A figure of 10,000 dead, while still tragic, would reduce Sobibor to near-insignificance in the Holocaust story, and to complete irrelevance in the larger tragedy of World War II.

Excavations (III)—Treblinka

Given the huge numbers involved, Treblinka should have been the easiest camp of all to excavate and find clear and decisive evidence of mass murder. And indeed there were excavations—again, three separate efforts.

(1) After the Soviet army captured Treblinka in August 1944—about one year after cremations ended—a joint Soviet-Polish team immediately began excavations; evidence of mass murder by one's enemies is always good PR. As described in Mattogno and Graf (2010: 77), they found a total of three mass graves:

---

[136] "A voice for the dead." Posted at www.spiegel.de (26 Sep 2014).
[137] Page 129, note 18.

- Grave #1: 10 × 5 × 2 m deep, with 105 corpses.
- Grave #2: 10 × 5 × 1.9 m deep, with 97 corpses.
- Grave #3: 10 × 5 × 2.5 m deep, with 103 corpses.

With a studied conservatism, the Soviet report stated the following:

> The camp… was an enormous death combine… The death factory in which the SS men ruthlessly and zealously exterminated millions of people was in operation around the clock for 13 months… The extent of the extermination of human beings was monstrous: about three million. (*ibid*: 78-80)

Clearly the team had no compunction about exaggerating, and yet they would only claim three mass graves, with a total of some 300 bodies. Perhaps most revealing was this statement:

> [Excavations] from the pits confirm that there were ovens in the camp where people were cremated. … At present it is difficult to uncover the traces and secrets of this oven for the cremation of people, but based upon the available data, one can picture it.

In other words—they found nothing. The team did claim to find "cinders and ash" on the road between the two parts of the camp (Treblinka 1 and 2), to a depth of 7–10 cm (3–4 inches). But even if true, this would not amount to more than a fraction of the total ash produced. And it would have been even more incriminating than burying the ash. How foolish could those Germans have been?

(2) The second excavation occurred a year later, when a Polish team investigated the camp during the course of the Nuremberg trial. Judge Lukaszkiewicz and his team conducted a five-day examination of the death-camp grounds. Mattogno and Graf (2010: 84-86) reproduce the whole report. Some highlights:

> 9 November 1945: Following witnesses, digging begun at a mass grave location. Found numerous coins and bits of containers. Digging halted at 6 meters (20 ft). "No human remains were found."

> 10 November 1945: Digging continued, same location. Found kitchen utensils, household objects, clothing. Bottom reached at 7 meters. Found: documents, coins. No remains.

> 11 November 1945: Again based directly on witness instructions, "test excavations" at the presumed site of the gas chambers, looking for foundation walls. Dug pits 10–15 meters long, 1.5 meters deep, uncovering only "undisturbed layers of earth." Also, a bomb crater was examined, finding "the presence of a large quantity of ashes as well as [unburned] human remains"—number and quantity unstated. Digging halted at 7.5 meters.

13 November 1945: Digging in a refuse pit. Found documents, kitchen containers, rags, coins. No bodies or ashes. Digging halted at 5 meters.

Underwhelming, to say the least. In his concluding statement Lukaszkiewicz wrote: "with great probability no mass graves are any longer to be found on the grounds of the former camp today..."

For decades thereafter, there were no attempts at further excavation. In the mid-1960s there were two notable Treblinka trials in West Germany. Their official findings were based on second- and third-hand witness accounts—but not one attempt to excavate. Mattogno asks a pointed question:

> What is to be thought of a judiciary that relies upon rumors and hearsay in a trial dealing with the murder of at least 700,000... instead of proposing an investigation of the scene of the crime, and suggesting to the Polish authorities... joint excavations to determine the size and position of the mass graves? (Mattogno and Graf 2010: 166)

When one is in possession of the legally-mandated truth, further evidence is unnecessary.

(3) Finally, beginning in 2007, a modern-day investigation was initiated. A 20-something British archaeologist, Caroline Sturdy Colls, was somehow enlisted to conduct the first investigation of Treblinka since the war years. Her work, called the "first-ever excavation" of the camp, has been rolling along at a low boil for some eight years now, with precious little analysis to show for it. To date she has published nothing of substance.[138] Her chief purpose seems to be to produce media stories and 'documentaries' of the camp that promote the traditional viewpoint.

Sturdy Colls's efforts have yielded inconsequential and even embarrassing results. For example, rather than digging at the site of the mass graves—which is conveniently covered over in concrete—she conducted a small excavation nearby, at the site of a pre-war cemetery. She found... human remains. A greater embarrassment was her finding of a fragment of an orange tile "with a Star of David on it." Such tiles, she says, "fit in with the idea that we are in the area of the gas chambers." She adds that this reminds her of claims that Stars of David were placed on the outside of the gas chambers, to lull the Jewish victims into a sense of complacency. But she got it all wrong. In reality, the tile was a product of a long-established Polish ceramics firm, *Dziewulski i Lange*. Their brand logo was a six-sided mullet star that

---

[138] Her 2012 article, "Holocaust archaeology," for example, is nearly useless as a quantitative study. It devotes a mere two pages of text to Treblinka, saying nothing of value. She claims to have found "over one hundred features" of the camp using her ground-penetrating radar, though no details are provided. Notably, all talk of gas chambers is absent. Colls's most recent work, *Holocaust Archaeologies* (2015), is more a discussion of methods than actual results; it has few details on Treblinka.

resembles the Jewish star, though having no connection to it. It was stamped on the back of their tiles.[139]

And yet the media continue to trumpet her findings as if of great significance. The Web-based media organization LiveScience, for example, headlined this story on 27 March 2014: "First-ever excavation of Nazi death camp Treblinka reveals horrors." The opening paragraph reads,

> The first-ever archaeological excavations at the Nazi death camp Treblinka have revealed new mass graves, as well as the first physical evidence that this camp held gas chambers, where thousands of Jews died.

All this is untrue, incidentally. The piece goes on to plug Sturdy Colls's new documentary *Treblinka: Hitler's Killing Machine*, produced by the Smithsonian Channel.[140] As before, the article provides no concrete information at all. The final section, "Finding the Gas Chamber," includes this statement:

> The second two trenches [excavation sites], however, revealed a brick wall and foundation. The gas chambers were the only brick buildings in the camp, Colls said. The excavations also revealed orange tiles that matched eyewitness descriptions of the floor of the killing chambers. Chillingly, each tile was stamped with a Star of David, likely part of the Nazi subterfuge that the building was a Jewish-style bathhouse.

Of the stunning finding of the foundations of the gas chamber, we get nothing: no size, no location, no structure, no maps, no photos, no surrounding artifacts—nothing. Of the orange tiles, no mention of the Polish firm that created them long before the war. All in all, an appalling bit of pseudo-archaeology and a risible piece of reporting.

A Better Account…

For all that, *something* happened at those Reinhardt camps. But it seems not to have been mass murder. If we take Hitler's words literally, he wanted to drive the Jews out of the German-controlled regions of Europe. As I have emphasized, on the revisionist view, the ghetto system initiated this process by concentrating Jews into small, well-defined areas. Once deportations began, they were shipped to the East via a few designated gateway transit

---

[139] A 5-minute video clip of this little incident is on Youtube: "Excavating a secret gas chamber." Her 2015 book offers a brief explanation of this embarrassing incident.

[140] The entire Smithsonian institution seems to have adopted as its mission the promotion of Holocaust orthodoxy.

camps—the Reinhardt camps. There they would be showered and disinfested of any disease-bearing lice, and then shipped further on eastward to other ghettos or labor camps.

The ideal location for such transit camps would be on the eastern edge of German territory, as of late 1941. In fact, all three Reinhardt camps were located on or near the eastern boundary of the General Government region of occupied Poland—the perfect location for shipment into newly-captured Russian territory. I further note that they would have had to disembark there anyway, in order to transfer to new trains that ran on the larger-gauge Soviet rail system.[141]

Interestingly, then, *all three camps should be expected to have had gas chambers*—but chambers that gassed clothing and personal items, against the disease-carrying lice. Similarly, all three camps should be expected to have had shower rooms—*real* showers, ones that washed the often-filthy new arrivals. Thus we should not be surprised if the likes of Kola, Haimi, or Sturdy Colls find evidence of 'gas chambers' or 'shower rooms.' In fact we should expect it.

The entire layout of the camps—the incoming quarantine area, the 'tube,' the gas chambers and showers, and the isolated exit zone—all make complete sense as transit stations. And as noted, it furthermore explains the perceptions of the eyewitnesses: friends and family members separated, sent down the tube, 'gassed,' never to be seen again. Separately they hear (true) stories of dead bodies being buried and/or burned. And a terrible smoke and the smell pervade the camp. What else are they to conclude? It is entirely understandable—but entirely wrong.

We must keep in mind: Many Jews undoubtedly died in those camps. Some perished *en route* to them. Some came sick with typhus, dying soon after arrival. Some, assuredly, were killed. Based on the lack of crematoria at all three camps, the Nazis were clearly expecting only a small and scattered number of dead; they probably assumed that ad hoc burials on site would suffice. We can easily imagine that, as the pace of deportation accelerated, so did the number of dead. Burials, therefore, would at some point have become insufficient—at different times, for each of the three camps. There being no alternative, we can thus understand the move toward limited burnings on open fires.

How many died, or arrived dead, on the revisionist thesis? We have already seen an estimate for Sobibor: 10,000. Regarding Belzec, Mattogno (2011: 91) says, "it is possible to infer... an order of magnitude of several thousands, perhaps even some tens of thousands." Somewhat arbitrarily,

---

[141] Of interest is a revisionist documentary, *The Treblinka Archaeology Hoax*, by Eric Hunt (online at: www.gaschamberhoax.com). Hunt examines the testimony of several witnesses who transited through Treblinka. He also debunks the work of Sturdy Colls.

let's assume a number of 40,000, as a working estimate. This is consistent with the general revisionist line that actual deaths are around 10 percent of conventional estimates. As to Treblinka, revisionist Thomas Kues has estimated total Jewish deaths at 20,000 to 30,000;[142] let me take 25,000 as a nominal figure.

In each of the three camps, we can state with confidence that the actual data from excavations and archaeological studies are much closer to revisionist than to conventional figures. If the experts were more objective about their findings, they would reduce their estimates to better align with the data. We await this development.

Closing the Camps, Tracking the Deportees

At the start of this chapter, I listed the closing dates for each camp. This in itself is another problem for orthodoxy. If in fact these camps were key elements in a Reich-wide extermination scheme, why did they close so soon? Belzec was done gassing by December 1942, but there were still nearly 2 million Jews to be killed, at least. Sobibor had the longest life of the three, but even this camp was out of commission by September 1943, when there were more than 1 million Jews left.

Treblinka, though, is the most troubling case. For all practical purposes, this latest and greatest death camp lasted just eight months; extensive gassings were essentially over by March 1943, with plenty of war to come and well over a million Jews remaining. Given the exigencies of an extermination program, it would have made no sense whatsoever to shut down the camps. Instead the Nazis largely halted the killings there and concentrated on burning the corpses. On the other hand, revisionists say this fits perfectly well with the thesis that Treblinka, like the others, was simply a temporary transit camp. When the conditions for mass deportation changed—because of Soviet advances in the East—the camps shut down.

I give the final word on the Reinhardt camps to traditionalism. Just as the orthodox historians have a hard time explaining the absence of human remains, revisionists have a hard time explaining where the Jews went. If they were funneled on to the East, we should have some record of large numbers of Jews showing up in specific ghettos or labor camps. But we lack documents of mass movements out of these camps, and we have few details regarding where the people ended up. Zimmerman (2000: 14-19) hammers on this point:

---

[142] Personal communication (1 Mar 2010).

This has always been the biggest problem for deniers. The Jews were not in concentration camps... So where were all the Jews? None of the German documents which talk about movements to the east give a location. ... [A]ll of the transports end at Belzec, Sobibor and Treblinka. ... [N]othing is said about where these Jews were "resettled." ... [T]he resettlement of millions of people would not have gone unnoticed. Yet, there is not a single document relating to such a resettlement. ... Deniers... argue that it made no economic sense to murder all of the Jews. However, from a cost standpoint it would have been much more costly and time consuming to resettle them. The only denier argument remaining is that these Jews were simply shoved across the border into the Soviet Union and abandoned.

Mattogno and Graf largely agree. Regarding Treblinka they write: "It is entirely unclear where the Jews deported to Treblinka ultimately wound up. That Treblinka served as a transit camp is proven, but for the most part we are still in the dark as to the details..." (2010: 301). More generally the same concern exists: "The fate of the Jews deported to the east is one of those questions for which there is no sure answer, due to the lack of documents" (*ibid*: 293). But they also state:

> In view of the paucity of existing documentation, we cannot determine with certainty what the final destination of this deportation was, but there exist various pieces of evidence, which make it possible for us to draw plausible conclusions. (*ibid*: 253)

They cite documents supporting the movement of thousands into the Ukraine. There are also references to floating labor camps in captured Soviet territory, and to newly established Jewish ghettos in the Baltics, Byelorussia, and the Ukraine. One can imagine that in newly captured territory there would be little infrastructure in place to track movements of people—especially Jews, who would have been seen as finally 'rid of' once crossing into former Soviet lands. For all practical purposes the deportees were permanently banished from the Reich the moment they departed, crossing immediately into a foreign land with little hope of return. When the Jews left the Reinhardt camps, the job was done; there was no further need to follow or record their movements.

Still, it is a large unanswered question. But it is a question that both sides must face. In a sense, both sides are missing the victims, and hence this issue counts against each case. But it has much more force against traditionalism, which makes positive, verifiable assertions about the fate of the victims.

The End of the Line

Each of the three Reinhardt camps came to a rather strange, if not bizarre end—in fact, the *same* bizarre end. Mass killings at Belzec were over by the end of 1942; for all intents and purposes Treblinka was done by February 1943; Sobibor was out of business by September of the same year. Things were not going well for the Germans by that time, but there was no reason to expect an imminent end to the war; in reality, it was to go on a full year and a half after the closing of the last Reinhardt camp.

In each of the three cases the Nazis, upon burying the victims' ashes, set about dismantling the camp and removing all traces of its existence. The first to go, Belzec, was initially just abandoned. But this strategy didn't work. Local farmers, thinking there was money or gold buried on the grounds, embarked on some ferocious wildcat digging. This inevitably scattered the ashes, giving the impression of a much broader burial area. "To put an end to this," says Arad (1990a: 179), "the Germans posted a Ukrainian guard, converted the grounds into a farm, and gave it to the guard. The area was plowed under and sown, and trees planted on it." Apparently this was the best that the SS could come up with.

Sobibor was dismantled in late 1943. Again, Arad explains:

> By the end of 1943 no trace was left; the camp area was plowed under, and crops were planted in its soil. A farm was put up in its place, and one of the Ukrainian camp guards settled there. (1990b: 1378)

As before, the vaunted Nazis murder hundreds of thousands of people, bury their ashes in the very spot where they murdered them, and leave a lone Ukrainian to raise beans there.

The Treblinka story has a slight twist. With the exhumations and burnings approaching an end in July 1943, a prisoner rebellion began brewing. The revolt came in August, during which many buildings were set afire and several hundred prisoners escaped. The camp held on for three more months, but then in November the SS "blew up the camp" (Laqueur 2001: 179). And then? We can guess:

> The grounds were plowed under and trees were planted; the camp was turned into a farm, and a Ukrainian peasant family was settled there. (Arad 1990c: 1487)

No need to change a winning strategy, apparently.

Chapter 9: Majdanek

Once a bright star in the Holocaust firmament, Majdanek[143] has fallen mightily. It is now almost inconsequential for the big picture—at least with respect to the Jewish Holocaust. Based on the latest 'official' estimate, the camp's 59,000 Jewish fatalities represent less than 1 percent of the total Holocaust. Other estimates are perhaps double this, but they are still the smallest of any of the six death camps.

Unlike the others, Majdanek was not a 'pure extermination' camp; it served multiple purposes, including concentration of Poles, Jews, and POWs, and implementation of forced labor. It was the largest of the six death camps, covering roughly 2.7 square kilometers (667 acres)—over 10 times the size of Sobibor and 35 times Belzec. Perhaps because of its size, no attempt was made to hide or disguise the location. It was located close to the city of Lublin, on the major Lublin-Chelm-Zamosc highway, and very near the Lublin train station and local airstrip. As Marszalek describes it, "Because of its location, the camp could be seen from almost all sides... The whole area is entirely open" (1986: 23).

Construction began in October 1941, and the first inmates began arriving by late November. The alleged gassings did not start until nearly a year later, in September 1942. They ran at a relatively slow and steady pace for some fourteen months, ceasing in October 1943.

The *New York Times* first reported on Majdanek in July 1943. They wrote that "the German murder toll in Poland is reaching a new high... including 1.8 million Jews [in all camps]"—according to the Polish Minister of Home Affairs.[144] He tells of men, women, and children "deported to the Majdanek death camp in the Lublin district, where they were slaughtered in masses in death chambers." On two days in July, "more than 3,000 persons were murdered in gas chambers. Such executions are taking place every day."

But it got worse. One year later, the NYT had precise details. "Victims put at 1,500,000 in huge death factory of gas chambers and crematories,"

---

[143] Pronounced 'my-DON-ek.' Also occasionally spelled 'Maidanek' or 'Maydanek.' Some writers (e.g. Hilberg) refer to it by the camp's German name, Lublin.

[144] 27 July (p. 9). Once again, we have no independent verification of this estimate.

178   THOMAS DALTON · *DEBATING THE HOLOCAUST*

screamed the headline.[145] The camp had recently been 'liberated' by the Russians, and they invited Western reporters to see the horror firsthand. As reporter Bill Lawrence wrote,

> I have just seen the most terrible place on the face of the earth—the German concentration camp at Maidanek, [at which] as many as 1,500,000 persons from nearly every country in Europe were killed in the last three years. I have been all through the camp, inspecting its hermetically sealed gas chambers, in which the victims were asphyxiated, and five furnaces in which the bodies were cremated.

He went to a nearby forest, where he saw 10 open mass graves—though only 368 bodies. "In this forest," he said, "the authorities estimate there are more than 300,000 bodies." The victims were of assorted nationalities: "Jews, Poles, Russians" and others. Perhaps we should have known then that something was amiss.

The Death Matrix

As always, we find a wide range of death figures. This is especially true for Majdanek. The range of conventional figures is shown in Table 24.

Table 24: Majdanek: Death Estimates	
DEATHS	SOURCE
1,700,000	Lipstadt (1983)
1,500,000	persons; NYT (30 Aug 1944)
1,380,000	persons; Dawidowicz (1986: 149)
360,000	persons; Laqueur (2001: 233)
235,000	persons; Rajca (1992: 129)
170,000	persons; Kranz (2003: 230)
> 120,000	Laqueur (2001: 233)
110,000	Rajca (1992: 129)
100,000	Pressac (2000)
80,000	Kranz (2003: 222)
< 72,000	USHMM (Web 2015)
60,000	Shermer and Grobman (2000: 128)
59,000	Kranz (2007)
> 50,000	Hilberg (2003: 1320)
(Jews only, unless stated otherwise)	

Again recall that, for present purposes, I am assuming a figure of 75,000 Jews.

---

[145] 30 August 1944 (p. 1).

Perhaps due to the relatively low Jewish death toll, Majdanek was, for many years, largely ignored by researchers on both sides of the Great Debate. Until recently the best traditionalist source was probably Marszalek's *Majdanek: The Concentration Camp in Lublin* (1986), even though it is now nearly 30 years old. In 2007 camp director Tomasz Kranz released a new book, *Extermination of Jews at the Majdanek Concentration Camp*; this now serves as the work of reference, even though it is hard to obtain and rarely cited by our orthodox historians.

On the revisionist side, we have one recent and detailed study—Graf and Mattogno's *Concentration Camp Majdanek* (2012).

As for the anti-revisionists, only Shermer and Grobman (2000) address the camp in any detail, and even then in only five pages. Zimmerman (2000) virtually ignores it. Longerich (2010) grants it scattered reference on six or seven pages; the same holds for Bartov's (2015) anthology.

Regarding the killings, Majdanek was unique in four respects. First, unlike the four previous camps, there were in fact a number of non-Jewish deaths there—some 19,000, according to Kranz (2007: 107). Second, a large portion of the total Jewish fatalities is claimed to have occurred on a single day: 3 November 1943, when 18,000 were allegedly machine-gunned in ditches.[146] Third, fully 60 percent of the victims died of natural causes, including disease, exhaustion, and privation; the remaining 40 percent died from gassings or shootings.[147] And fourth, the gas chambers allegedly operated on both Zyklon B and carbon monoxide (CO)—the only camp in which this was done.[148]

When the above specifics are combined into a death matrix, a few points immediately stand out. Consider Kranz's estimate of 59,000 Jewish victims. In order to accept his number, we need to know how and when these people died. But even he gives us a rapidly shifting story. In 2003 he wrote that "60 percent of the victims in Majdanek died as a result of starvation, forced labor, maltreatment, and illness" (2003: 230). Assuming this holds for the Jews as well, it means some 35,000 died of these natural causes, while the remaining 24,000 died by gassing or shooting. But if 18,000 Jews were shot

---

[146] See Kranz (2007: 108). This event, commonly known as *Operation Erntefest* ('Harvest Festival'), has a relatively fixed death toll among the various sources, varying only by 1,000 or so. All accounts of this event are based on the 1947 testimony of an imprisoned SS officer, Erich Mussfeldt. Graf and Mattogno reprint an extended excerpt (2012: 214-223), and by analyzing it conclude that the testimony is incoherent and contradictory, and thus likely coerced. Incidentally, one wonders why it is the *revisionists* who give us these details, and not their opponents? Traditionalists seem to prefer to simply repeat, in a parrot-like fashion, the general account of such an event without giving the reader the whole story, and without subjecting it to any critical scrutiny.

[147] *Encyclopedia of the Holocaust* (1990: 939). See also Kranz (2003: 230).

[148] Kranz, incidentally, has abandoned all claims about homicidal Zyklon use at the camp. He now argues that only CO gassing occurred.

during the 'Harvest Festival,' this leaves only, at most, (24,000 – 18,000) = 6,000 Jews who were gassed or shot prior to that date.

But Kranz could evidently see that this caused a problem for the conventional view, which demands large numbers of Jews gassed at each of the six death camps. If only 6,000 were 'shot or gassed,' and if, say, one or two thousand of these were shot, this leaves only perhaps 4,000 that were gassed—unacceptably low for our traditional historians. This is likely why, in 2007, Kranz backpedaled. He now makes no claims about gassings versus shootings or other causes. He simply says, "We do not, after all, have at our disposal any data documenting deaths by dividing them into various forms of killing" (2007: 104). In a footnote he adds that "estimates concerning the numbers of mass prisoner shootings and gassing... are very general estimates and are not supported by source research." Therefore such figures "should be considered of little use." In other words, we know *almost nothing* about *how* the Jews died; it is all speculation. But if this is true, how can he be so confident of his 59,000 figure?

Body disposal is also a huge question. There are highly contradictory reports of temporary crematoria, pit burnings, and mass burials in nearby forests—such that it is impossible to make a coherent estimate of this aspect of the camp. Even Graf and Mattogno do not provide clear information on this matter. But this is perhaps unimportant, given the relatively low numbers involved.

Staying with my initial death estimate of 75,000, and assuming no shooting deaths apart from the November massacre (highly unlikely), implies the provisional death matrix shown in Table 25.

We see that the average daily gassing total was never over 70, and for most of the life of camp was under 35. These facts are utterly incompatible with such claims as:

- "seven gas chambers," in camouflaged buildings.
- "ever-increasing quantities of Zyklon B" for "disinfection" (that is, gassings).
- "continual efforts were made to maximize [gas chamber] capacity... Even the space between the ceiling and the heads of standing people was used."
- "up to 1,000 Jews a day were being suffocated in the gas chambers."

—all from the *Holocaust Encyclopedia* (2001: 233). They seem to be anxious to play up the gas chambers far beyond that which is warranted. But then again, gas chambers are at the core of the traditionalist account. Thus, even though the role of the alleged gas chambers was minimal at best, it is instructive to briefly examine some of the relevant issues in order to see how the current story has evolved, and to introduce the (alleged) basic operation of such chambers.

Table 25: Death Matrix for Majdanek

By Category	1942 S	O	N	D	Total 1942	1943 J	F	M	A	M	J	J	A	S	O	N	Total 1943	Total
* natural causes:	3,000	3,000	3,500	3,500	13,000	3,000	3,000	3,000	3,000	3,000	3,000	3,000	3,000	3,000	3,000		30,000	43,000
* shooting:					0											18,000	18,000	18,000
* gassing:	500	500	500	500	2,000	1,000	1,000	1,000	2,000	2,000	1,500	1,500	500	500		12,000	14,000
Total Deaths:	3,500	3,500	4,000	4,000	15,000	4,000	4,000	4,000	5,000	5,000	4,500	4,500	4,500	3,500	3,500	18,000	60,000	75,000
# of gas chambers:	2	3	3	3		?	?	?	?	?	?	?	?	?	?			
gassings/day (total):	16.7	16.7	16.7	16.7		33.3	33.3	33.3	66.7	66.7	50.0	50.0	16.7	16.7	16.7			

Majdanek is further unique because its primary gas-chamber facility—so-called Bath and Disinfection I—is the best-preserved of any camp. Thus we have an unprecedented opportunity to directly examine the conditions of these chambers and their alleged operation. The fact that this is also the camp where homicidal gassings have been reduced down to near-insignificance is perhaps no coincidence. The more facts we can confirm, the more the revisionist claims are generally substantiated—and the lower the death toll.

The Seven Chambers of Majdanek

As this is the first time I have addressed in detail the question of Zyklon B gassing, I need to make a few general points about such chambers.

1. No one disputes that there were Zyklon chambers. Revisionists say they were strictly for delousing clothing and personal items. Traditionalists say they also served a homicidal role.
2. Zyklon is very poisonous and must be handled with great care. For delousing clothing it was sufficient to sprinkle the pellets on the chamber floor—while wearing a gas mask—and walk out of the room. After a two-hour gassing period, the room would have to be aired out, either with an air circulation system or by simply (and cautiously!) opening the doors and windows, and waiting several more hours. Only then would the chamber be safe to enter, and clothes retrieved.
3. Homicidal Zyklon gassing would have been very different. First the chamber would be packed solid with people, and the door locked, safely holding in a potentially panicking crowd. Then there would have to be some means to introduce the poison—which, practically speaking, could only happen by (a) piping in the gas via some ductwork, or (b) inserting the Zyklon pellets directly, through some opening in the wall or ceiling. Despite rumors of gas coming in through showerheads, no serious researcher on either side accepts this today. Hence, by common agreement, the pellets were directly introduced into the chamber.
4. Mass gassing requires *rapid killing*, and *rapid ventilation*. Otherwise the entire purpose is defeated. Rapid killing requires high—that is, immediately fatal—doses of Zyklon, quickly diffused throughout the packed chamber. Afterward, a powerful forced-air ventilation system, with fresh-air intake, would be needed to quickly clear the gas.
5. Zyklon pellets continue to release cyanide for as long as two hours. Even if, hypothetically, the victims were dead in five minutes, and thus ready for removal, the pellets in the room would still be releasing

their poisonous gas. Even after one hour (at room temperature), only 75 percent of the gas would have been evaporated.[149] Thus even a ventilation system would not be truly effective, since, until scooped up and contained, the pellets would continue to emit the gas. This is a huge practical problem, one that none of our orthodox historians addresses.

6. Any extensive use of Zyklon leaves a very durable telltale marker: intense blue coloration or staining of the wall surfaces, known as 'Prussian blue.'

The standard account of the seven Majdanek gas chambers originated from a Soviet-Polish report of August 1944. Apparently this had gone unpublished until being reprinted in Graf and Mattogno (pp. 119-128). It describes in detail the whole alleged gassing process, using both CO and Zyklon. The former was said to kill its victims in 5 to 10 minutes;[150] the latter in just 3 to 5 minutes.[151] Of course, the Soviets displayed a marked penchant for exaggeration, falsification of evidence, and revenge, so we should hardly expect much accuracy in such a report.[152] Yet it stands as the basis for the whole traditionalist view. As recently as 2003, Kranz wrote, "It appears most likely that altogether seven gas chambers were constructed, of which three were used for mass killing..." (2003: 229).

The alleged seven gas chambers fall into three groupings, according to the commonly accepted numbering:

➢ Chambers 1–4: in the building Bath and Disinfection I ("B&D I," a.k.a. Barrack 41)
➢ Chambers 5–6: in the building Barrack 28 (near the so-called old crematorium)
➢ Chamber 7: in the "new crematorium"

As homicidal mass-gassing facilities, they all have serious problems. I will take them in reverse order, leaving the most important for last.

---

[149] See the vaporization chart in Rudolf (2003c: 352).
[150] However, this is presumed at a stated concentration level of 0.5%, which is completely false. Even a 1% level would take 30 minutes to kill, perhaps an hour—see discussion in Chapter 5. The Flanagan study (1978) suggests that even a 5% concentration might take 20 minutes or more. Depending on the oxygen content, at 0.5% CO the victims could be expected to survive for an hour or more.
[151] Assuming a concentration of 0.3 mg per liter, or, 0.03%.
[152] Notably, even the Soviets, those masters of hyperbole, presumed no more than 6 bodies per square meter of chamber area. Compare this to the conservative number of 10 per square meter allowed by the revisionists, and figures of 20, 30, or even 40 per square meter promoted by the traditionalists.

Chamber 7: Located in the new crematorium. Area of 35 square meters.

The "new" crematorium dates to about September 1943, very late in the life of the camp. It held five single-muffle furnaces.[153] Each muffle is designed to burn one body at a time, and therefore the whole facility could nominally burn five at once. Burning time is a big issue in the debate; revisionists say "one body per hour," while their opponents claim an astonishing 5 or 10 per hour—more on this in the next chapter.

Claims of homicidal use for this chamber have largely been abandoned, even by the traditionalists. Pressac (1990) explains the situation concisely:

> The seventh alleged execution gas chamber is located in the new crematorium... The acting Director of the [Majdanek] museum has informed this author that this gas chamber saw only little—really very, very little—use, which means, plainly speaking, that it was not used at all. This fiction is maintained in order to preserve the popular belief that a crematorium must necessarily have included a gas chamber...
>
> If anyone had wanted to kill human beings with Zyklon B in this locale, its enclave-like location inside the building... would perforce have required an artificial ventilation system, of which, however, there is not a trace to be found.

Graf and Mattogno add: one finds "not even the slightest trace of Prussian Blue"; there is a crude post-war hole cut in the ceiling, in the attempt to create a means for introducing the Zyklon; there are open (unsealed) peep-holes leading into the adjoining mortuary room, which would have made gassing impossible. Notably, Shermer and Grobman (2000) completely ignore this chamber.

Chambers 5 and 6: Located in Barrack 28. Area of 71 sq m each.

Barrack 28 is described as a wooden structure, supposedly located 150 meters from the original ('old') crematorium, which consisted of two mobile single-muffle furnaces. According to Pressac, the gas-chamber building reportedly functioned on both carbon monoxide and Zyklon. He claimed that the structure was still extant, and proceeded to explain that this building, with its numerous windows, would have been utterly unusable as a gassing facility.[154] There seems to be no agreement on exactly where this Barrack 28 was located, nor is there any physical evidence of such a structure anywhere near its alleged location. Graf and Mattogno state, flat out, that all claims about the chambers in this barrack "are devoid of any historical foundation"

---

[153] A 'muffle' being the space or cavity into which the corpse is placed; also called a 'retort.'

[154] Graf and Mattogno correct him, stating that Barrack 28 no longer exists; hence we do not know to which building Pressac refers.

(p. 140). Rudolf (2005: 301) concurs: "no documentary or material trace exists of them." It seems likely that 'Barrack 28' was an invention of the Soviets.

Now to the alleged main gassing facility at Majdanek. As noted above, this building, fortunately, is almost completely intact today, and hence available for detailed examination—see Illustration 7.

Chamber 4 (room C): The largest of the four gassing rooms in B&D I (75 square meters). Allegedly used Zyklon only, no carbon monoxide. Contains an original, large glass window. Shows intense blue coloration on the walls and ceiling. But by common agreement on both sides, this room was used *only* for delousing of clothing. Reasons: (1) window could have easily been broken by victims; (2) no rapid ventilation system; (3) one door opens in and cannot lock; (4) ceiling openings were only added when the facility was converted to a hot-air delousing facility (no blue stains), hence were used for ventilation rather than insertion of Zyklon B. As Shermer and Grobman admit, "casual inspection of [this] large gas chamber room shows that its use was for delousing clothing and blankets, not for mass extermination…" (p. 162).

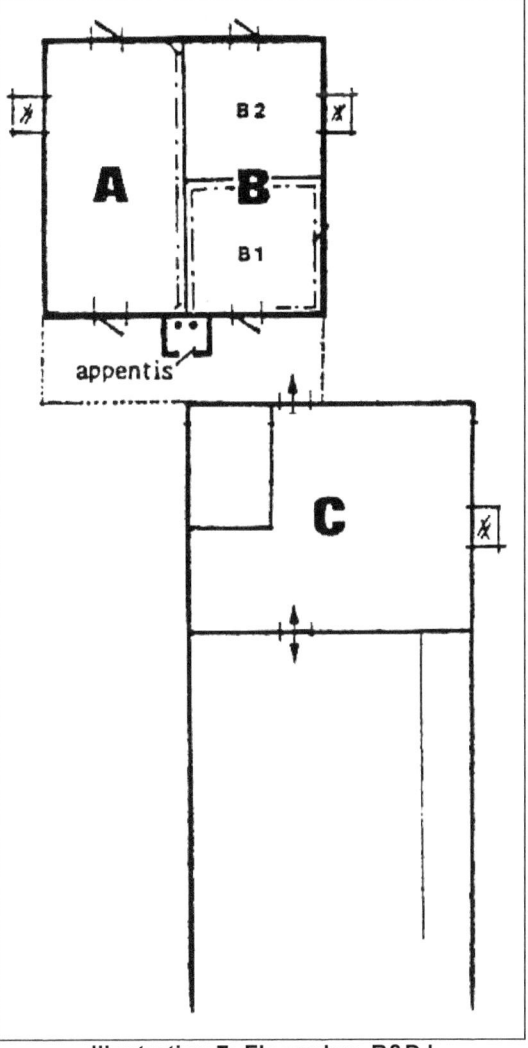

Illustration 7: Floor plan, B&D I

We are left then with the last three chambers, located at the rear of B&D I. Shermer and Grobman claim that they were built "for the express purpose of gassing prisoners" (p. 163). Pressac offers a different story. According to him they were all originally hot-air delousing chambers. They were then converted for use with Zyklon—still primarily for delousing—and later still to homicidal use with carbon monoxide.

The basic statistics on the three rooms are as follows:

<u>Chamber 1</u> (room B1): 17 sq m. Blue staining (slight). Lockable steel door. Alleged Zyklon and CO. Small (unsealable) window. Small, crude postwar holes in ceiling. No ventilation.

<u>Chamber 2</u> (room B2): 17 sq m. Blue staining (slight). Entrance via rear. Alleged Zyklon. Small, crude postwar holes in ceiling. No ventilation.

<u>Chamber 3</u> (room A): 35 sq m. Blue staining. Lockable steel door. Alleged Zyklon and CO. No ceiling holes.

Regarding homicidal Zyklon use, Pressac says: "It is difficult to say whether [these] rooms... were used as homicidal hydrogen cyanide gas chambers. This question remains open" (in Graf and Mattogno: 143). All three lacked wartime ceiling holes, which would have been essential for homicidal gassing. Pressac concludes:

> I do not believe that Section A [Chamber 3] could have served for homicidal Zyklon B gassings. In rooms B1 and B2 [Chambers 1 and 2] this seems to have been technically possible, but it is unlikely that these facilities were really used for this purpose. (in *ibid.*)

Graf and Mattogno add that the Prussian blue staining in Chambers 1 and 2 is relatively slight, and most likely resulted from diffusion from Chamber 3 rather than through use in the rooms themselves. In addition, neither chamber had a system of forced ventilation for rapid clearing of the toxic gas.

Therefore, homicidal Zyklon use seems largely ruled out for all three chambers. This leaves the alleged carbon monoxide poisoning. Rather than use a diesel engine as in the Reinhardt camps, the method at Majdanek is claimed to have been bottled (liquefied) carbon monoxide. This in itself is problematic, since bottled gas was very expensive, and the Germans had far better and cheaper means at their disposal—such as the producer-gas systems discussed in Chapter 5. Still, the fact remains that two of the rooms—Chambers 1 and 3—have perforated piping running around their base. They were connected to, allegedly, "CO gas cylinders" located in a tiny cell just outside the rooms ("appentis" in Illustration 7).[155]

The Soviet report of 1944 mentions that "five dark red bottles" were found in another location altogether ("Barrack 52"), labeled as carbon monoxide—though why these had any connection to Barrack 41, that is, Bath and Disinfection I, is left totally unexplained. Two of these five were then

---

[155] See also the documentary by Hunt, *The Majdanek Gas Chamber Myth* (on Youtube).

placed in the small cell outside Chambers 1 and 3; the other three have mysteriously vanished. But there is a big problem here: the two bottles located there today "are engraved with the label CO_2, i.e. carbon dioxide." Unlike carbon monoxide, carbon dioxide is not poisonous.[156]

Why would carbon dioxide be connected to rooms 1 and 3? Graf and Mattogno offer an explanation: The increasing number of natural deaths periodically overloaded the crematoria, and required the temporary storage of bodies. Bottled CO_2, when injected into an enclosed room, had two beneficial effects: it cooled the room slightly, and it displaced some oxygen, sufficient to delay somewhat the decomposition of the bodies. In fact, fruit growers use this technique all the time when they want to store fresh fruit over the winter; they use large carbon-dioxide coolers. Thus Chambers 1 and 3 could have functioned as temporary overflow morgues. When no longer needed as such, they could be returned to their original use, namely disinfestation with Zyklon B.

This furthermore helps to explain witness accounts. The rooms had dead bodies (true), they were 'gassed' (true, after they were already dead), and the bodies were eventually burned in crematoria (true). The individual facts are true, but they do not add up to 'homicidal gas chambers.'

Thus there is good reason to doubt *any* kind of mass gassing, by *any* means, in any of the "seven gas chambers" of Majdanek. Now, of course this does not and cannot rule out sporadic attempts to kill handfuls of people with gas. But the whole notion of "industrial, production-line gassing" at this camp seems to be completely out of the question. Conventional historian Tregenza sums it up:

> Majdanek was not a major gassing camp on the order of camps like Auschwitz. At Majdanek gassings were rather irregular. ... I hesitate to say that there was a regular gassing program there. (in Shermer and Grobman, p. 164)

To which the revisionists might add: "to say the least."

Unlike the other camps, revisionists have a reasonably precise estimate of Jewish deaths at Majdanek. In spite of traditionalist estimates claiming

---

[156] A close-up photo of the cylinder is available here: http://www.fpp.co.uk/docs/Irving/RadDi/2011/100911.html. The quote is from Graf and Mattogno (2012: 145). This is not to say that people cannot die from excess CO_2. As discussed in Chapter 7, breathing air in an enclosed space rapidly converts oxygen to carbon dioxide; this situation becomes fatal when CO_2 reaches 10 percent. However, simply squirting carbon dioxide into a room filled with people has no immediate effect. This gas could be used to accelerate asphyxiation, perhaps, through some complex process of pumping out normal air and substituting it with CO_2. But (a) there are easier ways to asphyxiate people, and (b) there is no evidence that such an approach was used. Interestingly, the Web site www.judaism.about.com shows a photograph of a sign with the cryptic wording "carbon oxide"—as if the kind of oxide was irrelevant.

360,000 or more fatalities at the camp, existing documentation points to a much smaller and more precise figure: 42,200. Of this total, Graf and Mattogno (2012: 265) calculate that 66 percent, or some 27,900, were Jews.

The bottom line is that Majdanek has sunk to irrelevance in the larger Holocaust story. The death of less than 28,000 Jews would come to about 0.4 percent of the '6 million,' an utterly inconsequential amount. Thus it is not without good reason that we hear very little about the camp any more from our traditional historians.

Chapter 10: Auschwitz

Sometimes it seems, with the Great Debate, to be feast or famine. After struggling to find traditional replies to the serious revisionist problems raised regarding the other five death camps, we come now to Auschwitz. Here we find a veritable deluge of information. As the biggest and baddest of all the camps, everyone's eyes are on Auschwitz. It is here that traditionalism is most self-confident, and most explicit. They *know* what happened there. They have hundreds of witnesses. They have photographs. Several key buildings, and some very relevant ruins, still exist. Literally thousands of books have been written on, or touch on, this camp. Here is the strongest evidence for the Holocaust. Some say the entire Holocaust story stands or falls on the shoulders of Auschwitz.

Precisely for this reason, some of revisionism's biggest guns have targeted this camp. They know that by attacking Auschwitz's credibility the whole edifice starts to quiver, and perhaps eventually falls. As before, the revisionists have strong counterarguments to the conventional story, though in this case almost every one is met with an attempted reply. Thus it is here that we have, at last, the makings of a real debate.

In a sense it is futile to attempt to address all the charges and counter-charges regarding Auschwitz in a single chapter. Doing justice to both sides would take an entire book in itself. Nevertheless, I will offer here those arguments that, in my judgment, are the strongest on each side. Secondary issues will be noted where possible, and reference made to other sources for follow-up by the reader as appropriate.

The Essentials of the Auschwitz Story—The Main Camp

As with the Holocaust as a whole, it is best to start with a quick overview of the basic facts. To reiterate several points made early on, there were three main areas of the Auschwitz complex:

- ➤ Auschwitz I (main camp, or *Stammlager*), opened in May 1940. Served as administrative center.

- Auschwitz II (Birkenau), opened in late 1941. Alleged to have served as extermination camp.
- Auschwitz III (Monowitz), opened in May 1942. Served as labor camp. Largely irrelevant for the Holocaust debate.

Auschwitz I existed for some sixteen months before the first alleged experimental Zyklon gassing occurred there, on 3 September 1941. Owing to the 'success' of this experiment, systematic gassings began there in February 1942. A single gas-chamber room of 78 square meters in area was used. Bodies were disposed of in the main camp's lone crematorium, 'Krema 1.'

Note that, formally speaking, a crematorium is simply a facility for incinerating dead bodies. It has no necessary connection to either gas chambers or any evil intent. Likewise, a 'gas chamber' could be any room with a means for entrapping people and subjecting them to lethal quantities of a poisonous gas; it has no necessary connection to a crematorium. Traditionalists claim, however, that the Nazis wanted to streamline the whole process by combining gas chambers and cremation furnaces in a single building. Hence all five Auschwitz crematoria, explained below, are also alleged to have had gas-chamber rooms. Revisionists argue that in the case of Kremas 2 & 3, the so-called gas chamber was simply a morgue or a temporary storage room for corpses. Such rooms would, of course, have been necessary for any building that was incinerating large numbers of bodies. In the case of Kremas 4 & 5, revisionists argue that the claimed gas-chamber rooms were either disinfestation or shower rooms.

Alleged gassings in the main camp averaged roughly 2,000 per month for most of 1942. The chamber room itself was about 78 square meters in area. If we assume that such a chamber could hold ten people per square meter, each gassing could then kill up to 780 people. Hence only two or three gassings occurred per month, on the orthodox view. In total, some 19,000–20,000 Jews were killed that year.

Perhaps due to the development of Birkenau, the main camp effectively ceased gassing by December. Sometime thereafter, the alleged gas chamber was converted into an air-raid shelter. The building survived the war largely intact.

In the 1950s and 1960s, Krema 1 was reconstructed for public display in order to mimic the claimed original design. Visits to the camp today are focused on Krema 1 as 'the' gassing facility of Auschwitz—as explained below, the Birkenau crematoria are in ruins, and hence not easily displayable. Unfortunately, many aspects of Krema 1's rooms were changed to accommodate visitor expectations and official historiography, and consequently the facility as it exists today is significantly different than the original—see

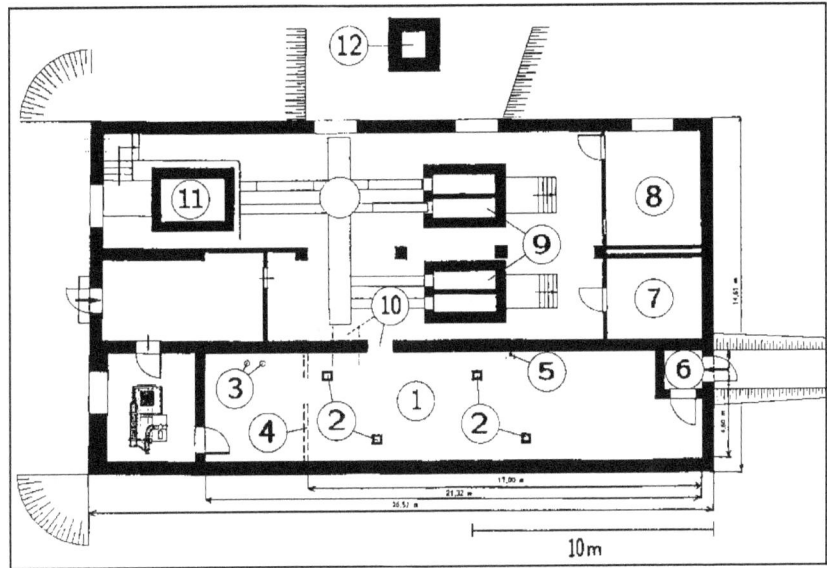

Illustration 8: Floor plan of Crematorium I at Auschwitz I/Main Camp today, after postwar alterations ("reconstruction"), following Pressac (1989: 159); taken from, Rudolf (2011: 76); numbers added as follows: 1: "gas chamber"; 2: postwar-made Zyklon B introduction holes; 3: toilet drains; 4: former partition morgue-washroom; 5: ventilation chimney of former air raid shelter; 6: air lock, today referred to as victims' entryway; 7: urns, 8: coke; 9: badly reconstructed cremation furnaces; 10: postwar-added entry to furnace room; dotted lines: location of original entry; 11: remains of former third furnace; 12: postwar-constructed, detached chimney.

Illustration 8. Sadly, it is not made clear to visitors that they are seeing a *reconstructed, redesigned* gas chamber; though, if they ask, they are told—if they ask.

In 1995, French anti-revisionist Eric Conan wrote:

> [S]everal buildings... were reconstructed with major errors and presented as authentic. [These include] gas chambers for delousing, which were sometimes presented as homicidal gas chambers. ... The example of crematorium 1 is typical. ... Everything there is false... [including] the dimensions of the gas chamber, the location of the doors, the openings for the introduction of Zyklon B, the furnaces [and] the height of the chimneys. ... For the moment, this remains as it is, and nothing is said to the visitors. That is too complicated. (cited in Rudolf 2011: 59)

Conan exaggerates—not *everything* about it is false, but it is deceptive in important ways:

> The current gas-chamber room is about 20 percent larger than the original morgue room.

Chart 10: Camp Area (Acres)

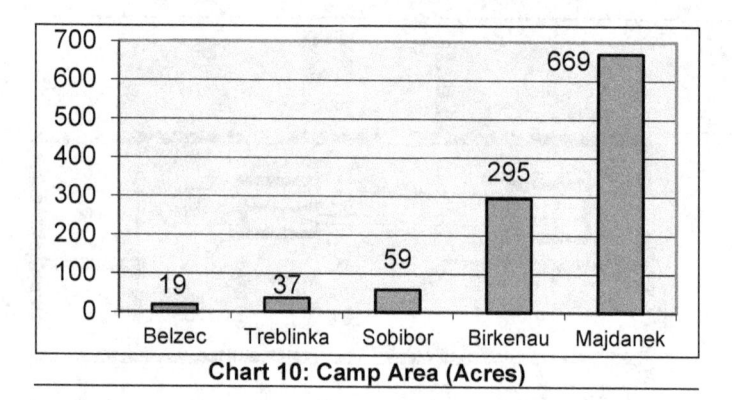

Camp	Acres
Belzec	19
Treblinka	37
Sobibor	59
Birkenau	295
Majdanek	669

- An exterior entrance door to the gas chamber, presently labeled "victim's entrance," was only added during the conversion to an air-raid shelter; it was not there during the earlier, allegedly homicidal, phase. Notably, an interior entrance door would have been highly impractical for mass murder.
- Entrance to the furnace room is in the wrong location, and has no door at all.
- Reconstructed furnaces have no exhaust flues and no hearth.
- Newly built chimney is not connected to the furnaces.
- Most importantly, four 'Zyklon-introduction holes' were added to the roof; they were never in either the original morgue or the air-raid shelter.[157]

Floor plans of the original building layout and the air-raid shelter renovation are given in Rudolf (2011: 198, 199).

Though the alleged gassings in Krema 1 ended in late 1942, the crematorium furnaces—six muffles in total—continued to dispose of bodies well into 1943. Over its functional life the crematorium incinerated some 65,000 Jewish corpses, on the traditional view. This comes to about 3,600 per month, or 120 per day on average.

Birkenau—Alleged Extermination Camp

Birkenau, or Auschwitz II, is the centerpiece of the Auschwitz Holocaust story; it was the site of nearly all the alleged 1 million Jewish deaths. It was a large camp, though not as big as Majdanek, and held perhaps 150,000 people at its peak. The comparative areas of the extermination camps (excluding Chelmno) are shown in Chart 10.

---

[157] There were four small holes originally, but these were not added until the air raid shelter renovation, and in any case are inappropriately placed to serve as Zyklon holes.

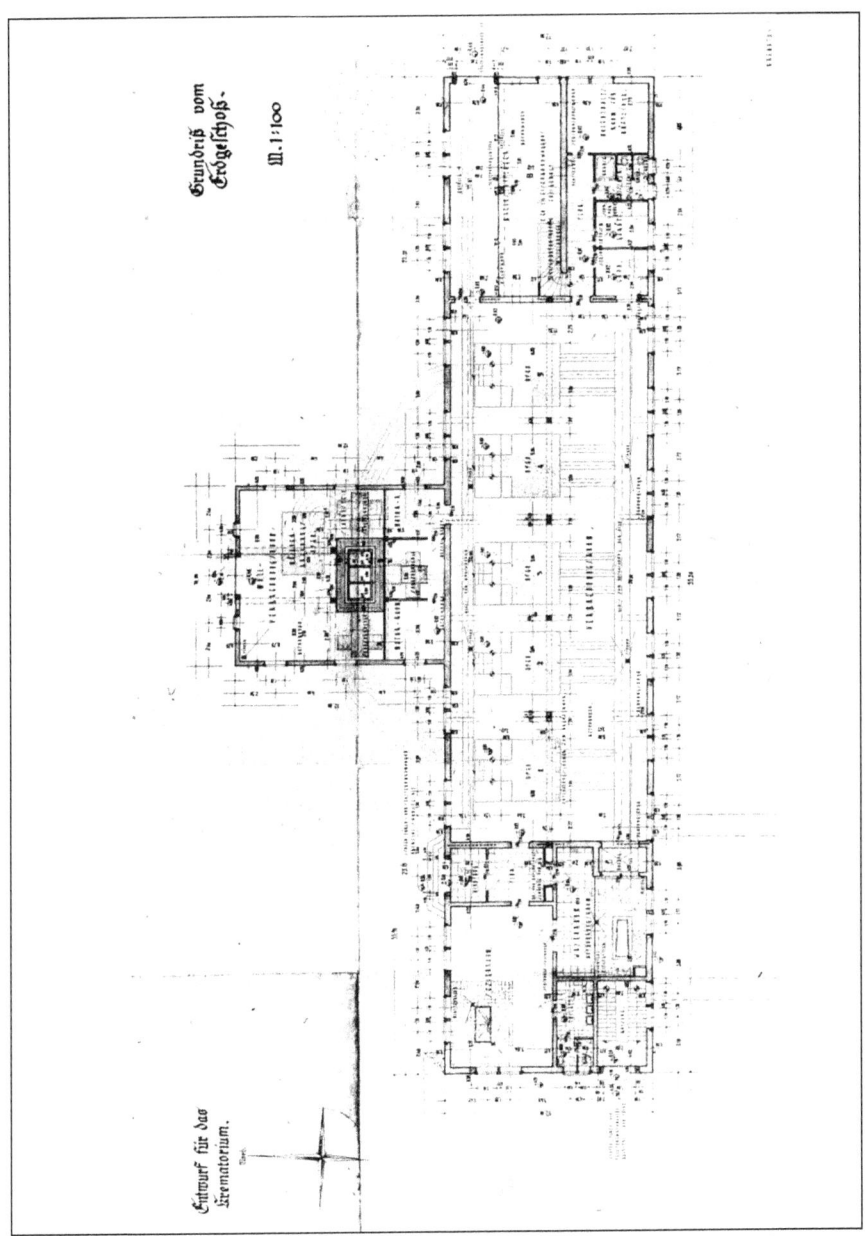

Illustration 9: Project of the new crematorium at Auschwitz (future Kremas 2/3 at Birkenau). Floor plan of the first floor. Drawing 933 by the Central Construction Office of 19 January 1942. Source: Archives of the Auschwitz Museum, negative no. 20818/4. The large hall in the center is the furnace hall with five triple-muffle furnaces, fed by a corpse introduction cart running on 3×5 set of rails. Taken from Mattogno (2015: vol. 2, Doc. 222)

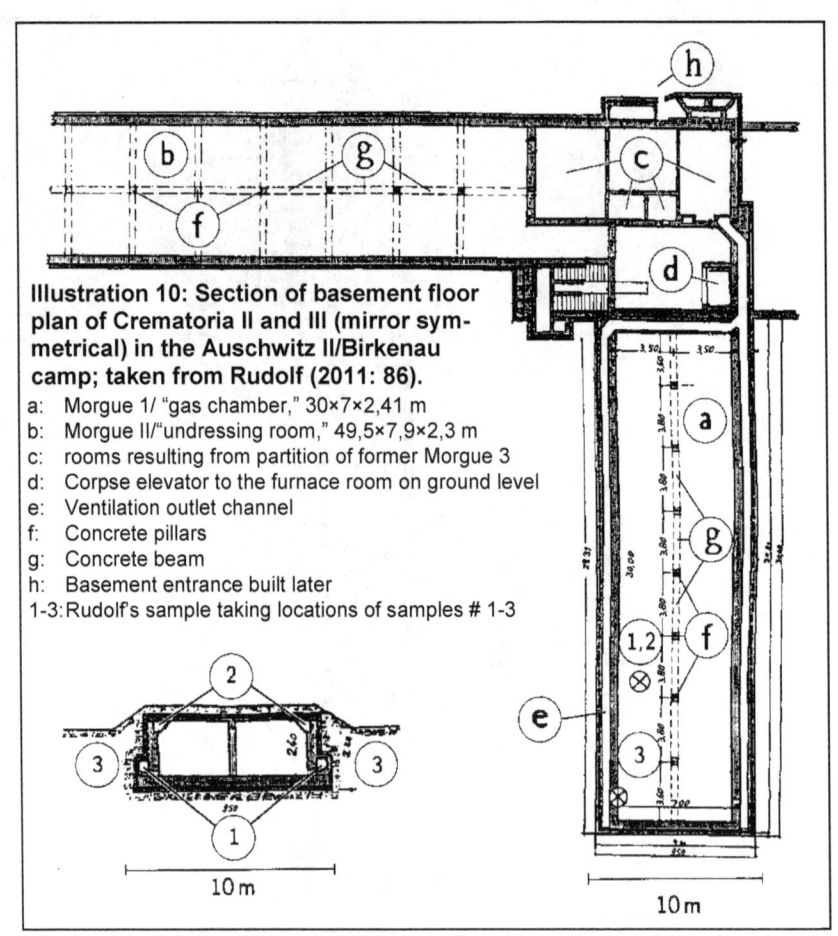

Illustration 10: Section of basement floor plan of Crematoria II and III (mirror symmetrical) in the Auschwitz II/Birkenau camp; taken from Rudolf (2011: 86).
a: Morgue 1/ "gas chamber," 30×7×2,41 m
b: Morgue II/"undressing room," 49,5×7,9×2,3 m
c: rooms resulting from partition of former Morgue 3
d: Corpse elevator to the furnace room on ground level
e: Ventilation outlet channel
f: Concrete pillars
g: Concrete beam
h: Basement entrance built later
1-3: Rudolf's sample taking locations of samples # 1-3

Illustration 11: Cross section through Morgue 1 (alleged "gas chamber") of Crematoria II and III (mirror symmetrical) in Auschwitz II/Birkenau camp; taken from Rudolf (2011: 86).
1: Ventilation outlet; 2: ventilation inlet; 3: soil

Even according to orthodoxy, Birkenau was not originally planned to be an extermination camp; it gradually "evolved" into that role. The successful gassings in the main camp encouraged development of a similar facility, and so in early 1942 two old farmhouses, or bunkers, at Birkenau were selected as preliminary gas chambers. The first of these, Bunker 1 (also known as the "red" bunker), with chamber area of 60 square meters, went into operation in February. The larger Bunker 2 ("white"), 90 square meters in area, came online in July. By the end of 1942, Bunker 1 had allegedly exterminated 50,000 Jews; Bunker 2, about 90,000.

The rapid accumulation of dead bodies quickly exceeded Krema 1's incineration capacity. For a while, bodies were buried on-site—to be burned

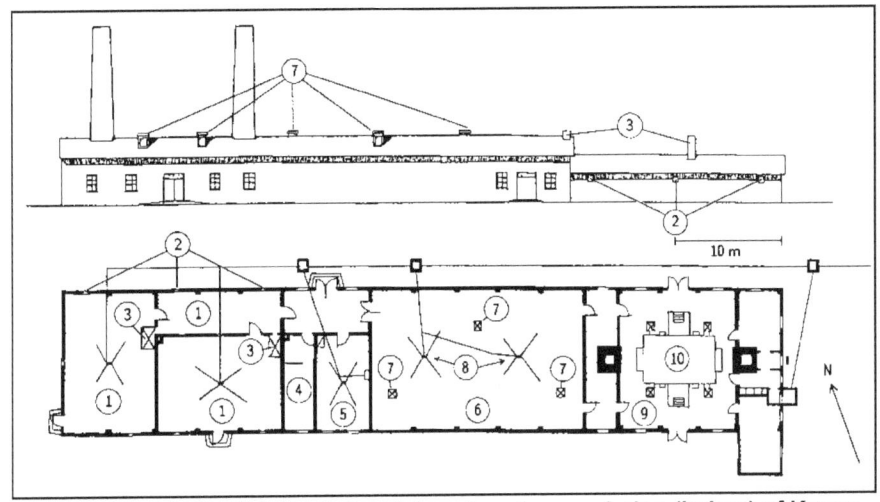

Illustration 12: North lateral view (above) and ground plan (below) of Krema 4 and/or 5 (mirror image) in Auschwitz II/Birkenau camp. (cleaned-up plans as they can be found in Pressac (1989: 401), taken from Rudolf (2011: 459); numbers added as follows:
1: Alleged "gas chambers"; 2: Alleged Zyklon B introduction hatches; 3: Heating stoves; 4: Coke room; 5: Doctor's office; 6: Morgue; 7: Ventilation chimneys; 8: Drains; 9: Furnace room; 10: Cremation furnaces

in late 1942—but more important, the decision was made to construct four new crematoria at Birkenau, in two phases. Phase 1 consisted of a single new crematorium, Krema 2, but soon thereafter a further decision was made to construct three additional facilities: a mirror-image twin of Krema 2—now designated Krema 3—and another mirror-image pair of buildings of a different, simpler design, Kremas 4 and 5. On the standard view, the first two were designed as normal crematoria, and only later evolved into their homicidal role. The latter two were designed as homicidal facilities from the start, complete with dedicated gas chambers. The layout plans of Kremas 2/3 and 4/5 are shown in Illustrations 9-12.

Allegedly, all four new crematoria had internal rooms that served as homicidal gas chambers; this was intended to streamline and "industrialize" the killing process. Kremas 2 and 3 each had a single, large underground room with an area of 210 square meters that operated as the gas chamber. Kremas 4 and 5 had three smaller rooms each, totaling 236 square meters per building. If these latter two were truly "dedicated homicidal facilities," then this larger gassing capacity would make sense. Oddly, though, the *cremation* capacity of these two was smaller than that of the former pair, by nearly half: a total of fifteen muffles in each of Kremas 2 and 3, compared to just eight muffles in Kremas 4 and 5. And cremation capacity was the constraining factor, as I will explain. This is only the first of several inconsistencies.

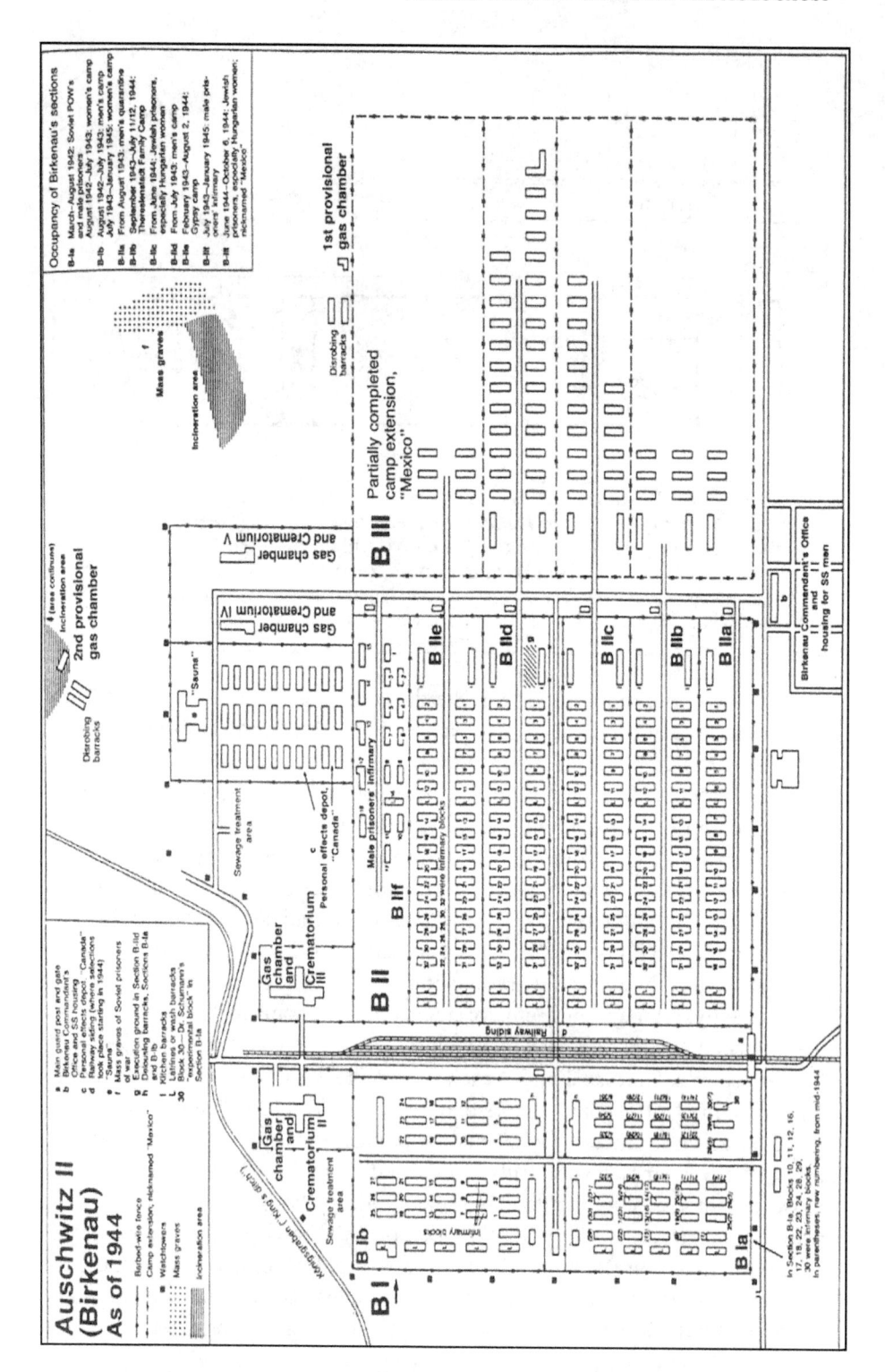

Auschwitz II (Birkenau) As of 1944

Occupancy of Birkenau's sections

B-Ia: March–August 1942: Soviet POWs and male prisoners
August 1942–July 1943: women's camp
B-Ib: August 1942–July 1943: men's camp; July 1943–January 1945: women's camp
B-IIa: From August 1943: men's quarantine
B-IIb: September 1943–July 11/12, 1944: Theresienstadt Family Camp
B-IIc: From June 1944: Jewish prisoners, especially Hungarian women
B-IId: From July 1943: men's camp
B-IIe: February 1943–August 2, 1944: Gypsy camp
B-IIf: July 1943–January 1945: male prisoners' infirmary
B-III: June 1944–October 6, 1944: Jewish prisoners, especially Hungarian women; nicknamed "Mexico"

1st provisional gas chamber
2nd provisional gas chamber

Mass graves
Incineration area
Disrobing barracks

Gas chamber and Crematorium V
Gas chamber and Crematorium IV
"Sauna"
Personal effects depot, "Canada"
Male prisoners' infirmary

B IIf B IIe B IId B IIc B IIb B IIa
B III — Partially completed camp extension, "Mexico"

Gas chamber and Crematorium III
Gas chamber and Crematorium II

B II
Sewage treatment area
Railway siding
Kitchen barracks
Latrines or wash barracks
Block 30 – Dr. Schumann's "experimental block" in Section B-Ia

B Ib   B Ia
Infirmary blocks

Birkenau Commandant's Office and housing for SS men

a Main guard post and gate
b Birkenau Commandant's Office and SS housing
c Personal effects depot, "Canada"
d Railway siding (where selections took place starting in 1944)
f Mass graves of Soviet prisoners of war
g Execution ground in Section B-IId
L Disrobing barracks, Sections B-Ia and B-Ib
30 Block 30 – Dr. Schumann's "experimental block" in Section B-Ia

In Section B-Ia, Blocks 10, 11, 12, 16, 17, 18, 22, 23, 24, 29, 30 were infirmary blocks.
In parentheses: new numbering, from mid-1944.

--- Camp extension, nicknamed "Mexico"
··· Barbed-wire fence
■ Watchtowers
▨ Mass graves
▦ Incineration area

Illustration 13 (left): Official Auschwitz museum map of of PoW camp Auschwitz II/Birkenau, approximately 2 km north-west of the main camp, construction situation as of late 1944. (taken from http://heatherdune.com/wp-content/uploads/2011/02/birkenau.jpg).

A layout map of Birkenau is shown in Illustration 13. The map shows Kremas 2 and 3 (upper left), Kremas 4 and 5 (upper middle), Bunker 1 at the right ("1st provisional gas chamber") and an approximate location for Bunker 2 ("2nd provisional gas chamber", top middle).

Figures are detailed below, but in terms of relative importance, Kremas 2 and 3, and Bunker 2, together account for nearly 85 percent of the total alleged gassings. The other three facilities—Kremas 4/5 and Bunker 1—are of minor significance to the overall story.

Bunker gassing shut down in early 1943, just as the four new Kremas were ramping up.[158] They (mostly 2 and 3) carried the gassing load for the remainder of that year and through the end of 1944, peaking with the extermination of the Hungarian Jews in the summer of 1944. The last gassings, and last cremations, supposedly occurred in November of that year. The four crematoria were then largely destroyed, although fortunately there are some significant remains of Krema 2. The Soviets captured Auschwitz on 27 January 1945. And some 7,500 inmates—all potential eyewitnesses to mass murder—were inexplicably still there, waiting to tell their stories.

Estimated Fatalities

Death figures vary more dramatically at Auschwitz than at any other camp. At the Nuremberg trials, estimates ranged from 2 million to 8 million. The highest known figure is 9 million, promoted in the 1955 documentary film *Night and Fog*, still widely shown. This incredible overestimate is all the more surprising given that two years earlier, Reitlinger (1953) had completed his initial detailed study of Auschwitz, finding 'only' some 900,000 Jewish deaths there. Over the past couple of decades the trend has clearly been downward, culminating in a widely discussed estimate of just 356,000 gassed Jews—see Meyer (2002). And all this from orthodox writers.

---

[158] Bunker 2 is said to have been reactivated in May 1944 for the alleged murder of the Hungarian Jews—discussed below.

Table 26: Auschwitz: Death Estimates

DEATHS	SOURCE
9,000,000	persons; *Night and Fog* (1955)
8,000,000	persons; French Research Office (1945)
6,000,000	Kremer (in Nyiszli 1951: 1655)
5,000,000	NYT (12 Apr 1945)
4,700,000	*Le Monde* (20 Apr 1978)
4,000,000	persons; Soviet report (1945)
3,000,000	Susskind (1986)
2,000,000	persons; Poliakov (1951: 496)
1,500,000	persons; NYT (27 Jan 2015)
1,352,980	Wellers (1983)
>1,100,000	Yad Vashem (Web 2015)
1,000,000	Hilberg (1961: 572; 2003: 1320)
960,000	USHMM (Web 2015)
< 900,000	persons; Reitlinger (1968: 500)
< 800,000	persons; Pressac (1993: 148)
< 710,000	persons; Pressac (1994: 202)
510,000	persons; Meyer (2002)

(Jews only, unless stated otherwise)

As with the other camps, death figures can be confusing due to the conflation of several categories of deaths, including:

- Jews versus non-Jews.
- "Killed" versus "died" (of natural, non-homicidal causes).
- Gassed versus non-gassed (including shootings, hangings, etc.).

The current orthodox consensus is that a total of 1.1 million people died at Auschwitz, of whom about 1 million (90 percent) were Jews. Of the 1 million Jewish deaths, about 900,000 (90 percent) were by gassing, and 100,000 by other means, including shootings, disease and deprivation.

The Death Matrix

In my master plan of the Holocaust, I assume a round figure of 1 million Jewish Auschwitz deaths. This, again, is consistent with most current thinking. I now attempt to lay out the monthly details of deaths and body disposal, this time including the breakdown by crematorium and bunker, as appropriate. Table 27 covers nearly three full years: January 1942 through December 1944.

Table 27: Death Matrix for Auschwitz from 1942 to 1944 (in thousands)

	1942 J	F	M	A	M	J	J	A	S	O	N	D	Total 1942	1943 J	F	M	A	M	J	J	A	S	O	N	D	Total 1943	1944 J	F	M	A	M	J	J	A	S	O	N	D	Total 1944	Total
Gassing:																																								
Bunker 1 (Red)–60m²:	1	5	5	5	5	5	5	5	5	5	5	4	50	5												10													0	60
Bunker 2 (White)–90m²:					15	15	15	15	15	15	15	15	90	15	15											30					15	20	15						50	170
K1 (78 m²)–1 chamber:	1	2	2	2	2	2	2	2	2	2	2	2	19													0													0	19
K2 (210 m²)–1 chamber:													0			6	6	6	6	6	6	5	5	5	5	51	5	5	5	6	40	90	40	30	18	3	2		244	295
K3 (210 m²)–1 chamber:													0				4	5	5	5	5	5	5			34	5	5	5	6	40	90	40	30	18	3	2		244	278
K4 (236 m²)–3 chambers:													0			3	3	1	1	1	1	1	1	1	1	16	1	2	3	3	5								14	30
K5 (236 m²)–3 chambers:													0				2	2	2	2	2	2	2	2	2	18	2	2	3	3	6	6	6	3	2	1			34	52
Subtotal gassings:	0	2	7	7	7	22	22	22	22	22	22	19	159	20	20	3	11	11	13	14	14	14	13	13	13	159	13	14	16	18	106	206	101	63	38	7	4	0	586	904
Non-Gassing: (shooting, typhus)	2	2	3	3	3	3	3	3	3	3	2	1	31	0	0	3	5	7	4	2	2	2	2	2	2	31	3	3	3	3	4	4	5	4	1	0	0		34	96
TOTAL DEATHS:	2	4	10	10	10	25	25	25	25	25	24	20	190	20	20	6	16	18	17	16	16	16	15	15	15	190	16	17	19	21	110	210	105	68	42	8	4	0	620	1,000
Body Disposal:																																								
Krema 1:	1	1	2	2	2	4	4	4	4	4	4	4	36	8	8	2	3	4	3	3						31													0	67
Krema 2:													0				6	6	5	5	6	6	6	6	6	52	6	6	7	8	9	9	9	9	9	3	2		77	129
Krema 3:													0					5	5	5	6	6	6	6	6	40	6	6	7	8	9	9	9	9	9	3	2		77	117
Krema 4:													0			4	4			4						12													0	12
Krema 5:													0				3	4	4	3	4	4	3	3	3	31	4	5	5	5	6	6	6	6	6	2			51	82
Total in crematoria:	0	1	1	2	2	4	4	4	4	4	4	8	36	8	6	16	18	17	16	16	16	15	15	15	166	16	17	19	21	24	24	24	24	24	8	4		205	407
Buried:	2	3	9	8	8	21	21																																	
Exhumed & pit burned:							27	27	26																															
Direct. gas ch. to pit burn:								21	21	20	12			12	12											24					86	186	81	44	18				415	
Total pit-burnings:	0					48	48	46	12					12	12	0	0	0	0	0	0	0	0	0	0	24	0	0	0	0	86	186	81	44	18	0	0	0	415	593

Both the gassing and body-disposal sections are more detailed than for the other camps, because we have far more specifics for Auschwitz—so much so that I will need to give a relatively in-depth discussion of these two areas separately. I begin with the gas chambers, to be followed by an elaboration of the issues surrounding disposal of the corpses.

Death Matrix (I): The Gas Chambers

First, a little background on the gassing claims in general. The very first mention of 'gassed Jews' seems to have been in April 1942, when the *Times of London* reported on 740 Dutch Jews, "some of whom were used as human subjects for experiments with poison gas" (2 Apr, p. 3). In June of that year, the *New York Times* first reported that 700,000 Polish Jews were killed by the Nazis; to accomplish this evil deed, "every death-dealing method was employed, [including] gas chambers…" (27 Jun, p. 5). Further reference came in the so-called Bund Report of July 1942, but these were evidently the gas vans allegedly used at Chelmno.

Late that year, the first story on "great crematoriums at Oswiencim"—or rather "Oswiecim," the Polish name for Auschwitz—and of "gas chambers" there, appeared in the NYT (25 Nov, p. 10). A follow-up article referred to Belzec and its "lethal gas chambers" (28 Nov, p. 7). Reference to chambers at Treblinka appeared by June 1943; at Majdanek, by July.

Near the end of 1943, the *Black Book of Polish Jewry* again identified Oswiecim as one of the Nazi death camps. In June 1944 the NYT reported that "victims were dragged to gas chambers in the notorious German concentration camps at Birkenau and Oswiecim" (20 Jun, p. 5). One month later they wrote that "cyanide gas caused death" in three to five minutes (3 Jul, p. 3). Also that month the NYT printed an account of an actual delousing procedure at Auschwitz:

> On arrival… the refugees are sorted into batches of 100 or so and taken to "bathing" sheds, where, after having been stripped and completely shaven, they are "deloused" with a solution of strong disinfectant and carbolic acid that burns their skins off. On leaving this shed they pass through a tunnel to a second "enumeration" shed with a typewritten slip bearing a serial number "proving" that they have been deloused. (6 Jul, p. 6)

Apart from the "burning their skin off" remark, this is likely a true account of events.

On 26 November 1944 the first detailed document on Auschwitz was released by two Jewish escapees, Rudolf Vrba and Alfred Wetzler. Today this report is known variously as the Vrba-Wetzler Report, the War Refugee Board Report, or the Auschwitz Protocols. According to Zimmerman (2000: 82), "The authors described the actual gassing procedures which, [however,] they never personally observed, but learned about from other prisoners…" The report opens with a firsthand account of a conventional delousing operation, followed by a series of extremely precise details about various camp activities. Much of the report has no quarrel with revisionism—right up until the part where it says, "… and then they were gassed." Revisionists point to a number of serious errors in the report: see Appendix B and the discussion below. Zimmerman acknowledges these "technical inaccuracies" (p. 83) and gives a brief summary of them, but offers no analysis at all. The implication is that these were all honest mistakes, and that the bulk of the document is literal truth.

Two months later, in January 1945, Auschwitz was liberated by the Soviet army, and more reports started to filter out. On April 12 the NYT ran a headline: "5,000,000 [Jews] reported slain at Oswiecim" (p. 6). Though outrageously false, this story set one of the high-water marks for the alleged camp death toll.

In light of this background and public hysteria, the Soviets issued their official government report on 6 May 1945.[159] This report "is probably the most important document ever issued on the gas extermination claim," according to Crowell (2011: 60). But not, of course, because of its veracity. Among other outrageous claims, it established as "fact" that "over 4 million people" were killed there. The Soviets interrogated 2,819 survivors, examined corpses, and pored over documents. They pieced together all the basics of the conventional story: the fake "bath" signs, the Zyklon poison, the open-air burning pits, the crematoria—which they claimed could burn an absurd 10,000 to 12,000 bodies per day; see below—the flaming chimneys, the sadistic medical experiments, the tossing of live children into burning pits.

Some further points stand out. First, there is only a single passing mention of Jews in the entire report ("a Jewish woman named Bella…"). Second, the Soviets autopsied 536 corpses and found not a single death due to cyanide poisoning. Instead, the most frequent cause of death was "exhaustion." This was no exception. Crowell (p. 58, n. 226) states that "no autopsy from any camp has ever yielded a verdict of cyanide poisoning"—an astonishing fact. Of course, traditionalists simply reply that all gassing victims were burned. The total elimination of evidence is a convenient trump card.

Lacking incriminating documents and forensic evidence, the Soviets had to rely on their witnesses. This procedure was adopted at Nuremberg, where

---

[159] Online at <www.codoh.com/library/document/225/>. This document was subsequently submitted to the IMT as document 008-USSR.

the *entire* case for homicidal gas chambers rested solely on eyewitness accounts. "It is surprising to note that it appears no documents referencing gas chambers were entered into the record of the IMT, if we exclude affidavits and testimony," says Crowell (p. 87). The situation was little better at the subsequent twelve NMT trials; "of the seven hundred documents entered by the prosecution, only four can be interpreted as referencing gas chambers." Three of these are clearly irrelevant to the homicidal claim, and the fourth—with its ambiguous mention of a *Vergasungskeller*, or "gassing cellar"—is likely a reference to fumigation or air raid protection, not murder.

And what about the decades since then? One could perhaps understand the lack of verification so soon after the war, but surely one would expect decisive evidence to come forth in the intervening years. But not so:

> The most troubling aspect of the mass gassing claim is not that it was made on the basis of slender or non-existent evidence. It is rather that nothing has been produced over the past 50 years that supports the claim. (*ibid.*, p. 93)

Neither the opening of archives nor such documents as transcripts of intercepted German radio transmissions have helped the cause.[160] This situation casts a large shadow over the entire Auschwitz story:

> This should represent a serious problem for historians. To maintain the gas extermination claim, purely on the basis of the documentation at Nuremberg, is to also maintain that it was carried out with such stealth and cunning that no record was ever made, not even in secret radio traffic or eavesdropped conversations. Because of the broad currency of the gassing claim, it is sometimes said that to deny it is to accuse the Jewish people of a grand conspiracy to create it. But the truth would seem to be the other way around: given the lack of evidence, it is those who assert that mass gassings took place who are in the position of having to explain why the evidence does not exist. They are the ones who end up asserting the existence of a grand conspiracy. (*ibid.*)

So it comes down to the eyewitnesses. But as we know, they are not without their difficulties. Traditionalism has an immediate problem: *its best witnesses would have perished during the event*. Camp survivors, by definition, did not experience the gassing routine, and hence are not truly firsthand witnesses. They can report only hearsay, rumor, and disconnected facts of observation—people disappearing, corpses, crematory smoke. Traditionalism has to settle for second-best.

---

[160] For a good discussion of the British decrypts, see Kollerstrom (2014).

Star Witnesses

The conventional view has it that about 200,000 Jews survived Auschwitz, and hence were 'witnesses.' Only a small fraction of these, however, have gone on record. Yad Vashem claims a total of 20,000 testimonies, for all aspects of the Holocaust; surely not more than 5,000 of these can be from Auschwitz. And the vast majority of these are likely useless, owing to lack of details, inconsistencies, and obvious absurdities—see the following chapter for more on witness problems. The bottom line is that we have only a few dozen useful witness statements for Auschwitz, and of these, there is heavy reliance on literally a handful of people. This is surprising, to say the least.

Who, then, are these star witnesses, upon whose fragile shoulders the entire Auschwitz gassing story—and hence the better part of the Holocaust—rests? The aforementioned Vrba and Wetzler are two. Elie Wiesel is the most famous Auschwitz survivor, but his statements and books are full of bombast and hyperbole.[161] And his best-known book, *Night*, is notorious for including no mention of gas chambers. We also have the noted psychologist Viktor Frankl, whose memoirs implied a lengthy stay at the camp, but was in fact later revealed to be all of two or three days—after which he was deported to a labor camp. Frankl also claimed that the "real extermination" took place at the smaller camps, not Auschwitz; this came as quite a shock to our orthodox historians. Then there is the novelist Primo Levi and his famous book *If This Is a Man*, reprinted as *Survival in Auschwitz*. Unfortunately he spent his entire time in Camp III (Monowitz), which never experienced gassings or mass murder. Indeed, it was not until after the war that Levi even learned about the alleged gassings at all. And we have the doctor Miklos Nyiszli, but his testimony too is rife with exaggeration; Pressac argues that every major fact he reports was magnified by at least a factor of four.

There was, however, a second group of Jews who were, in theory, virtually direct witnesses: the so-called *Sonderkommandos*, or "special commandos." These were inmates who were charged with the task of hauling the dead bodies out of the chambers and over to the crematoria furnaces or burning pits. Most *Sonderkommando* members were, allegedly, themselves gassed, but a few survived to tell their tale. Two of these are important to the orthodox view: Henryk Tauber and Filip Müller. Other important statements came from Bendel, Dragon, Feinsilber and a few others. Again, a very small number of individuals.

Rather than recount the many pros and cons of these people here, I have summarized the main points of their testimonies in Appendix B. Suffice it

---

[161] For a detailed examination of the many issues with Wiesel, see Routledge (2015).

to say that the problems are significant enough that we must demand independent confirmation of the main points.

Apart from the Jewish inmates, we have, of course, the Germans. They ran the camp and thus certainly must have known what was happening. But there are problems here too. Considering the legal indiscretions at Nuremberg, it is clear that any given individual could likely be pressured into admitting almost anything—especially when tempted with vague promises of reprieve from a death penalty. But even this seems to have been less than successful. Of the dozens of Nazi personnel captured, a mere handful ever 'admitted' the presence of mass gassing. In fact, the bulk of the German testimony rests on *just three individuals*: Commandant Rudolf Höss, camp doctor Johann Kremer, and SS private Pery Broad. Unfortunately for traditionalism, all three 'confessions' contain obvious exaggerations and blatant falsehoods.[162] Again, rather than elaborate all their claims here, reasonable or otherwise, I have summarized the pros and cons of the most-important witnesses in Appendix B.

Gassing Capacity and 'Actual' Usage

According to current orthodoxy, then, something like 900,000 Jews were gassed at Auschwitz over 34 operational months—February 1942 through November 1944. Astonishingly, nearly half of these allegedly occurred during just the eight-week Hungarian operation in the summer of 1944. Apart from this brief paroxysm of killing and its immediate aftermath, monthly gassings were never higher than 25,000 per month, or about 830 per day—and usually much less. Put another way, for 30 of 34 operational months, the average number of gassings was relatively small: about 14,300 per month, or 475 per day.

Compare this to the camp's alleged capacity. Under the '10-per-square-meter' rule, the maximum capacity for a single gassing would have been as follows:

Bunker 1:	600 persons
Bunker 2:	900 persons
Krema 1:	780 persons
Krema 2:	2,100 persons
Krema 3:	2,100 persons
Krema 4:	2,360 persons
Krema 5:	2,360 persons
TOTAL:	**11,200 persons,** per single gassing cycle

---

[162] In addition to these men, traditionalists occasionally cite a few lesser individuals, including Fritz Klein, Hössler, Klehr, Stark, Kaduk, Erber, and Baer.

According to Piper, the Nazis could have conducted five or six gassing cycles per day, bringing the theoretical Auschwitz capacity to an astounding 65,000 or more per day. Evidence of a monstrous killing machine, traditionalists say. And yet, such a figure is completely irrelevant—in more ways than one. For 90 percent of the camp's life, the Nazis never gassed more than an average of some 475 per day—about 0.8 percent of theoretical capability. Kremas 2 and 3 each gassed about 5,000 per month, allegedly, but this could have easily been done in a single day—three gassings, 2,000 each. For the other 29 days, the chambers sat empty and unused. Kremas 4 and 5 were used even less frequently; not more than one single gassing per month would have been necessary. Bunker 2 would have been the most heavily used, requiring some fifteen gassings monthly. But even this could have been done in just three days, leaving 27 days idle.

Therefore, on the conventional view, the Nazis had an incredible overcapacity of gas chambers, to the point that establishing Auschwitz as a dedicated extermination camp centered on poison gassings seems unbelievable. Furthermore, this severely undermines witness claims about repeated, rapid gassings of 2,000 or 3,000 people at a time, which would only have happened over a very short period of time, at the very peak of the Hungarian action. For the vast majority of the time, the vaunted Auschwitz gas chambers sat empty—even according to orthodoxy, whether they wish to admit it or not.

The situation during the brief Hungarian operation, however, was far different from usual. For those eight weeks in the summer of 1944—from mid-May to mid-July—Kremas 2 and 3 must have peaked at nearly 100,000 people gassed per month, or 3,300 per day. Bunker 2 was supposedly reactivated to help handle the load. But even at this incredible rate, Kremas 2 and 3 required no more than 50 gassing cycles per month—about 10 days' worth—and Bunker 2 only about 22 gassings, or some four days per month.

Thus we see that, even then, the gassing facilities were not heavily taxed. In fact, even in the single worst month—June, with 206,000 gassing deaths—the entire gassing load could have been easily handled by just Krema 5 alone. It would have taken about 85 gassing cycles, which could have been completed in just about 15 days. Half the month would have been empty.

Finally, consider tiny Bunker 1. With its single 60-square-meter chamber, Bunker 1 could have, in principle, gassed 3,600 per day, or 100,000 per month. *This bunker alone could have handled the entire Auschwitz gassing load, including the Hungarian massacre.*[163] After Bunker 1, there was no

---

[163] This would have required holding some Hungarian Jews for a short time, which would certainly not have been a problem. Over four months, Bunker 1 could have gassed 400,000 persons, enough capacity for the period of May–July 1944. There is, however,

need for any additional gas chambers—and yet the Nazis allegedly built eight more. It could be argued that they needed crematoria, not gassing facilities; but then why did they allegedly build them with gas chambers? Or some might claim that they needed buildings with combined gas chambers and crematoria, to better "industrialize" the killing process. But in this case, a single chamber in any one of the four would have more than sufficed.

Probably the best argument for chambers in each crematorium is this: no single crematorium could keep up with the gassings. One crematorium's chamber could have handled all the gassing, but then the bodies would have had to be distributed amongst multiple buildings to accomplish the necessary incineration. *The constraining factor, by far, was the furnaces, not the chambers.* But this again assumes incredibly poor planning by the Nazis. Surely they would have known about these constraints, and sought to match the gassing capacity with the furnace capacity. They would have had a few, small gassing rooms, and a large number of incineration muffles. And yet we see wildly disproportionate capacities—gas chambers too large and too numerous, and furnaces far too few. This suggests, once again, that they had no grand plans for mass murder.

The Mechanics of Gassing

In addressing the gassing process we must grapple with two distinct problems: (1) how to get the Zyklon gas *into* the chamber, and (2) how to get it *out* of the chamber.[164] In order to be effective for mass murder, both had to happen rapidly, reliably, and safely.

In principle the can of Zyklon pellets could have been opened in a room adjacent to the gas chamber itself, and then the gas pumped or circulated into the chamber. Despite rumors to this effect, no one on either side of the debate accepts this method. Rather, the pellets themselves were introduced directly into the room. Death allegedly came to everyone within five to twenty minutes "at most."

The only effective way to get such pellets into a room packed with frightened people would be from above: either through holes in the ceiling, or high on a side wall. In fact both of these methods were allegedly used:

---

an additional problem that may have made it utterly impractical to consider using only Bunker 1, namely, the inability to ventilate the Zyklon after each gassing. Revisionists disagree on how important ventilation would have been, but any building intended for high utilization over long periods of time would likely have needed an effective venting system—which Bunker 1 did not have. Lacking this key element, it was likely rarely used, if at all.

[164] There would have been other ancillary problems, of course, including how to keep a large number of panicky victims in the room.

> In Krema 1, four (or perhaps six) openings were chiseled into the ceiling, not having been designed in from the start; the pellets were simply sprinkled over the heads of the people below.
> For Bunkers 1 and 2, "trained SS disinfectors wearing gas masks discharged the contents of Zyklon B cans into each bunker room through vents in the side walls" (Piper 1994b: 162). Again—pellets just dumped onto the floor.
> Kremas 4 and 5 were similar to the bunkers: "When the chamber was full, the SS guards shut the doors, and one of them, wearing a gas mask, climbed a ladder or a chair [next to an outside wall of the chamber]. When the SS doctor on duty gave a sign, the SS man would pour Zyklon B pellets into the opening" (*ibid*: 172).

Revisionists point to some obvious concerns here. First, it seems like an entirely unprofessional and even amateurish way of injecting the pellets, especially in Kremas 4/5, which were supposedly designed as homicidal facilities from the start. One would have expected a fully automated and well-designed procedure, which is clearly lacking here.[165] Furthermore we would expect some means of swiftly gathering up and disposing of the deadly Zyklon pellets; such means are also completely absent. Lacking such means, the pellets would have continued to emit deadly gas for two hours or more, dramatically slowing down the whole operation.

Second: As explained above, the dirty work of removing the dead bodies was assigned to a select group of Jewish inmates, widely called *Sonderkommandos*—though the Germans never used this term. Just 30 minutes after the start of gassing, they entered the room, with gas masks on, to begin removal. But the loose pellets were still in the room, scattered amongst the dead bodies and emitting deadly gas. Incredibly, neither the bunkers nor Kremas 4/5 had any powered ventilation system. The SS simply opened doors and windows, and let the room air out. Granted the SS didn't care much about the *Sonderkommandos*' health, but nonetheless, it could well have been fatal to work under such conditions—even slaves are no use dead. And this is not to mention the risk to the SS men standing nearby. Hence we find an expert like Piper (1994b: 171) having to admit that a fully packed chamber of 2,000 people could take four hours to unload. This is hardly the streamlined, high-speed assembly line of death that is advertised. Finally, at the end of the clearing-out, the loose pellets would have had to be swept up and discarded; but no witness has ever described this process. All this is difficult to believe, given that two simple and obvious changes—remote gassing and a ventilation system—could have solved many problems at once.

---

[165] Though, for some strange reason, the Dachau delousing chambers and many others located throughout the Third Reich had precisely such devices. If Dachau could figure out how to do it for clothes, why not Auschwitz for homicides?

Kremas 2 and 3 were allegedly, and inexplicably, different. Their gas chambers had four interior, wire-mesh columns that extended from the floor to openings in the ceiling. From above, the SS would dump the pellets into a smaller wire-mesh cage and then lower it into the column, down into the room. After the 10- or 20-minute gassing period, the little cage was lifted out and carefully disposed of.

This process, at least, makes more sense, and seems more appropriate for high-volume killing. Unfortunately there are several problems here as well:

> The case for these columns rests on just two witnesses: Tauber and Michal Kula. In their testimonies they described similar devices inside the chambers. As a member of the *Sonderkommando*, Tauber had access to the inside; Kula worked in the metal fabrication shop. For traditionalists, any pair of corroborating witnesses is more than enough to establish truth. Revisionists demand further evidence, given the many problems with every significant witness.
> There is no unambiguous documentation of these columns. They are not shown on any drawing or blueprint, and are not mentioned in any communication. The closest thing found was a single inventory sheet that listed "4 wire-mesh insertion devices." However, the inventory sheet was for the nearby "undressing room," or morgue #2, *not* the alleged gas chamber room (morgue #1).[166]
> The columns were allegedly anchored to the gas chamber floor. Yet in the floor of these chambers, accessible today, no one has found any evidence of attachment points. Nor do the roof remains show any evidence of attachment.
> There exist today no physical remains, nor any components, of these columns. Not one physical trace of them has turned up.

No Holes?

The problem of the wire-mesh columns is closely related to perhaps the most famous and most contentious issue of the Birkenau crematoria, specifically for Krema 2: *no holes in the ceiling*.

On the standard view, Kremas 2 and 3 were originally conceived and designed as ordinary crematoria with two underground corpse rooms, or morgues, to temporarily hold the bodies. In late 1942, as they were nearing

---

[166] Pressac (1989) argues that the clerk who filled out the inventory sheet simply made a mistake and assigned them to the wrong room. Rudolf responds that the other inventory items were assigned correctly, hence it is unlikely that only this one item was misplaced.

completion, the Nazis allegedly decided to convert them to homicidal facilities.[167] After completion in early 1943, both buildings were modified for this purpose—including, importantly, the chiseling of four holes in the 45-cm (18-inches)-thick concrete ceiling of cellar #1, and the addition of the wire-mesh columns.

Illustration 14: Under the collapsed roof of the furnace hall of Krema 2, Auschwitz-Birkenau.

Illustration 15: The collapsed reinforced concrete roof of morgue #1 of Krema 2 at Birkenau in August 2000.
© Carlo Mattogno; from Rudolf/Mattogno (2011: 320).

---

[167] See van Pelt (2002: 369).

When the Nazis destroyed the crematoria with dynamite in 1945, they collapsed the ceilings of the Krema 2 and 3 semi-underground chambers. Krema 3's ceiling was utterly destroyed, but Krema 2's ended up shattered but somewhat intact—sufficiently so that it retains some evidentiary value, even today; see Illustrations 14 and 15.

We should find evidence, then, of four regularly spaced holes in the ceiling of Krema 2's Morgue #2, square in shape, and 25 cm (10 inches) on a side.[168] In fact, nothing like this exists. Of course there are holes—dozens of holes of various sizes, in all parts of the roof. But the question is if any of the holes (a) are generally in the expected location, (b) are of expected size, and (c) appear to be original, that is, chiseled out by the Nazis in early 1943, and suitable for use as Zyklon-insertion holes. Or better yet: that they were actually built in place.

As far back as the 1970s revisionists have argued that the alleged holes could not be found. Mattogno and Rudolf visited the site in 1990 and 1991, looking to confirm the claims. Rudolf (2011: 191) reports that in 1991 he found just two possible Zyklon holes. But they had several problems: crudely chiseled, wrong dimensions, bent-back reinforcing rods still present—see his photos. Furthermore, the roof did not fracture *through* the holes during the blast, as would be expected due to the structural weakness caused by the presence of such a hole. All indications point to the two holes being created after the war, possibly in the course of the Polish or Soviet investigations. In both Rudolf's and Mattogno's judgment, the ceiling never had any holes.

Without holes, there could be no gas chamber. Without a gas chamber, no mass murder. And with no mass murder at Auschwitz, the entire Holocaust story is undermined. Thus Faurisson's famous quip: "no holes, no Holocaust." Obviously an oversimplification, but the general point has merit: The missing holes at Krema 2 are very important for the entire debate.

Do we have any tangible evidence, then, that the holes actually existed? Only indirectly, via photographs. There exist a handful of photos—one terrestrial, and a few aerial—showing objects of some sort on the roof of cellar #1 of Krema 2. First of all we have the so-called train photograph from February 1943; see Illustrations 16 and following. It shows a narrow-gauge construction train in the foreground, and in the background the back of Krema 2 with the newly finished underground cellar #1 still protruding a couple feet from the soil.[169] In the detail photo (Illustration 17), we see three or four—the fourth partially hidden by the train's smokestack—unevenly spaced,

---

[168] There is some dispute among traditionalists as to the size of the holes. As we will see, Keren *et al.* (2004) argue that they were 50 × 50 cm, considerably larger than Provan's figures.

[169] It would eventually be covered with soil and perhaps grass.

Illustration 16: So-called train photo with Krema 2 in the background. From Rudolf (2011: 103)

Illustration 17: Section enlargement of Illustration 16. Taken from Rudolf/Mattogno (2011: 382).

squarish objects on the roof. Could these be the small "chimneys" or vents through which the Zyklon was dumped into the mesh columns below?

The second photograph was taken from the air on 25 August 1944, just after the end of the Hungarian operation—see Illustration 18 (Krema 3 on left, Krema 2 on right.). It shows four elongated dark smudges above each cellar #1.[170] Could these be the Zyklon vents? This was the claim of two CIA analysts who first published the photo in 1979.

---

[170] Frequently overlooked is the fact that Krema 3 also shows four dark smudges on its cellar #1 roof. But strangely, these are clearly more widely staggered than the Krema 2 marks. This would make no sense, given that both crematoria were designed and built as mirror-images. We would expect that any objects built into or added onto the cellars would be identical in each case.

Illustration 18: Section enlargement of Allied air photo RG 373 Can F 5367, exp. 3185, of the Birkenau camp, taken on August 25, 1944, showing Kremas 2 (left) and 3 (right). The added black arrows point to the underground morgues #1 with dark smudges on their roofs; see text. From Rudolf (2011: 106)

We can identify the undressing rooms [cellars #2], gas chambers [cellars #1], and crematoria sections as well as the chimneys [of the crematoria themselves]. On the roof of the sub-surface gas chambers, we can see the vents used to insert the Zyklon B gas crystals. (Brugioni and Poirier 1979: 10f.)

Revisionist John Ball disagrees: "It is obvious that these patches cannot be input hatches" (2003: 277). He argues that they would have to be either the vents themselves, or shadows of the vents. But the smudges are roughly three to four meters (ten to twelve feet) in length, far too long to be the actual vents, which would have been less than one meter high. If the smudges are shadows, they are irregular, too long, and at the wrong angle with respect to the sun—compare to the central chimney's shadow angle. Thus they cannot be from the small, rectangular Zyklon vents. But if they are neither vents nor shadows, what are they? Ball cites a 1996 letter from Brugioni to Provan, in which Brugioni interprets the marks "as including the shadows of the vents, but also including roof discoloration marks, perhaps from people walking around the area of the vents..." And yet nothing else in the photo indicates dark smudges from foot traffic. This would be expected, for example, from the hundreds of thousands who marched to their deaths in the gas chambers. Furthermore the smudges are largely disconnected and show no access route.

What about confirmation from other photos? Two are relevant. One from 31 May 1944, at the height of the Hungarian action, shows only a *single* large black mark on the roof—see Mattogno (2005c: 318). Second, in an air photo of September 13, just three weeks after the August 25 shot, the Krema 2 smudges have mysteriously vanished; this part of that photo was curiously cropped out by Brugioni and Poirier. In Ball's opinion, the August 25 smudges are simply forgeries, added to the negatives sometime afterward. The photos are thus ambiguous, but tend to favor the revisionist view. The existence of the holes remains in doubt.

"Fixing a Hole…"

What do the anti-revisionists have to say about all this? There have been three attempts in recent years to account for the holes: (1) Charles Provan's study in 2000; (2) van Pelt's analysis in 2002, as part of the Lipstadt trial; and (3) Keren, McCarthy, and Mazal's study of 2004. All three have been analyzed by Rudolf and Mattogno.

First: Provan's study appeared in 2000 as a self-published brochure.[171] I will draw on Mattogno's (2005c) analysis for a revisionist critique. Provan begins with a number of witness statements, but as we know, the revisionists give little plausibility to any potentially self-serving claims that cannot be verified with either photographic, documentary, or physical evidence. He then addresses the air photos, siding with the revisionists on the August 25 shot: "No matter what one thinks of the authenticity of the smudgy marks, it is impossible to view them, whether authentic or not, as 'vents'" (in Mattogno 2005c: 291). Likewise with the terrestrial photos: the openings themselves are not visible, and the roof objects, "whatever they are, they are not the Zyklon B insertion chimneys…" (p. 297).

This leaves only a study of the ruins. During a trip to Birkenau in early 2000, Provan picked out eight holes as being manmade (#1–8), three of which—numbers 2, 6, and 8—he determined were original Zyklon holes. These are shown in Illustrations 19-21. Mattogno examines each of these:

> Hole #2 (= Rudolf's Hole #1). It has the same problems noted above, in particular: Measured dimensions of roughly 89 × 52 cm, according to Provan, are far too large to be an original 25 × 25 cm Zyklon hole. The hole is, in fact, over seven times too large. Provan's explanation: the blast enlarged the hole. Mattogno shows that several other holes for air vents, heater exhaust, etc.—none "Zyklon"—in both Kremas 2 and 3, survived without being enlarged in the least, and thus Provan's conclusion is unfounded. Also, Mattogno has a series of photos of this hole over a period of ten years (1990–2000), which clearly shows signs of being tampered with. "Between 1992 and 1997, the hole has

---

[171] A version is online at: <http://mailstar.net/holocaust-debate20.html>

Illustration 19: Collapsed concrete roof of morgue #1 of Krema 2 in Birkenau. Provan's opening #2 in October 1991. © Carlo Mattogno; from Rudolf/Mattogno (2011: 336)

been coarsely enlarged and squared by blows with a chisel" (p. 309). This is a serious problem with all of the Birkenau remains; they are virtually unprotected and subject to unknown modifications.

- Hole #6 – As Mattogno describes it: "Hole no. 6 is a crack clearly caused by the collapse of this part of the roof... This does not even have a definite shape..." (p. 312). This conclusion is confirmed by the photo.
- Hole #8 – This hole "forms a part of a long fracture in the roof of the morgue... [It] is a simple fracture, without definite shape." It furthermore is crossed by four iron reinforcing bars, and thus could never have served as a Zyklon hole.

Provan's case is very weak, though perhaps he has done the best possible with limited evidence.

The second assessment was made by van Pelt in defense of Lipstadt against the Irving libel suit. In reviewing the remains of the chamber ceiling, van Pelt concluded that the Zyklon holes simply were *no longer there*: "Today, these four small holes that connected the wire-mesh columns and the chimneys cannot be observed in the ruined remains of the concrete slab" (2002: 464). The only possibility, according to van Pelt, is that the SS filled in the holes with concrete, just prior to blowing up the building: "it would have been logical to attach at the location where the columns had been, some formwork... and pour some concrete in the hole and thus restore the slab." In Mattogno's opinion, this is completely absurd. One cannot repair a hole in an 18-inch-thick reinforced concrete slab without leaving some obvious evidence:

> [A] large area of the ceiling is preserved around pillar no. 1, a zone in which the first hole for the introduction of Zyklon B should be found.

Illustration 20: As above, Provan's opening #6 in June 1990. © Carlo Mattogno; from Rudolf/Mattogno (2011: 336)

Illustration 21: As above, Provan's opening #8 in August 2000. © Carlo Mattogno; from Rudolf/Mattogno (2011: 338)

Yet from the inside, the ceiling shows no sign of having been closed again... (2005c: 313f.)

Mattogno concludes that van Pelt's theory "is therefore totally untenable."

The third and most-detailed study was that of Keren *et al.* in 2004. The report is striking, if for no other reason than that it completely ignores the analyses by Mattogno, Rudolf and Provan. This immediately marks it as questionable scholarship. However, the authors do mention the thesis that the holes were filled in just prior to demolition (Keren 2004: 73). But they immediately dismiss it. Interestingly, they do not cite van Pelt by name; evidently his work has no credibility with them either.

Consequently, they proceed to break with standard traditionalism by assuming that the Zyklon holes were *cast in place* when the concrete ceiling was poured in January 1943. Their key finding, though, was their claim to have located three of the four holes in the ruins of the cellar. They call their study "the first to add physical confirmation to the testimonial and photographic evidence for the location of the holes" (*ibid*: 68).

Their analysis is based on a three-way comparison between the train photo, the aerial photo of August 25, and the ruins. They begin with a novel interpretation of the train photo. Of the three visible objects—#1, 2, 3, moving right to left—it is clear that the shadows fade from darker to lighter. The first two the authors interpret as vents 1 and 2, and they are in fact in roughly the expected position, at least with respect to the *angular* location. The actual location along the line-of-sight, however, is difficult or impossible to determine. Of the third object, which is in an inconvenient position, they say: "This does not correspond to an introduction port [vent]... It may be an object on or near the roof of the gas chamber. It is lower and narrower than Chimneys 1 and 2" (p. 71). This comes off as merely dismissing a troublesome piece of data. If this object is not a chimney, perhaps the others are not either.

Half-hidden by the train's smokestack, on the left, is an object that Keren and colleagues declare to be the fourth vent. Again, it appears to be close to the expected location, in terms of angular measure. The third vent would then have to be hidden just behind the left edge of the smokestack. This indeed is their determination. It is perhaps an odd coincidence that they found holes in the ruins corresponding to the locations of Objects 1, 2, and 4. Like the vent itself, hole #3 could not be identified.

Just by way of comparison: van Pelt evidently disagrees with Keren. He claims (2002: 340) that Objects 1, 2, and 3 are Zyklon chimneys, and that #4 is hidden. Keren's #4 he totally ignores. But never mind; according to van Pelt's view of the photo, "it proves the existence of these [wire mesh] columns beyond reasonable doubt." He evidently has a low standard of proof.

Mattogno's critique (2005c: 365f.) of Keren's analysis is not entirely convincing. He claims that Object 1 is farther back along the line of sight, placing it on the eastern half of the roof, and much closer to Object 2. In fact there is no way to confirm this. Object 4, he says, is at the rear of the ceiling, actually touching the wall of the building—and hence in completely the wrong location for vent #4. Again, this is possible, but we have no way of confirming it. One intriguing bit of evidence in support of his view is a January 15 photo of the cellar that shows some boxes stacked against the wall, exactly where Mattogno argues Object 4 is situated. This is the same photo, incidentally, that shows a clean, flat roof, with no sign of Zyklon chimneys. Finally, Mattogno argues that the shadows of Objects 1, 2, and 4 correspond better to cylindrical objects than rectangular; hence his opinion that they were storage barrels or drums. This is difficult to determine either way.

The aerial photograph, with the four dark smudges, causes problems for Keren and colleagues. They claim that the marks alternate over the centerline of the cellar, and correspond to the hole locations. In fact they all appear to lie on the eastern half of the roof. The authors' explanation: "Heaped earth obscures the east edge of the gas chamber, making holes appear farther east" (p. 82). Also, the marks are clearly not spaced identically with the alleged vent locations. Thus their explanation that the smudges represent trampled soil or vegetation from the repeated walking around the vents and dumping of Zyklon.

Of course, the vents must also be there in the smudges, somewhere. Keren *et al.* first admit that the vents cannot be seen in the photo: "It is impossible to observe the Zyklon holes themselves in any of the aerial photographs" (p. 95). But they quickly add, "certain phenomena associated with the holes can be identified." It took some effort and imaginative thinking, but

> after careful study [photo analyst] Lucas identified four small objects within the smudges, all slightly elevated above the level of the roof. … In all probability, these correspond to the four 'chimneys' above the holes in the roof.

A miraculous finding, which Mattogno rightly dismisses: "In other words, 'the four small objects' cannot be seen, but—in an act of faith—they still have to be there!"

The authors then address one more problematic issue: the May 31 photo, which shows only the single large mark, and no evidence of the four dark smudges. They have a ready explanation: "the camouflage in the Crematorium area in general, and the gas chamber in particular, changed over time." That is, the soil covering was not added until after May 31, which was then tamped down to the point of striking visibility in the August 25 shot. An odd act of camouflage: one that made the homicidal gassing vents *more* visible, not less.

Finally they address the ruins themselves and their finding of three holes corresponding to vents 1, 2, and 4. As may be expected, there is some overlap with previous studies, which we can confirm by comparing photographs:

> Hole #1 (= Provan #2, = Rudolf #1): Same issues as cited above. One difference, though: Keren *et al.* assume that the holes were uniformly sized 50 × 50 cm, not the 25 cm square that Provan believed. Hence this opening is closer to their expected size. They add: "Portions of straight, flat edges and a 90-degree angle survive intact…" This is difficult to fathom from the photograph, especially given that other verified holes—such as furnace vent holes—survived to be clearly identifiable as square, pre-blast openings.

Illustration 22: Collapsed concrete roof of Morgue #1 of Krema 2 in Birkenau. Keren's opening #4. From Keren *et al.* (2004: 85)

- Hole #2 (= Provan #6): Same issues as above—it is clearly a cracked opening, without definite shape. Keren's photo #12 (p. 85) is laughable; in a pile of rubble the authors show, with a dashed line, where the nice, square hole once existed.
- Hole #3: Only a "projected location," and a photo of a pile of rubble. No analysis possible.
- Hole #4: There is no actual concrete hole, but only "a pattern in the rebar," that is, a squarish opening in the reinforcing rods—see Illustration 22. The bent-back rods, which would appear to a casual observer as signs of ad hoc post-construction work, are viewed by the authors as "proof" that the Nazis cut but did not remove the rebar, bent the rods back, and then poured concrete over them. No one would construct a concrete hole in this manner. Their explanation, in the words of Mattogno, is "frankly ridiculous."

Mattogno's critique of Keren *et al.* may be summarized as follows:

> [T]hey have simply selected from the large number of holes and cracks of all sizes and shapes... those that are closest to their assumed positions of the alleged openings for the introduction of Zyklon B. (2005c: 372)

Furthermore, "the authors assume that the ruins at the time of their investigations (1998–2000) were exactly the same as those at the end of 1944 when the SS blew up the crematorium II... a totally unsound hypothesis."

So: Whither the holes? Photos are ambiguous. *One* ground photo shows objects on the roof, others do not. *One* air photo shows four dark smudges—which are possible forgeries—and others do not. The ruins have many holes, none of which is as clear as known and proven holes that survived similar destruction in other parts of the crematorium. And the lack of supporting evidence—chimneys themselves, concrete chimney lids, chimney attachment marks on floor or ceiling, wire-mesh columns, column attachment marks—is damning for the traditional case. We can understand Faurisson's insistence: "No holes, no Holocaust."

The Leuchter Report

Finally, a brief comment on some well-known chemical analyses that were performed on the remains of the gas chambers. In 1988 an American "execution technician," Fred Leuchter, traveled to Auschwitz to test for the presence of cyanide residue in the delousing and gas chambers. He extracted samples from the ruined walls of the chambers in Kremas 1 through 5, as well as a known delousing facility. His results were striking: concentration levels from the alleged gas chambers for every sample (some 16 in total) were all less than 10 mg/kg, and around 2 mg/kg on average. For the known delousing room, it was 1,050 mg/kg—roughly 500 times greater than the chambers. Leuchter's conclusion: Zyklon gas was never or only very rarely used in the alleged gas-chamber rooms; hence they could not have served their alleged function of mass murder. His results were published in 1988,[172] causing outrage amongst the Holocaust establishment.

In the early 1990s the expert chemist Rudolf also went to Auschwitz seeking to confirm these results using a more carefully controlled process. His samples from the Krema 2 chamber were completely consistent with Leuchter's. He furthermore took some twelve samples from the delousing room, all of which equaled or exceeded the levels found earlier—and in some cases, were higher by a factor of ten. Hence the same overall conclusion.

Traditionalist critics have responded in three ways. First, they argue that it is natural for a delousing chamber to have higher concentrations of cyanide because killing lice requires a much higher air-level concentration than killing people. Furthermore, the normal delousing procedure let the rooms soak for a few hours before clearing, causing high levels of residue to build up on the walls. This much is true, and admitted by Rudolf. In fact the levels must nominally be about one hundred times greater to kill lice in one hour than to kill people in one hour—see Rudolf (2011: 179f.). But he adds that, because of the need to kill *everyone* in a densely crowded room in *minutes*, not hours, the practical concentration levels would have to be at least ten times higher than the minimum lethal levels—and perhaps as high as that used against lice. And, given the alleged 'production-line' nature of the human gassing, the gas chambers would have been exposed much more often than the delousing room.

Second: Traditionalists ask, Why any residue at all? If the revisionists claim that there were no gassings, as some do, and that the gas-chamber rooms were actually morgues, then there should be no cyanide residue whatsoever. However, this conclusion is not quite correct. In fact it was likely that even corpse rooms were fumigated periodically. This would not have been necessary to kill germs—Zyklon has no effect on them, as traditionalists gleefully point out—but to kill the lice that infested the dead bodies. Arad (1987: 128) quotes a Jewish prisoner: "the corpses were dirty and full of lice…" Clearly it was an issue that had to be addressed by occasional delousing actions in the morgues.

Third, a subsequent official analysis of the chamber walls was performed by a Polish team led by J. Markiewicz in the early 1990s. The results, published in 1994, show equally low cyanide levels in all rooms, thus apparently

---

[172] Revised in 2012, 3rd edition.

vindicating the traditionalist view. But as so often happens in the Holocaust saga, there is more to the story. The Polish team had used a different technique that looked only for *unstable* cyanide compounds—ones that, conveniently, would not survive the 50 years of time.[173] Sure enough, they found virtually no residue. Their data was duly published in 1994. "Case closed," according to traditionalism.

From an objective standpoint it is difficult to know what to make of such results. Crumbled ruins, sitting for decades in the open air; samples that are sensitive to location, depth, porosity, and so on; nuances of chemical analysis—all these factors make it hard for the average person to draw conclusions. If the entire revisionist case rested on such data, they would be on shaky ground. But that is not so. Hence this aspect of the debate is relatively indeterminate, but at the very least stands as yet one more curious element in the larger drama that has become the Great Debate.

Death Matrix (II): Body Disposal

With more than 1 million alleged fatalities overall, Auschwitz had the biggest disposal problems of any camp in the Reich: the biggest fuel problem, the biggest burning-time problem, the biggest ash problem. Without an adequate resolution, the traditional Auschwitz story threatens to collapse. And as I noted earlier, if Auschwitz collapses, the entire Holocaust story is put at risk.

Since it was intended from the start to hold many thousands of inmates, Auschwitz was anticipated to experience many thousands of deaths, by a variety of causes. The planners knew that the bodies would have to be hygienically disposed of. There would be neither time nor space for cemeteries or careful, civilian-style cremations. Mass graves were useful only as a short-term solution, and then only in early 1942—if for no other reason than the high water table, which was only about one meter below the surface. This mitigated any thoughts of 'normal,' deep mass graves. Burials were thus neither pragmatic nor preferable. Therefore, high-volume crematoria were the best alternative. This in itself indicates no evil intent; it is simply a consequence of housing thousands of people under wartime conditions.

Every corpse at Auschwitz was eventually burned. So of the 1 million or so deaths that allegedly occurred there, we must account for... 1 million burnings. The crematoria were the first choice, but for two periods in the life of the camp they were inadequate. When the crematoria furnace capacity was exceeded, the bodies were burned in the open air, either in pits or on

---

[173] See Rudolf/Mattogno (2011): 45-67. Prussian blue is a famously stable and persistent form of cyanide residue.

makeshift pyres. Thus we have two separate and distinct disposal problems: (1) How many were burned in the crematoria? and (2) How many were burned in the open air? The issues in each case are very different, and we must have an adequate account of both.

There were problems from the very start. For all of 1941, 1942 and the first two months of 1943, Auschwitz had only the single unit Krema 1. It began operation with two muffles[174] and expanded to six by mid-1941, but even these were not enough to keep up with the alleged gassings. Consequently, for the entire first year of 'mass killing' there was insufficient capacity. For the first eight months, the excess bodies—some 80,000 to 100,000—were buried in shallow graves. Then it was decided to create open-air pits or pyres beginning in October 1942. These would burn not only the exhumed corpses but the continuing overflow as well.

With the activation of Kremas 2–5 in early 1943, there was sufficient furnace capacity for the first time. Hence the initial period of open-air burnings ceased. Unfortunately for the Germans, the furnaces of Kremas 1 and 4 had to be decommissioned by mid-1943, setting the stage for another shortfall. The second overflow period came a year later, with the surge in deaths attributed to the Hungarian action. For eight weeks in May, June, and July 1944, huge numbers of bodies were allegedly burned in the pits.

Despite all the notoriety surrounding the crematory furnaces, the two overflow periods required many thousands to be burned in the open, if we are to properly account for the 1 million deaths alleged by the traditionalists. In fact, by the end of the camp's life, *more bodies had been burned in the open air than in all the crematoria combined.* And by a significant margin: 41 percent in the crematoria, versus 59 percent in the open air—see the death matrix for details (p. 199). This fact is almost completely unknown by revisionists and traditionalists alike. Only Zimmerman seems to have an appreciation of it, but even he underestimates the open-air burnings because he clings to unrealistic furnace capacities.[175]

---

[174] As explained in Chapter 9, a muffle is the entry cavity into which the corpse is placed. Also called a 'retort,' and occasionally (and confusingly), an 'oven'—Zimmerman (2000: 205) baldly states "each muffle can be considered an oven," and so he proceeds to use the words interchangeably. Van Pelt (2002) unfortunately does the same. *More correctly*, a cremation oven (or better, cremation furnace) refers to a physical unit that may have one or more heat sources and one or more muffles. A furnace heated with coke, like the Auschwitz models, could have one or more fireplaces (hearths). The Auschwitz 8-muffle furnaces, for instance, had four hearths, one for each pair of muffles. Some cremation furnaces had one muffle but two hearths. Hence a cremation furnace can potentially burn more than one adult body simultaneously, depending on the design, but a standard 'muffle' is designed to cremate only one corpse at a time. To use the words muffle and oven/furnace interchangeably is, in effect, to deliberately confuse the reader.

[175] The 59/41 split assumes the lower crematoria capacity figures favored by revisionists. As I will explain shortly, there were at least two higher estimates, from Bischoff and Höss. Using the Bischoff figures, 37 percent would have been burned in the open. With

Furnaces and Capacity

Let me address the furnaces first. Regarding my above comment, I want to be very clear on the furnace/muffle breakdown by crematorium:

Krema 1: One 2-muffle furnace at first; two more
  furnaces added later. Total: 3 × 2 each   = 6 muffles
Krema 2: Five 3-muffle furnaces. Total: 5 × 3   = 15 muffles
Krema 3: Same as K2   = 15 muffles
Krema 4: One 8-muffle furnace. Total: 1 × 8   = 8 muffles
Krema 5: Same as K4   = 8 muffles

The reader is invited—nay, challenged—to find an unambiguous presentation of even this elementary information in a published traditionalist account of Auschwitz. There is a reason for this: transparency leads to difficult questions being asked.

For a good example of this apparently deliberate obfuscation, see Piper (1994b). His article, "Gas chambers and crematoria," is one of the more authoritative sources of information on Auschwitz, given his status as chief historian for the camp museum. He first speaks of "five furnaces" for Krema 3 (p. 165), and then refers to "12 crematoria furnaces (ten three-retort and two eight-retort)" for Birkenau—but without details. Later (p. 168) he refers to the furnace room of Krema 2: "It housed five furnaces, each with three retorts." No reference to Krema 3 anymore, other than that it was "nearly identical" to K2. Coming to the common design for Kremas 4 and 5, he refers to "one eight-retort furnace with four coke hearths" (p. 169). But he offers few other details. Though his facts are all correct, piecing together the whole picture can be almost impossible for the uninformed reader.

With respect to the debate, a major question is this: How long did it take to burn one body? This gets at the crucial matter of *furnace capacity*, which bears directly on the open-air burnings, and which must be understood to grasp what may or may not have happened at Auschwitz. A related question of interest—that of fuel consumption and corresponding *efficiency* of the furnaces—will have to be passed over here in the interest of space. Suffice it to say that, given known records of coke deliveries to the camp and minimum required consumption per body, only about 10 percent of the claimed cremations can be accounted for.

Revisionists are firm in their conviction that, for an average adult, it took one hour per body, per individual muffle. Clearly the muffle design called for one body at a time. The arched muffle entrance was about 60 × 60 cm (2

---

the Höss numbers, this would drop to 26 percent—still, a large proportion of total burnings. And as I will show, the revisionist depiction of events has only 10 percent of all burnings in the open air.

× 2 feet), and some of this space was taken up by rollers for the metal corpse stretcher. The stretcher itself was not more than two meters (6½ feet) in length.

An especially contentious issue in the debate is this: Could the Nazis burn multiple bodies at once? If this were possible on an extended basis, it would support the traditional picture, since it would allow very high burning capacities and thus very short 'per body' burning times, as well as lower fuel consumption. Traditionalists cite witnesses who claim that two, three, or even eight bodies were loaded at a time.[176] The only way to even approach such numbers would be with the bodies of children or infants, which certainly happened periodically. By general agreement, up to one-third of the population was children under age 16. Allowing that the average child weighs half an adult, an individual muffle could burn, on average, 1.2 bodies per hour, instead of one.[177] This is the figure that Mattogno uses.

Traditionalists, however, like to take the witnesses literally and assume that two, three, or more *adult* bodies could be loaded at once. Mattogno responds by showing that it would be pointless to attempt this, even assuming that one could fit them in the muffle, because it would inevitably be accompanied by a roughly proportional *increase* in burning time. For example, loading and burning two adult male bodies at once would take nearly two hours, thus yielding no increase in average burning time.[178]

Furthermore, once the bodies did begin to catch fire, the ensuing heat and flames would exceed the physical design standards of the interior of the furnace and flue, resulting in premature damage and shorter operational life. Even two adult corpses at once, over an extended time, would have this effect. Rudolf (2011: 385) cites a statement from 1946 by the lead furnace designer, Kurt Prüfer:

> [I]n Auschwitz in my presence two corpses were inserted into each muffle instead of just one, and that the furnaces of the crematory could subsequently not stand the strain…

---

[176] The Sonderkommando member Henryk Tauber testified that up to eight at once could be loaded; cited in Rudolf (2011: 382).

[177] If, say, 2 of every 6 people were children (33 percent), and if, on average, 2 children weighed as much as 1 adult, then those 6 bodies could be burned thusly: 4 adults, one hour each; 2 children at once, in one hour. Hence 6 bodies in 5 hours, or 1.2 per hour.

[178] See Mattogno's discussion in Rudolf and Mattogno (2011: 148-151). He summarizes: "[B]y increasing the load of organic burning material, one increased either the corresponding fuel consumption or the duration of the combustion process. Hence, should 'multiple' cremations in the Birkenau furnaces have been successful, this would not have been of any effective advantage… 'Multiple' cremations would only have multiplied the duration of the cremation process and the coke consumption by the number of corpses loaded into the muffle."

But the SS evidently did not heed this warning, at least at first. The first two of the new crematoria to become operational, Kremas 2 and 4, were apparently run with multiple bodies; Krema 2 incurred major damage during the first few weeks of operation and had to be repaired for months, while Krema 4 lasted just three months before becoming permanently disabled. It seems that the Nazis learned their lesson, as the other three crematoria continued in operation, off and on, until the very end. Hence in all likelihood they rarely ran multiple bodies.

Traditionalists disagree. On their view, multiple bodies were the norm, at all crematoria, throughout the life of the camp. As evidence they cite the Bischoff letter of 28 June 1943, in which Krema 1's capacity was 2.8 bodies per hour per muffle, and Kremas 2–5s' capacities were an amazing 4.8 per hour. As if these numbers weren't high enough, van Pelt promotes the literal truth of a statement by Commandant Höss, who claimed—under coercion—that Kremas 2 and 3 could each burn an incredible 2,000 per day (= 6.7 bodies/hour), and Kremas 4 and 5 each 1,500 per day (= 9.4 bodies/hour).

We therefore have three sets of estimates of capacity.[179] If we assume an average working month of 25 days, given downtime for failures, repairs, extended maintenance, occasional fuel shortages, and so on, we can obtain a projected monthly capacity for each of our three estimates. These are summarized in Table 28.

Table 28: Claimed Auschwitz Cremation Capacities
per hour, day and month (/hr, /d, /m)

		Mattogno			Bischoff			Höss		
		per muffle		per Krema	per muffle		per Krema	per muffle		per Krema
Krema	Muffles	/hr /d	/d /m		/hr /d	/d /m	/hr /d	/d /m
1	6	1.2 24	144 3,600	2.8 57	340 8,500	(6.7)(133)	(800)(20,000)
2	15	1.2 24	360 9,000	4.8 96	1,440 36,000	6.7 133	2,000 50,000
3	15	1.2 24	360 9,000	4.8 96	1,440 36,000	6.7 133	2,000 50,000
4	8	1.2 24	192 4,800	4.8 96	768 19,200	9.4 188	1,500 37,500
5	8	1.2 24	192 4,800	4.8 96	768 19,200	9.4 188	1,500 37,500

How realistic are these estimates? A detailed analysis is beyond the scope of this book, but Mattogno makes a strong case that the Bischoff hourly rates are impossible, and the Höss figures ridiculous.[180] But with the acknowledgment of substantial open-air burnings, the actual crematoria capacity is no

---

[179] Four, if we count the Soviet Special Commission report of 1945. They claimed outrageously high rates for each of the five Kremas: K1: 9,000 per month; K2/3: 90,000 per month; and K4/5: 45,000 per month. Total alleged capacity: 279,000 per month—almost 50 percent higher than Höss's figures.

[180] Independent evidence suggests that Mattogno's estimates are the more accurate. During 1942, Krema 1 began operation with 2 muffles and then expanded to 6. During the first phase it could handle, according to Mattogno, a maximum of perhaps 1,200 bodies per

longer that critical an issue in the debate. The main value is as a test of the trustworthiness of the source; anyone claiming or endorsing unrealistic, or physically impossible, burning rates is perhaps not reliable on other points.

Finally, a brief mention is also warranted for one well-known revisionist argument: All the Auschwitz crematoria, combined over their operational lives, could not have disposed of the 1 million bodies. Here is the calculation: As per the death matrix, we can see the maximum time period that each Krema was operating. If we assume that each Krema operated for 25 days during its months of operation (an overestimate, in fact), then we can calculate the maximum number of possible Auschwitz cremations, for each of the estimates—see Table 29:

Table 29: Claimed or Implied Operational Lifetime Capacity of the Auschwitz Crematoria

Krema	Months	Mattogno	Bischoff	Höss
1	18	64,800	153,000	360,000
2	20	180,000	720,000	1,000,000
3	18	162,000	648,000	900,000
4	3	14,400	57,600	112,500
5	19	91,200	364,800	712,500
	Totals:	512,400	1,943,400	3,085,000

Sure enough, on the revisionist view 'only' half a million bodies could have been incinerated. But the traditionalists have two possible replies: (1) The Bischoff (or Höss) estimates are the more realistic, hence it was no problem to burn 1 million corpses; (2) there were large numbers of open-air burnings, hence any limitation on crematoria capacity is irrelevant. The first option is a very tough case to make, but the second is an obvious way out. If it were believed that only very few open-air burnings took place, then the revisionist argument would be quite serious. But as it is, with the admission of numerous such burnings, crematoria limitation becomes largely irrelevant.

---

month; in the second phase, up to 3,600 per month. As I have shown in the death matrix, K1 was thus running at capacity for virtually the entire year. The excess bodies had to be buried, and then later pit-burned. Yet if K1 had the higher Bischoff or Höss capacities, then there would have been no excess at all. This is incompatible, however, with the widely-accepted fact that some 80,000 bodies were buried that year.

I further note that the matrix shows an unacceptably high figure of 8,000 monthly burnings for three months, but this is required by other traditionalist claims about it. In all likelihood the actual rate was much lower than this.

The Hungarian Operation

What about body disposal during the Hungarian operation? Here we are told that about 400,000 Hungarian Jews were killed between mid-May and mid-July 1944. This was in addition to the 'normal' load of about 6,000 non-Hungarians per week. Over a period of just eight weeks, then, the Nazis managed to kill and burn over 55,000 people per week, or about 7,800 daily. *In just eight weeks, 45 percent of Auschwitz's entire death toll occurred; the remaining 55 percent were spread out over the other 128 weeks.* This is a wild disparity, and alone should cause us to ask some tough questions about the validity of the traditionalist account.

A brief historical comment is warranted here. It may seem odd that the Hungarian Jews were not deported *en masse* until such a late date; after all, the war had been under way for nearly five years by that time. The reason was that Hungary was a member of the Axis for most of the war, and as such was left alone by the Nazis. Requests for deportation of Jews were subtly resisted. By the time the war started to go bad for Germany, in mid-1943, Hungary wanted out. They initiated secret armistice negotiations with the Allies, and began to further resist German demands. By early 1944 Hitler got wise to the situation. He invaded Hungary in March; mass Jewish deportations commenced within two months.[181]

Gassing the 400,000 Hungarians would not have been a problem, as explained above. Kremas 2 and 3 were each gassing about 3,000 per day, on average. This could have easily been handled with two gassing cycles. Krema 4's chambers apparently dropped out after the first week, for unknown reasons. Krema 5 was gassing about 320 per day, a mere 1 percent of its alleged capacity. Bunker 2 chipped in with about 650 per day—a single gassing.

Burning the bodies would have been a huge problem, however. The three operating crematoria (2, 3, 5) were already running near capacity—per Mattogno—before the first Hungarians arrived. Thus, in effect, nearly every Hungarian body had to be burned in the open air.[182]

If the over-extended crematoria could handle, say, 90,000 bodies in total for those three months, then roughly 350,000 bodies had to be pit-burned—most in just eight weeks. Take the single worst month, July 1944. Here we have over 180,000 bodies burned in 30 days: 45,000 a week or almost 6,500 per day, on average. Piper (1994b: 173) claims that at its peak the camp was

---

[181] Butz (2003: 167-231) has an excellent and lengthy chapter on the Hungarian Jews. Of particular interest is his analysis of an ICRC report claiming that persecution of the Jews began only *after* October 1944—and hence that any reference to a summer massacre was largely propaganda.

[182] Even so, in the death matrix, I allow for pushing the kremas slightly beyond capacity.

burning an incredible 10,000 bodies per day in the open air! These are huge numbers, on par with Treblinka's alleged 7,500 daily average. Consequently, all the problems of the Reinhardt burnings recur here:

- Extremely inefficient to burn mass bodies in pits, or on pyres.
- Can't burn all layers at once.
- Can't stack bodies very high.
- Huge amounts of wood required: 1.1 million kilograms (1,200 tons) per day. No evidence of this entering the camp, or being processed there. This would have been 69,000 tons in total, equivalent to nine Eiffel Towers—in just eight weeks.
- Can't burn bodies fast enough. It would take 12–14 pits burning simultaneously, for 20 hours per day, just to burn up that much wood.
- Huge amounts of ash produced: 60,000 kilograms (67 tons) per day. Must be sifted for bones and teeth, which must then be ground to dust.
- Must dispose of the ashes: 160 cubic meters, every day.

This last issue is particularly contentious. With no mass-grave space into which the ashes could be dumped—as for the Reinhardt camps—other solutions were required. Piper (1994b) explains that the crematoria ashes, and presumably also the pyre ashes, were first dumped into shallow holding pits, and then later removed. Ultimately, "they were poured into the Vistula River or nearby ponds. Sometimes they were used to prepare compost; other times they were used directly to fertilize the fields of the camp farms" (p. 171). So we have four different alleged destinations for the ash—three of which are in principle available for forensic examination to this day. What Piper does not tell the reader is that he is utterly lacking in any hard evidence that these things are true. He in fact has no idea where, or how much, ash was disposed of.

Van Pelt (2002: 269) has different ideas: "Outside Bunker 2 were large burning pits where bodies were cremated in the open. The remains of these pits, together with the ashes, are still visible today." A rather shocking statement—the ashes are still there to this day! Thus a forensic examination can begin in short order, and confirm all the orthodox details of open-air burnings. Except that no such examination has ever been conducted, nor even discussed, to my knowledge.[183]

---

[183] Rudolf (2001) gives a good summary of forensic examinations at Auschwitz. Considering the magnitude of the alleged crime, examinations to date have been shockingly inadequate. There have been just three minor efforts since the war: (1) For the 1946 Krakow Trial, hair samples and a metal cover plate were tested for cyanide residue; all came up positive, but with neither quantifiable results nor reproducibility. (2) In 1966, possibly in connection with the ongoing Frankfurt Trial, a Polish company was commissioned to drill soil samples and analyze them. But the results were never made public or published; they have "vanished into the museum's archives"—suggesting that the diggers did not

If we conservatively assume a complete combustion of corpses cremated in the Auschwitz cremation furnaces, resulting in 5% ash mass of the initial average corpse mass of 50 kg, this then comes to about 2.5 kilograms per body. For the bulk of 1943 and 1944 (apart from the Hungarians), with some 500 corpse cremations per day, this would yield about 1,250 kilograms per day. At the peak of the Hungarian action with 800 furnace cremations daily, it would have been 2,000 kg daily (2.2 tons), in addition to the 65 tons from the open-air pyres[184]—resulting in a total of over 67 tons per day. All of this had to be sifted and crushed, every day, and then disposed of in one of the four ways.

Finally, one last major problem with open-air burnings:

> Smoke signals: continuously, from the open-air pits, for over four months. This is in addition to the almost-continuous smoke from the Birkenau crematoria chimneys, which is alleged to have poured out every day for two years. In which case we would expect to find…

Air Photo Evidence

Smoke signals from masses of burning bodies, and from smoking crematoria chimneys, are relatively easy to spot from the air. Because Auschwitz was an industrial work camp, it was the target of several Allied reconnaissance flyovers. Photos were taken on ten dates in 1944. Table 30 gives these dates, and summarizes the alleged activity that was occurring at the time.

Table 30: Summary of Auschwitz Air Photos

PHOTO DATE	CLAIMED ACTIVITIES DURING THAT MONTH
4 Apr 1944	21,000 deaths, all cremated—700 per day.
31 May 1944	First month of Hungarian operation; 110,000 deaths (3700/day), 24,000 cremations, 86,000 pit-burned.
26 Jun 1944	Peak month of Hungarian operation; 210,000 deaths (7000/day), 24,000 cremations, 186,000 pit-burned.

---

find what they wanted. (3) Lastly, the Markiewicz studies of 1990/1994, looking for cyanide residue on the wall of the gas chamber—described earlier. Were I the family member of an Auschwitz victim, I would be outraged at this audacious and deliberate lack of will to investigate the scene of the greatest crime in history.

[184] See data for June 1944 in Table 27, p. 199: 186,000 corpses in 30 days=6,200 per day; 50 kg per average corpse, reduced to 5% ashes: 6,200×50×0.05 = 15,500 kg; plus 3.5-times the amount of seasoned wood (175 kg per corpse) reduced to 4% wood ash (see values given in Appendix A): 6,200×175×0.04=43,400 kg; this yields a total of 58,900 kg of pyre cremation remains, or some 65 US short tons. If assuming incomplete combustion of the corpses on pyres resulting in 10% corpse cremation remains, this value would rise to 74,400 kg or 82 US short tons.

Photo Date	Claimed Activities During That Month
8 July 1944	Continuation of Hungarian operation; 105,000 deaths, 24,000 cremations, 81,000 pit-burned. (German photo)
20 Aug 1944	68,000 deaths (2300/day), 24,000 cremations, 44,000 pit-burned.
23 Aug 1944	Same as 20 Aug
25 Aug 1944	Same as 20 Aug
13 Sep 1944	42,000 deaths (1400/day), 24,000 cremations, 18,000 pit-burned.
29 Nov 1944	4,000 deaths/cremations (135/day).
21 Dec 1944	Few killings or burnings, if any.

What do the photos show us? Without the full, original photos this is hard to tell. Each side of the debate obviously shows only those photos, or portions of photos, it chooses. Still, we can assume that the strongest evidence is presented by each side. The best images of the most important photos are shown in Illustrations 23-28.

April 4: Shows main camp (Auschwitz I) only. Krema 1 clearly visible—no activity. This is as expected; by this date K1 was neither gassing nor cremating anyone. No evidence of any mass extermination.

May 31: (Illustration 23) Birkenau camp, late May, near peak of Hungarian killings. Kremas 2, 3, 4, 5 clearly visible—*no smoke from any chimneys*. However, there is "a long thin smoke plume" (Zimmerman 2000: 290) coming from a small area, possibly a pit or pyre, near Krema 5, see Illustration 23b. Compare to Birkenau camp layout.

June 26: (Illustration 24) Auschwitz I + II. During the peak of the Hungarian action—*no smoke (either chimneys or pits), nor any evidence of mass killing*.

July 8: (Illustration 25) Birkenau. Peak of Hungarian action. Wisp of smoke near K5 (top right)—somewhat broader than May 31 photo, from small pit. *No smoking chimneys*.

August 20: (Illustration 26) Birkenau. Smoke near K5. Additionally, smoke seen coming from the K3 chimney.[185] According to Rudolf and Mattogno, this is the only known air photo of a smoking chimney. Thus, it does prove that (a) chimneys did smoke when operating, and (b) the smoke was visible from the air. Incidentally, Rudolf also shows a ground photo of a darkened K2 chimney, proving again that they did in fact smoke when operating.

August 23: (Illustration 27) Birkenau. *No smoking chimneys*. Smoke near K5.

---

[185] Not visible in figure. Described in Rudolf (2011: 165). Photo enlarged in Mattogno (2010). Contested as scratches on photo by Bartec (2012).

August 25: Auschwitz I + II. K2 and 3 visible—see Illustration 18 for Kremas 2 and 3. *No smoking chimneys, no smoking pits in visible area (K4 and 5 are not included)*.

September 13: (Illustration 28) Birkenau. All Kremas clearly visible. *No smoking chimneys, no smoking pits.*[186]

November 29: Birkenau. All Kremas clearly visible. *No smoking chimneys, no smoking pits.*

December 21: Minimal alleged killing activity, if any. *No smoking chimneys, no smoking pits.*

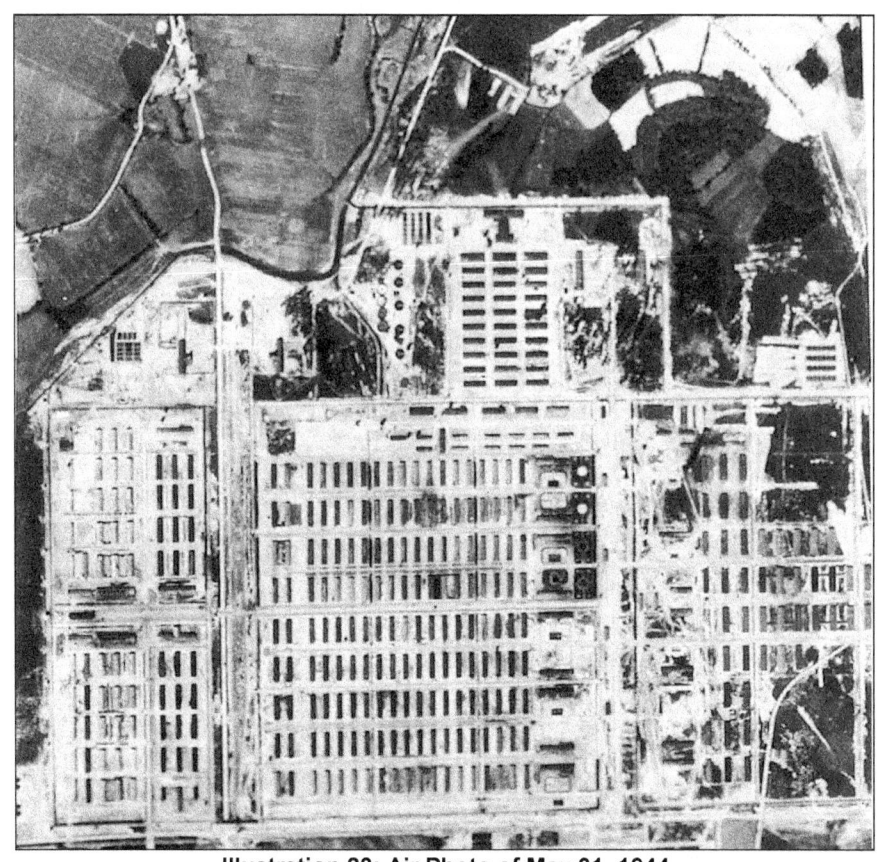

Illustration 23: Air Photo of May 31, 1944

---

[186] Note also the cluster of bombs in mid-air, ominously encircling K2. These were destined for Monowitz, however, and not Birkenau.

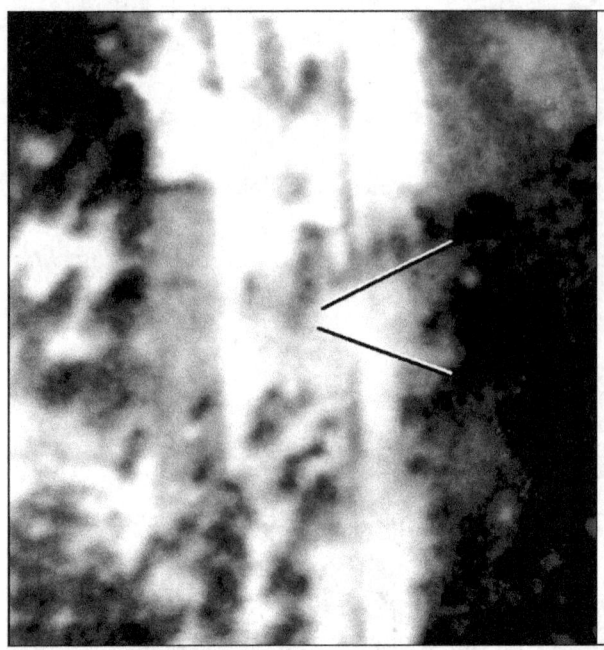

Illustration 23b: Section enlargement of Illustration 23 showing Krema 5 (left) with smoke rising from its backyard (marked with lines by the author)

Illustration 24: Air Photo of June 26, 1944, section showing Birkenau only.

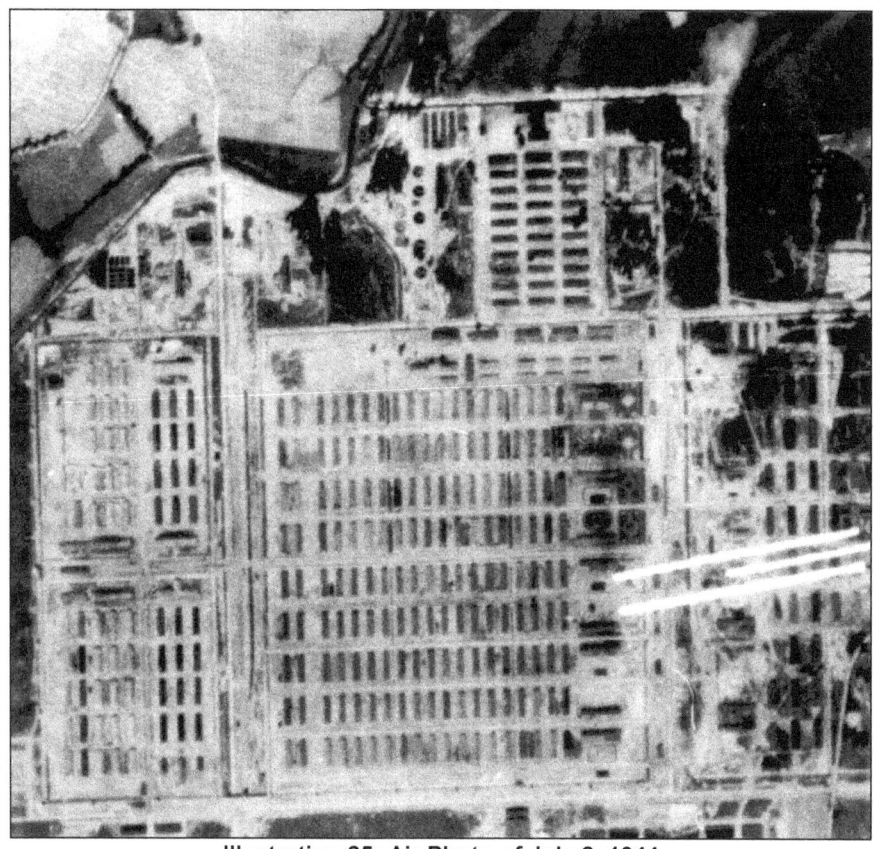

Illustration 25: Air Photo of July 8, 1944

Illustration 26: Air Photo of August 20, 1944

Illustration 27: Air Photo of August 23, 1944

Illustration 28: Air Photo of September 13, 1944

In summary: Ten air photos, and of all four chimneys in all three functional crematoria, only *one* photograph shows *one* smoking chimney. The conclusion must be that the crematoria really were not used very often at all. Either that, or it was incredibly bad luck for the traditionalists—that the photos just happened to be shot on just the day, and at just the time, when there was no crematoria activity. Unlikely, to say the least.

Furthermore, four photos show open-air incinerations, but these from only a single very small area. This is entirely incongruous with the conventional account in which thousands of bodies were burned every single day. Most damning is the June 26 photo. By standard accounts, it should have shown us three heavily smoking crematoria and several ongoing open pit fires.[187] Instead we find—*no smoke whatsoever.*

Van Pelt's handling of the air photos is interesting. The August 25 photo of the four smudges appears twice in the book (pp. 175, 353), to bolster his case for the Zyklon holes. Apart from this he includes only two other photos: May 31 and June 26. His image of the former appears near the end of the book (p. 449); it is a later exposure than Illustration 23 and the wisp of smoke is not visible. The June 26 shot (p. 91) shows the full ground image, leaving a tiny Birkenau camp at the top. Of note: There is no discussion whatsoever of these two photos in the text. The reader has no idea that these were taken at the height of the Hungarian massacre, or that they show no evidence at all of mass burnings—and hence mass murder.

How does Zimmerman respond? Regarding the May 31 photo he simply says, "Neither the transports nor the gassings occurred when the photo was taken" (p. 51). But this much is obvious. Regarding the June 26 photo he offers only this: "on this particular day there were no arrivals from Hungary" (*ibid.*)—bad luck! Of the July 8 photo he refers to the presence of "heavy smoke" (p. 245), which, for him, "confirms all aspects of the eyewitness accounts about the open-air burnings…" The other photos merit no discussion at all.

Significantly, there is not a single photograph of any kind reproduced in Zimmerman's book. No air photos, no ground photos—nothing. It is almost as if he really doesn't want the reader to judge for himself. We are simply expected to take his word for everything. And he is not alone. Neither Longerich (2010) nor Bartov (2015) saw fit to include a single air photo—

---

[187] Consider the following "eyewitness testimony" from one Professor B. Epstein: "For several months we saw long lines of people sent to their death in the crematorium [only one?]. Especially large groups were killed in May, June, and July 1944. During this time the crematorium worked day and night, as we could see from the flames which shot out of the chimneys…. In this time, we saw two gigantic fires in the open, which blazed brightly during the night, in addition to the flames that shot out of the crematorium chimneys" (cited in the official Soviet Special Commission report of 1945).

Illustration 29: Photo allegedly taken by the Polish resistance group at Auschwitz. This allegedly shows corpses being burned in a pit located north of Krema V. Taken from Rudolf (2010: 264)

nor any photos at all. Instead, it is to the revisionist sources that we must turn, if we want to find the actual photographs. This is highly revealing.

Finally, speaking of ground photos, there are two very similar photographs alleged to show open-air burnings of bodies near Krema 5—see Illustration 29. Strikingly, this is the only alleged corpse photo at any of the six death camps. The smoking area in the photo is claimed to correspond to the small burning area seen in the May, July, and August 20-23 air photos. Revisionists point out a number of odd things in this photo, suggesting that it may have been doctored: inhuman-looking corpses, man with a weirdly bent elbow, mismatched lighting of standing figures, wrong fence posts. But in the end, these are largely irrelevant. Even if completely authentic, the photo shows only a few dozen bodies, heaped on the ground, next to some nondescript smoking pit. And this much can be accepted by revisionists with little problem.

What can we conclude about those alleged open-air burnings? If the death matrix is close to correct, nearly 600,000 bodies were burned in the open air.

This is a huge number, and critical to the entire Auschwitz story. It is revealing, then, to look at what some of the leading traditionalists have to say about these burnings.

Three of the most important recent works on Auschwitz are Zimmerman (2000), van Pelt (2002), and Hilberg (2003). Since they were published successively, each should have been able to build upon the other and reinforce its views. In summary, here's what they have to say on this most-vital aspect of the Holocaust:

> - Zimmerman dedicates one section—about 14 pages—to the topic, and makes a reasonable attempt to reply to Mattogno's charges. But he gives no specifics on open-air totals, so we are not really sure which view he is advocating, or how his calculations are performed.
> - Van Pelt offers passing commentary on all of four pages, out of 570. Of the first open-air period he simply states that he accepts Höss's figure of 107,000 buried and then burned. Of the second period, he says only this: "During the Hungarian Action, when the daily number of gassed Jews far exceeded the official incineration capacity of the crematoria, open-air pyres took care of the excess" (2002: 256). That's all—no numbers, no specifics, no analysis. This demonstrates an astounding lack of scholarship, if not a deliberate effort to mislead the reader. Furthermore he apparently has no regard for prior research. In his entire book there is not a single mention of Mattogno, or even a single mention of Zimmerman. As for Rudolf, van Pelt discusses him only in the appendix, and then only his chemical analysis of the gas chambers; but nothing on his many other contributions.
> - Hilberg is the most revealing. Not one word on Mattogno, not one word on Zimmerman, not one word on van Pelt. This, out of three volumes and over 1,300 pages. On the whole topic of open-air burnings Hilberg offers us one single sentence: "From the end of summer to November 1942, the accumulated decomposing bodies infested with maggots had to be uncovered and burned" (2003: 942). One single sentence to elaborate on the alleged disposal of nearly 600,000 Jews. Traditionalism, it seems, has run out of things to say on this most important issue.[188]

Finally, what about physical evidence? Surely if that many people were burned there would be some evidence, somewhere—even if only in the "ponds," "compost heaps," and "farm fields" mentioned by Piper. Earlier I cited van Pelt's astonishing claim that the ashes "are still visible today," but

---

[188] Though perhaps we should be grateful for even a sentence. Longerich (2015) offers us not one word at all.

apparently no one has ever bothered to quantify them. Nor have any significant excavations ever been conducted at Birkenau.[183] Perhaps the Auschwitz authorities can enlist the services of Mr. Kola, Mr. Haimi, or Ms. Sturdy Colls—if they are up to the task.

Overall conclusions: If Auschwitz was truly a mass-extermination death camp, it was incredibly poorly designed. The Nazis obviously had no idea how many Jews would be coming into the camp, how they would be killed, or how to dispose of the bodies. The total capacity of all the alleged gas chambers—approaching 65,000 per day—is absurd. No one in their right mind would plan for such levels of killing. The corresponding crematoria could handle barely more than 1,200 bodies per day, combined—if they were all working. And they were never all operational at the same time. This is an incredible mismatch with gassing capacity. Again, no rational person would design such an inept system of mass murder. Either we greatly overestimate the capability of the Germans, or something is seriously wrong with the conventional account of Auschwitz.

A Revisionist Auschwitz

Where, then, does all this leave the revisionists? They accept that large numbers of people, including Jews, were killed or died at the camp. But in combining all available data on crematoria operation, registrations and arrivals data, and air photo evidence, they arrive at much smaller figures. Faurisson (2005: 64, 114) has suggested a number of 150,000 deaths. Mattogno (cited in Rudolf 2011: 423) and Graf (2003: 298) argue that in fact the documented number of official deaths is correct: 136,000. Let me, then, take a figure of 140,000 as a kind of consensus.

On this view, roughly 90 percent of the 140,000 bodies were disposed of in the crematoria furnaces (126,000), and the remaining 10 percent (14,000) on open-air pyres. Individual Krema burnings never exceeded 3,000 per month, and the most heavily used was #1, which had to carry the full burning load for an entire year. During the Hungarian peak, Kremas 2 and 3 were burning about 3,000 bodies monthly, but this required only nine days per month. This could explain why aerial photos showed no smoking chimneys during that two-month window—there was only a one-third chance of finding them in operation. For the other months of 1944, Kremas 2 and 3 were running, on average, only five days per month; hence, even less chance of photographing them. By luck, one was caught on August 20.

Regarding open-air burnings, some 11,000 bodies were burned in late 1942, and another 3,000—about 1,000 per month—during the Hungarian action. Again, the burning of 1,000 per month is entirely consistent with air photos showing a small smoke trail rising from the camp (May 31, July 8, and August 20 and 23).

These details on Auschwitz allow us to complete the revisionist account of Holocaust deaths. I describe this new picture of events in the following chapter.

PART III

THE FUTURE OF THE DEBATE

Chapter 11: "Storytellers Supreme"

> *"Instead of idols and passions, I worshipped words and argument, becoming part of an unashamedly Jewish verbal invasion of American culture... Inspired by our heritage as keepers of the book, creators of the law, and storytellers supreme..."*
>
> —Max Frankel, Executive Editor, New York Times[189]

People love stories. We love happy stories, sad stories, heroic stories, tragic stories. Storytelling is a central element in every human culture that has ever existed. It is as old as language itself, and perhaps even older. It may well be that images like the Lascaux cave paintings relayed a kind of visual story to our human ancestors of 30,000 years ago. Storytellers are honored and respected in all societies, as entertainers, educators, and carriers of cultural traditions.

Jewish culture is particularly enamored of stories and storytellers. Storytelling plays a large role in sustaining their values and traditions, and in realizing a shared experience of Jewish life. We see evidence of this in modern society, in the great success of Jews in literature, cinema, and media generally. By at least one admission, they are "storytellers supreme," and they are lavishly recognized and rewarded for these accomplishments.

But what is a story, after all? Up until the sixteenth century a story was literal 'history,' that is, a true recounting of actual events. But then it began to change to its more modern sense of a fictional narrative meant to entertain or amuse. Of course, any good story is a little bit of both. The best stories have a grain of truth at their core, around which the storyteller weaves a fantastic elaboration of ideas and images intended to bring a vividness and luster to that truth.

The Holocaust is a kind of story. It is a tale of tragedy and woe, of a heroic and innocent people set upon by monstrous forces, and subjected to

---

[189] Frankel (1999: 400).

the most horrendous fate imaginable. It makes for marvelous novels and motion pictures. But those interested in truth have other aims. We want to know precisely what that grain of truth at the center of things is, and how much is fanciful elaboration. This is the real challenge for Holocaust scholars on both sides of the debate.

The best way to unravel the story is to put everything under scientific and logical scrutiny. Certain things are physically impossible, others highly unlikely, some entirely feasible. Some events leave clear and decisive evidence, others none at all. Much of my discussion in Part II was intended to employ some of these scientific and logical tests to the conventional story in order to judge its trustworthiness. We found many improbabilities and impossibilities, and these help us to better understand the whole event that was the Holocaust.

The Problem of the Witnesses

When these issues of scientific or material counterevidence are raised, traditionalism has always had recourse to a putatively definitive source: eyewitnesses. The victims, the survivors... they were there, they saw it with their own eyes. They are key—decisive, in fact—to the entire traditional picture of events. These people are the original storytellers from whom the larger narrative of the Holocaust is woven. At least within the Jewish community, survivors are secular saints today. Like St. George, they fought the dragon with their own hands and lived to tell about it. It is unfortunate that, due to this sainthood status, there is a strong incentive for survivors to recount the most horrific stories in the greatest possible detail. In fact the more terrible a survivor's tale, the more he or she is revered as a miraculous one who lived to tell.

Yet from an objective standpoint we have to ask difficult questions. With the myth of St. George we are entitled to ask, for example, "Do dragons really exist?" If the answer is no, then a central pillar of the myth is discredited. Perhaps George fought and killed some wild animal—still a brave act, no doubt, but certainly a different story than the usual one. With the Holocaust we are entitled to ask questions about what *exactly* the witnesses saw, how *exactly* they came to their conclusions, and if perchance there might not be some fanciful elaborations slipping into their stories, whether deliberate or not.

Professional sociologists and psychologists have long known of such problems, and lately they have begun to acknowledge the many issues with wartime witnesses. Beim and Fine (2007), for example, write the following in the context of the Holocaust:

> Although seeing something "with my own eyes" is a powerful claim of facticity, scholars recognize that eyewitness testimony is problematic. Indeed, memory is distorted, often a function of political perspective, emotional stress, prejudicial beliefs, or even the form in which memory is requested. ... In addition, witnesses can provide inaccurate testimony through "repressed memories." Research on testimonies in the courtroom demonstrates that a testifier's confidence in his account is unrelated to the account's accuracy. (pp. 56f.)

They summarize the point by stating that "a testimony is a speech act, rather than just a descriptive statement." Lindemann (1997: 530) makes a similar observation.

> Some Holocaust survivors are patently not infallible witnesses, since... they contradict one another and 'remember' things that can be proved not to have happened. ... Memory plays tricks on us... especially when observation is under the pressure of powerful emotions. Victims are not automatically reliable observers or saints.

Precisely how many witnesses are "not infallible" is an open conjecture.

In the case of Holocaust witnesses there were, and are, many reasons for both *deliberate* and *unintentional* exaggeration of events. And in some cases, perhaps even outright falsification. Obviously, as victims of Nazi persecution, Jews had a strong motive for revenge; many undoubtedly deliberately falsified aspects of their stories to more strongly implicate the perpetrators. Some may have lied for status reasons, simply to acquire the standing of 'secular saint' within their community. Others saw a profit motive and stood to make a lot of money from books and movies. Yet others may have had political or ideological motives for falsifying their accounts.

Surely only a small minority of witnesses committed such deliberate falsification. More troublesome are cases in which the witnesses are unintentionally mistaken in important ways—even as they fully believe the things they say are true. A frequent problem was that of rumors taken as literal truth. These stories continue to recur, even today. A 2008 CNN story on an American soldier, Anthony Acevedo, described his three-month captivity in a Buchenwald sub-camp.[190] He recounts his experience of eating bread "made of redwood sawdust, ground glass, and barley." The Nazis, he says, used "wooden bullets" to inflict extra damage on their victims. He heard the usual rumors: "peeling the skins of people, humans, political prisoners, making lampshades." Taken to the main camp one day, Acevedo recalls seeing a building with "large pipes":

> We thought we were going to be gassed when we were told to take our clothes off. We were scared. We were stripped. Rumors were

---

[190] "WWII vet held in Nazi slave camp breaks silence." CNN (11 Nov 2008).

around that this was where the political prisoners would be suffocated with gas. It turned out to be a shower...

Similar accounts are repeated over and over by survivors, who nonetheless continued to believe that actual gassings occurred "somewhere else."

We have other troublesome scenarios. There are cases in which factual events, in themselves nothing sinister, are wrongly pieced together. There is the potential for false memories to be implanted in people via mass media, suggestive or leading questioners, or fellow storytellers. And then there is the simple fact that memory is fallible—we all have had experiences in which something we were certain was true turned out to be false. We can only begin to imagine how hard it must have been, under extraordinarily difficult conditions of pain, illness, and death, to retain and recall factual details about the camps.

No doubt much of what the witnesses stated was true. But it is equally certain that much of what they said was false. To be honest with ourselves, we must find a way to confirm what was said. The mere fact that a certain statement by Witness A was repeated by Witness B does *not* mean that the statement is 'confirmed.' There are many other reasons why a given account would be repeated by others:

- Both witnesses heard, and believed, the same rumors.
- Both witnesses misinterpreted the same set of isolated factual events.
- Witness B was influenced, consciously or otherwise, by Witness A.
- Both witnesses had similar motives and reasons to reach a similar conclusion.
- Both witnesses were coached by a common third party.

To state the obvious, just because two witnesses claim to have seen something technically or physically impossible, this does not mean that it happened. Even if a dozen people claim to have seen a flying pig, this does not establish as fact that pigs can fly.

Holocaust survivors have not claimed that Nazi pigs were flying, but they have said some fairly outrageous things. I already mentioned a few such cases—those of Robert Spitz, Shaul Ladany, and most notably Moshe Peer, who claimed to have survived fully six gassings at Belsen, a camp with no homicidal gas chambers at all.[191] Here are a few other infamous examples of outrageous stories that have since been definitively rejected:

- Soap made from Jewish human fat (claimed by famed Nazi-hunter Simon Wiesenthal).[192]

---

[191] See Chapter 5 for details.

[192] Wiesenthal is a story in himself. Recently he was exposed by Guy Walters (2010) as "a liar—and a bad one at that." Wiesenthal would "lie repeatedly" about his Nazi-hunting exploits; he would "concoct outrageous stories about his war years"; indeed, "there are

> Lampshades, book bindings, gloves, purses, and other personal items made from Jewish skin (claimed at Nuremberg).
> Blood gushing out in "fountains" from mass graves (claimed by Elie Wiesel).
> Human fat ladled from open-air cremations and used to hasten the burning of corpses (claimed by Höss, Tauber, and others).
> Babies tossed in the air and shot like clay pigeons (claimed at Nuremberg).
> Sausage made from Jewish flesh (claimed by David Olère).
> 20,000 Jews annihilated by some kind of atom bomb (claimed at Nuremberg).

To this day, we continue to see a string of absurd statements by putative witnesses. Felix Brinkmann managed to avoid death at three Nazi camps, including Auschwitz. "Five times he had been slated for the gas chambers, but each time he used his fluency in German to talk his way out," according to CNN. (One wonders: Was it really so easy to dupe the Germans?) Years later he was "stunned" to find out that his wife, also sent to Auschwitz, "was alive and well in Poland."[193]

Greek Jew Yitzchak Ganon claimed, incredibly, that "Mengele stole my kidney." Allegedly chosen as a human guinea pig, Ganon recalls lying on an operating table when "he cut into me without anesthetic." "Then I saw my kidney pulsating in [Mengele's] hand." After the operation, Ganon was selected for the gas chamber as the 201st man of the day; "but it was full after 200," he said.[194] Most fortunate.

Recently we read reports of an Auschwitz survivor who "walked out of [the] gas chamber alive." Gena Turgel, then age 21, was herded naked into the gas chamber with hundreds of other victims. "Yet Turgel... walked out alive." "She had no idea the Nazis had tried to kill her until a woman she knew said, 'Don't you know what has just happened to you? You were in the gas chamber!'" Turgel's simplistic explanation: "it must not have worked." The absurdity of this story is astounding—and yet NBC News reported it as fact.[195]

Such cases are remarkable but not exceptional. And it's not only a few obscure survivors who have made questionable claims. Virtually all of the prize witnesses have made blatantly false statements and engaged in gross exaggeration and rumor-mongering. Appendix B summarizes some key points made by all of the lead witnesses for each of the six death camps.

---

so many inconsistencies... that it is impossible to establish a reliable narrative." See also the news story "Head Nazi-hunter's trail of lies", *Times Online* (18 July 2009).

[193] CNN (1 Aug 2009).
[194] *Daily Mail* (UK—11 Dec 2009).
[195] NBC News (26 Jan 2015).

Again, this is not to suggest that all these witnesses are liars, or that everything they said is false; it only implies that close scrutiny and independent verification are required before we should accept their accounts as truthful.

Elie and Viktor

Even Elie Wiesel, the most famous of all Auschwitz survivors and recipient of the Nobel Peace Prize, has made some very dubious claims—in addition to the above comment on the "fountains of blood." Consider his most famous book, *Night* (1960), which has sold some 10 million copies. It is well known for such imagery as flaming crematoria chimneys:

> "Jews, look! Look through the window! Flames! Look!" And as the train stopped, we saw this time that flames were gushing out of a tall chimney into the black sky. (p. 25)[196]

In fact, crematoria chimneys *never* spew flames unless they have accumulated a large amount of soot which somehow catches fire and burns out, which can happen occasionally. He further describes giant flaming pits into which the Nazis were throwing… "Babies! Yes, I saw it—saw it with my own eyes…" He himself was marched toward the flaming pits of death, only to be miraculously diverted, just "two steps from the pit." Interestingly, in Wiesel's entire book there is not a single mention of a gas chamber at Auschwitz. Only the flaming pits of death.

Upon leaving Auschwitz, Wiesel claims he was sent to Buchenwald. He stayed there for some two months in early 1945, until the camp was liberated by the Americans. Of his time there, Wiesel (1985: 79) has written that, "In Buchenwald they sent 10,000 persons to their deaths each day." This is quite impossible, given no more than 13,000 people died there in all of 1945.[197]

Fellow traditionalist Vidal-Naquet had this to say about Wiesel's fantastic tales: "… a man like Elie Wiesel, who tells all sorts of things… One only has to read a few descriptions in *Night* in order to know that some of his depictions are not true, and that at the end he has turned into a Shoah peddler" (in Faurisson 2003a: 141). Wiesel himself virtually admitted as much, in describing an encounter with a rabbi:

> "What are you writing?" the Rabbi asked. "Stories," I said. He wanted to know what kind of stories: true stories… "About things that happened?" "Yes, about things that happened or could have happened."

---

[196] In Wiesel's account, a crazed woman is the first to shriek about the "flaming chimneys." They all think her mad, until Wiesel "sees" them himself. In the cited quote he alleges to be giving us his first-hand account.
[197] See Graf (2003: 298).

"But they did not?" "No, not all of them did. In fact, some were invented from almost the beginning to almost the end..." "That means you are writing lies!" I did not answer immediately. The scolded child within me had nothing to say in his defense. "Things are not that simple, Rabbi. Some events do take place but are not true; others are [true]—although they never occurred." (1982: viii)

Perhaps it is just such a flexible notion of "truth" that led Wiesel to argue for deliberate ignorance when it comes to the Auschwitz gas chambers. In his 1995 book *All Rivers Run to the Sea*, he is at the brink of describing the very chambers that were so conspicuously absent in *Night*, when he writes: "No, let us go no further. Decency and custom forbid it.... Let the gas chambers remain closed to prying eyes, and to the imagination. We will never know all that happened behind those doors of steel" (p. 74). In other words, the traditional story is set in concrete, and let no one dare to raise troubling questions.

Of late, there have emerged credible claims that Wiesel fabricated much of his life history, and actually stole the identity of a real Auschwitz survivor. In early 2009 Hungarian media reported on one Miklos Grüner, a survivor who had befriended a fellow Auschwitz inmate named Lazar Wiesel in 1944. In the mid-1980s Grüner had an opportunity to meet his old friend, now going by the name Elie Wiesel. But upon meeting him, says Grüner, "I was stunned to see a man I didn't recognize at all." Apparently Elie had simply adopted the persona and life history of Lazar.

These remarkable charges appear to be substantiated by one astonishing fact: Elie Wiesel has no Auschwitz tattoo. Revisionists have posted a number of photos of him, sleeves rolled up, and the alleged number A-7713 nowhere to be seen.[198] And there are other problems: signatures that don't match, inconsistencies with the famous Buchenwald 'bunk' photo, Wiesel's alleged time at the Sorbonne... the list goes on. We can rest assured, however, that our mainstream media will not raise such troubling issues anytime soon.

A second prime witness to Auschwitz was the Viennese psychiatrist Viktor Frankl. His most famous account, *Man's Search for Meaning* (1947), was declared in 1991 to be one of the ten most influential books in America.[199] And yet, as Pytell (2000) explains, there are problems. Frankl strongly implies that he spent an extended time at the camp, when in fact he was there for only two or three days. His short time there was marked by odd events:

> In Auschwitz, Frankl recalled (although he sometimes wondered if he had imagined it) being selected by Joseph Mengele "to the left for the

---
[198] See www.eliewieseltattoo.com and Routledge (2015).
[199] See "Book Notes," *New York Times* (20 Nov 1991, p. C26).

gas chamber." But he "switched behind Mengele's back" to the right-hand line where he recognized his friends. (pp. 296f.)

Improbable, to be sure. Furthermore, "Frankl never explicitly described how he managed to escape from Auschwitz." Apparently the chance arose to join a departing transport, "but no one knew if this transport was just a 'ruse' to get more work out of the sick or really a trip to the ovens." (Obviously the former.) According to Pytell (p. 299), "the truth is that he escaped (or denied) the worst of the horrors of the camps." In fact, in Frankl's view, Auschwitz was not even a true death camp; as he says, "most of the [extermination] events described here did not take place in the large and famous camps, but in the small ones where most of the real extermination took place." As I mentioned in the previous chapter, this statement is utterly unsubstantiated by anything in the Auschwitz orthodoxy. But again, we have no way to know how much of Frankl's story to believe. In general Pytell calls it an "embellished" account, and describes Frankl's personality in terms of "opportunism, self-protection and naiveté" (p. 282)—bad qualities for a star witness.

From Bad to Worse

Then we have cases of outright fraud. A number of Holocaust books from alleged witnesses turned out to be heavily falsified or pure fabrications. The 1965 book *Painted Bird* by Jerzy Kosinski was passed off as the true account of a child survivor until exposed in the early 1990s. Binjamin Wilkomirski's *Fragments* (1996) was published to widespread acclaim. Translated into nine languages, it won a number of awards including the National Jewish Book Award (US), Prix Mémoire de la Shoah (France) and the *Jewish Quarterly* prize (UK). The book was exposed in 1999; it turns out that Wilkomirski spent the war years safely tucked away in Switzerland. And then there was Bernard Holstein's book *Stolen Soul* (2004), which fooled people for only a few months until he was discovered. Apparently the fake Auschwitz serial number tattoo on his arm had convinced publishers of his authenticity.

Recently we have seen other examples of blatant fraud. First, Misha Defonseca's book *Misha: A Mémoire of the Holocaust Years*. Published in 1997, this work stood for ten years as a true account of a child survivor, one who, after the murder of her parents, was forced to wander the forests of Europe for four years—and was adopted by a pack of wolves, no less. It has been translated into eighteen languages and was made into a French feature film. Defonseca earned millions as a result. In February 2008 it was revealed that the author was in fact a Belgian woman named Monique de Wael, who was not even Jewish, and who had fabricated the entire story. Of her childhood experiences in wartime Europe she said, "[I] *found it difficult to differentiate between what was real and what was part of my imagination*"—a canonical statement, one that may well hold true for many Holocaust witnesses.

Then there is the tale of Herman Rosenblat. An AP report of 13 October 2008—"Amazing Holocaust love story lives on"—described Rosenblat's imprisonment in a Buchenwald sub-camp, and of receiving apples and bread from a local Jewish girl, handed through the camp fence, over a period of several months. Soon separated, the couple allegedly came together again in 1958 on a blind date, and eventually married. Rosenblat went public with his story in the 1990s, and it was turned into a 2008 children's book, *Angel Girl*. Rosenblat's own book, *Angel at the Fence,* was scheduled for release in February 2009. And plans were in the works for a feature film, *The Flower of the Fence.* Few questioned his account. It was endorsed by influential talk show host Oprah Winfrey, who called it the greatest love story she had ever seen. Holocaust expert Michael Berenbaum "saw no reason to question it." "Crazier things have happened," he said. Indeed.

On December 26, the AP reported: "Author defends disputed Holocaust memoir." Questions had arisen about Rosenblat's story, especially the fact that the fence in question was located directly adjacent to an SS barrack: "the layout of the camp... made it virtually impossible that Rosenblat could have approached the fence without being spotted."

Just two days later, according to the AP, "Rosenblat acknowledged that he and his wife did not meet... at a sub-camp of Buchenwald." Rosenblat "described himself as an advocate of love and tolerance who falsified his past to better spread his message." His publisher, Penguin Group, promptly cancelled his forthcoming book. Of particular concern was the fact that no one felt free to question details of the story. As Holocaust specialist Ken Waltzer stated, "All this shows something about the broad unwillingness in our culture to confront the difficult knowledge of the Holocaust." "I was burned," added Berenbaum.[200]

The situation has grown to the point that virtually all Holocaust memoirs are now suspect. In 2013 the British paper *Daily Mail* ran a story titled, "Could there be anything more twisted than these Holocaust fantasies? How more and more people are making up memoirs about witnessing Nazi crimes" (21 June). The reporter, Guy Walters, notes that nearly every such work includes standard scenes, such as Nazi guards killing babies and

---

[200] After the truth came out, Rosenblat was interviewed by Dan Harris of ABC News. This remarkable interview, which has since been pulled from the ABC archive, is still on Youtube under the title "Herman Rosenblat about his holocaust lies on ABC TV." Harris's reaction alone is worth the viewing.

firsthand accounts of Josef Mengele. Walters closes the piece with this comment: "Anybody reading these books should stop and ask themselves whether what they hold in their hands is, in fact, true."

Such cases have seriously undermined the overall credibility of the witnesses, and caused revisionists to demand solid, objective confirmation of all witness statements. And not only revisionists: traditionalists, too, have been exasperated by the frequent unbelievability of witness statements. Here is a sampling of what some prominent traditionalists have had to say about "survivor narratives":

> [M]ost of the memoirs and reports [of survivors] are full of preposterous verbosity, graphomanic exaggeration, dramatic effects, overestimated self-inflation, dilettante philosophizing, would-be lyricism, unchecked rumors, bias, partisan attacks and apologies. (Gringauz 1950: 65)

> A certain degree of reserve is necessary in handling all [Holocaust evidence], and particularly this applies to [survivor narratives]. For instance, the evidence concerning the Polish death camps was mainly taken after the war by the Polish State Commission or by the Central Jewish Historical Commission of Poland. The hardy survivors who were examined were seldom educated men. Moreover, the Eastern European Jew is a natural rhetorician, speaking in flowery similes. ... Sometimes the imagery transcends credibility... (Reitlinger 1968: 581)

> Many thousands of oral histories by survivors [exist] around the world. Their quality and usefulness vary significantly according to the informant's memory, grasp of events, insights, and of course accuracy. Also important... is the interviewer's ability to pursue lines of inquiry that elicit information that has been subconsciously or deliberately suppressed, or that supplements an already accumulated body of information on a given subject or place. The longer the time elapsed, the less likely that the informant has retained freshness of recollection... The transcribed testimonies I have examined have been full of errors in dates, names of participants, and places, and there are evident misunderstandings of the events themselves. (Dawidowicz 1981: 177)

> Sources for the study of the gas chambers are at once rare and unreliable. ... Most of what is known is based on the deposition of Nazi officials and executioners at postwar trials and on the memory of witnesses and bystanders. This testimony must be screened carefully, since it can be influenced by subjective factors of great complexity. ... [T]here is no denying the many contradictions, ambiguities, and

errors in the existing sources. These cannot be ignored... (Mayer 1988: 362f.)

Even the Holocaust experts at Yad Vashem are frustrated. An Israeli article on the first Demjanjuk trial had this to say:

> Over half of the 20,000 testimonies from Holocaust survivors on record at Yad Vashem are "unreliable" and have never been used as evidence in Nazi war crimes trials [according to archives director Shmuel Krakowski]. Krakowski says that many survivors, wanting "to be part of history," may have let their imaginations run away with them. "Many were never in the place where they claim to have witnessed atrocities, while others relied on second-hand information given them by friends or passing strangers... A large number of testimonies on file were later proved inaccurate..."[201]

Recently a German 'blue-ribbon' committee was formed to combat anti-Semitism. In arguing for a reduced role for the survivors, one German-Jewish committee member, Elke Gryglewski, stated that "they are not objective and too emotional." "One cannot expect that survivors are objective," she added.[202]

This whole situation imposes a terrible burden on researchers trying to get to the truth of things, especially when constrained by social and legal restrictions on what can be said and on what questions can be asked. Such a dilemma has led one researcher, survivor Michel de Boüard, to exclaim:

> I am haunted by the thought that in 100 years or even 50 years the historians will question themselves on this particular aspect of the Second World War which is the concentration camp system, and what they will find out. *The record is rotten to the core.* [There exists] a considerable amount of fantasies, inaccuracies, obstinately repeated (particularly concerning numbers) heterogeneous mixtures, generalizations... (italics added; cited in Rudolf 2011: 125)

I emphasize that these are not the voices of revisionists, but of those in charge of defending and sustaining the orthodox story.

So how can we discern the truth of witness statements? The best way is through scientific analysis and forensic examination, just as would be done in any normal criminal investigation. This approach was discussed in detail in Part II.

---

[201] *Jerusalem Post* (17 Aug 1986, p. 1). It is true that Krakowski attempted to repudiate the story a week later, in a letter to the editor (21 Aug, p. 10). He now claimed that "very few" of the testimonies were "inaccurate," but otherwise did not dispute the statements made in the original article.

[202] "German committee: Shoah survivors lack objectivity." *Jerusalem Post Online* (6 Dec 2009).

There is, however, one other accepted method for uncovering the truth of witness statements: cross-examination under oath, in a court of law. Given the many postwar camp trials and the numerous legal actions against revisionists, one would expect that many witnesses have taken the stand to defend their stories. But this is not the case. Many hundreds of witnesses have testified, to be sure, but they were apparently never subjected to rigorous cross-examination.

In fact it appears that only two witnesses to the gas chambers have ever faced such cross-examination: Arnold Friedman and Rudolf Vrba. Germar Rudolf (2011: 317) recounts events at the Zündel revisionism trial in Canada in 1985. According to Rudolf, Friedman had to admit that he had not personally seen the smoking, flaming chimneys of the crematoria, but was simply relating what he heard from others. Vrba as well was compelled to admit that he had not seen the chambers, and was guilty of applying "poetic license" to various rumors he had heard at the camp. Vrba's original postwar account of events, discussed in Chapter 10, included such "facts" as 1,765,000 gassed Jews at Auschwitz by April 1944 (versus just 350,000, on the standard view); incorrect maps of the camp; wrong drawings of crematoria furnaces; and a 3-minute gassing-execution time.

But this 1985 court case was an absolute exception to the norm. There seems now to be a general position held by courts of law around the world: Holocaust witnesses shall not be interrogated. They can testify, but they can never be subjected to rigorous cross-examination. Apparently the feeling is that they have been too traumatized by the entire event to withstand hostile questioning, and so their statements go unquestioned—to the detriment of us all.

Moving Ahead: A Revisionist Holocaust

If the witness statements are frequently unreliable and must all be subjected to independent evaluation, and if, per Part II, there are many gaping holes in what was physically and technically possible at the camps, then we are compelled to accept that revisionism offers a potentially viable account of the Holocaust. If the orthodox story is suspect, alternative interpretations may be more-nearly correct.

How might we move forward on this conflict? One simple thing we could do is agree on a common, and reasonable, definition of 'Jewish Holocaust victim/survivor.' Regarding who counts as a Jew, it is probably unreasonable, for the purposes of the debate, to include a person with one Jewish grandparent. 'Jewish' should refer only to those of majority Jewish heritage—say, 50 percent or more.

Likewise, a 'victim' has to be defined in a commonsensical and relevant way. Here is a proposal: A Holocaust victim is any Jewish person, per above, directly killed by the Nazis in a ghetto or camp, or who died from preventable causes while in their custody. Jewish soldiers killed on the battlefield are not Holocaust victims. Jews who died after fleeing the Nazis are not victims. Jews who simply happened to die during Hitler's time in power are not victims. Jews killed due to Allied bombings and other attacks are not victims.

Similarly, a 'Holocaust survivor' cannot reasonably include the broad DellaPergola definition mentioned in Chapter 3. A survivor should be defined narrowly, as one who escaped from a situation in which his or her life was immediately at risk, or who lived under directly life-threatening conditions. It appears that such a situation existed only in the worst camps and the worst ghettos. Many camps and ghettos seem to have been relatively benign, and Jews were under no immediate threat—even though they were held against their will, and perhaps employed in forced labor. Those who fled to safety as the Germans approached are not survivors. Those who simply outlived Hitler are not survivors.

Finally, how about a criterion for victory in this debate? Given that this competition rather resembles a tug-of-war, I propose drawing the finish line in the middle. If the traditional account is of 6 million deaths, and the revisionists argue for around half a million, then let us place the goal line at 3 million. That is, should it ever come to pass that society accepts a figure of less than 3 million Jewish victims (defined above), then—the revisionists win. Until such time, traditionalism holds the upper hand. Let us see how long the status quo reigns.

And where does revisionism stand at the present? Throughout Part II, I made corresponding estimates of the revisionist Jewish death tolls for each camp. These figures are summarized in Table 31.

Table 31: Revisionist Death Estimates (Camps)	
Chelmno:	2,000
Belzec:	40,000
Sobibor:	10,000
Treblinka:	25,000
Majdanek:	28,000
Auschwitz:	140,000
TOTAL:	245,000

But we still have the two other major categories of deaths. First are the Einsatzgruppen actions and other shootings. I examined details of these shootings in Chapter 4. Any Holocaust total of 6 million demands something like 1.6 million shooting deaths overall. But as I noted, evidence of such a number is utterly lacking. Based on the sketchy evidence presented to date, we can presume that between 100,000 and 150,000 Jews died from Einsatzgruppen and other shootings. I will take a figure of 140,000 as a representative total, until further evidence appears.

Secondly we have the roughly 1 million ghetto deaths, on the standard view. Again in Chapter 4, I generated a revisionist estimate of about 145,000 such deaths. These figures, combined with the above camp numbers, give us a snapshot look at the revisionist assessment of the Holocaust—see Table 32. In total, revisionism points to an overall death toll of about 570,000 Jews.

Table 32: Revisionist Death Estimates (Overall)	
Death camps:	245,000
Other camps:	40,000
Ghettos:	145,000
Shootings:	140,000
TOTAL:	570,000

Breaking these down into a high-level 'revisionist death matrix' gives us the assessment shown in Table 33. Lacking further details and physical evidence, there is not much benefit in breaking these down into monthly figures, as I have done for the orthodox view.

Table 33: Revisionist Death Matrix (000)							
	Pre-1941	1941	1942	1943	1944	1945	**Totals**
Ghettos	8	45	50	20	15	7	145
Shootings	9	35	70	18	5	3	140
Camps	5	10	140	65	55	10	285
Totals	22	90	260	103	75	20	**570**

Again, this matrix points to a Jewish death toll of some 570,000. I emphasize that such a breakdown is very preliminary. It is a very rough first approximation to revisionist claims, as best I can discern. I would hope that they would take it upon themselves to improve these numbers and to further justify their claims. Only then can we truly assess the validity of the revisionist view.

Chapter 12: Hoax? Fraud? Conspiracy?

In this final chapter I want to bring some closure to the issues raised, and to address the big cloud hanging over this entire debate.

Assume for the moment that the worst-case scenario comes to pass—namely, that the revisionists are proven right: that the number of Jewish victims is eventually accepted to be on the order of 500,000, rather than something like 6 million.[203] This, as I have stated repeatedly, is the likely outcome of the debate. Future historians will then ask themselves this question: How was it possible that, for over, say, 100 years, a badly mistaken view of events was so widely accepted as the truth?

This is not just a question for some hypothetical future. Many people today, convinced that revisionists are largely correct, ask the same question. And some of them have answers. These answers go by such names as 'hoax,' 'fraud,' and 'conspiracy.' The 'Holohoax,' they say, is a gigantic fraud, perpetrated by a global Jewish conspiracy whose leading figures reside in Israel and the United States. Anyone with even a passing awareness of the Holocaust debate has heard these charges. They strike some as outrageous, others as racist, and yet others as eminently plausible. Any discussion of the Great Debate would be incomplete without addressing this most contentious and explosive issue.

Let's examine this whole claim in a bit of detail. In Chapter 1, I dismissed the notion that the Holocaust was a hoax. I explained that a hoax is a contrived situation intended to deceive someone for profit or gain. And as far as we know, there is no evidence that any significant aspect of the Holocaust was fabricated or contrived explicitly in order to deceive. I stand by that earlier statement, and reiterate here that, in my opinion, the Holocaust was not a hoax.

A 'fraud' is essentially the same as a hoax—that is, a deception or trickery intended to deceive, for the purposes of personal gain. But it lacks the benign origins of the latter word, and hence should be taken as involving a more explicitly malevolent intention. For the same reasons as above, however, I think it is equally incorrect to call the Holocaust a fraud.

---

[203] Odd that the view claiming the *least* number of deaths is considered the 'worst case'—but I let that pass for now.

But under our assumption above, and in the analysis of the preceding chapters, the standard view of the Holocaust is grossly mistaken. Statements about it are patently untrue. Dismissals of revisionism are thus utterly unjustified; in our hypothetical (and likely) future, the revisionists are proven correct. Past criminal charges brought against individuals for speaking about that which, it turns out, is now accepted as true are themselves criminal. Clearly something has gone dramatically wrong. How can we understand this phenomenon?

Some will resort to base charges: The Jews *lied* about the Holocaust. They lied for reasons of revenge, profit, and fame. They lied to protect their power, and to cover their own misdeeds. If the traditional view turns out to be wrong, we will hear it over and over: The Jews lied.

But is this fair? It is difficult to say, given that the whole notion of lying is quite ambiguous. In most manifestations, a lie involves someone knowing the truth of something and then saying otherwise. But there are many grey areas here. Is a half-truth a lie? Is an exaggeration a lie? Is a dissembler a liar? And then there is the question of intent. Is a 'noble' lie any less pernicious than an 'ordinary' lie? And how are we to judge intention?

Apart from all these issues is the question of what is sometimes called an *honest lie*: of someone who legitimately and honestly believes they are stating the truth, but in fact are wrong. I suspect that many academics and media persons fall into this category. Being generally lazy thinkers and unwilling to undertake a critical examination of things, they simply accept the standard view and repeat it verbatim.

The problem here is that, in the context of the great Holocaust debate, very few people know the truth. Those few are the people whom I cited in Chapter 1, along with a small number of others. For all the rest there is mass reliance on this handful of individuals, and on a small set of standard reference works. Academics cite each other incessantly, in a circular parade of fallacious reasoning. They either cannot be troubled to investigate the truth or are afraid of what they might find. And so they simply fall in line.

But let me be clear: There are Holocaust liars out there. They fall into two main categories. Many survivors are outright liars; they know what actually happened, and they consciously and willfully state facts to the contrary. They may have benign or 'noble' motives, but liars they are. Other survivors are less to blame: those who simply make unwarranted inferences—about homicidal gas chambers, for instance—or who suffer from false memories. They are weak-minded dupes, perhaps, or manipulated simpletons, but not liars per se. The lying survivors, though, are the most dangerous and are fully to blame for their distortions of the truth.

The second group of liars is the clique of Holocaust specialists—those academics and researchers who are directly and intimately acquainted with the issues. Many of these men and women are intelligent individuals. They surely understand the revisionist charges, and yet they ignore or falsely disparage them. In this category I place all those mentioned in Chapter 1: Arad and Lipstadt, Shermer and Zimmerman, van Pelt and Kershaw, Browning, Evans and Longerich. I have to assume they know the truth, but choose to say otherwise. In my opinion, they are outright liars.

Their only conceivable excuse—to claim ignorance—is to surrender their entire claim to expertise. For the experts to somehow claim that they 'did not know' about these issues is to admit gross incompetency, if not sheer idiocy. Thus our experts are caught in a terrible bind: either they are outright, malicious liars, or they are gross incompetents. Needless to say, the future does not bode well for their reputations.

A 'Jewish Conspiracy'?

What about that most serious charge: that the Holocaust is a Jewish conspiracy, intended to benefit individuals, Jewish groups, and the state of Israel? Jewish conspiracy theories have a long history, and could be the subject of their own book. They go back at least to the charge that Jews were the murderers of Jesus Christ. They would include the infamous "Protocols of the Elders of Zion," a 1900-era document of uncertain origin, describing Jewish plans for world domination. Such theories seem to have developed because Jews have been extremely successful in many cultures throughout history, their minority status notwithstanding. But is there anything to this specific notion of a Holocaust conspiracy?

The short answer is no... and yes. A Holocaust conspiracy theory can take one of two forms. The first is the idea of a small group of powerful and influential Jews who work together, in secret, to concoct a plan of action that benefits them in some way. To refer to the Holocaust as a 'Jewish conspiracy' implies that this small group of Jews acted together during and immediately after the war, concocted the Holocaust story, the gas chambers, the 6 million deaths, etc. because they knew that it would lead to global sympathy for Jewish people, to financial reparations, and perhaps even to the final consent to the creation of a Jewish Zionist state of Israel. Well, in fact all those things happened—but we are utterly lacking any evidence that it was planned that way. Unless someone can produce clear evidence of a pre-planned Holocaust, it would be best to drop all such talk.

The other aspect of a conspiracy is the notion of some on-going action, by writers, historians, business leaders, governmental leaders, media CEOs, and the like, in which they are all in on the scam, and are consciously sustaining a false story simply for the benefit of the Jews. This one is more interesting. There is a kind of ad hoc conspiracy at work here, both among Jews and non-Jews. Jews feel an intense sense of unity and cohesion, and will rarely seriously oppose one another; when push comes to shove, Jews stick together.[204] They cover each others' lies, and they deflect any seriously critical attacks. This is true not only for the Holocaust but with any issue pertaining to broadly Jewish interests.

Among non-Jews, we know that there are very many influential and wealthy people who do indeed derive their wealth and power from Jews. They understand all too well that one does not bite the hand that feeds. Even these non-Jews, who know nothing about the Holocaust, will reflexively defend the traditional story—and attack those expressing any doubt about it—simply to protect their benefactors. This happens frequently in government, academia, the media, and entertainment, where so many depend heavily upon Jewish largess. And all this in addition to the reaction of many liberals and leftists, who have been more or less brainwashed into believing that all Holocaust critics are evil.

Thus, in a functional sense, there is a kind of conspiracy—a conspiracy of silence. Holocaust witnesses and liars will not be challenged, revisionist issues will not be discussed, and revisionists themselves will be censored, defamed, or jailed. It is not a conspiracy to deliberately and consciously sustain a false Holocaust story, but rather one to defend Jewish interests generally by stifling critics.

All this is possible because of the role and pervasiveness of Jewish influence. Hence the first step is to inquire into the actual state of affairs. It is a fact that Jews have substantial influence, directly and indirectly, in virtually all Western nations. If we are to understand the broader context of the Holocaust, we have to know the truth about this influence.

The root of the problem, as just mentioned, is that Jews have been a minority in many cultures, and yet have succeeded. And not just a minority, but a *small* minority. And not just successful, but *spectacularly* successful. Such a situation is a breeding ground for conspiracy theories. But more importantly, it begs an explanation: How, precisely, does this influence operate?

A fundamental principle of democracy, and of justice, is embodied in the phrase: one man, one vote. According to this principle each person has some say in the governance of his or her society, and each person counts equally. Anything less would be to favor certain persons or groups, or to disenfranchise others. A practical consequence of this principle is that of proportional representation: each subgroup of people has a voice proportional to their number. Men and women, being roughly equal in number, should have

---

[204] The Jewish 'Law of Moser,' among other dictates, proscribes turning on or betraying a fellow Jew to a non-Jew.

roughly equal say in society. Ethnic or racial minorities are full and equal participants in the life of society—each individual allowed one vote—but as a group, their influence should only be comparable to their size within a given nation.

A corollary to this principle of equal representation, or rather, its justification, is the idea that all human beings are intrinsically equal. We accept that women are fully equal to men in a social, political and legal sense. We believe that they are equally intelligent and creative. We believe that they should receive equal pay for equal work. We furthermore expect that women will be more or less equally represented in social organizations and institutions.

The same holds for blacks, Hispanics, Turks, Arabs—any minority or subgroup of the population. We believe that each subgroup is intelligent, creative, and politically and legally equal to each other. Consequently, we expect that, in line with their numbers, ethnic minorities should be proportionately represented in our social institutions.

If any one group is overrepresented, then necessarily some other group is underrepresented. If men constitute 80 percent of a corporation's executives, or 80 percent of a nation's legislators, then women are obviously unfairly represented. If blacks are a 15 percent minority and yet whites comprise, say, 95 percent of executives or legislators, then blacks are unfairly represented. In a truly just and democratic society, each subgroup will be at least roughly represented according to its numbers.

Hence the obvious concern here: if Jews are overrepresented in a given society, then, *necessarily*, other groups are underrepresented. If the Jewish voice carries more weight than others, then, *necessarily*, others will not be treated fairly or justly. This is elementary math.

Before examining the details of one nation in particular—the United States—consider the following. The global Jewish population is about 13 million. Relative to a worldwide total of 7.2 billion people, Jews represent just 0.18 percent, and shrinking. Compare this to their global influence. One measure of such influence is given in a survey by *Vanity Fair* magazine. Its editors periodically compile a list of the "100 most powerful people in the world"—in the sense of social or cultural influence. A recent survey, from 2007, included a list that was over 50 percent Jewish. Specifically, out of 106 names (a few of the "individuals" were actually pairs), 57 are Jewish—or 53 percent. The highest ranking of these are: Google founders Sergey Brin and Larry Page; private equity megalith Blackstone's owner Stephen Schwarzman; film director Steven Spielberg; New York mayor Michael Bloomberg; designer Ralph Lauren; media tycoon Barry Diller; fashion maven Diane von Fürstenberg; and Hollywood super-agent David Geffen. Granted, *Vanity Fair* has a very shallow notion of power. And granted that it is part of the Jewish (American)-owned Condé Nast empire. Even so, this is a striking statement of Jewish influence.

Then consider Jews' standing today as an ethnic minority. Apart from Israel, they are less than a 2 percent minority in every country of the world. The nations with the highest Jewish percentage are as follows:[205]

1. USA   1.80%
2. Canada   1.09%
3. France   0.74%
4. Uruguay   0.51%
5. Australia 0.49%
6. Hungary   0.48%
7. UK   0.45%
8. Argentina 0.43%
9. Latvia   0.28%
10. Belgium   0.27%

Based on such numbers, we would normally expect Jews to have a corresponding influence in the political and business affairs of each nation. Again, this would reflect the general principles of equality, democracy, and justice that all these nations extol. But this is not the case. Jewish influence undoubtedly exceeds these numbers in every instance, considerably so in the major world powers—US, Canada, France, UK, and Australia. Thus we might inquire as to just how extensive that influence is, and how it is manifest. This should tell us something about the kernels of truth behind a putative 'Holocaust conspiracy.'

Covering All the Bases

The United States has the largest Jewish population of any nation on Earth—Israel included—and the largest percentage of any country apart from Israel. Hence we have good reason to look at Jewish influence there. Additionally, (1) it is the lone military superpower; (2) it is the global center for Holocaust study and scholarship; (3) American (primarily Jewish-American) money and influence are leading factors in promoting the Holocaust; and (4) extensive data are readily available. First I will examine the general matter of

---

[205] 2014 data (www.jewishvirtuallibrary.org). The percentage for the US is disputed, given the wide range of estimates for the Jewish population. The stated 1.8% is based on a total of 5.7 million. However, other estimates give higher numbers, over 6 or even 7 million. The fact that all numbers are reported by Jewish agencies, and the question of mixed heritage, cause significant problems in reaching definitive numbers for all countries.

Jewish influence in the US, and then I will look at how it affects the Holocaust debate.

To begin with, here is one clue. A 1996 *New York Times* column by Jewish writer Ari Shavit discussed the recent Israeli killing of some one hundred Lebanese civilians. There was initially some concern about the potential American reaction to such killings, but Shavit writes, resignedly: "Believing with absolute certitude that now, with the White House, the Senate, and much of the American media in our hands, the lives of others do not count as much as our own."[206] Here we have a rather shocking statement by a foreign observer. Was it—*is it*—really possible that the White House, the Senate, and the American media are "in the hands" of the Israelis, or Jews in general? What could prompt such a statement?

That Jewish influence is extensive in American society is well known, certainly in the areas of economics, politics, and intellectual and cultural life.[207] In 2013, Vice President Joe Biden made some impolitic remarks

---

[206] 27 May, p. 19.

[207] Regarding economics: Without digressing into crude generalizations about 'rich Jews,' let me just cite a few relevant statistics. Overall, Jewish income is considerably above average. In the early 1990s it was fully 50 percent higher than the national median (Kosmin and Ritterband 1991: 21). Regarding the very wealthy, *Forbes* magazine compiles an annual list of the world's richest people, with details by individual country. Kosmin and Ritterband (p. 24) cite a study of the 400 wealthiest Americans; of this list, 92 were identified as Jews (23 percent). Of the top 40 names, 16 (40 percent) were Jews.
The trend continues today. *Forbes*'s 2012 list of the world's billionaires includes 1,426 names in total, including 442 Americans. Roughly 17 percent of the global list, and 35 percent of the Americans, are Jews. Their 2014 list of the richest Americans includes at least 15 Jewish names among the top 40: Ellison, Bloomberg, Zuckerberg, Adelson, Page, Brin, Soros, Icahn, Ballmer, Blavatnik, Dell, Bren, Perelman, Murdoch, and Schwarzman. But even this is misleading; the Walton family, for example, takes four of the top ten names, even though it is a single family enterprise.
As to intellectual and cultural life, one measure of this was cited above: *Vanity Fair*'s 2007 list of the world's 100 most powerful, or influential, individuals, 53% of whom are Jewish—and most of these Jewish-Americans. An earlier study (Zuckerman 1977: 68) noted that Jews made up 27 percent of all US-born Nobel Prize winners, and 40 percent of winners in science and economics. Lipset and Raab (1995: 26) state that Jews account for 20 percent of professors at leading universities—with certain disciplines considerably higher than that. Generally, at least since the 1970s, they have "composed about half of the American intellectual elite" (Kadushin 1974: 23). This was still true in the mid-1990s: "during the last three decades Jews have made up 50 percent of the top two hundred intellectuals…" (Lipset and Raab, p. 26).
The entertainment industry is worthy of a brief remark. The fact that "Jews control Hollywood" is neither controversial nor even disputed today. In fact it is openly discussed. An opinion piece by Joel Stein in the *Los Angeles Times* ("How Jewish Is Hollywood?" 19 Dec 2008) explained matter-of-factly that "Jews totally run Hollywood." Stein cited the names of the major studio bosses, and every one was Jewish: Chernin (20th Century Fox), Grey (Paramount), Iger (Disney), Lynton (Sony Pictures), Meyer (Warner Bros.), Moonves (CBS), Sloan (MGM), Zucker (Universal), and Bob and Harvey Weinstein (The Weinstein Co.). And this does not include numerous other influentials, including Gary Barber (MGM), Jon Feltheimer (Lionsgate), Ryan Kavanaugh (Relativity Media),

along this line in a public speech. "Jewish heritage is American heritage," he opined, trying to flatter his most important constituency. After elaborating on the important Jewish role in such areas as civil rights, immigration, women's rights, and gay rights, Biden said, "I think behind all of that, I bet you 85 percent of those changes, whether it's in Hollywood or social media, are a consequence of Jewish leaders in the industry. The influence is immense, the influence is immense."[208] Occasionally, it seems, our politicians do tell the truth.

For present purposes, however, I will briefly examine two broad sectors of American society: media and government. In all cases we should bear in mind the baseline measure of Jewish-Americans as representing less than 2 percent of the population.

Media Dominance

The Jewish role in American media has long been a topic of discussion. In the early 1920s, Henry Ford issued a number of scathing critiques of Jewish control in newspapers, radio, theater, and motion pictures.[209] In the midst of World War Two, Joseph Goebbels commented on their influence in his personal diary: "Some statistics are given to me on the proportion of Jews in American radio, film, and press. The percentage is truly frightening. Jewry controls 100% of the film business, and between 90 and 95% of press and radio."[210] Though perhaps an exaggeration, such numbers give some indication of Jewish dominance at the time.

Without question, their role has strengthened over time. As a general measure we can refer to Lipset and Raab's (1995: 27) claim that nearly 60 percent of leading directors, producers, and writers, in both television and cinema, are Jews. This is reflected in Jewish influence in the major media corporations. Here are the largest in the United States, along with their leading executives:

1) <u>Time-Warner</u>: Jeff Bewkes, Jeff Zucker.
2) <u>Disney</u>: Robert Iger (for the previous 20 years, Michael Eisner).

Avi Lerner (Nu Image), Lawrence Bender (producer), Tom Rothman and Amy Pascal (Sony), Haim Saban, and Marc Graboff (Core Media). Stein closed his piece with this cute little comment: "I don't care if Americans think we're running the news media, Hollywood, Wall Street or the government. I just care that we get to keep running them."

[208] "Jewish heritage is American heritage" (www.politico.com, 21 May 2013).

[209] See Ford's book *The International Jew*, which is a collection of weekly essays over a period of some two years. For a good discussion, see Kevin MacDonald's review article in *The Occidental Quarterly* 2(4).

[210] 24 April 1942. For the full context see Dalton (2010).

3) 21ˢᵗ Century Fox and News Corp: Rupert, James, and Lachlan Murdoch.
4) Viacom: Sumner Redstone, Philippe Dauman.
5) CBS Corp: Sumner Redstone, Leslie Moonves.
6) Comcast/NBC: Brian Roberts, David Cohen, Mark Lazarus, and Robert Greenblatt.

All these individuals are Jewish.[211] This general power structure has been in place for much of the past three decades.

Of special interest is the status of the three major American television networks, each of which is firmly under Jewish control: Disney owns ABC, Comcast owns NBC, and CBS—previously owned by Viacom—is now an independent but still Jewish-run enterprise. There are two additional major news channels: CNN and Fox News. CNN is owned by Time-Warner, and Fox News by 21ˢᵗ Century Fox.[212] Thus there are no truly independent major television or news networks left in the US.

Regarding print media, Jewish influence has an especially long history. It goes back at least to the late 19ᵗʰ century, when Adolph Ochs purchased the *New York Times* in 1896. The *Times* has been pro-Israel and pro-Zionist ever since; the current owner, publisher and chairman is Arthur Sulzberger. Alsatian Jew Eugene Meyer purchased the *Washington Post* in 1933. Both the current publisher—his great-granddaughter Katharine Weymouth—and chief editor Martin Baron are Jewish. Until recently purchased by the Zionist Murdoch, the *Wall Street Journal* was owned by the Jewish Kann family. Mort Zuckerman owns the *New York Daily News*, the third-largest New York paper. Ownership and management at other major papers have varied recently, but it has widely been observed for years that such papers as the *Los Angeles Times* and the *Chicago Tribune* have reflexively supported Jewish and Israeli views.

Regarding magazines and journals, the Condé Nast empire—which includes *Vanity Fair*, *The New Yorker*, *Wired*, and *Vogue*—is owned by Samuel ("Si") Newhouse.[213] In addition to the *New York Daily News*, Zuckerman also owns *US News and World Report*. Other periodicals, such as *The New Republic*, *Commentary*, and *The Weekly Standard*, are chronically pro-Israel and pro-Jewish.

---

[211] With the possible exception of the Murdochs; their ethnicity is uncertain, although Rupert has long been an avid supporter of Israeli and Zionist causes.
[212] The Fox name comes from William Fox (1879-1952), the Hungarian-Jewish founder of Fox Films.
[213] This, in addition to "dozens of newspapers," according to Wikipedia.

As to radio, perhaps the most striking example is National Public Radio. Anecdotally, the on-air staff at NPR is over half Jewish.[214] Is it not uncommon to hear a Jewish program host interviewing a Jewish expert about some other prominent Jewish-American. References to the Holocaust or Judaism pop up frequently, even in stories that have no ostensible connection. And NPR's influence is substantial. Affiliate stations are widely distributed throughout the country, reaching some 26 million listeners. With 860 stations—an average of 17 per state—it is often possible to pick up identical programming on three or more stations simultaneously. In response to charges that NPR is pro-Israel or pro-Jewish, Jewish groups launch counterattacks, preposterously claiming that it is pro-Muslim or pro-Arab. Station managers thus get complaints from both sides, and thus falsely conclude that their coverage is 'about right.' It seems that a strong offense is often the best defense.

Finally, there is considerable Jewish influence in a number of other technology companies which, though not strictly media, nonetheless play an important role in the media infrastructure. The three clearest such examples are (1) *Google*, run by Sergey Brin and Larry Page; (2) *Facebook*, with CEO Mark Zuckerberg and COO Sheryl Sandberg; and (3) *Oracle*, led by Larry Ellison and co-CEO Safra Catz. Others of significance include Michael Dell, owner and CEO of Dell Computer. Wikipedia, managed by co-founders Jimmy Wales and Lila Tretikov, is notably sensitive to Jewish and Israeli concerns. Participant Media is run by founder Jeff Skoll, formerly of eBay. The software company Asana is run by Facebook castoffs Dustin Moskovitz and Justin Rosenstein. And debate continues to swirl around Amazon CEO Jeff Bezos, regarding whether or not he is Jewish.

Dominance in Government

Jewish influence in American government was hidden in the shadows for many years, rarely spoken of and even less often written about. Finally, in 2006, John Mearsheimer and Stephen Walt published a groundbreaking article, "The Israel Lobby and US foreign policy," incorporating extensive research on the issue. They documented and consolidated information that had previously been dispersed amongst many sources—information that had been often discussed elsewhere, though not necessarily in a scholarly fashion. Details of the article were subsequently elaborated in their 2007 book of the same name.

---

[214] And this does not include non-Jews, such as Cokie Roberts, who have Jewish spouses or relatives.

Prominent Jewish-Americans focus their efforts on the support and defense of Israel—hence the term 'Israel Lobby,' sometimes called the 'Jewish Lobby'—but they also seek to combat perceived anti-Semitism, promote Jewish interests and support the traditional Holocaust story. The Lobby has had high-level contacts in government since the beginning of the twentieth century, and has exercised considerable power. For a detailed discussion of the substantial Jewish role in both world wars, see my essays (2013, 2014). With the defeat of Hitler, the Lobby became increasingly emboldened.

Into the 1950s, Jewish influence was well attested to by Secretary of State John Foster Dulles. Israel invaded Egypt in October 1956, capturing the whole of the Sinai Peninsula. UN resolutions were passed demanding a withdrawal; these had the full support of both Eisenhower and Dulles. But the Jewish Lobby had other ideas. In a phone call of 11 February 1957 to Harry Luce, Dulles said, "I am aware how almost impossible it is in the country to carry out a foreign policy not approved by the Jews. Marshall and Forrestal learned that. I am going to try to have one."[215] A conversation the next day included a complaint about "the terrific control the Jews have over the news media, and the barrage which the Jews have built up on Congressmen." A week later, in a phone call with a church leader, Dulles said,

> I am very much concerned over the fact that the Jewish influence here is completely dominating the scene and making it almost impossible to get Congress to do anything they don't approve of. The Israeli Embassy is practically dictating to the Congress through influential Jewish people in the country. (*ibid.*)

This was a remarkably blunt assessment by a knowledgeable insider.

And yet the power of the Lobby grew even stronger during the Johnson Administration of the 1960s. The Six-Day War in 1967 galvanized Jewish-Americans, catapulting the Lobby to the top of the Washington power pyramid, where it remains today.

In its present form the Israel Lobby consists of several components: individual Jewish-Americans, pro-Israel think tanks, Jewish organizations, prominent intellectuals,[216] and sympathetic non-Jews, such as Christian Zionists. The whole process is coordinated by an umbrella organization, the American Israel Public Affairs Committee (AIPAC). For at least the past 20 years, AIPAC has been one of the most powerful and most feared organizations in Washington. A 1997 *Fortune* magazine poll rated them the second-

---

[215] Cited in Neff (1981: 433). 'Marshall' is former Secretary of State and Defense George Marshall. 'Forrestal' is former Secretary of Defense James Forrestal. Both men held office in the late 1940s. See also Neff (1995: 99).

[216] Including the notorious 'neo-conservatives,' who are predominantly Jewish but include a minority of non-Jews.

most powerful lobby, behind only the 38-million-member American Association of Retired Persons (AARP). This ranking was confirmed in 2005.[217]

Jewish influence can be examined separately in the Congress and the White House. Congressional influence is driven by AIPAC and by the campaign money that it directs to favored candidates. AIPAC conducts a rigorous vetting process to determine who are the 'true friends' of American Jews, and these candidates, once 'certified kosher,' can expect financial support from around the entire country. Mearsheimer and Walt (2007: 155) relate the case of a 1990 Democratic Senate candidate from Oregon, Harry Lonsdale, who got invited to AIPAC headquarters in Washington. "I was told what my opinion *must* be, and exactly what words I was to use to express those opinions in public," he said. Having passed the test, Lonsdale was given a list of likely donors; "I called; they gave—from Florida to Alaska." The fact that people "from Florida to Alaska" have no equity in the state of Oregon is apparently of no concern to AIPAC.

Conversely, if a candidate is perceived to be an enemy of the Jewish people, for instance by opposing unconditional aid to Israel, or by insisting on just treatment for Palestinians, then AIPAC and the Lobby will pull out all the stops to defeat him by giving massive support to an opponent. Mearsheimer and Walt cite a number of such victims, including McKinney, Findley, Hilliard, McCloskey, Fulbright, Jepson and Stevenson. One notable example, the 1984 defeat of Senator Charles Percy, had AIPAC crowing: "All the Jews in America, from coast to coast, gathered to oust Percy. And the American politicians... got the message." One Jewish editor said in 2002, "There is this image in Congress that you don't cross these people or they take you down." "The bottom line," according to Mearsheimer and Walt, "is that AIPAC... has an almost unchallenged hold on Congress" (p. 162). They quote an anonymous staffer: "We can count on well over half the House—250 to 300 members—to do reflexively whatever AIPAC wants." And they recount an incident with AIPAC chief Steven Rosen in which he places a napkin on a table, saying, "In 24 hours, we could have the signature of 70 senators on this napkin" (p. 10). Both houses of Congress are thus well covered, from the Jewish perspective.

In addition to being held in thrall to AIPAC-coordinated funds, a growing number of Jewish Americans have been directly elected to Congress. The 2006 midterm election was notable in this regard. Shortly after the election the *Jerusalem Post* (4 Jan 2007) ran an article: "Most Jews Ever Set to Enter Congress." The overall number was 43, including 13 Senators and 30 members of the House. This trend continued in 2008: "Record Number of Jews Elected to Congress" (*Jerusalem Post*, 5 Nov 2008). The new total was 48: 15 in the Senate, and 33 in the House. Nearly all of these were Democrats.

---

[217] See Mearsheimer and Walt (2007: 117).

Accordingly, then, this Jewish contingent suffered a minor setback in 2014, as Republicans swept into power. Approaching the 2016 election, there currently are just 30 Jews in Congress—11 in the Senate and 19 in the House. But of course, when Jewish Lobby money can purchase congressmen, there is no need to hold office yourself.

So much for the legislative branch. What about the judiciary? Only one striking fact need be mentioned. The current US Supreme Court has, among its nine justices, three Jews: Stephen Breyer, Ruth Ginsburg, and Elena Kagan. Thus the highest court in the land is 33 percent Jewish—in a nation of 1.8 percent Jews.

Then we have the executive branch. What about American presidential candidates, and the White House? Mearsheimer and Walt open their book with some reflections on the 2008 presidential election. They note that, despite the many differences between Democrats and Republicans, there is "one subject [on which] the candidates will speak with one voice. ... [They] will go to considerable lengths to express their deep personal commitment to one foreign country—Israel..." (p. 3). McCain, Obama, Romney and Edwards are all quoted as to their passionate dedication to the Jewish state.

Hillary Clinton in particular has made a notable shift to the pro-Jewish side; consequently, she was "expected to snare the lion's share of the Jewish community's substantial political donations in the race for the 2008 Presidential nomination."[218] Though she failed to get the Democratic nomination, Clinton went to great lengths to earn Jewish support. And as if political reasons were insufficient, since 2010 she has had a Jewish son-in-law, Marc Mezvinsky. This development has surely cemented her commitment. Unsurprisingly, she is a lock for the Democratic nomination in the 2016 race.

Clinton's shift, late in the 2008 campaign, to a rabidly pro-Israel stance was nothing short of astonishing. Speaking at a debate in Philadelphia on the topic of the alleged Iranian threat to Israel, she said, "An attack on Israel would incur massive retaliation from the United States..."[219] This in itself is striking, given that there is no mutual defense pact with Israel as there is with the NATO countries. And it is utterly irresponsible, since "massive retaliation" would constitute an act of war requiring Congressional approval. Wanting there to be no doubt as to her commitment to the Jewish state, Clinton added this comment a week later: "If Iran were to launch a nuclear attack on Israel... we will attack Iran.... [W]e would be able to totally obliterate them." This, of course, is highly revealing. Such a statement can *only* be explained as obsequious pandering to the Israel Lobby, for whom no amount of saber rattling is too extreme.

---

[218] Mearsheimer and Walt (2007: 159).
[219] 16 April 2008.

Republican nominee John McCain was also eager to display his fealty. Early in the nomination race he traveled to Israel, seeking endorsement: "When it comes to the defense of Israel, we simply cannot compromise" (in Mearsheimer and Walt 2007: 4). He gave a lengthy interview to *Atlantic Monthly* journalist Jeffrey Goldberg, heaping praise upon Israel, and sprinkling in references to the Holocaust.[220] After declaring the Zionist cause to be "just," McCain explains that he recently visited the Yad Vashem memorial. He relates his admiration for Auschwitz survivors Wiesel and Frankl, adding, "I think about Frankl all the time." (That's a bit weird.) And in a discussion on the mortal threat posed by Iran, McCain exclaims: "The United States of America has committed itself to never allowing another Holocaust. [This has been true] ever since we discovered the horrendous aspects of the Holocaust."

In the 2012 presidential race, Republican Mitt Romney dutifully made his own trip to Israel, to fund-raise and earn the support of the Israeli leadership. He pledged to use "any and all measures" against Iran, presumably including military attack. Tough talk paid off at home. His top individual donor was Jewish casino mogul Sheldon Adelson, who gave in excess of $34 million.

And then we have President Barack Obama, a man who has had a number of his own 'Jewish moments.' In a 2008 interview, with the Democratic nomination still undecided, Obama made a point of emphasizing his support for Israel—embracing the racist notion of Israel as a "Jewish state," and declaring it to be "a fundamentally just idea." He added: "If you're waiting for America to distance itself from Israel, you are delusional."[221] Immediately upon earning the nomination in June 2008, Obama's very first act was a meeting and speech at AIPAC. There he pronounced himself a "true friend of Israel" and promised his "unshakeable commitment to Israel's security." Suggesting a near-religious devotion, he publicly declared that its security is "sacrosanct."[222] One month later, during his first major overseas trip, Obama spent a day in Israel, during which he found the time to lay a wreath at the Yad Vashem Holocaust monument—while dutifully wearing a white Jewish skull cap.[223] This astoundingly crass act of obeisance to the Israel Lobby dashed any remaining hopes that Obama might be free of their influence.

---

[220] Online interview, "McCain on Israel, Iran, and the Holocaust" (30 May 2008). See: <http://www.theatlantic.com/international/archive/2008/05/mccain-on-israel-iran-and-the-holocaust/8346/>

[221] Online interview, "Obama on Zionism and Hamas" (J. Goldberg, 12 May 2008): <www.theatlantic.com/international/archive/2008/05/obama-on-zionism-and-hamas/8318/>

[222] UPI (4 Jun 2008).

[223] Reuters (23 Jul 2008).

In August 2008 Obama named Joe Biden as his running mate. As an Irish Catholic from working-class Scranton, Pennsylvania, one might have thought that Biden would be disinclined to be reflexively pro-Israel. But that's not how it works in Washington. In a recent interview on the Jewish (American) cable network Shalom TV, Biden admitted, "I am a Zionist. You don't have to be a Jew to be a Zionist."[224] True enough. But Obama knew that he was facing a tight race, and it would have been unwise to select anyone other than a 'true friend' of Israel.

In his nearly 8-year tenure, Obama has made numerous Jewish appointments to key positions. Past and present staff members include Rahm Emanuel (chief of staff), Mary Schapiro (SEC), Ben Bernanke (Fed chair), David Axelrod (senior advisor), Elena Kagan (solicitor general), Peter Orszag (OMB), Larry Summers (NEC), Dennis Ross (special assistant), Jonathan Greenblatt (special assistant), Tony Blinken (NSA), Jack Lew (Secretary of Treasury), David Plouffe (senior advisor), Gene Sperling (NEC), Janet Yellen (Fed chair), and David Cohen (CIA). Special mention goes to Secretary of State John Kerry; few realize that his family's original surname was Kohn, and that his father was a full Jew. And such a list does not include those non-Jews with Jewish spouses, such as former Secretary of Treasury Tim Geithner and current UN Ambassador Samantha Power. We can be sure that such individuals are highly attuned to Jewish and Israeli concerns.[225]

Why do American presidential candidates bow before the Lobby like this? Because in huge national campaigns, money is critical. The 2008 race exceeded $1 billion in total cash raised, smashing all previous records. The 2012 campaign surpassed $2 billion, with each candidate individually raising over $1 billion. The upcoming 2016 presidential race will surely set another record.

But the key fact is this: The bulk of the money, *for both parties*, comes from Jewish donors. This has been true for at least the past 50 years. Jimmy Carter's chief of staff, Hamilton Jordan, wrote:

> In 1976, over 60 percent of the large donors to the Democratic Party were Jewish... Over 75 percent of the monies raised in Humphrey's 1968 campaign was from Jewish contributors; over 90 percent of the monies raised by Scoop Jackson in the Democratic primaries was from Jewish contributors...

Even Carter, from a region with a very small Jewish population, drew 35 percent of his funds from them. And it was not just Democrats. Jordan notes,

---

[224] See, for example, Weitzel's online article "Biden and Israel": <http://www.counterpunch.org/weitzel09022008.html>

[225] Obama's late 'break' from the pro-Israel line is more show than substance. His occasional public tiffs with Israeli Prime Minister Netanyahu are only about the degree, not the fact, of compliance.

for example, that "over 60 percent of the monies raised by Nixon in 1972 was from Jewish contributors."[226]

This trend accelerated in the 1990s. Regarding Bill Clinton's 1992 victory, the *New York Times* reported: "Jews contributed about 60% of Mr. Clinton's non-institutional campaign funds" (5 Jan 1993). Consequently, Clinton appointed many Jews to high-ranking positions: Robert Reich (Labor), Madeleine Albright (State), Robert Rubin (Treasury), William Cohen (Defense), Dan Glickman (Agriculture), David Kessler (FDA), Arthur Levitt (SEC chairman), Alan Greenspan (Federal Reserve), and (unsuccessful) attorney general nominee Zoe Baird—along with advisors Dennis Ross, Martin Indyk, Sandy Berger and Rahm Emanuel.

In the 2000 presidential election, Al Gore, with the election seemingly in the bag, nominated orthodox Jew Joseph Lieberman as running mate. Such a decision would not have happened without an eye to Jewish donors and the Lobby generally. Unfortunately for Gore, he lost what should have been a landslide victory. As with Hillary's 2008 run, sometimes even the money of the Lobby is not enough to turn the trick.

But of course, the joke was on us all. The 2000 winner, George W. Bush, turned out to be even more sympathetic to Jewish concerns than Clinton or Gore. Bush made a number of high-level Jewish appointments, including Michael Chertoff (Homeland Security), Michael Mukasey (Justice), Samuel Bodman (Energy), and Ben Bernanke (Federal Reserve). But perhaps more important were the many Jewish neo-conservative advisors and staffers that influenced White House policy: Elliot Abrams,[227] Doug Feith, Aaron Friedberg, John Hannah, Scooter Libby,[228] Richard Perle, Paul Wolfowitz, David Wurmser, David Brooks, Charles Krauthammer, William Kristol, Norman Podhoretz, Eliot Cohen, Bernard Lewis, Max Boot, David Frum, Robert Kagan, and Daniel Pipes. These individuals were decisive in the decisions to go to war with Afghanistan and Iraq, and perhaps had a role to play in the 9/11 attacks.

Since 2000, the prominent Jewish role in fundraising has continued unabated. In 2003 the *Washington Post* reported: "Democratic presidential candidates depend on Jewish supporters to supply as much as 60% of the money raised from private sources" (13 Mar, p. A1). *The Hill* reported the next year

---

[226] Mearsheimer and Walt (2007: 407, note 55).
[227] Abrams seems to have a particularly galling notion of Jewish exceptionalism. He wrote that "there can be no doubt that Jews... are to stand apart from the nation in which they live. It is the very nature of being Jewish to be apart... from the rest of the population" (cited in Mearsheimer and Walt 2007: 167).
[228] I. Lewis "Scooter" Libby committed a federal offense in 2005 by leaking the identity of CIA agent Valerie Plame. He was sentenced to 30 months in prison, but Bush commuted the jail term in 2007. When you commit crimes for the president, you need not worry about prosecution.

that "an estimated 50 to 70 percent of large contributions to the Democratic Party and allied political units came from Jewish donors" (30 Mar 2004, p. 1). Feingold (2008: 4) writes that "The role of campaign contributions given by Jews deserves special mention. Over 60 percent of the campaign funds collected by the Democratic Party, and a respectable percentage of Republican funds, stem from Jewish sources." And in 2011 the *Jewish Telegraphic Agency* noted, "Obama captured 78 percent of the Jewish vote in 2008, and estimates over the years have reckoned that Jewish donors provide between one-third and two-thirds of the party's money" (7 Jun).

With such a system in place, pandering to Jewish interests is certain to continue for the foreseeable future. Jimmy Carter nicely summarized the situation in a March 2008 television interview with the Arab news organization Al Jazeera:

> You have to understand that in the US it is impossible for any candidate for president, governor, Senate, or House of Representatives to get elected if they publicly contradict the policies of the Israeli government.

This influence has clear and undeniable effects on US policy, especially foreign policy. Consider, for example, foreign aid. Despite the many impoverished nations around the world, Israel has been for decades the number one recipient of US aid money. It receives $3 billion annually in military aid, and another $2–3 billion in indirect aid and benefits—upwards of $6 billion per year, every year. On a per capita basis this works out to an astonishing $1,200 annually for every Israeli man, woman and child. Right behind Israel on the recipient list, though receiving much less money, are America's Arab and Muslim client states—Egypt, Jordan, Pakistan. These countries toe the American line, and hence this aid indirectly serves to benefit Israel as well.

With respect to the United Nations, the US can be counted on to cover for any and all Israeli crimes. Since 1972, the US has vetoed 42 Security Council resolutions critical of Israel—more than all other vetoes from all other permanent members combined. In the General Assembly, the US often finds itself virtually alone, siding with Israel and a handful of dependent micro-nations against overwhelming world opinion.

Perhaps most important, Jewish influence was decisive in causing the United States to start—and continue—the Iraq war. In March 2003, US Representative James Moran said, "If it were not for the strong support of the Jewish community for this war with Iraq, we would not be doing this."[229] The comment caused such a stir, and hit so close to the bone, that Colin Powell himself was forced to publicly deny it. The decisiveness of the Lobby in this matter has been recognized worldwide. In late 2003, with the war well

---

[229] *Washington Post* (11 Mar 2003).

underway, outgoing Malaysian president Mahathir Mohamad said the unspeakable: "Today Jews rule the world by proxy. They get others to fight and die for them."[230] Mearsheimer and Walt (2007) are clear in their overall assessment: "the war would almost certainly not have occurred" without pressure from the Lobby; they were the "critical element." They dismiss as well the common liberal fantasies that Iraq was a "war for oil," or was part of some evil Republican scheme to frighten the public and thus maintain power.

Most telling is the behavior of the American government since 2003. Despite campaign pledges to oppose war and to bring troops home, Congress has been more than happy to allow Obama to conduct military attacks in several countries—Iraq, Afghanistan, Pakistan, Yemen, Somalia, and Libya all experience on-going drone strikes. The Americans ousted Muammar Gaddafi of Libya in 2011, turning that region into a state of chaos. Since 2014, the US has led the attack on the Islamic State, or ISIS. And it continues to make belligerent overtones toward Syria and Iran.

Thus we have a strange situation: Congressional Republicans and Democrats, who disagree on nearly every aspect of governmental action, readily find common cause when it comes to war. This fact is explicable in only one way: both parties are beholden to the same lobby, a lobby that likes to have wars that kill Muslims and disrupt enemies of Israel.[231]

Exploiting the Holocaust

It is clear that Jewish-Americans have massive, disproportionate and decisive influence at many levels of American society—despite being a sub-2-percent minority. The Lobby's influence on each level tends to reinforce and support that of other levels, resulting in a kind of matrix of control over the

---

[230] AP (16 Oct 2003).
[231] Lest we have any thoughts that Congress is acting out of humanitarian concern, we should recall that this is the same system that: conducted a crushing eight-year sanction policy on Iraq in the 1990s, resulting in the death of more than 500,000 Iraqi children ("As many as 576,000 Iraqi children may have died since the end of the Persian Gulf war because of economic sanctions imposed by the Security Council, according to two scientists who surveyed the country for the [UN] Food and Agriculture Organization," NYT, 1 Dec 1995), and then declared the action "worth it" (to quote Madeleine Albright); fired a cruise missile into the only pharmaceutical plant in Sudan, leading to thousands of indirect deaths; gave chemical weapons to Saddam Hussein when he was "our man" fighting Iran; supplied weapons and money to Osama bin Laden when he was "our man" in Afghanistan fighting the Russians; and generally opposes every conceivable humanitarian action when it comes to the Palestinians. The American government holds Arabs and Muslims in very low regard.

largest issues and most-sensitive topics. Hence, for example, political corruption by Lobbyist money is not reported in the media. Jewish and Israeli crimes are underreported, misrepresented, or ignored. 'Good' Holocaust stories get substantial airplay, while 'bad' ones get nothing. Laws are passed in support of Israel, or against anti-Semitism, with little or no public comment. The image of Jewish-Americans in the media is unfailingly positive—and that of Arabs or Muslims rarely so.

I emphasize here: This does not constitute a 'Jewish conspiracy.' It is a simple consequence of two factors. The first is the age-old and universal tendency of minority groups to favor their own. Every minority gives preferential treatment to their fellows, and Jews are no different. The fact that they may be more tenacious on this point is incidental.

Second, it is not a conspiracy of Jews, but rather a *conspiracy of money*. The American system is built on free-market capitalism and the power of capital. Money rules, both in the marketplace and in the halls of government. This is widely known and accepted, if implicitly, by the American public, who have been largely brainwashed as to its adverse effects and possible alternatives; the capitalist system does a very good job at sustaining and defending itself. In a system where money rules, those with the most money, and the will to spend it, have the most influence—period. The Israel Lobby leads the pack, and they are rewarded with dominant control over foreign policy and many domestic issues. The only way that this can change is for another lobbying group to outspend them, or for the American public to wake up from their bad dream and decide that a corrupt, centralized federal government is unacceptable. Barring a miracle or total disaster, neither of these is likely in the near term.

How, then, does all this translate into support for the conventional story of the Holocaust? The strategy works on at least three levels:

1. Universal agreement to ignore, censor, or harass revisionists and revisionism generally.
2. The creation of a 'Holocaust Industry.'
3. The deployment of the Holocaust story toward political ends.

I emphasize that there is no evidence to suggest that these things are centrally coordinated by AIPAC or some secret Jewish cabal. Rather, they are commonly understood by all.[232] Dissenters from these implicit strategic objectives can be sure to receive gentle 'reminders' should they stray.

The first point is self-evident. Public discussion of revisionism is literally nonexistent. Even when prominent figures like Mahmoud Ahmadinejad,

---

[232] I am tempted to call it 'mind-reading by a far-flung bureaucracy,' but that phrase has already been taken.

Bishop Williamson, or Jean-Marie Le Pen[233] breach the taboo, we never get the slightest indication that there might actually be something to their claims. Earlier I cited the legal attacks against prominent revisionists; these continue to the present day. Even this very book will be sure to be ignored or censored, simply because it dares to take revisionism seriously, and to examine its claims in an unbiased manner.

The second point was brought into some prominence in 2000 with Norman Finkelstein's book *The Holocaust Industry*. He argues that a kind of cult has been cultivated around the Holocaust that serves to deflect criticism from Jews and from Israel, and to perpetuate certain organizations and institutions that exist only for this purpose: "The Holocaust was therefore a ploy to de-legitimize all criticism of Jews; such criticism could only spring from pathological hatred" (p. 37). Though showing no sympathy to revisionism, he nonetheless observes that "much of the literature on Hitler's Final Solution is worthless as scholarship. Indeed, the field of Holocaust studies is replete with nonsense, if not sheer fraud" (p. 55).

Like any industry, this one centers on money. The primary source is so-called reparations money paid by the European nations. Germany of course was the prime target; their original 1952 settlement of $522 million pales in comparison to actual payments to date. Finkelstein notes that "with little if any external pressure, [Germany] has paid out to date some $60 billion" (p. 84). Rudolf (2011: 45) puts the actual figure at $100 billion, and in recent public lectures Finkelstein raised the estimate to over $120 billion.

But a single payment, even a large one, was insufficient for the Lobby. They found in reparations a colossal cash cow that could be milked indefinitely. Finkelstein describes it as "an outright extortion racket" (p. 89). Even Hilberg denounced it as "blackmail"; he added, "I cannot accept the thesis that blackmail methods were the only way to deal with this issue."[234] Finkelstein describes in nauseating detail the Jewish attack on Switzerland, a neutral country, which evidently did not work hard enough to repel Nazi demands, or to recover lost Jewish bank accounts. Starting in 1995, Edgar Bronfman and the World Jewish Congress hammered on the Swiss government, bluntly rejecting offers that increased from $30 million to $600 million. Then in 1998, "the Swiss finally caved in" and agreed to pay $1.25 billion.

But the reparations game never ends. In Chapter 1, I cited a news item in which Belgium, a nation invaded and occupied by Germany, was recently compelled to pay out $170 million. In 2007, *Ha'aretz* reported that "Israel

---

[233] In early 2015, Le Pen reiterated his infamous view that the gas chambers were merely a "detail" of the war. See, for example, *The Australian* (3 Apr).

[234] Swiss weekly *Weltwoche* (28 Jan 1999). Quoted in *The Journal of Historical Review* (Jan/Feb 1999; p. 14).

seeks fresh Holocaust reparations deal with Germany" (11 Sep). The Israeli government demanded that Germany cancel an outstanding debt of 500 million euros—about $750 million—due to "unanticipated" costs associated with repatriating Holocaust victims. When told that German officials rejected this demand, Israeli Minister Rafi Eitan responded, "So just give us the money." The Germans balked, but Eitan was unconcerned: "ultimately, Germany will agree to the demands." Such is the arrogance of the Lobby.

And if this wasn't enough, we now have a situation in which the *children* of survivors are filing their own claims, asking payment for their psychological pain and suffering. The AP reported (15 Jul 2007) on a group of 4,000 Israelis called "second-generation survivors" who are seeking about $10 million annually from Germany. These children are "incapable of working," "live with an irrational fear of starvation," and suffer "bouts of depression." They "cannot ride buses because it reminds them of the transports their parents took to the concentration camps"; they also "fear dogs because they were used by the Nazis to control crowds." The Germans viewed this as "opening an indefinite channel for future claims"—as indeed it does.

But the gravy train rolls on. "Israel to seek another 1 billion Euros in Holocaust reparations from Germany," wrote *Ha'aretz* in late 2009. "Survivors sue Hungarian railway in US court," said *Agence France Presse* in early 2010; this time the plaintiffs sought $1.24 billion. "US survivors to receive federal funds," reported the *Jerusalem Post* in 2011—as if German money was insufficient. In 2012, *Ha'aretz* wrote that "Germany agrees to $300 million more in restitution to Jews." And in late 2014, "Germany announces $250 million fund for child Holocaust survivors," according to *The Forward*.

All these billions of dollars work to perpetuate the conventional Holocaust story, and to further entrench the power of the Industry generally. This money works its way back into PACs and lobbyists that coerce legislators to support the Lobby, to censor revisionism, and to overlook Israeli crimes in the Middle East. The money funds endowed chairs at American universities, and centers for Holocaust studies, which are widespread.

The money also goes to fund the various Holocaust museums and memorials, which are further bastions of the traditional story. An umbrella group called the Association of Holocaust Organizations (www.ahoinfo.org) tracks and coordinates global activities. As of 2015, they list 320 member and affiliated organizations worldwide, with fully 223 of these in the US alone. The global centerpiece, of course, is the US Holocaust Memorial Museum. Its $55 million annual budget—paid for by US taxpayers—is in addition to a "$540 million comprehensive campaign" of endowment funds. For those in the Holocaust Industry, every year is a good year.

A New World Order

What we have, then, is not merely an 'industry'; it is nothing less than a Holocaust propaganda machine. I use this term in the literal sense, as a system that promotes and propagates a particular ideology to the exclusion of others.[235] Like all propaganda machines, this one traffics in half-truths, partial truths, mistruths, distortions, exaggerations and outright lies. It operates in all forms of media: television, radio, motion pictures, print and press. And it engages in ruthless suppression of dissidents.

The effect on printed material is particularly striking. The sheer number of Holocaust books published each year is staggering. From 1960 onward there has been an exponential growth in the annual output; only in the past few years has this acceleration slowed. Consider just library-caliber books. The database WorldCat is one of the most extensive online references. A search for English-language books on the Holocaust reveals the following average annual number of publications, by decade:

1960s:	135	(per year)
1970s:	341	(per year)
1980s:	828	(per year)
1990s:	1,484	(per year)
2000s:	2,088	(per year)
2010-2014:	1,737	(per year)

It is hard to appreciate just how prodigious this output is. From 2000 through 2014, a total of 29,574 English-language Holocaust books have been released by major publishers.[236] This works out to an average of *5.4 new Holocaust books per day, every single day, for 15 consecutive years.* In total, WorldCat now lists over 58,000 entries. Apart from the sheer number of trees pulped on behalf of this cause, this represents thousands of books that might have been published on other worthy subjects, but were not.

A search of Amazon.com yields comparable numbers. Searching on 'Holocaust,' 'English,' 'all formats' (books, tapes, videos, etc.), we find the annual output rising from 11 per year in the 1960s to 525 annually between 2000 and 2010. And between 2010 and 2015 alone, the figure is up to 1,180 per year.

Or perhaps I underestimate. On 25 January 2014, the *New York Times* quoted the director of Yad Vashem, Avner Shalev, as saying, "Every year we have 6,000 books published about the Shoah." (There's that '6' again.)

---

[235] 'Propaganda,' after all, derives from the Latin Catholic phrase *propaganda fide*: "propagating the faith."

[236] Of course, not all these are unique titles. Many are new editions, translations, re-printings, etc.

If true, this astounding figure is considerably higher than either of my above estimates. This would imply that roughly 90,000 Holocaust books have been published just since the year 2000. Somebody out there is very busy.

Finally, all propaganda systems ultimately have political objectives. In our case, the orthodox Holocaust story is used as a means to achieve political ends that favor Israel and Jewish interests in general. This is clear if we recall that the Holocaust is a "major basis for the founding of the State of Israel," according to an official US government statement.[237] It is thus central to that nation's legitimacy. Undermining the Holocaust story means undermining Israel's *raison d'etre*, and this has enormous consequences for the Middle East.

Furthermore, the Holocaust casts a huge burden of implicit guilt over Western nations, most of all Germany, and thus applies moral coercion to support Israel and Jews. Billions of dollars of 'restitution' and 'reparation' funds flow to them without challenge. Western nations are very slow to criticize the Jewish state, and slower still to take meaningful action against it. They allow atrocities in the occupied territories to continue, with only the mildest of complaints.

But it is not only guilt that holds the other nations back; it is the financial threat from the United States. The US has tremendous economic leverage at its disposal, and is quick to use it if a given nation fails to toe the line. Ultimately, of course, this is the fault of the other nations, primarily those of Europe, which became enmeshed in the US financial system after World War II, and thus subject to economic blackmail. Only by disengaging from the US-centered financial system can they regain a measure of freedom from coercion, not to mention self-respect.

But there is perhaps a higher objective still. Some see the Holocaust as the foundation for a "new world order" that was envisioned after the fall of Eastern European communism—evidently an order in which Jewish/Israeli influence plays a large role. For example, in a 1991 *Toronto Star* op-ed piece titled "Memory of the Holocaust Central to New World Order," B'nai Brith director Ian Kagedan laid out his grand vision.[238] He condemned the "effective denial of the Holocaust" by the former Communist regimes, and issued a directive to the new democratic governments: "In the moral reconstitution of Eastern Europe, coming to terms with the Holocaust must figure prominently." Kagedan closes with this:

> The Holocaust stands as Western Civilization's greatest failure. It was a natural outcome of centuries of racism and of anti-Semitism. To deny the Holocaust is to deny racism's capacity to undercut our civilization's basic values and to destroy democracy. Achieving our quest

---

[237] *Contemporary Global Anti-Semitism*, US Department of State, 2008 (p. 23).
[238] 26 Nov 1991 (p. A17).

of a "new world order" depends on our learning the Holocaust's lessons.

A striking statement: Revisionists not only "destroy democracy," but they stand in the way of the new (Jewish-influenced) American world order. In this new order, Jewish and American influence extends across the globe, recasting all issues and conflicts to its advantage. In the 25 years since this piece was published we must acknowledge that Kagedan's vision has largely materialized; hence we can understand Mahathir Mohamad's comment, cited earlier: "The Jews rule the world by proxy."

Ironic—the one sentence here that revisionists may perhaps agree with: "The Holocaust stands as Western Civilization's greatest failure." If revisionism ever becomes close to being accepted, there is no doubt: the entire Holocaust episode will stand as a *monumental failure* in world history—a failure of honesty, of integrity, of morality, of principle, of justice, of freedom. It will be a colossal indictment of a system that proclaimed such lofty ideals and then proceeded to crush them when they became inconvenient to those in power. If such a day does come about, we can only hope that the leading players will still be alive, in order to witness firsthand the consequences of their actions—and perhaps to atone for them.

I believe that day will come. Like all good stories, the traditional Holocaust story will come to an end. Common sense, critical thinking and clear reason will ultimately win out. On that day, the people of the world will begin to understand the price that was paid for subservience to a story that was accepted, without challenge, by all.

Epilogue

"Holocaust denial is ideologically motivated. The deniers' strategy is to sow seeds of doubt through deliberate distortion and misrepresentation of the historical evidence. Teachers should be careful not to unwittingly legitimize the deniers through engaging in a false debate. Care must be taken not to give a platform for deniers—do not treat the denial of the Holocaust as a legitimate historical argument, or seek to disprove the deniers' position through normal historical debate and rational argument."
—Guidelines for Teaching about the Holocaust (2004)

"These Holocaust deniers are very slick people. They justify everything they say with facts and figures."
—Steven Some, chair New Jersey Commission on Holocaust Education[239]

When I began my research for this book, I expected to find a well-documented, clear, coherent picture of the Holocaust, as recounted in the traditional view. I expected to find strong evidence—documentary, material and forensic—that supported it. I expected to find solid justification for the death tolls (especially the '6 million'), and solid rationales for the methods of killing and body disposal. Naturally there would be some incomplete aspects of the overall picture, but this was to be expected, given the horrendous circumstances. I expected in turn to find these shortcomings ruthlessly exploited by a handful of fanatical zealots, the 'deniers,' long on insults and short on brains. I expected to find strong traditionalist counterarguments that

---

[239] *The Star-Ledger* (Newark, NJ), 23 Oct 1996, p. 15.

directly responded to, and decisively defeated, revisionist claims. In fact I found none of these things.

Instead I found a Holocaust story in tatters. I found that many aspects of the traditional view had serious, unresolved problems. I found that the vast majority of Holocaust writers completely ignored revisionist challenges—a situation explicable only as either complete ignorance, or worse, deliberate deception. In the few cases where the revisionists were addressed, I found crude polemics and name-calling rather than reasoned counterarguments. I found an avoidance of the strongest challenges and the ablest critics. I found a traditionalism that was unafraid to deploy its considerable power, contacts, and resources to keep the upper hand. I found, by all accounts, a movement with something to hide.

On the revisionist side, I found solid challenges and well-argued and articulate concerns. I found these issued by a small number of hardy and increasingly sophisticated individuals, who displayed an unflagging commitment to the pursuit of truth—often at a high personal cost. I also found a revisionist movement that was highly argumentative and combative, divided, unwilling to compromise, and overly confident in their own conclusions. I found some of them a bit too specialized and lacking in their own 'big picture' of events.

And I found a large middle ground of people who feign disinterest, who take no stand. I found people who are "not political"—a perfect excuse to avoid involvement. I found people unwilling to talk about the Holocaust, even in private, for fear of... *something*. I found people willing to overlook shoddy research, logical absurdities, unethical practices, moral outrages, and crimes against humanity, all because it might cause them some personal inconvenience. I found that the more 'important' a person was, the less of a backbone they had. I found cowardice where I expected bravery, and capitulation to money and self-interest where I expected principled, ethical behavior. I found people who should have known better—but said nothing.

In short, I found a debate unlike any other in modern society. And it was all the more striking, owing to the great importance of this debate for the present-day world. The Great Debate is a kind of gigantic magnifying glass; it brings many issues to a single focal point, one that turns on our most basic understanding of a series of events that happened 70 years ago. I found in this debate a kind of key to understanding one aspect of the structure and operation of the Western powers—a key with the potential to open a Pandora's Box of troubles for those at the top.

* * *

In the contentious atmosphere of this debate, it is easy to overlook the areas of common ground. With few exceptions, I think it is fair to say that all parties agree that:

- Hitler and his top men despised the Jews, and wanted a society cleared of them.
- As a consequence, they initiated a ruthless de facto policy of ghettoization, deportation, forced labor, and murder.
- Many thousands of Jews died of non-homicidal causes while in German custody—in the ghettos, in the camps and in transit. They died from typhus, exposure, exhaustion and related ills.
- Many thousands more were directly killed through mass shootings, hangings and torture.
- Of these alleged crimes against the Jews, there is a near-complete lack of material evidence—especially for the death camps, the bodies and the means of killing.
- The total number of Jews who died, or were killed, is not known with any certainty.

A few other points also must be agreed to, by anyone willing to rationally consider the facts: The '6 million' has little basis in fact, and rather seems to have been invoked as a symbolic figure; the Auschwitz 'gas chambers' were used far less often than is commonly portrayed; the mass disposal of bodies—in particular, the open-air burning—is unlikely to have happened in the manner described; and the Auschwitz air photos are disturbingly calm for an alleged death camp at the height of its activity.

The main points of contention, then, are really very few:

- The total number of Jewish deaths.
- The number of Jewish deaths, by cause, at each location or camp.
- The use of Zyklon gas chambers for mass murder.
- The use of diesel engine exhaust for mass murder.
- The veracity of the eyewitnesses, and the postwar testimonies.
- The method, and quantity, of bodies incinerated—both in crematoria and open-air.

The key to understanding these issues is the death matrix. By showing estimated deaths and disposals by month and by cause, we gain a very clear picture of what is alleged to have happened. We can see what was possible, and under what conditions. Obvious problems are thereby made transparent. And at the highest level—of the entire Holocaust—it forces us to create a complete and coherent picture of events.

I believe the present work is the first on either side of the debate to have introduced this device. This, to me, is quite surprising, considering how obvious a technique it is. But on the other hand, it is perhaps not so surprising; the death matrix has a power of transparency that can quickly expose absurdities, and can quickly undermine an inconsistent position. One's pet theory can easily crumble. In one glance it exposes all the dark corners of the Holocaust story. The shell game is over; all the cups are overturned. There is nowhere to hide, no hidden recesses in which to stash the bodies. And I emphasize that this criticism holds for both sides of the debate, each of which has failed to put it to use.

* * *

In my research, and in my own attempt to come to conclusions, I was struck time and time again by items and facts that were either clearly at odds with the standard account, or were otherwise revealing of the reality of the situation. Here are a few topics that stand out for me, even though I was not able to explore them in detail.

1. Nazi concern for inmate welfare
On 26 October 1943, Senior Group Leader Oswald Pohl—reporting directly to Himmler, and head of the entire camp system—wrote a secret letter to all camp commandants. It was recapped by Danuta Czech in her book, *Auschwitz Chronicle* (1990). The letter is rather shocking, in that Pohl admonishes the commandants for the high death rates in the camps. There is an urgent need for labor, and thus all camps are ordered to take necessary actions to reduce deaths and improve inmate health. As Czech recounts:

> Pohl states that… the concentration camps have become a significant factor in the German war effort. Henceforth, it is imperative to take all care not only that previous performance be maintained, but also increased. Commandants, SS Commanders, and Camp and Garrison Doctors are to be concerned primarily with maintaining the health and performance capability of the prisoners. Not out of any false sentimentality but rather because their arms and legs are needed… The first goal is to decrease by one tenth the number of inmates unable to work because of illness. All those responsible must achieve this goal. Indispensable for this are:
> 1. Proper and appropriate nourishment.
> 2. Proper and appropriate clothing.
> 3. Utilization of all natural means to encourage health.

4. Avoidance of every effort unnecessary for the performance of labor.
5. Use of performance prizes.

These points are treated in full by Pohl on three pages of instructions in which he even deals with how potatoes are to be stored, peeled, and prepared so that they are tasty and nourishing. ... Pohl emphasizes that he will personally supervise the execution of the orders transmitted in the letter. (p. 515)

Hardly the words expected from one of the supposed "leading architects" of mass murder.

Traditionalists, however, have a ready response: all this applies only to the labor force—the extermination actions at Auschwitz and Majdanek would continue (the other death camps having been shut down by this point). But the letter makes no distinctions. Clearly labor was badly needed by this time, and a large majority of the Auschwitz Jews, for example, could have contributed.

Pohl's letter is so damning to the traditional point of view that Czech felt compelled to add a footnote, "explaining" the situation for us: "the shortage of labor prompted Pohl to write this letter to the Commandants. It does not change anything in the camp conditions... The behavior of the SS men trained in ruthlessness and horror cannot be changed with a single letter..." Thus, in spite of what the letter actually says, Czech is convinced that its purpose "is not to stop the extermination, direct or indirect." Its whole point, she says, is simply to "lead to a more intensive exploitation of the prisoners' labor"—a process by which they would literally be worked to death.

To read this letter in such a way is indicative of someone with rigid and preconceived ideas—someone unable to read things as they are, and who sees only secret, hidden meanings in place of clear and explicit text. It is, in fact, the mindset of someone who sees anti-Jewish conspiracies in every nook and cranny. This point is underappreciated: The greatest conspiracy theorists are the *traditionalists*, not their opponents.

Lest we think this an aberration, Graf and Mattogno (2003: 16) cite the following letter from Pohl to his boss, Himmler, from April 1942. This was a full year and a half prior to the above, a time when the war was still going well for Germany—and Auschwitz, Chelmno, Belzec, and Sobibor were allegedly murdering thousands per day:

The war has brought a visible change in the structure of the concentration camps and has fundamentally altered their responsibilities with regard to the use to which the inmates may be put. The detention of inmates solely for security, educational or preventive reasons is no longer in the fore. Emphasis has shifted to economic concerns. Mobilizing *all* inmate labor, first of all for war-related tasks (increased armaments production) and *later on for tasks of peacetime*, is becoming more and more important. ... This realization results in certain necessary measures requiring a gradual restructuring of the concentration camps from their former, one-sidedly political form into an organization appropriate to the economic tasks. [italics added]

Clearly no plans for imminent "extermination."

And Pohl's right-hand man, Richard Glücks, issued this decree to all camps a few months later, in December 1942:

> The First Camp Physicians are to use all means at their disposal to effect a considerable decrease in the mortality figures in the individual camps... The camp physicians are to pay greater attention to the inmates' rations than heretofore, and shall submit proposals for improvements to the camp commandant, in agreement with the administration. These improvements must not remain on paper only, but must be regularly verified by the camp physicians. Further, the camp physicians shall see to it that working conditions at the various work sites are improved as much as possible... The Reichsführer-SS [Himmler] has ordered that mortality absolutely must decrease.

We must ask ourselves: Are these the words of men intent on mass murder? We find no reference at all to gassings or mass killings, even in these high-level, top-secret correspondences. It should be obvious that every healthy inmate—Jew or otherwise—was a valuable asset, not to be squandered. If you're going to kill them, for God's sake wait until the war is over! Why annihilate your slave labor when you need it most?

2. Postwar memoirs of three top Allied leaders—Eisenhower, Churchill, and De Gaulle—contain no mention of the Holocaust

Eisenhower's book, *Crusade in Europe* (1948), is a single volume of some 550 pages—the smallest of the three. Reviewing the index, one finds no listing for either 'Auschwitz,' 'Holocaust,' or 'gas chambers.' The single entry on Jews refers to the following paragraph:

> Of all these displaced persons, the Jews were in the most deplorable condition. For years they had been beaten, starved, and tortured. Even food, clothes, and decent treatment could not immediately enable them to shake off their hopelessness and apathy. They huddled together—they seemingly derived a feeling of safety out of crowding together in a single room—and there passively awaited whatever might befall. To secure for them adequate shelter, to establish a sys-

tem of food distribution and medical service, to say nothing of providing decent sanitary facilities, heat, and light was a most difficult task. They were, in many instances, no longer capable of helping themselves; everything had to be done for them. (pp. 439f.)

No mention of extermination, mass murder, gassing, crematoria—nothing. Only "beaten, starved, and tortured"—which, given the alternative, isn't so bad.

Charles de Gaulle's work, *The Complete War Memoirs* (1954/1964), consists of three volumes and a total of more than 2,000 pages. In the index we again find no reference whatsoever to 'Auschwitz,' 'Holocaust,' or 'gas chambers'—nor this time even to Jews. This being the latest-written of the three works (French original in 1954), De Gaulle obviously had plenty of time to reflect on the Holocaust; evidently it merited no discussion at all.

The largest memoir was written by Churchill. *The Second World War* (1948-1953) is a massive, six-volume account of the war, consuming nearly 4,500 pages of text. Once again, the indices (one per volume) have no entries at all for 'Auschwitz,' 'Holocaust,' or 'gas chamber.' There are a few references to Jews, but most are simple passing comments. Only one entry, out of six volumes, addresses Jewish persecution. In Volume 1, page 58, we find one single phrase: "brutalities towards the Jews were rampant."[240]

These men all knew what transpired at Nuremberg. They saw the concentration camp photos and they personally visited some of the sites. They had access to the most confidential information available. And yet, no extermination camps, no '6 million,' no gas chambers, no Auschwitz—only beatings, starvation, and assorted brutalities. It is almost as if they thought there was no Holocaust at all.

3. Postwar German leaders have feared, and continue to fear, Jewish power

One may ask: Why don't postwar German leaders expose the Holocaust story? Surely they would like to clear their collective reputation, not to mention save billions in reparations. But in reality, the opposite is true: they vigorously defend the orthodox account. Why is this?

It seems that, in large part, they have been bullied and blackmailed into sustaining the conventional story. Consider a few representative examples. The first postwar chancellor of West Germany, Konrad Adenauer, eagerly

---

[240] There is one further reference, not in the main text but in the Appendix to Volume 6. In a short note to Anthony Eden, allegedly referring to the Hungarian operation at Auschwitz, Churchill wrote, "There is no doubt that this is probably the greatest and most horrible crime ever committed in the whole history of the world, and it has been done by scientific machinery by nominally civilized men in the name of a great State and one of the leading races of Europe" (p. 693). Notably, there is no explicit mention of either Auschwitz, gas chambers, or Jews.

sought reconciliation with world Jewry. In a speech of 6 September 1952, he elaborated on the "great moral obligation" held by Germany toward Israel and Jews generally. He urged his government to quickly approve a reparations plan:

> I hope that the cabinet will not make things difficult for me. If the cabinet did cause problems, it would be a foreign policy disaster of the first order. … Let us be clear that now, as before, the power of the Jews in the economic sphere is extraordinarily strong, so that this… reconciliation with the Jews is an absolute requirement [for Germany].[241]

The deal, known as the Luxembourg agreement, was signed just four days later.

Wearing a Jewish skullcap, Chancellor Helmut Kohl pronounced Germany's "never ending shame" for the Holocaust in 1985. "We must not nor shall we ever forget the atrocities committed under the Hitler regime," he said.[242]

In a 2005 speech, Chancellor Gerhard Schröder accepted responsibility for "the greatest crime in the history of mankind," one that involved "the murder of millions." Camps such as Auschwitz were "a manifestation of absolute evil." Jews and others "were exterminated with cold industrial perfection." Germans today "bear a special responsibility" for the Holocaust; they must say "never again."

And in 2014, Angela Merkel vowed to strenuously fight a burgeoning German anti-Semitism. "I will personally do everything I can—as will my entire government—to ensure that anti-Semitism doesn't have a chance in our country." Of the growing Jewish population and culture there, she added, "We are proud and pleased that it was possible for that to grow in recent years."[243] This, in a nation with a mere 0.14% Jewish constituency.

It is hard to say whether such supplication is the result of cowardice, pragmatism or some sort of subtle brainwashing of the German elite. Pragmatic issues certainly loom large; the American Jewish Lobby would undoubtedly exact fierce economic retribution if German leadership were ever to waver in their commitment to orthodoxy. Either way, it is clear that the Jewish Lobby still has a stranglehold on the German government.

4. Certain Holocaust statistics have fallen dramatically over the years
Some may find it hard to believe that hundreds of Holocaust experts could be profoundly in error with respect to the '6 million,' or the death statistics

---

[241] In Stackelberg and Winkle (2002: 400).
[242] See, for example, *Los Angeles Times* (22 Apr 1985).
[243] Quoted by LiveMint.com (6 Sep 2014).

for the ghettos, the shootings, or the camps. But in fact they have been proven wrong, and dramatically so, on at least three occasions.

I mentioned the first case in Chapter 2 in my side comment on Auschwitz. Recall that, prior to 1990, many popular sources held that the camp witnessed 4 million total deaths (Jews and non-Jews).[244] On 17 July of that year, the *Washington Times* announced: "Poland reduces Auschwitz death toll estimate to 1 million." With little fanfare, the most infamous of death camps saw a 75-percent reduction in its fatalities. Worse yet, the reduction came entirely on the non-Jewish side of the ledger; these figures plummeted by over 90 percent.

The second example was discussed in Chapter 9. Majdanek came to world attention with 'authoritative' claims of 1.5 million killed. Even as late as 1986, experts estimated 1.38 million Jewish deaths there. Today the curator of the camp museum claims just 59,000 fatalities—a reduction of 96 percent.

As a third example, consider another group allegedly targeted by Hitler: homosexuals. In 1975 the *New York Times* reported that "nearly a quarter of a million homosexuals were executed by the Nazis between 1937 and 1945" (10 Sep, p. 45). Six years later, Rector (1981: 116) wrote, "It seems reasonable to conclude that at least 500,000 gays died in the Holocaust because of anti-homosexual prejudice that consequently led to a Nazi policy of gay genocide…" "Actually," he adds, "500,000 may be too conservative a figure." Seventeen years later, however, Grau (1998: 140) admitted this: "An examination of the Third Reich's trial statistics… reveals that these numbers are wildly exaggerated." Putting hard figures to it, Novick (1999: 223) says, "The actual number of gays who died or were killed in the camps appears to be around five thousand, conceivably as high as ten thousand." Another astonishing development. Here we see a drop from a "conservative" 500,000 to perhaps 5,000—the actual figures now coming in at a mere 1 percent of prior estimates.[245]

Thus we should not be too surprised if the overall Jewish death toll ultimately drops by 90 percent or more. Given the facts, it seems inevitable.

5. Objective data, when it comes to light, virtually always supports the revisionist position

Here is a good example: In 1990, forensic archaeologist Richard Wright was enlisted to find and excavate a rumored mass grave in the Ukraine, one which was the alleged work of the Einsatzgruppen. Recalling this event in

---

[244] Though some historians, like Hilberg and Reitlinger, had long argued for lower numbers.
[245] Similarly, estimates of gypsy deaths have dropped from more than 500,000 to something like 50,000.

2010, Wright emphasized that the question "Where are the bodies?" is essential in proving war crimes. Eyewitness statements, he said, are "particularly vulnerable." This poses a problem: "Without the bodies as material evidence of events such as the Holocaust, those who wish to deny that they happened can—and have tried hard to—set up a contest" in which both sides argue about the truth (Wright 2010: 99).

Wright traveled to Serniki, Ukraine, in an attempt to confirm reports of a then-16-year-old witness who had been conscripted to fill in an Einsatzgruppen mass grave in 1942. The young man reported that "the grave was some 50 meter long, 5 meters wide, and 2-3 meters deep. It contained up to 800 bodies, and was probably dug to below the local water table" (p. 98). We can do some quick calculations here. Assuming a 2.5 meter depth, the grave would have been (50×5×2.5=) 625 cubic meters in volume. At a presumed density of seven bodies per cubic meter, such a grave could theoretically hold 4,375 bodies. And yet the claim was only of 800 bodies.

"Locating and excavating such a site promised to be a formidable job," says Wright. But find it he did, and this allowed a proper excavation that would confirm or refute the witness story. The grave "turned out to contain some 550 bodies and not the 800 he had estimated." Furthermore, "the grave was some 10 m shorter than he said." As Wright sees it, the witness is vindicated; despite the small errors, his general claims were "materialized in the soil"—in particular, "the general size and shape of the mass grave [and] the fact that there were hundreds of bodies in it." In other words, close enough.

But Wright glosses over the critical calculation. The actual grave was found to be (40×5×2.5=) 500 cubic meters. This grave held 550 bodies, resulting in a density of *only 1.1 bodies per cubic meter*. This is an astonishingly low figure, far below even the revisionist estimate.

If all Einsatzgruppen mass graves were of this density, or all death camp graves, it would mean the complete end of the traditional story. If the Einsatzgruppen killed, say, 1.5 million Jews, it would have required 1.36 million cubic meters to bury them all; or some 2,700 mass graves of the kind at Serniki. If all 900,000 alleged Treblinka victims were buried at a comparable density, it would have required 818,000 cubic meters, or some 1,600 Serniki-style graves. Such figures are sheer fantasy. They are utterly impossible.

And it makes sense that the Serniki grave was of typical density. Having shot 550 people, for whatever reason, it would not be reasonable to dig a smallish 80 cubic meter grave—perhaps of dimensions 10 × 4 meters and 2 meters deep—in which to hide them. The victims would be packed to within inches of the surface, and this would have been pointless as a means of hiding the bodies. Clearly you would want them all to be at least two meters below ground. In this case, the Serniki grave was the ideal size: wide enough for one or two layers of bodies at the bottom, and space to cover with two meters of soil. It makes sense—but then the whole traditionalist case falls apart.

Thanks to Wright's work, revisionists now have one more solid, objective, irrefutable piece of data suggesting that they are right.

6. The anti-revisionist response is highly revealing
Since the year 2000, there have been only a few attempts by orthodox historians to respond directly to revisionist challenges. Two of these are particularly instructive: Richard Evans's book *Lying about Hitler* (2001), and Deborah Lipstadt's entry on "Denial" in the 2010 Oxford University *Handbook of Holocaust Studies*. Their tactics betray the many weaknesses of the conventional account.

In Chapter 4 of his book—"Irving and Holocaust Denial"—Evans attempts to summarize and rebut the revisionist point of view, with the ultimate goal of proving David Irving a 'denier.' In order to do so, he must define 'Holocaust denial,' show that it is wrong, and demonstrate that Irving supported it. On the first count, Evans proposes four pillars of denial: (1) less than 6 million Jews killed; (2) gas chambers were not used to any large degree; (3) the National Socialists' intention was deportation and not mass murder; and (4) the Holocaust story is "a myth invented by Allied propaganda," and "the supposed evidence... was fabricated after the war" (p. 110). We can agree with the first three, but the last is not defended by any revisionist of the past 30 years or so.

Evans then reviews the revisionist movement, employing a number of deceptive tactics. First, he liberally sprinkles his text with *ad hominem* attacks and other slanders, beginning with the generous use of the term 'denier.' The deniers, he says, "inhabit an intellectual world that [is] far removed from the cautious rationality of academic historical scholarship. What moved them seemed to be a strange mixture of political prejudice and bitter personal experience" (p. 105)—though one might wonder how Evans could know such things. They offer "a perverse kind of entertainment," something that belongs "to what some have called a paranoid style of historical writing." Deniers live in a kind of fantasyland; they claim "that virtually nothing of what [the survivors] had suffered had ever happened." More hyperbole from Evans; no serious revisionist has claimed that "nothing ever happened" to the Jews, or that they did not suffer greatly. But he goes on. "A good deal of [revisionist writing] seemed to be linked to racial hatred and antisemitic animosity in the most direct possible way." Another false statement, and tellingly, he offers neither citations nor any evidence to support this charge. In sum, says Evans, we must beware of the "weird and irrational world of Holocaust denial" (p. 110).

Next, Evans runs through a brief roll-call of prominent revisionists, but he gives an entirely misleading view of the field. He covers five individuals: Rassinier, App, Stäglich, Butz, and Faurisson. Certainly these men were important in the early development of revisionist ideas, but today only Faurisson is active—and remarkably so for a man of 85. Butz is alive and well, but only playing a secondary role in revisionism. Critically, Evans elects not to mention *any* of the leading present-day revisionists. Mattogno, Graf, Rudolf, Kues, and Berg are nowhere to be found in the chapter.[246] Neither are their arguments.

Apart from his *ad hominem* attacks and distorted presentation of revisionism, Evans deploys a third common traditionalist tactic: silence on the key issues at hand. For example, he tells us nothing of the long and discrediting history of the '6 million'; nothing of the true meaning of vital German words such as *Ausrottung* and *Vernichtung*; nothing of what Hitler actually said about the Jews; nothing of the deportation plans such as Madagascar; nothing of the Auschwitz air photos; and nothing of the absence of bodies or remains at nearly every phase of the Holocaust.[247]

Finally, a fourth tactic: straw-man argumentation. Evans's final pillar of denial is that the Holocaust is a "myth" and the evidence "fabricated." He elaborates: "Reading through the work of Holocaust deniers like Arthur Butz, it was more than clear that they wanted their readers to believe that the evidence for the Holocaust was all fabricated" (p. 128). Later he refers to "the common position of Holocaust deniers that evidence for the Holocaust has been fabricated" (p. 139). These statements are utterly false, as should be clear from the entirety of the present work. Evans lays out an argument that revisionists *do not make*, knocks it down, and then declares victory. It is a classic logical fallacy. The fact that Irving—not a serious Holocaust revisionist—made two or three ill-considered remarks does not grant Evans license to smear the true revisionists with the same broad brush.

For a Cambridge historian, all this is completely unacceptable. Evans is either ridiculously ignorant of his subject matter, or is deliberately misinforming the reader by excluding nearly all of the most relevant information. Either way, he has lost all credibility.

---

[246] Mattogno and Berg appear in three footnotes later in the book, but only with regard to their oldest work.

[247] Interestingly, he does touch briefly on the decisive issue of diesel gassing—though giving just the slightest hint of the difficulties involved. Evans writes: "Irving also denied that diesel engines could be used for killing operations. 'These engines,' he [Irving] said, 'exhaust non-lethal carbon dioxide, and only minute quantities of toxic carbon monoxide'" (p. 123). True, as we have seen. Evans's reply? Nothing. He loftily declares Irving's argument to be "specious and derivative," and leaves it at that. This is actually quite common among orthodox historians. When compelled to discuss an inconvenient issue, they will mention it very briefly, explicitly or implicitly deem it false, and then drop it.

More recent is Lipstadt's 2010 essay. A professor of theology and a Zionist Jew, she has long promoted herself as an expert on the Holocaust and Holocaust denial. Here, if anywhere, we would expect to find a rational, logical and disinterested treatment of the many troublesome issues. But again we are disappointed. In her very first sentence, Lipstadt manages to deploy three argumentative fallacies. The "deniers" (slander) are led by a small group of men, including "Faurisson, Butz, and Irving" (misleading names), who "spread the notion that the Holocaust... never happened" (straw man and flat-out lie). A poor start, to be sure.

She then offers a list of 12 points of alleged commonality amongst all deniers. Of these, only five are legitimate and relevant: (1) no genocide took place, (2) homicidal gas chambers did not exist, (3) Jewish fatalities were much less than 6 million, (4) there are non-sinister explanations for many issues, including Zyklon use against typhus and the fact that *ausrotten* means 'uprooting,' and (5) the Nuremberg trials were a "victors' court" that involved torture to extract false confessions. Her remaining points are irrelevant, deceptive, or misleading.

The bulk of her piece focuses on "deniers' tactics." The list below summarizes these, and provides some obvious responses.

> ➤ Deniers often refer to "immoral equivalencies," that is, downplaying Jewish persecution by the Germans because all parties in the war did terrible things. Response: Irrelevant to the Holocaust story and to revisionist arguments.
> ➤ "Deniers cast themselves as academics engaged in a reasoned pursuit of historical truth" (p. 563). Response: True and accurate. Why this is a problem is unclear—except that it makes the job of traditionalists like Lipstadt much harder.
> ➤ Survivor testimony "is ignored, discredited, or dismissed unless it can be interpreted as indicating that the Holocaust did not happen." Response: Partly true. Outrageous, contradictory, or blatantly false testimony is disregarded. Some testimony is useful, but must always be subjected to scrutiny. In no case is testimony used to support the idea that the Holocaust "did not happen."
> ➤ "Deniers rely on verbal obfuscation," as when they discuss the meaning of 'final solution' or 'special treatment.' Response: It is not "obfuscation" to refer to the actual words used by the Germans and to examine their true meanings in context. Notably, she does not mention here the issues with *ausrotten* and *vernichten*.
> ➤ Minor errors in either National Socialist or survivor testimony are used to discredit the entire testimony. Response: False. Each specific

claim must be examined on its own merits. However, a statement containing even one flagrant falsehood must immediately be suspected of containing other falsehoods.

- ➢ Deniers try to exonerate leading National Socialists by attributing the murder of Jews to rogue elements of the army or to German allies. <u>Response</u>: Jewish deaths resulted from a wide variety of causes—none of which derived from explicit orders from the top. Call this 'exoneration' if you like.
- ➢ Related to the above, deniers emphasize that no one has found a Hitler order for mass murder, nor even reference to such an order. <u>Response</u>: True, and a significant fact, as I explained in Chapter 5. Lipstadt tries to brush away this inconvenient matter by stating that "reputable historians seldom base their conclusions on the existence, let alone the absence, of a single document" (p. 566). But no revisionist has ever based his claim on this single fact. It is only one of many that point to mass deportation, not mass murder.
- ➢ Deniers say that the Auschwitz Krema 2 ruins have no evidence of ceiling holes into which the Nazis poured the Zyklon pellets. Without such holes, there was no mass murder at Birkenau. And disproving mass murder at Auschwitz undermines the entire Holocaust story. <u>Response</u>: True, and another difficult fact for Lipstadt and her colleagues. She claims to know of "a wide variety of evidence that attests to their existence and location." She points to one air photo allegedly showing something on the Krema 2 roof, and one ground photo showing "chimneys" under construction, but these fail to prove her case. In the end, the stubborn fact remains: if there were holes in the ceiling of Krema 2, there would almost certainly be some tangible evidence today. But there is none.

Thus we can see the same deceptions at work here as in Evans's book. (A) *Ad hominem* attacks abound: revisionists are 'deniers,' 'anti-Semites,' and 'racists.' (B) Misleading presentation of revisionism and the leading revisionists: no mention at all of Mattogno, Rudolf, Graf, Kues, or Berg, nor anything at all on their many important publications through 2010. (C) Silence on many of the same key issues: nothing on the '6 million,' Hitler's actual words, deportation plans, air photos, or the glaring absence of bodies or remains. And (D) straw-man arguments: emphasis on 'hoax,' 'myth,' evidence fabrication, and the idea that 'the Holocaust never happened.' Such is the state of orthodox replies to revisionism.

* * *

In completing my inquiry into the Holocaust, let me return to a passing comment I made in Chapter 8. There, in the discussion of wood requirements for burning corpses to ash, I noted the striking contrast between revisionist claims of 160 kg of wood per typical 45 kg corpse (3.5-to-1 ratio) and orthodox claims that the same body requires only 25 kg of wood (0.56-to-1). Köchel (2015) analyzed actual incinerations of diseased farm animals in 2001, and his work roughly confirmed the revisionist position. I then suggested a little burning experiment to settle this issue.

Let me repeat and expand upon that idea. I hereby propose what I call the "Grand Holocaust Experiment." Its purpose would be to confirm the critical gas-bury-exhume-burn sequence of the three Reinhardt camps. Here's how it might go: Purchase 1,000 live hogs of various sizes, in a weight range of 10 to 200 lbs. Herd them tightly into an enclosed room, with a ceiling slightly higher than the largest hog. Ensure that the room is 'hermetically sealed.' Take a large modern diesel engine, remove the catalytic converter, and then route the exhaust pipe into the room. Record what happens. As we recall, on the traditional view, all the animals will be expected to die within 10 or 20 minutes. If, however, the engine repeatedly stalls, or the walls are blown out, or the animals simply refuse to die after, say, 1 hour, then just shoot each one.

Dig a pit in the ground of size 145 cubic meters—roughly 6m × 6m, and 4m deep. Pack all 1,000 dead hogs into the pit; this would approximate the claimed seven bodies per cubic meter. Cover the pit with dirt and wait six months.

Construct a typical Reinhardt-like pyre, using metal rails about 30 meters in length. Exhume the dead hogs, and weigh each corpse. Then stack as many as possible on the pyre, in any configuration desired. Record the maximum number stacked, if less than 1,000. Presuming all 1,000 can be piled up, then load the pyre with approximately (1,000 × 45 × 0.56 =) 25,000 kg of dry hardwood.[248] Light the pyre, and record what happens.

If the traditionalists are right, the hog corpses will be largely burned to ash—except for their teeth and large bones. Gather up and weigh the full mass of ash, teeth, and bone. Then sift through the entire mass and extract all teeth and bones; weigh these. Pulverize the teeth and bones to dust, using only hammers or a 1940s-era grinder. Combine this pulverized mass with the other remaining ash, return to the original pit, measure the volume, and bury with dirt. Take core samples every, say, five years, and record the results.

Either side may conduct this Grand Experiment, but with their far greater financial resources, I would suggest that our orthodox defenders undertake

---

[248] This is equivalent to about 46 cubic meters of solid wood. This would just about perfectly fill the space below a 30m × 2m pyre that was one meter high.

it. Or better: that they fund a neutral party to conduct it. Either way, this relatively simple procedure could resolve many unanswered questions and contentious claims. It would go a long way toward settling the Holocaust debate. May the best man win.

* * *

As I stated at the beginning of this book, I have tried to serve as an objective party. My goal was to observe and analyze the arguments on each side from a neutral vantage point. As to the total number of Jewish victims, I have deferred in making definitive pronouncements. Given the ensemble of facts, however, the overall death toll is certainly less than 3 million, and very likely under 2 million. And in my estimation, there is a 50/50 chance that it is lower than 1 million. The difference between the 1 and 2 million range is likely to turn on the definition of 'victim.' Using a reasonably stringent definition—say, any Jew who was directly killed at the hands of the Nazis, or who died while in their custody—will likely lead to the lower figure; a more generous definition, such as DellaPergola's (see Chapter 3) will push toward the higher.

The reader is perhaps concerned that the arguments presented here favor revisionism, and that this somehow compromises my neutrality. I would beg to disagree. The arguments are what they are. It is up to the traditionalists—the experts—to respond. If they have no good response, the revisionist arguments stand. The situation presented in this book is simply a consequence of both parties laying out their best charges and countercharges. I have done my best to present the strongest and most complete case on each side. If there appear to be winners and losers, the praise (or blame) goes to the parties themselves, not to me.

In a criminal (non-jury) trial, a judge listens to both sides, dispassionately, weighs the evidence, and then reaches a determination. The fact that he makes a decision for one side or the other *does not invalidate his objectivity*. It does not mean that he 'favors' one side, or is in cahoots with them. If the best evidence on each side has been laid out and cross-examined, then we can expect that most rational, unbiased judges would reach a common conclusion. And I think the same is true here in the Great Debate—even though I have done less than offer judgment on it.

Here, each reader must be his own judge. Each must determine for himself which account of events—traditionalist, revisionist, or something else altogether—is most likely true.

Because of its reliance on censorship, polemics, and bullying rather than on rational objectivity, traditionalism is currently in a sorry state. But its advocates can take specific actions to regain some dignity in this whole affair:

- ➢ Put an end to the name-calling, censorship, and harassment of revisionists.
- ➢ Deal directly with the strongest and latest revisionist arguments in a clear and objective manner.
- ➢ Utilize a death matrix, or related technique, to clearly show the entire picture.
- ➢ Conduct large-scale, scientific studies on the gassing and burning of animal corpses under death camp conditions; in other words, conduct the Grand Experiment. Analyze fuel consumption, burning time, ash content and mass.
- ➢ Conduct scientific excavations at Auschwitz, Sobibor, Treblinka, and Chelmno, taking soil samples and analyzing them for ash content and human remains.
- ➢ Admit the weaknesses in the standard view.
- ➢ Admit when you are wrong, and revise the story accordingly.

Alas, this is perhaps asking too much. With so much time, money, power and blood invested in the standard view, I'm afraid that few traditionalists will find it worthwhile to approach this debate in such a dignified manner. In which case, as usual, it is up to the rest of us.

Annex

Appendices

Appendix A: Calculation Assumptions

Quantity	Metric	US	Accepted by:
Estimated Values			
Max density of living bodies (in enclosed space, i.e. "gas chamber")			
– Soviet-Polish report of 1944	6 per sq m	0.6 per sq ft	
– Revisionist:	10 per sq m	0.9 per sq ft	All revisionists
– Traditionalist:	22 per sq m	2 per sq ft	Düsseldorf court
	28 per sq m	2.6 per sq ft	Provan; Muehlenkamp
	38 per sq m	3.5 per sq ft	Gerstein
Max density of dead bodies (in mass graves)			
– Revisionist:	6 per cu m	1 per 6 cu ft	Ball (2003: 270); Rudolf (2005: 284)
	8 per cu m	1 per 4.5 cu ft	Mattogno and Graf (2005: 317)
– Traditionalist:	15 per cu m	1 per 2.4 cu ft	Gerstein (implied); Muehlenkamp
	19 per cu m	1 per 1.9 cu ft	Provan
	22.5 per cu m	1 Per 1.6 cu ft	Harrison et al. (2011: 418, 421)
Average weight of gassing victim (30% children)			
– Revisionist:	50 kg	110 pounds	Mattogno and Graf
– Traditionalist:	35 kg	77 pounds	Provan; Muehlenkamp
Average weight of partially decomposed corpse			
– Revisionist:	45 kg	100 pounds	Mattogno and Graf (2005: 145)
– Traditionalist:	25 kg	55 pounds	Muehlenkamp
Amount of seasoned (dry) wood, to completely burn 1 kg animal flesh (fixed-height pyre, open air)			
– Revisionist:	3.5 kg		Mattogno and Graf (2005: 148f.)
	11 kg		onethirdoftheholocaust.com
– Traditionalist:	2 kg		Muehlenkamp max
	1 kg		Muehlenkamp min
	0.56 kg		Harrison et al. (2011: 467)
Burning time: Amount wood burned in one hour, in one square meter			
– Revisionist & Traditionalist:	80 kg	176 pounds	Mattogno and Graf (2010: 149)
Ash data			
Wood ash: Remainder by weight	8 %		Revisionist (high): Mattogno (2004c)
	0.33 %		Revisionist (low): Neumaier (2003: 496)
	4 %		Revisionist (mean)
Wood ash: Density	340 kg / cu m	21 lbs / cu ft	Accepted by all parties
Corpse ash: Remainder by weight	5 %		Accepted by all parties
Corpse ash: Density	500 kg / cu m	31 lbs / cu ft	Accepted by all parties
Total ash density	375 kg / cu m	23 lbs / cu ft	Mattogno and Graf (2010)
Total ash (wood + corpse), per average body			
– Revisionist (mean):	8.6 kg / body	18.8 lbs / body	
– Traditionalist:	2.8 kg / body	6.1 lbs / body	Muehlenkamp

Appendix B: Major Death Camp Witnesses – Pro & Con

Witness / Status	Testimony supporting orthodoxy	Revisionist Critique
AUSCHWITZ		
Höss (commandant)	– Multiple dates (3/16/46; IMT on 4/5/46; memoirs). – Covers all major aspects of extermination story. – "2.5M Jews gassed, 0.5M other ways." (IMT) – "1.13M Jews killed in total." (memoirs) – Memoirs are "extremely reliable." (Zimmerman, p. 236)	– Nothing new in any of his testimonies. – Memoirs are "model of incoherence and contradiction, containing a number of demonstrable untruths" (Crowell). – "No material or documentary support for the [memoir] claims" (Crowell). – The "3M" killed (IMT) is exaggerated by 200%. – Mentions only 1 Zyklon hole in K1 roof. – In IMT, mentions 3 other camps: Treblinka, Belzec, and "Wolzek" – no such camp ever existed. – Claims to have visited above camps in 1941 – neither Treblinka nor Sobibor existed until 1942. – Claims Sonderkommandos "ate and smoked" (no gas masks) while unloading gas chamber – would have been fatal. – Describes "self-burning corpses"; use of "waste oil" and "methanol"; use of dynamite – all ludicrous claims for body disposal. – Exaggerated numbers of Jews living in Europe by a factor of 10.
Kremer (Nazi doctor)	– 2 sources of information: diaries, and 3 trial testimonies (Krakow/1947, Münster/1960 and Frankfurt/1964). – Diaries describe quarantine and gassing against typhus and lice. – Diaries mention "special actions" (Sonderaktion) – presumed to mean homicidal gassing. – Describes Auschwitz as worse than Dante's Inferno; calls it "anus mundi," and "camp of annihilation." – Confirmed "extermination" interpretation of diaries during trials.	– "Gassings" only mentioned once in diaries, in connection with fumigation for lice. – Was only in Auschwitz for 10 weeks, then returned to University job – unlikely that he would have been allowed to return after witnessing mass murder. – Letter of 10/21/42 describes only typhus and typhoid fever as reasons for "Auschwitz hell." – Use of phrase "bei einer Sonderaktion AUS Holland" refers to a deportation action, not murder. – Coerced into admitting "extermination" thesis; otherwise faced "merciless punishment." – Claimed 6 million Jewish deaths at Auschwitz versus 1 million accepted today.
Broad (SS private)	– Testified at NMT, and in 1959 and 1964. – Described mass shooting, cremation in pits. – Describes gassing at Krema 1. – "More thorough" than Höss. (Zimmerman)	– Claimed 4-6 bodies at once in muffle – impossible. – Claimed "flames" shooting out of chimneys – pure myth. – Claimed 4,000 people at once in chambers – an impossible 19/sq m. – Claimed 2-3 million Jews exterminated – vastly overestimated. – Described 6 Zyklon holes in KI, for "aeration" – wrong, and inconsistent with Höss. – Claimed gassing death came within 4 minutes – impossible. – Claimed Hungarian deaths up to 10,000/day – gross exaggeration. – Claimed Hungarians arrived Mar/Apr 1944 – actually, May-July.
Vrba (Jewish prisoner)	– Aka Walter Rosenberg. – Leading author of "Auschwitz Protocols" (aka War Refugee Board Report). – Describes gassing procedure,	– Sketch of camp is ridiculously inept. – No mention of gassing at Krema 1 in main camp, even though this went on for nearly 1 year. – Drawing of Krema 2/3 layout is completely wrong, both inside and out. Claims that muffles burned "3 normal

Witness / Status	Testimony supporting orthodoxy	Revisionist Critique
	even though never personally witnessed it.	corpses" at once, in 1.5 hours – gross exaggeration. – Describes krema furnaces as "9 furnaces, each with 4 openings" – in fact, 5 furnaces with 3 openings each. – Claims that chambers gassed 2,000 in 3 minutes – technically impossible. – Claims a total of 1.76M gassed, up to April 1944 – impossibly high, and about 3x current orthodoxy.
Tauber (Jewish Sonderkommando)	– "Best witness for gassing" (Pressac). – Describes 4 Zyklon holes, fake showers. – Mentions 5 incineration pits near K5.	– Burned 4-5 corpses per muffle, sometimes up to 8 – impossible. – Claimed that trench-burning was more efficient than kremas – wrong. – Trenches near K5 never found. – Talks about ladling of liquid human fat from trenches to speed up burning – impossible. – Never actually witnessed a gassing. – Claimed 5-7 minutes/body cremation – impossible.
Müller (Jewish Sonderkommando)	– Claims to have spent 3 years in Auschwitz. – Mentions 4 incineration pits near Bunker 2. – Mentions 5 pits (50m long) near K5.	– Unbelievably long time as Sonderkommando (normal was 3 months). – Bunker trenches never found. – K5 trenches never found. – Describes pits with boiling liquid human fat – impossible. – Claims pits were 2.5m deep – impossible, since water table only 1m deep. – Describes several quasi-pornographic gas chamber scenes. – Describes doctors cutting warm flesh from dead bodies, causing buckets to jump. – Claims furnace burning time of 7-12 minutes per body – impossible. – Describes wire-mesh Zyklon columns as having "spirals" in them, rather than moveable cages. – Claims that gassing victims were blue – does not happen. – Describes 6 holes in K1 roof – inconsistent with Höss. – Never testified until his 1979 book – 35 years late.
Bendel (Jewish Sonderkommando)	– Aka Charles Sigismund. – Describes gassing procedure. – Describes 1000 people gassed at once, in Bunkers (27). – Mentions 3 pits, 12m long.	– Claims K2/3 gas chamber was 10m long actual, 30m. – Claims train tracks ran "up to the door" of K2/3 – wrong. – Claims K2/3 burn rates of 2,000/day comparable to impossible Hass numbers. – Describes 2 Zyklon holes "actually", 4. – Said pits can burn 1000 bodies/hour impossible. – Describes ladling of liquid fat from pits impossible.
S. Dragon (Jewish Sonderkommando)	– Most important witness for Bunkers, even though worked there only 3 days. – Gave 2 testimonies: Feb. and May 1945. – Described fake signs "Zum Baden" and "Desinfektion." – Claims 1700 people gassed in B1, and 2500 in B2 – Describes B1 burning pits: 4 pits, 35 m long. – Describes B2 burning pits: 4 (later, 6) pits, 35 m long.	– Nothing in either testimony describes Bunker locations; never accompanied investigators to personally locate them. – 2 testimonies show many discrepancies. – Inconsistent distance between Bunkers – first 500m, then 3 km. – Can't pack so many people into each Bunker – approx. 25/sq m (impossible). – Said gas smells "sweet" –actually, bitter almond smell. – Claimed to be with Mengele during selection in 12/42, but Mengele was not at Auschwitz until 5/43. – Claimed that Sonderkommandos could clear B1 in 2-3 hours – but from his own details, it would have taken 60-80 hours. – Mentions ladling of human fat from pits – impossible. – Burning pits never found. – Claimed B1 pits burned 7-8,000/day – impossible.

Witness / Status	Testimony supporting orthodoxy	Revisionist Critique
		– Claimed B2 pits burned 10,000/day – impossible. – Claimed both Bunkers combined burned up to 28,000/day – impossible!
Nyiszli (Jewish doctor)	– Claims to have worked with Mengele. – Describes 2 burning pits at Bunkers, each 50m long; could burn 5-6,000/day. – Described fake "Bath/Baden" signs.	– Claimed Birkenau kremas could burn up to 10-20,000 bodies per day – vast exaggeration. – Pits never found; can't burn that many bodies. – Described poison gas as "chlorine" – wrong (this was a standard WWI gas). – Mentions 4 elevators to lift bodies from chambers to furnaces – wrong (actually 1). – According to Pressac, all claims are "exaggerated by a factor of 4." – Said all 4 kremas had 15 muffles – actually, only K2/3. – Claimed gas chamber room was 200 m long actually, 30 m. – Said Theresienstadt arrivals lived "2 yrs" in camp actually, 8 months.
Wiesel (Jewish inmate)	See text.	See text.
Levi (Jewish inmate)	– Spent 11 months at camp; liberated by Soviets. – Describes chambers as fake showers.	– Expressed regret for being too sick to leave with the Nazis, prior to Soviet takeover! – Never set foot in Birkenau (only at Auschwitz III-Monowitz). – Only learned about gassings after the war. – Primary book (1947/1959, 1996) speaks rarely and vaguely of "the" gas chamber; however, 1976 Appendix suddenly has many details of the chambers. – Claims 24,000 Auschwitz deaths in one day – gross exaggeration.
V. Frankl (Jewish inmate)	– Spent 2 years at Theresienstadt ghetto, and 2 or 3 days at Auschwitz. – Claimed that "real extermination" took place at the smaller camps, not large ones like Auschwitz.	– No discussion of the "facts" of Auschwitz. – Misleadingly implies he spent months there. – Never describes how he got out of the camp. – Claimed to see flaming chimneys.
Feinsilber (Jewish Sonderkommando)	– Aka: Fajnzylberg, Jankowski, Kaskowiak. – First to use term "Bunker."	– Claimed up to 12 corpses/muffle – impossible. – Claimed Birkenau kremas could burn up to 8,000 per day – vast exaggeration. – Describes 2 holes in K1 roof – inconsistent with Höss, Müller, Broad. – Claimed Hungarian deaths up to 18,000/day – gross exaggeration.
BELZEC		
Gerstein	See text.	See text.
Reder	See text.	See text.
Pfannenstiel (SS doctor)	– Witnessed gassing w/ Gerstein.	– Likely coerced, threatened w/ prosecution.
Oberhauser (SS Lt.)	– Claimed avg. 150 Jews killed per transport.	– Possible.
Schluch (SS Sgt.)	– "Showed Jews to the chambers."	– Delousing chambers.
Klukowski (Polish dr.)	– Diary reports that 40 train cars/day arrived, people killed with "electricity."	– Electricity myth completely rejected.
SOBIBOR		
Stangl (commandant)	– "Never denied his crimes"	

Witness / Status	Testimony supporting orthodoxy	Revisionist Critique
Lambert (Sgt.)	– Constructed gas chambers.	– Delousing chambers
Fuchs (SS)	– Witnessed test gassing of 30-40 women.	
Bauer (SS)	– "Gasmeister"	– Claimed 350,000 total victims – gross exaggeration.
TREBLINKA		
Gerstein	See text.	See text.
Wiernik	– Spent 1 year in camp, before escaping during prisoner revolt. – Published influential booklet, "Year in Treblinka" (1944). – First to cite "engine exhaust" as killing method.	– Describes gassing engine as from "dismantled Soviet tank" – highly improbable. – Claims 500 people in 25 sq m chamber – impossible 20/sq m. – Claims 1200 people in 49 sq m chamber – even more impossible 24/sq m. – Claims victims "suffered for hours" in closed chamber when engine failed, when they would have suffocated within 30 minutes. – Camp map plagiarized from a 1942 report. – Describes gassing victims as "yellow from the gas" – they would have been red or pink. – Claimed "millions" of deaths – gross exaggeration. – Claimed up to 20,000 gassed per day – gross exaggeration. – Describes burning 3,000 bodies per pyre – impossible. – Claimed that women's bodies burned easier than men – nonsense.
Rajzman	– "Nestor of Treblinka survivors." – Spent 10 months at camp. – Describes "fake train station" to fool Jews.	– Claims gassed 10-12,000 per day average, and up to 25,000 per day – gross exaggeration. – Describes killing by "pumping out air" from chambers, and use of "chlorine gas" and "Cyklon." – Failed to locate mass graves during postwar investigations. – Claimed 2,775,000 total victims – gross exaggeration. – Described burning pits of 300 m long, and 6 m deep – impossibly large.
Stangl (commandant)	Same as Sobibor	
Franz (2nd in comm.)	– "cannot say how many were gassed."	Agreed.
Mentz (SS)	– "Gunman of Treb." Shot people.	Agreed.
Mattes (SS)	– Mentions 6 chambers, holding 300 people each.	
Horn (SS)	– "describes gassing procedure."	
Bomba (inmate)	– "Barber of Treblinka"	– Describes a 16 sq m (12' × 12') haircut room with 16 barbers and up to 70 (naked) women – over 5 people per square meter.
CHELMNO		
(none)		
MAJDANEK		
(none)		

Bibliography

Traditionalist Sources—Cited or for Further Reading

Arad, Y. 1987. *Belzec, Sobibor, Treblinka*. Indiana University Press.
Arad, Y. 1990a. "Belzec." In Gutman (ed.), *Encyclopedia of the Holocaust*. Macmillan.
Arad, Y. 1990b. "Sobibor." In Gutman (ed.), *Encyclopedia of the Holocaust*. Macmillan.
Arad, Y. 1990c. "Treblinka." In Gutman (ed.), *Encyclopedia of the Holocaust*. Macmillan.
Arad, Y. 1990d (ed.). *The Pictorial History of the Holocaust*. Macmillan.
Atkins, S. 2009. *Holocaust Denial as an International Movement*. Praeger.
Bartov, O. 2015. *The Holocaust: Origins, Implementation, Aftermath*. Routledge.
Beim, A. and Fine, G. 2007. "Trust in testimony: The institutional embeddedness of Holocaust survivor narratives." *Archives of European Sociology*, 48(1): 55-75.
Bem, M. and Mazurek, W. 2012. *Sobibor: Archeological Research Conducted on the Site of the Former German Extermination Centre, 2000-2011*. Foundation for Polish-German Reconciliation.
Benz, W. (ed.). 1991. *Dimension des Völkermords*. (in German) Oldenbourg.
Berenbaum, M. 1993. *The World Must Know*. Little, Brown.
Bezwinska, J. and Czech, D. (eds.) 1984. *KL Auschwitz Seen by the SS*. H. Fertig.
Blatt, T. 1998. *Sobibor: The Forgotten Revolt*. Elfin Cove Press.
Blech, B. 2004. *Secrets of Hebrew Words*. J. Aronson Inc.
Browning, C. 2004. *The Origins of the Final Solution*. University of Nebraska Press.
Browning, C. 2010. "Problem solvers." In Hayes and Roth (eds.), *Oxford Handbook of Holocaust Studies*.
Brugioni, D. and Poirier, R. 1979. *The Holocaust Revisited*. National Technical Information Service.
Bryant, M. 2014. *Eyewitness to Genocide*. University of Tennessee Press.
Buergenthal, T. 2009. *A Lucky Child*. Profile Books.
Burrin, P. 1989/1994. *Hitler and the Jews*. Edward Arnold.
Chernofsky, P. 2013. *And Every Single One Was Someone*. Gefen.
Cobain, I. 2012. *Cruel Britannia*. Portobello.
Corni, G. 2003. *Hitler's Ghettos*. Oxford University Press.
Czech, D. 1989. *Kalendarium der Ereignisse im Konzentrationslager Auschwitz-Birkenau*. (in German) Translated in English as Czech (1990).
Czech, D. 1990. *Auschwitz Chronicle*. H. Holt.
Dawidowicz, L. 1975. *The War against the Jews*. Holt, Reinhart, and Winston.
Dawidowicz, L. 1976. *A Holocaust Reader*. Behrman House.
Dawidowicz, L. 1981. *The Holocaust and the Historians*. Harvard University Press.
Dawidowicz, L. 1986. *The War against the Jews*. (2nd ed.) Bantam.
Dean, M. 2010. "Ghettos." In Hayes and Roth (eds.), *Oxford Handbook of Holocaust Studies*.
Desbois, P. 2008. *The Holocaust by Bullets*. Palgrave Macmillan.
Defonseca, M. 1997. *Misha: A Mémoire of the Holocaust Years*. Mt. Ivy Press.
Delarue, J. 1964. *History of the Gestapo*. Macdonald.
DellaPergola, S. 2003. Review of relevant demographic information on world Jewry. <icheic.org/pdf/ICHEIC_demography1.pdf>
Dimont, M. 1962. *Jews, God, and History*. Simon and Schuster.
Dodd, C. 2007. *Letters from Nuremberg*. Crown.
Donat, A. (ed.) 1979. *The Death Camp Treblinka*. Schocken Books.

Evans, R. 2001. *Lying about Hitler*. Basic Books. Republished as: *Telling Lies about Hitler* (2002), Verso.
Feingold, H. 2008. *Jewish Power in America*. Transaction.
Frankel, M. 1999. *The Times of My Life*. Random House.
Frankl, V. 1947/1959. *From Death-Camp to Existentialism*. Beacon. (Original German title: *Ein Psycholog erlebt das Konzentrationslager*.) Reprinted as Frankl (1947/1992).
Frankl, V. 1947/1992. *Man's Search for Meaning*. Beacon. (Reprint of Frankl, 1947/1959).
Friedman, P. 1954. "The Jewish ghettos of the Nazi era." *Jewish Social Studies*, 16: 61-88.
Gilbert, M. 1981. *Auschwitz and the Allies*. Rainbird.
Gilbert, M. 1988. *Atlas of the Holocaust*. Pergamon Press.
Gilead, I. *et al.* 2009. "Excavating Nazi extermination centres." *Present Pasts*, vol. 1: 10-39.
Goldberg, E. 2004. *Holocaust Memoir Digest*. Vallentine Mitchell.
Goldhagen, D. 1996. *Hitler's Willing Executioners*. Knopf.
Gordon, S. 1984. *Hitler, Germans, and the "Jewish Question."* Princeton University Press.
Gottfried, T. 2001. *Deniers of the Holocaust*. Twenty-First Century Books.
Grau, G. 1998. "Final solution of the homosexual question?" in *The Holocaust and History*, Berenbaum and Peck (eds.). Indiana University Press.
Griffin, S. *et al.* 2008. "Diesel fumes *do* kill." *Journal of Forensic Science*, 53(5): 1206-1211.
Gringauz, S. 1950. "Some methodological problems in the study of the ghetto." *Jewish Social Studies* (12): 65-72.
Gutman, Y. 1985. *Denying the Holocaust*. Hebrew University of Jerusalem.
Gutman, I. (ed.) 1990. *Encyclopedia of the Holocaust*. Macmillan.
Gutman, I. and Berenbaum, M. (eds.) 1994. *Anatomy of the Auschwitz Death Camp*. Indiana University Press.
Harrison, J. *et al.* 2011. *Belzec, Sobibor, Treblinka: Holocaust Denial and Operation Reinhard*. Available online: http://holocaustcontroversies.blogspot.com
Headland, R. 1992. *Messages of Murder*. Associated University Presses.
Hilberg, R. 1961. *The Destruction of the European Jews*. (1st ed.) Quadrangle.
Hilberg, R. 1985. *The Destruction of the European Jews*. (2nd ed.—3 volumes) Holmes and Meier.
Hilberg, R. 2003. *The Destruction of the European Jews*. (3rd ed.—3 volumes) Yale University Press.
Holstein, B. 2004. *Stolen Soul*. University of Western Australia.
Igounet, V. 2000. *Histoire du négationnisme en France*. (in French) Editions du Seuil.
International Military Tribunal (IMT). 1946/1947. *The Trial of German Major War Criminals*. 42 volumes. (Blue series).
Jewish Black Book Committee. 1946. *The Black Book: The Nazi Crimes against the Jewish People*. Jewish Black Book Committee.
Kadushin, C. 1974. *The American Intellectual Elite*. Little, Brown.
Keren, D. *et al.* 2004. "Ruins of the gas chambers." *Holocaust and Genocide Studies*, 9(1).
Kershaw, I. 2000. *Hitler, 1936-1945: Nemesis*. W. W. Norton.
Kershaw, I. 2008. *Hitler, the Germans, and the Final Solution*. Yale University Press.
Klee, E. *et al.* 1991. *The Good Old Days: The Holocaust as Seen by Its Perpetrators and Bystanders*. Konecky & Konecky.
Kogon, E. *et al.* 1993. *Nazi Mass Murder*. Yale University Press.
Kola, A. 2000. *Belzec: The Nazi Camp for Jews in the Light of Archeological Sources*. US Holocaust Memorial Museum.
Kosinski, J. 1965. *Painted Bird*. Houghton Mifflin.
Kosmin, Barry A. and Ritterband, Paul (eds.) 1991. *Contemporary Jewish Philanthropy in America*. Rowman and Littlefield.

Kovner, A. 1945/1976. "The mission of the survivors." In *The Catastrophe of European Jewry* (Gutman and Rothkirchen, eds.). Yad Vashem.
Krakowski, S. 2009. *Chelmno: A Small Village in Europe.* Yad Vashem.
Kranz, T. 2003. "Between planning and implementation: The Lublin district and Majdanek camp in Nazi policy." In *Lessons and Legacies,* vol. 14 (L. Thompson, ed.). Northwestern University Press.
Kranz, T. 2007. "Bookkeeping of death and prisoner mortality at Majdanek." *Yad Vashem Studies,* 35(1): 81-109.
Kranz, T. 2007b. *Extermination of Jews at the Majdanek Concentration Camp.* Państwowe Muzeum na Majdanku.
Langerbein, H. 2004. *Hitler's Death Squads.* Texas A&M University Press.
Laqueur, W. (ed.) 2001. *The Holocaust Encyclopedia.* Yale University Press.
Levi, P. 1947/1959. *If This Is a Man.* Orion. (Reprinted as Levi, 1993).
Levi, P. 1993. *Survival in Auschwitz.* Collier. (Reprint of Levi, 1947/1959).
Lindemann, A. 1997. *Esau's Tears.* Cambridge University Press
Lipset, S. and Raab, E. 1995. *Jews and the New American Scene.* Harvard University Press.
Lipstadt, D. 1983. "Holocaust: What we knew was too awful to imagine." *Los Angeles Times* (19 Apr, p. C5).
Lipstadt, D. 1993. *Denying the Holocaust.* Free Press.
Lipstadt, D. 2010. "Denial." In Hayes and Roth (eds.), *Oxford Handbook of Holocaust Studies.*
Longerich, P. 2010. *Holocaust.* Routledge.
Mankowski, Z. 1990. "Majdanek." In Gutman (ed.), *Encyclopedia of the Holocaust.* Macmillan.
Marszalek, J. 1986. *Majdanek: The Concentration Camp in Lublin.* Interpress.
Mason, A. 1956. *Harlan Fiske Stone: Pillar of the Law.* Viking.
Mayer, A. 1988. *Why Did the Heavens Not Darken?* Pantheon.
Meyer, F. 2002. *Die Zahl der Opfer von Auschwitz. Osteuropa,* 52(5): 631-641. In English at <www.vho.org/GB/c/Meyer.html>
Michman, D. 2011. *The Emergence of Jewish Ghettos during the Holocaust.* Cambridge University Press.
Montague, P. 2012. *Chelmno and the Holocaust.* University of North Carolina Press.
Morsch, G. et al (eds.) 2011. *Neue Studien zu nationalsozialistischen Massentötungen durch Giftgas* (in German). Metropol.
Muehlenkamp, R. 2006. Carlo Mattogno on Belzec archaeological research. <http://holocaustcontroversies.blogspot.com/2006/05/carlo-mattogno-on-belzec.html>
Müller, F. 1979. *Eyewitness Auschwitz: Three Years in the Gas Chambers.* Stein and Day.
Niewyk, D. 2000. *Columbia Guide to the Holocaust.* Columbia University Press.
Noakes, J. and Pridham, G. 1995. *Nazism, 1919-1945.* University of Exeter Press.
Novick, P. 1999. *The Holocaust in American Life.* Houghton Mifflin.
Nyiszli, M. 1951. "SS-Obersturmführer Doktor Mengele." *Les Temps Modernes,* March.
Nyiszli, M. 1993. *Auschwitz: A Doctor's Eyewitness Account.* Arcade.
O'Neil, R. 1998. "Belzec: The forgotten death camp." *East European Jewish Affairs,* 28(2): 49-62.
O'Neil, R. 1999. "Belzec: A reassessment of the number of victims." *East European Jewish Affairs,* 29(1-2).
Orth, K. 2009. "The genesis and structure of the National Socialist concentration camps." In G. Megargee (ed.), *Encyclopedia of Camps and Ghettos.* Indiana University Press.
Orth, K. 2010. "Camps." In Hayes and Roth (eds.), *Oxford Handbook of Holocaust Studies.*
Perry, M. (ed.) 2000. *Dachau Liberated.* Inkling.
Perry, M. and Schweitzer, F. 2002. *Antisemitism.* Palgrave Macmillan.
Piper, F. 1991. "Estimating the number of deportees to and victims of the Auschwitz-Birkenau camp." *Yad Vashem Studies* 21: 49-103.

Piper, F. 1994a. "The number of victims." In Gutman and Berenbaum (1994).
Piper, F. 1994b. "Gas chambers and crematoria." In Gutman and Berenbaum (1994).
Pohl, D. 2008. "The murder of Ukraine's Jews under German military administration." In Brandon and Lowers (eds.), *Shoah in Ukraine*, Indiana University Press.
Poliakov, L. 1971. *Harvest of Hate*. Greenwood Press. (Originally published in French as *Bréviaire de la Haine*, 1951.)
Pressac, J.-C. 1989. *Auschwitz: Technique and Operation of the Gas Chambers*. Beate Klarsfeld Foundation.
Pressac, J.-C. 1990. "Deficiencies and inconsistencies with the Leuchter Report." In Shapiro (1990).
Pressac, J.-C. 1993. *Les crématoires d'Auschwitz*. (in French) Editions du CNRS.
Pressac, J.-C. 1994. *Die Krematorien von Auschwitz*. (in German) Piper.
Pressac, J.-C. 2000. Interview. In Igounet (2000). (in French).
Provan, C. 1991. "Kurt Gerstein and the capacity of the gas chamber at Belzec." <holocaust.skeptic.net/documents/provan_Gerstein.html>
Provan, C. 2004. "The blue color of the Jewish victims at Belzec death camp—and carbon monoxide poisoning." *The Revisionist*, 2(2).
Pytell, T. 2000. "The missing pieces of the puzzle: A reflection on the odd career of Viktor Frankl." *Journal of Contemporary History*, 35(2): 281-306.
Rajca, C. 1992. "The problem of the number of victims in the camp at Majdanek." *Zeszyty Majdanka*, vol. 14. (In Polish).
Rector, F. 1981. *The Nazi Extermination of Homosexuals*. Stein and Day.
Reitlinger, G. 1953. *The Final Solution*. (1st ed.) Beechhurst.
Reitlinger, G. 1961. *The Final Solution*. (2nd ed.) A. S. Barnes.
Reitlinger, G. 1968. *The Final Solution*. (3rd ed.) Yoseloff.
Reitlinger, G. 1971. *The Final Solution*. (4th ed.) Sphere.
Reitlinger, G. 1987. *The Final Solution*. (5th ed.) Aronson.
Rhodes, R. 2002. *Masters of Death*. Knopf.
Robinson, J. 1976. "The Holocaust." In *The Catastrophe of European Jewry* (Gutman and Rothkirchen, eds.). Yad Vashem.
Romanov, S. 2006. Why the "diesel issue" is irrelevant. <www.holocaustcontroversies.blogspot.com>
Schelvis, J. 1993/2007. *Sobibor: A History of a Nazi Death Camp*. Berg.
Shapiro, S. (ed.) 1990. *Truth Prevails: Demolishing Holocaust Denial*. Beate Klarsfeld Foundation.
Shermer, M. and Grobman, A. 2000. *Denying History*. University of California Press.
Snyder, T. 2009. "Holocaust: The ignored reality." *New York Review of Books*, 56(12). (16 July).
Soviet Union Special Commission. 1945. Auschwitz Report by the Soviet War Crimes Commission (Document 008-USSR). Online: <www.codoh.com/library/document/225>
Specter, M. 2004. *Denialism*. Penguin.
Spitz, R. 1981. In S. Rothschild (ed.), *Voices from the Holocaust*. New American Library.
Stackelberg, R. and Winkel, S. (eds.). 2002. *The Nazi Germany Sourcebook: An Anthology of Texts*. Routledge.
Stern, K. 1993. *Holocaust Denial*. American Jewish Committee.
Sturdy Colls, C. 2015. *Holocaust Archaeologies*. Springer.
Susskind, D. 1986. *Le Nouvel Observateur* (May 30).
Tregenza, M. 2000. "Das vergessene Lager des Holocaust." In I. Wojak (ed.), *'Arisierung' im Nationalsozialismus, Volksgemeinschaft, Raub, und Gedächtnis*. Campus Verlag. (In German).
US Department of State. 1946. *Nazi Conspiracy and Aggression*. 10 volumes. (Red series).
US Department of State. 2008. *Contemporary Global Anti-Semitism*. <http://www.state.gov/documents/organization/102301.pdf>

US Government Printing Office. 1951–1952. *Trials of War Criminals before the Nuremberg Military Tribunals.* 15 volumes. (Green series).
Van Pelt, R. 2002. *The Case for Auschwitz.* Indiana University Press.
Van Pelt, R. and Dwork, D. 1996. *Auschwitz: 1270 to the Present.* Norton.
Vidal-Naquet, P. 1992. *Assassins of Memory.* Columbia University Press.
Walters, G. 2010. *Hunting Evil.* Broadway.
Webb, C. and Chocholaty, M. 2014. *The Treblinka Death Camp.* Ibidem-Verlag.
Wellers, G. 1983. "Essai de détermination du nombre des morts au camp d'Auschwitz." *Le Monde Juif*, Oct.-Dec.
Wiesel, E. 1960. *Night.* Hill and Wang.
Wiesel, E. 1982. *Legends of Our Time.* Schocken.
Wiesel, E. 1985. "Author, teacher, witness." *Time* (18 March; p. 79).
Wiesel, E. 1995. *All Rivers Run to the Sea.* Knopf.
Wilkomirski, B. 1996. *Fragments.* Schocken.
Wright, R. 2010. "Where are the bodies? In the ground." *The Public Historian* 32(1): 96-107.
Zimmerman, J. 2000. *Holocaust Denial.* University Press of America.
Zimmerman, J. 2004. "Fritjof Meyer and the number of Auschwitz victims: A critical analysis." *Journal of Genocide Research*, 6(2).
Zuckerman, H. 1977. *Scientific Elite.* Free Press.

Traditionalist Web Sites

www.deathcamps.org
www.hdot.org
www.holocaustcontroversies.blogspot.com

www.nizkor.org
www.ushmm.org
www.yadvashem.org

Revisionist Sources—Cited or for Further Reading

Alvarez, S. 2011. *The Gas Vans.* Barnes Review.
Ball, J. 2003. "Air photo evidence." In Rudolf (ed.), 2003.
Ball, J. 2015. *Air Photo Evidence* (3rd ed.). Barnes Review.
Bartec, R. 2012. "Smoking Crematory Chimney at Auschwitz: A Correction." *Inconvenient History* 4(4).
Berg, F. 1986. "The German delousing chambers." *Journal of Historical Review*, 7(1).
Berg, F. 1988. "Typhus and the Jews." *Journal of Historical Review*, 8(4).
Berg, F. 2003. "Diesel gas chambers: Ideal for torture—absurd for murder." In Rudolf (2003).
Berg, F. 2003b. "Poison gas *über alles.*" *The Revisionist*, 1(1).
Berg, F. 2008. "Nazi railroad delousing tunnels for public health, or mass murder?" Online: <http://www.nazigassings.com/railroad.html>
Butler, R. 1983. *Legions of Death.* Arrow Books.
Butz, A. 1976. *The Hoax of the Twentieth Century.* Historical Review Press.
Butz, A. 2000a. "On the 1944 deportations of Hungarian Jews." *Journal of Historical Review*, 19(4).
Butz, A. 2000b. "The greatest dirty open secret." *Journal of Historical Review*, 19(5).
Butz, A. 2015. *The Hoax of the Twentieth Century.* (4th ed.) Castle Hill.
Christophersen, T. 1973. *Auschwitz: Truth or Lie.* Samisdat.

Christophersen, T. 1985. "Reflections on Auschwitz and West German justice." *Journal of Historical Review*.
Crowell, S. 2000. "Bomb shelters in Birkenau: A reappraisal." Online at: <http://codoh.com/library/document/904/>
Crowell, S. 2001a. "The basement showers of crematorium III." *Journal of Historical Review*, 20(2).
Crowell, S. 2001b. "Beyond Auschwitz." *Journal of Historical Review*, 20(2).
Crowell, S. 2011. *The Gas Chamber of Sherlock Holmes*. Nine-banded Books.
Dalton, T. 2010. "Goebbels on the Jews." *Inconvenient History* 2(1).
Dalton, T. 2011. "Reexamining the 'gas chamber' of Dachau." *Inconvenient History* 3(4).
Dalton, T. 2013. "The Jewish hand in the world wars (Part I)." *Inconvenient History* 5(2).
Dalton, T. 2014. "The Jewish hand in the world wars (Part II)." *Inconvenient History* 6(2).
Faurisson, R. 1999. *Ecrits Révisionnistes (1974–1998)*. 4 volumes. Edition privée hors-commerce. English online: <http://vho.org/aaargh/fran/livres4/presenteRF.pdf>
Faurisson, R. 2001. "Shoah: Fictive images and mere belief?" *Journal of Historical Review*, 20(1).
Faurisson, R. 2002. "My revisionist method." *Journal of Historical Review*, 21(2).
Faurisson, R. 2003a. "Witnesses to the gas chambers of Auschwitz." In Rudolf (2003).
Faurisson, R. 2003b. "How many deaths at Auschwitz?" *The Revisionist*, 1(1).
Faurisson, R. 2004. "Treblinka: An exceptional guide." *The Revisionist*, 2(1).
Faurisson, R. 2005. "Reply to J.-C. Pressac on the problem of the gas chambers." In Rudolf, ed. (2005).
Finkelstein, N. 2000. *The Holocaust Industry*. Verso.
Flanagan, N. *et al.* 1978. "An unusual case of carbon monoxide poisoning." *Medicine, Science, and Law*, 18(2).
Gauss, E. See Rudolf, G.
Goebbels, J. 1942-1943/1970. *The Goebbels Diaries: 1942-1943*. (L. Lochner, trans. and ed.). Greenwood Press.
Goebbels, J. 1923-1945/1987. *Die Tagebücher von Joseph Goebbels* (The Diaries of Joseph Goebbels). E. Fröhlich (ed.). K. G. Saur.
Graf, J. 1994. *Auschwitz*. Würenlos.
Graf, J. 2000. "What happened to the Jews who were deported to Auschwitz but were not registered there?" *Journal of Historical Review*, 19(4).
Graf, J. 2003. "National Socialist concentration camps: Legend and reality." In Rudolf (2003).
Graf, J. 2015. *The Giant with Feet of Clay* (2nd ed.). Castle Hill.
Graf, J., Kues, T., and Mattogno, C. 2010. *Sobibor: Holocaust Propaganda and Reality*. Barnes Review.
Graf, J. and Mattogno, C. 2012. *Concentration Camp Majdanek* (3rd ed.). Barnes Review.
Graf, J. and Mattogno, C. 2015. *Concentration Camp Stutthof* (3rd ed.). Castle Hill.
Heddesheimer, D. 2011. *The First Holocaust* (2nd ed.). Barnes Review.
Hinsley, F. 1981. *British Intelligence in the Second World War* (vol. 2). Cambridge University Press.
Hitler, A. 2000. *Table Talk*. Enigma.
Holtz, J. and Elliott, M. 1941. "The significance of diesel-exhaust-gas analysis." *Transactions of the American Society of Mechanical Engineers* (February): 97-105.
Irving, D. 1977. *Hitler's War*. Viking Press.
Irving, D. 1978. *The War Path*. Viking Press.
Irving, D. 1996. *Nuremberg: The Last Battle*. Focal Point Press.
Jansson, F. 2014. "The origin of the Soviet report on the 'next generation' homicidal gas chamber at Sachsenhausen." *Inconvenient History* 6(4).
Köchel, H. 2015. "Outdoor incineration of livestock carcasses." *Inconvenient History* 7(1).

Köhler, M. 2003. "The value of testimony and confessions concerning the Holocaust." In Rudolf (2003).
Kollerstrom, N. 2014. *Breaking the Spell*. Castle Hill.
Kues, T. 2010. "Chil Rajchman's Treblinka memoirs." *Inconvenient History* 2(1).
Kulaszka, B. (ed.) 1988. *Did Six Million Really Die?* Samisdat.
Leuchter, F. *et al.* 2012. *The Leuchter Reports* (3rd ed.). Barnes Review.
Mattogno, C. 2003a. "The crematoria ovens of Auschwitz and Birkenau." In Rudolf (2003).
Mattogno, C. 2003b. "The gas chambers of Majdanek." In Rudolf (2003).
Mattogno, C. 2003c. "Auschwitz: Fritjof Meyer's new revisions." *The Revisionist*, 1(1).
Mattogno, C. 2003d. "The four million figure of Auschwitz." *The Revisionist*, 1(4).
Mattogno, C. 2004. *The Bunkers of Auschwitz*. Theses and Dissertations Press.
Mattogno, C. 2004b. *Special Treatment in Auschwitz*. Theses and Dissertations Press.
Mattogno, C. 2004c. "Combustion experiments with flesh and animal fat." *The Revisionist*, 2(1).
Mattogno, C. 2004d. "Flames and smoke from the chimneys of crematoria." *The Revisionist*, 2(1).
Mattogno, C. 2004e. "The 'gas testers' of Auschwitz." *The Revisionist*, 2(2).
Mattogno, C. 2004f. "The morgues of the crematoria at Birkenau in the light of documents." *The Revisionist*, 2(3).
Mattogno, C. 2004g. "No holes, no gas chamber(s)". *The Revisionist*, 2(4).
Mattogno, C. 2004h. "The openings for the introduction of Zyklon B – Part I: The roof of the morgue of crematorium I at Auschwitz." *The Revisionist*, 2(4).
Mattogno, C. 2005a. "Auschwitz: The End of a Legend." In Rudolf (ed.), 2005.
Mattogno, C. 2005b. "'Denying History?'—Denying evidence!" *The Revisionist*, 3(1).
Mattogno, C. 2005c. "The elusive holes of death." In Rudolf and Mattogno (2005).
Mattogno, C. 2010. *Auschwitz: Open Air Incinerations*. Barnes Review.
Mattogno, C. 2010b. *Auschwitz: Crematorium I*. Barnes Review.
Mattogno, C. 2011. *Belzec: In Propaganda, Testimonies, Archeological Research, and History*. Barnes Review.
Mattogno, C. 2011b. *Chelmno: A German Camp in History and Propaganda*. Barnes Review.
Mattogno, C. 2011c. *Auschwitz: The First Gassing* (2nd ed.). Barnes Review.
Mattogno, C. 2014. *Inside the Gas Chambers*. Barnes Review.
Mattogno, C. 2015. *The Cremation Furnaces of Auschwitz*. Castle Hill.
Mattogno, C. 2016. *Curated Lies: The Auschwitz Museum's Misrepresentations, Distortions and Deceptions*. Castle Hill.
Mattogno, C. 2016b. *Healthcare in Auschwitz: Medical Care and Special Treatment of Registered Inmates*. Castle Hill.
Mattogno, C. and Graf, J. 2010. *Treblinka: Extermination Camp or Transit Camp?* (2nd ed.) Barnes Review.
Mattogno, C., Graf, J., and Kues, T. 2013. *The "Extermination Camps" of "Aktion Reinhardt."* Castle Hill.
Mearsheimer, J. and Walt, S. 2006. "The Israel lobby and US foreign policy." *London Review of Books*, March. Online at: <http://www.lrb.co.uk/v28/n06/mear01_.html>
Mearsheimer, J. and Walt, S. 2007. *The Israel Lobby and US Foreign Policy*. Farrar, Straus, and Giroux.
Neff, D. 1981. *Warriors at Suez*. Simon and Schuster.
Neff, D. 1995. *Fallen Pillars*. Institute for Palestinian Studies.
Neumaier, A. 2003. "The Treblinka Holocaust." In Rudolf (2003).
Nowak, H.J. and Rademacher, W. 2003. "Some details of the Central Construction Office of Auschwitz." In Rudolf (2003).
Rassinier, P. 1978. *Debunking the Genocide Myth*. Noontide Press.

Rassinier, P. 1990. *The Holocaust Story and the Lies of Ulysses*. (2nd ed.) Institute for Historical Review.
Renk, B. 2001. "Convergence or divergence? Recent evidence for Zyklon introduction holes at Birkenau crematory II." *Journal of Historical Review*, 20(5/6).
Routledge, W. 2015. *Holocaust High Priest*. Castle Hill.
Rudolf, G. 1993. *Vorlesungen über Zeitgeschichte*. (Lectures on Contemporary History). Published under pen name "Ernst Gauss." Revised, in English, as Rudolf (2011).
Rudolf, G. (ed.) 1994. *Grundlagen zur Zeitgeschichte*. (Foundations of Contemporary History). Published under pen name "Ernst Gauss." Revised, in English, as Rudolf (2000, 2003).
Rudolf, G. (ed.) 2000. *Dissecting the Holocaust*. (1st English ed.) Revised as Rudolf (2003).
Rudolf, G. 2001. "A brief history of forensic examinations of Auschwitz." *Journal of Historical Review*, 20(2).
Rudolf, G. (ed.) 2003. *Dissecting the Holocaust* (2nd ed.). Theses and Dissertations Press.
Rudolf, G. 2003a. "The controversy about the extermination of the Jews – An introduction." In Rudolf (2003).
Rudolf, G. 2003b. "Holocaust victims: A statistical analysis." In Rudolf (2003).
Rudolf, G. 2003c. "Some considerations about the 'gas chambers' of Auschwitz and Birkenau." In Rudolf (2003).
Rudolf, G. 2003d. "Cautious mainstream revisionism." *The Revisionist*, 1(1).
Rudolf, G. 2004. "On the progress and propagation of Holocaust revisionism." *The Revisionist*, 2(3).
Rudolf, G. (ed.) 2005. *Auschwitz: Plain Facts*. Theses and Dissertations Press.
Rudolf, G. 2011. *Lectures on the Holocaust* (2nd ed.). Barnes Review.
Rudolf, G. and Lambrecht, W. 2011. *The Rudolf Report* (2nd ed.). Barnes Review.
Rudolf, G. and Mattogno, C. 2011. *Auschwitz Lies* (2nd ed.). Barnes Review.
Sanning, W. 1990. *The Dissolution of Eastern European Jewry*. (3rd ed.) Institute for Historical Review.
Stäglich, W. 1986. *The Auschwitz Myth*. Institute for Historical Review.
Walendy, U. 2003. "Do photographs prove the NS extermination of the Jews?" In Rudolf (2003).
Weber, M. 1992. "The Nuremberg Trials and the Holocaust." *Journal of Historical Review*, 12(2).
Weber, M. 2001. "Wilhelm Hoettl and the elusive 'six million'." *Journal of Historical Review*, 20(5/6).
Weber, M. 2002. "New 'official' changes in the Auschwitz story." *Journal of Historical Review*, 21(3/4).
Weckert, I. 2003a. "The gas vans: A critical assessment of the evidence." In Rudolf (2003).
Weckert, I. 2003b. "What was Kulmhof/Chelmno?" *The Revisionist*, 1(4).

Revisionist Web Sites

www.adelaideinstitute.org
www.codoh.com
www.eliewieseltattoo.com
www.fpp.co.uk
www.gaschamberhoax.com
www.germarrudolf.com
www.holocausthistorychannel.wordpress.com
www.holocausthandbooks.com
www.ihr.org
www.inconvenienthistory.com
www.nazigassings.com
www.revisionists.com
www.vho.org
www.zundelsite.org

General Index

Page numbers of entries in footnotes are set in italics.

— 2 —
21st Century Fox: 267

— A —
ABC Corporation: 267
Abrams, Elliot: 274
Acevedo, Anthony: 247
Adelson, Sheldon: *265*, 272
Adenauer, Konrad: 289
Afghanistan: *94*, 274, 276
Ahmadinejad, Mahmoud: 277
AIPAC: see American Israel Public Affairs Committee
air photos: 23, 212, 213, 219, 229, 237, 238, 241, 285, 294, 296
  Auschwitz: 229-240
Aktion 1005: 91
Aktion Reinhardt: see Operation Reinhardt
Albright, Madeleine: 274, *276*
Alvarez, Santiago: *41*, *113*, *118*, 119, *152*
American Israel Public Affairs Committee (AIPAC): 269-272, 277
Anselm of Canterbury: 54
Antin, Mary: 135
anti-Semitism: 24, 25, 31, 32, 62, 255, 269, 277, 281, 290, 296
  defined: 32
App, Austin: 294
Arad, Yitzhak: 34, 80, 128-137, *143*, 146-150, 153, 156-160, 164, 176, 220, 261
Arbeitsdorf: 99

Argentina: 264
Association of Holocaust Organizations (AHO): 279
Auerbach, Rachel: 130, 131, 149
Auschwitz: passim; see Chapter 10
  death matrix: 199
  estimated deaths: 198
  map (Birkenau): 197
  revisionist version: 240-241
  witnesses: 203-204, 250-252, 304-306
Auschwitz Protocols: see Vrba-Wetzler Report
ausrotten: 102-104, 294, 295
Australia: *15*, 264
Austria: *24*, 26, 62, 109
autopsy: 29, 201
Axelrod, David: 273

— B —
B'nai Brith: 281
Babi Yar: 90, 94
Baer, Richard: *204*
Baird, Zoe: 274
Balfour Declaration: 17, 45
Ball, John C.: 4, 212, 213, 303
Ballmer, Steve: *265*
Barber, Gary: *265*
Baron, Martin: 267
Bartec, Robert: *230*
Bartov, Omer: 22, 106, 124, 151, 167, 179, 237
Bauer, Erich: 130, 307
Becker, August: 119
Beim, Aaron: 246
Belgium: 16, *24*, 264, 278

Belzec: 23, 37, 41, 52, 55, 63, 75-78, 100, 118, *144*, *146*, 177, 200, 257, 287, 304, 306, see Chapters 6-8
  death matrix: 138
  estimated deaths: 130
  map: 132, 165
  mass graves: 149, 151, 156
Bem, Marek: 130, 167-169
Bendel, Charles S.: 203, 305
Bender, Lawrence: *266*
Benz, Wolfgang: 4, 55, 113, 130
Berenbaum, Michael: 22, 40, 41, 55, *112*, 253
Berg, Friedrich P.: 4, 30, 36, *107*, 108, 117, 152, 294, 296
Bergen-Belsen: 29, 41, 99, 111, 112, 248
Berger, Sandy: 274
Bernanke, Ben Shalom: 273, 274
Bewkes, Jeff: 266
Bezos, Jeffrey P.: 268
Bible, and prediction of "six million": 64
Biden, Joseph R.: 265, 266, 273
bin Laden, Osama: *276*
Birkenau: 99, 145, 190, 192-197, 200, 208, 209, 212-214, 218, 223, *224*, 229-231, 237, 240, 296, 306
  map: 197
  mass graves: 221
Bischoff letter, on gassing capacity: *222*, 225-226
Bischoff, Karl: 225

Blatt, Thomas: 128
Blavatnik, Len: *265*
Blech, Benjamin: 64
Blinken, Tony: 273
Bloomberg, Michael: 263, *265*
blue bodies, gassing victims: 148, 149, 152, 153, 305
blue wall coloration: see Prussian blue
Bodman, Samuel: 274
Bomba, Abraham: 307
Bonaparte, Napoléon: 107
bone grinder: 122
Boot, Max: 274
Bormann. Martin: 47
Brand, Joel: 63
Bren, Donald: *265*
Breyer, Stephen: 271
Brin, Sergey: 263, *265*, 268
Brinkmann, Felix: 249
Broad, Pery S.: 204, 304, 306
Bronfman, Edgar: 278
Brooks, David: 274
Browning, Christopher R.: 4, 35, *44*, 130, 261
Brugioni, Dino: 212, 213
Buchenwald: 41, 99, 111, 247, 250-253
Bug river: 94
Bund Report: 200
bunkers (Auschwitz gassing facilities): 194, 197-199, 204-207, 227, 228, 305, 306
Burrin, Philippe: 105
Bush, George W.: 274
Butz, Arthur R.: 4, 30, 36, 146-149, *227*, 294, 295

— C —

Canada: 25, 34, *148*, 256, 264
carbon dioxide: 187
carbon monoxide: 108, 116, *148*
  bottled: 108, 116, 179, 184, 186
  diesel exhaust: 23, 41, 116, 118, 124, 131, 143, 145-148, 151, 152, *294*
  engine exhaust: 116
  producer gas: 116
Carter, Jimmy: 273, 275

Catz, Safra: 268
CBS: *265*, 267
Central Intelligence Agency (CIA): 211, 273, *274*
Chavez Report: 110
Chelmno: 9, 23, 41, 55, 77, 78, 109, *112*, *124*, 129, 132, 141, 145, 157, 159, 192, 200, 257, 287, 299, 307, see Chapter 5
  death matrix: 123
  estimated deaths: 113
  map: 114, 115
  mass graves: 113, 115, 120, 122, 124
Chernin, Peter: *265*
Chernofsky, Phil: *56*
Chertoff, Michael: 274
China: *21*
chlorine gassings: 144, 306, 307
Chocholaty, Michal: 130
Chomsky, Noam: 26
Christ, Jesus: 261
Churchill, Winston: 289
Clinton, Hillary: 271, 274
Clinton, William: 274
CNN: 247, 249, 267
Cobain, Ian: 50
Cohen, David: 267, 273
Cohen, Eliot: 274
Cohen, William: 274
Cole, David: *24*
Cologne: 21
Comcast: 267
Conan, Eric: 191
Concentration camps history: 99
Condé Nast: 264, 267
Cooper, Abraham: *21*
Corni, Gustavo: 81-86
crematoria: 22, 29, 42, 44, 122, 158, 190, 285, 289
  Auschwitz: 22, *29*, 33, 37, 52, 120, 250, 256, see also Chapter 10
  capacity: 223-226
  Chelmno: 120, 121, 125, 157
  Dachau: 110
  Majdanek: 177, 183, 184, 187
Croatia: 74
Crowell, Samuel: *30*, 36, *107*, 201, 202, 304

cyanide gas: see Zyklon B
cyanide residue: see Prussian blue
Czech Repubic: *24*
Czech, Danuta: 80, 286, 287

— D —

Dachau: 41, 99, 108-111, *207*
  gas chamber: 110
Dalton, Thomas: 27, *45*, 103, *111*, *266*
Dauman, Philippe: 267
Dawidowicz, Lucy: 33, 64, 178, 254
de Boüard, Michel: 255
de Gaulle, Charles: 289
de Wael, Monique: see Defonseca, Misha
Dean, Martin: 82, 83
death matrix: 9, 78, 285, 299, see Chapter 4 and each camp
  Einsatzgruppen: 88, 90
  revisionist: 258
Defonseca, Misha: 252
Dell, Michael: *265*, 268
DellaPergola, Sergio: 66, 67, 257, 298
Demjanjuk, John: 163, 255
Desbois, Patrick: 88, 93-95
diesel exhaust: see carbon monoxide
Diller, Barry: 263
Dimont, Max: 111
Disney Corporation: 266, 267
Dodd, Christopher: 48
Dodd, Thomas: 48, 49
Donahue, Phil: *24*
Donat, Alexander: 128
Dragon, Shlomo: 203, 305
Dresden: 21
Dühring, Eugen: 59
Dulles, John F.: 269

— E —

Eden, Anthony: *289*
Edwards: 271
Egypt: 64, 269, 275
Eichmann, Adolf: 23, *44*, 56, 57, 63
Einsatzgruppen: 9, *56*, 74-78, 87-96, 120, 145, 257, 258

estimated deaths: 88
Eisenhower, Dwight D.: 269, 288
Eisner, Michael: 266
Eitan, Rafi: 279
electrocution: 143
Elliott, Martin: *117*, 152
Ellison, Larry: *265*, 268
Emanuel, Rahm: 273, 274
Epstein, B.: *237*
Erber, Josef: *204*
Evans, Richard: 35, 161, 261, 293-296
excavations: 174, 299
　Auschwitz: *228*, 240
　Belzec: 130, 163-167
　Chelmno: 115, 122, 124
　Einsatzgruppen: 93-95, 291-293
　Sobibor: 167-169
　Treblinka: 169-172

— F —

Faurisson, Robert: 4, 30, 33, 36, 37, 53, 106, 210, 219, 240, 250, 294, 295
Feingold, Henry: 275
Feinsilber, Alter: 203, 306
Feith, Doug: 274
Feltheimer, Jon: *265*
Findley, Paul: 270
Fine, Gary: 246
Finkelstein, Norman: 278
Flanagan, N.: 117, *183*
Flossenbürg: 99
Ford, Henry: 62, 266
Forrestal, James: 269
Fox News: 267
Fox, William: *267*
France: 24, 27, 47, 109, 252, 264
Frankel, Max: 245
Frankl, Viktor: 203, 251, 252, 272, 306
Franz, Kurt: 163, 307
fraud, in Holocaust literature: 252-254
free speech, right of: 16, 26, 282
Friedberg, Aaron: 274
Friedman, Arnold: 256
Friedman, Philip: 81, 83
Frum, David: 274
Fuchs, Erich: 147, 153, 307
Fulbright, J. William: 270

furnaces: *222*, see crematoria

— G —

Gaddafi, Muammar: 276
Ganon, Yitzchak: 249
Garaudy, Roger: 31
gas vans: 41, 88, 109, *112*, 113, 118-120, 123-125, 145, 200
Geffen, David: 263
Geithner, Tim: 273
Germany: 12, 16, 21, 24-27, *32*, 36, 41, 44, 48, 50, 56, 59-62, *66*, 87, 100-104, 109, 110, 135, 171, 227, 278-281, 287-290
Gerstein, Kurt: *137*, 144-150, 303-307
ghettos: 9, 41, 42, 56, 68, 74-78, 81-87, 96, 116, 119, 127, 172-175, 257, 258, 285, 291
　Bialystok: *81*, 87
　Czestochowa: *81*, 87
　Kaunas: *81*, 87
　Kielce: 87
　Krakow: 87
　Lodz: 81, 82, 87, 122, 125
　Lublin: *81*, 87
　Lvov: *81*, 87
　Minsk: *81*, 87
　Radom: *81*, 87
　Vilnius: 87
　Warsaw: 81-87, 143
Gilbert, Martin J.: 4, 113
Ginsburg, Ruth: 271
Glickman, Dan: 274
Globocnik, Odilo: 146
Glücks, Richard: 288
Goebbels, Joseph: 23, 103-105, 266
Golczewski, Frank: 130
Goldberg, Esther: 113
Goldberg, Jeffrey: 272
Goldmann, Nahum: 63
Gordon, Sarah A.: *27*, 70
Gore, Albert: 274
Göring, Hermann: 23, 47, 57
Graboff, Marc: *266*
Graf, Jürgen: 4, *27*, 37, 100, 112, 129, *131*, 135, 143-149, *157*, *162*, 167-171, 175, 179, 180, 183-188,
240, *250*, 287, 294, 296, 303
Grau, Günter: 291
Greece: *25*
Greenblatt, Jonathan: 273
Greenblatt, Robert: 267
Greenspan, Alan: 274
Grey, Brad: *265*
Griffin, Sean: 117, *148*
Gringauz, Samuel: 254
Grobman, Alex: 22, 34, 145, 152, 162, 178, 179, 184-187
Gröning, Oskar: *29*
Gross-Rosen: 99
Grüner, Miklos: 251
Gryglewski, Elke: 255
Guantanamo Bay: 99
Gusen: 109
Gutman, Yisrael: 34, 35, 146

— H —

Haimi, Yoram: 168, 169, 173, 240
Hamburg: 21
Hannah, John: 274
Harris, Dan: *253*
Harrison, Jonathan: *35*, 161, 303
Headland, Ronald: 88-90
Hertz, Joseph: 63
Herzogenbusch: 99
Hess, Rudolf: 47
Hilberg
　estimated deaths: 74
Hilberg, Raul: 4, 9, *13*, 23, 34, 37, *43*, 55, 63, 74-77, 82, 88-90, 105, 106, 111, 113, 130, 145, 147, 150-153, 161, 167, *177*, 178, 198, 239, 278, *291*
　death matrix: 74-79
Hilliard, Earl: 270
Himmler, Heinrich: 23, 35, *57*, 63, 115, 116, 286-288
Hinzert: 99
Hiroshima: 21
Hirszman, Chaim: *144*
Hitler, Adolf: 22, 23, 27, 31, 32, 43, 44, *47*, *48*, 54, 55, 62, 63, 100-104, 172, 227, 257, 269, 278, 285, 290, 291, 294, 296

missing extermination order: 23, 27, 52, 105-107, 115, 296
Höfle, Hermann: 75
holes, in gas chamber ceilings: 213-219
Holocaust: passim
 'Hoax': 30, 31
 definition: 21-22, 39-40
 education: 15, 283
 publications: 280, 281
 restitution: 16, 31, 45, 261, 278-281, 289, 290
 revisionist version: 26-28, 256-258
 start of: 41, 54
 survivors: 12, 16, 18, 23, 44-46, 52, 66, 67, 73, 112, 135, 201, 202, 246-250, 254-257, 260, 272, 279, 293
Holstein, Bernard: 252
Holtz, John: *117*, 152
Horn, Otto: 163, 307
Höss, Rudolf: 44, *47*, 51, 162, 204, *222*, 225, 226, 239, 249, 304-306
Hössler, Franz: *204*
Höttl, Wilhelm: 56, 57
Humphrey, Hubert: 273
Hungarian Jews, massacre of: 197, 204, 205, 211, 212, 222, 227-230, 237-240, *289*, 304, 306
Hungary: *25*, 63, 227, 237, 264
Hunt, Eric: *173*, *186*
Hussein, Saddam: *276*
hydrogen cyanide: see Zyklon B

— I —

Icahn, Carl: *265*
Iger, Robert: *265*, 266
Indyk, Martin: 274
International Military Tribunal (IMT): see Nuremberg trials
Iran: 271, 272, 276
Iraq: *276*
Iraq war: *94*, 274-276
Irving, David: 4, 25, 34-36, 57, 67, 105, 214, 293-295
Israel: 15-17, 24, 31, *32*, 44, 45, 259, 261, 264, 267-281, 290
Israel Lobby: 268-279, 290

— J —

Jackson, Robert H.: 57
Jackson, Scoop: 273
Jansson, Friedrich: *109*
Japan: 14, *21*
Jepson, Roger: 270
Jewish population, world: 67-72
Jordan: 275
Jordan, Hamilton: 273

— K —

Kaduk, Oswald: *204*
Kadushin, Charles: *265*
Kagan, Elena: 271, 273
Kagan, Robert: 274
Kagedan, Ian: 281, 282
Kann, family: 267
Kaplan, Benjamin: 49
Kauen: 99
Kavanaugh, Ryan: *265*
Keren, Daniel: *210*, 213, 216-219
Kerry, John: 273
Kershaw, Ian: 34, 105, 106, 261
Kessler, David: 274
Khvativ: 95
Kishinev: 60
Klehr, Josef: *204*
Klein, Fritz: *204*
Klukowski, Zygmunt: 306
Köchel, Heinrich: *162*, 297
Kohanski, Alexander: 57
Kohl, Helmut: 290
Köhler, Manfred: 51
Kola, Andrzej: 128, 164-168, 173, 240
Kollerstrom, Nicholas: *202*
Korherr, Richard: 82
Kosinski, Jerzy: 252
Kosmin, Barry A.: *265*
Kovner, Abba: 57
Krakowski, Shmuel: 44, 113, 114, 119, 123, 124, 255
Kranz, Tomasz: 9, 127, 178-180, 183
Krauthammer, Charles: 274
Kremer, Johann: 198, 204, 304
Kristallnacht: 54

Kristol, William: 274
Kubowitzki, Leon: 63
Kues, Thomas: 37, 129, *149*, 169, 174, 294, 296
Kula, Michal: 208
Kulmhof: see Chelmno

— L —

Ladany, Shaul: 112, 248
Lambert, Erwin: 307
Langerbein, Helmut: 95
Lanin, E.: *60*
Laqueur, Walter: 35, *43*, 109, 110, 113, 136, 137, 153, 176, 178
Latvia: 264
Lauren, Ralph: 263
Lawrence, Bill: 178
Lazarus, Mark: 267
Le Pen, Jean-Marie: 278
legislation, against Holocaust revisionism: 24-26, 51, 277
Lerner, Avi: *266*
Lestchinsky, Jacob: 58
Leuchter, Fred A.: 219-221
Levi, Primo: 203, 306
Levitt, Arthur: 274
Lew, Jack: 273
Lewis, Bernard: 274
Libby, Irve Lewis: 274
Libya: 276
Lieberman, Joseph: 274
Liechtenstein: *25*
Lindemann, Albert S.: 247
Lipset, Seymour M.: *265*, 266
Lipstadt, Deborah E.: 4, 24, 26, 34, 35, 152, 161, 162, 178, 213, 214, 261, 293-296
Lisinitchi: 94
Lithuania: *25*, 87
Longerich, Peter: 35, 81-83, 87-93, 111, 124, 151, 161, 167, 179, 237, *239*, 261
Lonsdale, Harry: 270
Lublin: see Majdanek
Luce, Harry: 269
Lukaszkiewicz, Zdzislaw: 130, *131*, 170, 171
Luxembourg: *25*, 290
Lynton, Michael M.: *265*

— M —

MacDonald, Kevin: *266*
Madagascar, as Jewish homeland: 27, 294
Majdanek: 37, 41, 52, 55, 77, 78, 85, 99, 108, 111, 145, 192, 200, 257, 287, 291, see Chapter 9
  death matrix: 181
  estimated deaths: 178
  mass graves: 178
  witnesses: 307
Malkinia: see Treblinka
Markiewicz, Jan: 220, *229*
Marshall, George: 269
Marszalek, Josef: 177, 179
Mason, Alpheus T.: 49
mass graves: 11, 22, 40, 52, 56, 82, 85, 86, 303, see each camp
  Einsatzgruppen:90-95, 291-293
  Stalin's: *93*
Mattes, Heinrich: 163, 307
Mattogno, Carlo: 4, *27*, *35*, 37, *90*, 112-116, *121*, 122, 125, 129-131, 135, 143-152, *157*, 161-175, 179, 180, 183-188, 193, 209-221, 224-227, 230, 239, 240, 287, 294, 296, 303
Mauthausen: 51, 99, 109, 111
Maxwell Fyfe, David P.: 57
Mayer, Arno: 255
Mazal, Henry: 213
Mazurek, Wojciech: 130, 167, 169
McCain, John: 271, 272
McCarthy, Jamie: 213
McCloskey, Paul N.: 270
McKinney, Cynthia: 270
Mearsheimer, John: 268-276
media, Jewish influence in: 266-268
Mengele, Josef: 249-254, 305, 306
Mentz, Willi: 163, 307
Merkel, Angela: 290
Meyer, Barry: *265*
Meyer, Eugene: 267
Meyer, Fritjof: *67*, 197, 198
Mezvinsky, Marc: 271
Michman, Dan: 82
microwave delousing: *108*

Mittelbau: 99
Mohamad, Mahathir: 276, 282
Mommsen, Hans: 106
Monowitz (Auschwitz III): 99, 190, 203, *231*, 306
Montague, Patrick: 113-124
Moonves, Leslie: *265*, 267
Moran, James: 275
Morsch, Günter: *124*, *152*
Moskovitz, Dustin: 268
Muehlenkamp, Roberto: *137*, 303
muffle: *222*, see crematoria
Mukasey, Michael: 274
Müller, Filip: 203, 305, 306
Murdoch, family: *267*
Murdoch, James: 267
Murdoch, Lachlan: 267
Murdoch, Rupert: *265*, 267
Mussfeldt, Erich: *179*

— N —

Nagasaki: 21
National Public Radio (NPR): 268
Natzweiler: 99, 109
NBC-Universal Corporation: 249, 267
Neff, Donald: *269*
neo-conservatives: *269*, 274
Ner River: 113
Netanyahu, Benjamin: *273*
Neuengamme: 99, 109
Neumaier, Arnulf: *122*, 303
Newhouse, Samuel ("Si"): 267
news corporations: 266
newspapers, leading American: 267
Nixon, Richard: 274
Noakes, Jeremy: 130
Novick, Peter: 291
Nowak, Hans Jürgen: *108*
Nuremberg trials: 21, 44, 47-52, *57*, 111, 197, *201*, 202, 295, 304
Nyiszli, Miklos: 198, 203, 306

— O —

O'Neil, Robin: 130, 164, 166
Obama, Barack: 101, 271-276

Oberhauser, Josef: 306
Ochs, Adolph: 267
Olère, David: 249
Opel Blitz: 118, 119
open-air burning: 121, 125, 131, 133, 136, 140, 155, 157-160, 162, 201, 222-230, 237-240, 285, 297, 303, 307
Operation Reinhardt: 128, 148
  camps: see Chapters 6-8
Oren, Michael: 17
Orszag, Peter: 273
Orth, Karen: 99, 118
Oswiecim: see Auschwitz
ovens: *222*, see crematoria

— P —

Page, Larry: 263, *265*, 268
Pakistan: 275, 276
Palestine, and Palestinians: 16, 17, 32, 45, 60, 64, 270, *276*
Pascal, Amy: *266*
Peer, Moshe: 112, 248
Peloponnesian War: 107
Percy, Charles: 270
Perelman, Ron: *265*
Pericles: *107*
Perle, Richard: 274
Perlman, Nathan: 57
Perry, Marvin: *30*, 152, 162
Perry, Michael W.: 110
Pfannenstiel, Wilhelm: 148, 306
Pinter, Stephen: 110
Piper, Franciszek: 4, 205, 207, 223, 227, 228, 239
Pipes, Daniel: 274
Plame, Valerie: *274*
Plaszow: 99
Plouffe, David: 273
Podhoretz, Norman: 274
Pohl, Dieter: 88, 89
Pohl, Oswald: 286-288
Poirier, Robert: 212, 213
Poland: *25*
Poliakov, Léon: 148, 198
Pope John Paul II: 42
Portugal: *25*
Powell, Colin: 275
Power, Samantha: 273
Pressac, Jean-Claude: 33, 113, 130, 178, 184-186,

191, 195, 198, 203, *208*, 305, 306
Pridham, Geoffrey: 130
producer gas generators: 116, 119, 152, 153, 186
Protocols of the Elders of Zion: 261
Provan, Charles D.: *137, 148*, 161, 210-219, 303
Prüfer, Kurt: 224
Prussian blue: 183-186, 219-221, *228*
Prützmann, Hans: *90*
pyres: see open-air burning
Pytell, Timothy: 251, 252

— R —
Raab, Earl: *265*, 266
Rademacher, Werner: *108*
Rajca, Czesław: 178
Rajchman, Chil: 149
Rajzman, Samuel: 130, 163, 307
Rassinier, Paul: 31, 36, 294
Rauff, Walter: 119, 120
Ravensbrück: 99, 110
Rawa-Ruska: 94
Rector, Frank: 291
Reder, Rudolf: 144-146, 150-153, 306
Redstone, Sumner: 267
Reich, Robert: 274
Reitlinger, Gerald: 23, 33, 34, *43*, 144, 197, 198, 254, *291*
Renouf, Michèle: 73
revisionism, core concepts: 26-28
Reynouard, Vincent: 26
Rhodes, Richard: 95
Riga: 99
Ritterband, Paul: *265*
Roberts, Brian: 267
Roberts, Cokie: *268*
Robinson, Jacob: 55, 57
Roman Empire: *45*
Romania: *25*, 59, 62, 74
Romanov, Alexander II, Czar: 60
Romanov, Sergey: 152, 153
Romney, Willard Mitt: 271, 272
Rosen, Steven: 270
Rosenberg, Elias: 145, 157
Rosenberg, Walter: see Vrba, Rudolf
Rosenblat, Herman: 253
Rosenstein, Justin: 268
Ross, Dennis: 273, 274
Rothman, Tom: *266*
Routledge, Warren: *203, 251*
Rubin, Robert: 274
Rudolf, Germar: 4, *12*, 25, 31, 37, 67, 105, 109, *111*, 117, 150, *183*, 185, 191-195, 208-221, 224, *228*, 230, 238-240, 255, 256, 278, 294, 296, 303
Russia: *25*, 107
  anti-Semitism in: 59-62

— S —
Saban, Haim: *266*
Sachsenhausen: 99, 109, 111
Sandberg, Sheryl: 268
Sanning, Walter N.: 65, 66
Sarkozy, Nicolas: *15*
Saurer trucks: *41*, 118, 119, 129
Schapiro, Mary: 273
Scheidl, Franz J.: 36
Schelvis, Jules: 128, 130, *159*
Schluch, Karl A.: 147, 148, 306
Schröder, Gerhard: 290
Schulman, Samuel: 102
Schwarzman, Stephen: 263, *265*
Schweitzer, Frederick: *30*, 152, 162
Sereny, Gitta: 128
Serniki, Ukraine: 292
Shalev, Avner: 280
Shapiro, Paul: 93
Shapiro, Shelly: 34
Shavit, Ari: 265
Shermer, Michael B.: 4, 22, *24*, 34, 145, 152, 162, 178, 179, 184-187, 261
Silberschein, Rabbi: 143
Sinai Peninsula: 269
Six Day War: 269
Six Million, origin: 58-64
Skoll, Jeff: 268
Sloan, Harry E.: *265*
Smith, Bradley R.: *24*
Snyder, Timothy: 88, 130
Sobibor: 23, 37, 41, 52, 55, 64, 77, 78, 100, 118, 177,
257, 287, 299, 304-307, see Chapters 6-8
  death matrix: 139
  estimated deaths: 130
  map: 133
  mass graves: 157
Somalia: 276
Some, Steven: 283
Sonderkommandos: 203, 207, 208, *224*, 304, 305
Soros, Georges: *265*
Soviet Union: *21*, 22, 27, 41, 47, 54, 87, 102, 175
Spain: *25*
Spanic, E.: 66
Specter, Michael: 23
Speer, Albert: 47
Sperling, Gene: 273
Spielberg, Steven: 263
Spitz, Robert: 112, 248
Stackelberg, Roderick: *56, 290*
Stäglich, Wilhelm: 36, 294
Stalingrad: 57
Stangl, Franz: 163, 306, 307
Stark, Hans: *204*
steam delousing: 28, 135, 144
steam gassings: 108, 143, 144
Stein, Joel: *265*
Stern, Kenneth S.: 34, 152, 162
Stevenson, Adlai: 270
Stone, Harlan F.: 49
Sturdy Colls, Caroline: 88, 171-173, 240
Stutthof: 37, 99, 108, 109
Sudan: *276*
Sulzberger, Arthur: 267
Summers, Larry: 273
survivors: see Holocaust, survivors
Susskind, David: 198
Switzerland: 16, *25*, 252, 278
Sydnor, Charles: 105
Syria: 276

— T —
Tacitus: 64
Tauber, Henryk: 203, 208, *224*, 249, 305
Theresienstadt: 74, 306
Time-Warner Corporation:

266, 267
Töben, Frederick: 26, 36
Transnistria: 74
Treblinka: 23, 37, 41, 52, 55, 63, 77, 78, 83, 85, 100, *103*, 111, 118, 200, 228, 257, 292, 299, 304, 307, see Chapters 6-8
  death matrix: 138
  estimated deaths: 130
  map: 134
  mass graves: 157
Tregenza, Michael: 130, 149, 166, 187
Tretikov, Lila: 268
Trunk, Achim: *118, 124, 152*
Turgel, Gena: 249
typhus: 28, 29, 61, *84*, 107, 108, 111, 135, 173, 199, 285, 295, 304

— U —
Ukeles, Jack: 66
Ukraine: 61, 89-93, 175
ultra-shortwave delousing: see microwave delousing
United Kingdom: 47, 70, 252, 264
United Nations: 15, 16, 45, 57, 269, 273-276
United States: 49, 259, 263, 281
  foreign aid to Israel: 17, 275
  Jewish influence in: 264-277
  Supreme Court: 49, 271
United States Holocaust Memorial Museum (USHMM): *21*, 22, 35, 56, 73, 76, 82-84, 88, 93, 94, 111, 113, 127, 130, 146, 148, 153, 167, 169, 178, 198, 279
Uruguay: 264

— V —
vacuum murder: 144
Vaivara: 99
van Pelt, Robert J.: 4, 34, 113, 130, 152, 161, 162, 167, *209*, 213-216, *222*, 225, 228, 237, 239, 261
Vergasungskeller: 202
Vernichtung: 101-103, 294, 295
VHF delousing: see microwave delousing
Viacom Corporation: 267
Vidal-Naquet, Pièrre: 24, 33, 250
Vistula river: 228
von Fürstenberg, Diane: 263
von Otter, Göran F.: 150
Vrba, Rudolf: 200, 203, 256, 304
Vrba-Wetzler Report: 201, 304

— W —
Wales, Jimmy: 268
Walt, Stephen: 268-276
Walters, Guy: *248*, 253, 254
Walton, family: *265*
Waltzer, Ken: 253
Wannsee Conference: 41, 54, 127, 128
War Refugee Board Report: see Vrba-Wetzler Report
Warsaw, camp: 99
Webb, Chris: 130
Weber, Mark: *24, 49*, 67
Weckert, Ingrid: 114, 119, 120
Weinstein, Bob: *265*
Weinstein, Harvey: *265*
Weiss, Shevach: 42
Weissmandel, Dov: 63
Weitzel, Robert: *273*
Weizmann, Chaim: 62, 63
Wellers, Georges: 198
Wennerstrum, Charles: 50
Wetzler, Alfred: 200, 203
Wewelsburg: 99
Weymouth, Katharine: 267
White House: 265, 270, 271, 274
Wiernik, Jankiel: 144, 145, 163, 307
Wiesel, Elie: 22, *48*, 203, 249-251, 272, 306
Wiesenthal, Simon: 248
Wilkomirski, Binjamin: 252
Willenberg, Samuel: 163
Williamson, Richard: 278
Wilson, Peter: 73
Wilson, Woodrow: 45
Winfrey, Oprah: 253
Winkle, Sally A.: *56, 290*
wire-mesh columns (for use with Zyklon): 208, 209, 214, 219, 305
Wise, Stephen: 60, 62
Wolfowitz, Paul: 274
World War I: 27, 45, 59, 61
Wright, Richard: 291-293
Wright, Robert A.: 57, 58
Wurmser, David: 274

— Y —
Yad Vashem: 34, 35, 44, 56, 65, 73, 76, 82, 88, 113, 130, 146-150, 153, 167, 169, 198, 203, 255, 272, 280
Yellen, Janet: 273
Yemen: 276

— Z —
Zabecki, Franciszek: 163
Ziereis, Franz: 51
Zimmerman, John C.: 31, 34, *105*, 111, 120, 124, 150-153, 163, 164, 174, 179, 201, 222, 230, 237, 239, 261, 304
Zionism: 17, 31, 32, 45, 57, 60, 72, *272*
Zucker, Jeff: *265*, 266
Zuckerberg, Mark: *265*, 268
Zuckerman, Harriet: *265*
Zuckerman, Mort: 267
Zündel, Ernst: 25, 256
Zyklon B: 23, 28, 42, 107-110, 116, 119, 135, 145, 147, 179-187, 190-192, 200, 201, 206, 207, 210-220, 237, 285, 295, 296, 304, 305

Free Samples at www.HolocaustHandbooks.com

HOLOCAUST HANDBOOKS

This ambitious, growing series addresses various aspects of the "Holocaust" of the WWII era. Most of them are based on decades of research from archives all over the world. They are heavily referenced. In contrast to most other works on this issue, the tomes of this series approach its topic with profound academic scrutiny and a critical attitude. Any Holocaust researcher ignoring this series will remain oblivious to some of the most important research in the field. These books are designed to both convince the common reader as well as academics. The following books have appeared so far, or are about to be released. Compare hardcopy and eBook prices at www.findbookprices.com.

SECTION ONE:
General Overviews of the Holocaust

The First Holocaust. The Surprising Origin of the Six-Million Figure. By Don Heddesheimer. This compact but substantive study documents propaganda spread prior to, during and after the FIRST World War that claimed East European Jewry was on the brink of annihilation. The magic number of suffering and dying Jews was 6 million back then as well. The book details how these Jewish fundraising operations in America raised vast sums in the name of feeding suffering Polish and Russian Jews but actually funneled much of the money to Zionist and Communist groups. 5th ed., 198 pages, b&w illustrations, bibliography, index. (#6)

Lectures on the Holocaust. Controversial Issues Cross Examined. By Germar Rudolf. This book first explains why "the Holocaust" is an important topic, and that it is well to keep an open mind about it. It then tells how many mainstream scholars expressed doubts and subsequently fell from grace. Next, the physical traces and documents about the various claimed crime scenes and murder weapons are discussed. After that, the reliability of witness testimony is examined. Finally, the author lobbies for a free exchange of ideas about this topic. This book gives the most-comprehensive and up-to-date overview of the critical research into the Holocaust. With its dialog style, it is pleasant to read, and it can even be used as an encyclopedic compendium. 3rd ed., 596 pages, b&w illustrations, bibliography, index.(#15)

Breaking the Spell. The Holocaust, Myth & Reality. By Nicholas Kollerstrom. In 1941, British Intelligence analysts cracked the German "Enigma" code. Hence, in 1942 and 1943, encrypted radio communications between German concentration camps and the Berlin headquarters were decrypted. The intercepted data

Pictured above are all of the scientific studies that comprise the series *Holocaust Handbooks* published thus far or are about to be released. More volumes and new editions are constantly in the works. Check www.HolocaustHandbooks.com for updates.

refutes the orthodox "Holocaust" narrative. It reveals that the Germans were desperate to reduce the death rate in their labor camps, which was caused by catastrophic typhus epidemics. Dr. Kollerstrom, a science historian, has taken these intercepts and a wide array of mostly unchallenged corroborating evidence to show that "witness statements" supporting the human gas chamber narrative clearly clash with the available scientific data. Kollerstrom concludes that the history of the Nazi "Holocaust" has been written by the victors with ulterior motives. It is distorted, exaggerated and largely wrong. With a foreword by Prof. Dr. James Fetzer. 4th ed., 261 pages, b&w ill., bibl., index. (#31)

Debating the Holocaust. A New Look at Both Sides. By Thomas Dalton. Mainstream historians insist that there cannot be, may not be a debate about the Holocaust. But ignoring it does not make this controversy go away. Traditional scholars admit that there was neither a budget, a plan, nor an order for the Holocaust; that the key camps have all but vanished, and so have any human remains; that material and unequivocal documentary evidence is absent; and that there are serious problems with survivor testimonies. Dalton juxtaposes the traditional Holocaust narrative with revisionist challenges and then analyzes the mainstream's responses to them. He reveals the weak-

ISSN 1529-7748 · All books are 6"x9" paperbacks unless otherwise stated. Discounts are available for the whole set.

HOLOCAUST HANDBOOKS — Free Samples at www.HolocaustHandbooks.com

nesses of both sides, while declaring revisionism the winner of the current state of the debate. 2nd ed., 332 pages, b&w illustrations, bibliography, index. (#32)

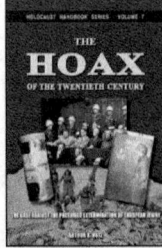

The Hoax of the Twentieth Century. The Case against the Presumed Extermination of European Jewry. By Arthur R. Butz. The first writer to analyze the entire Holocaust complex in a precise scientific manner. This book exhibits the overwhelming force of arguments accumulated by the mid-1970s. Butz's two main arguments are: 1. All major entities hostile to Germany must have known what was happening to the Jews under German authority. They acted during the war as if no mass slaughter was occurring. 2. All the evidence adduced to proof any mass slaughter has a dual interpretation, while only the innocuous one can be proven to be correct. This book continues to be a major historical reference work, frequently cited by prominent personalities. This edition has numerous supplements with new information gathered over the last 35 years. 4th ed., 524 pages, b&w illustrations, bibliography, index. (#7)

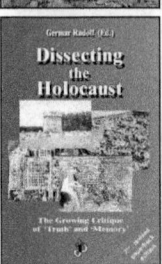

Dissecting the Holocaust. The Growing Critique of 'Truth' and 'Memory.' Edited by Germar Rudolf. *Dissecting the Holocaust* applies state-of-the-art scientific technique and classic methods of detection to investigate the alleged murder of millions of Jews by Germans during World War II. In 22 contributions—each of some 30 pages—the 17 authors dissect generally accepted paradigms of the "Holocaust." It reads as exciting as a crime novel: so many lies, forgeries and deceptions by politicians, historians and scientists are proven. This is the intellectual adventure of the 21st century. Be part of it! 2nd ed. 620 pages, b&w illustrations, bibliography, index. (#1)

The Dissolution of Eastern European Jewry. By Walter N. Sanning. Six Million Jews died in the Holocaust. Sanning did not take that number at face value, but thoroughly explored European population developments and shifts mainly caused by emigration as well as deportations and evacuations conducted by both Nazis and the Soviets, among other things. The book is based mainly on Jewish, Zionist and mainstream sources. It concludes that a sizeable share of the Jews found missing during local censuses after the Second World War, which were so far counted as "Holocaust victims," had either emigrated (mainly to Israel or the U.S.) or had been deported by Stalin to Siberian labor camps. 2nd ed., foreword by A.R. Butz, epilogue by Germar Rudolf containing important updates; 224 pages, b&w illustrations, bibliography (#29).

Air Photo Evidence: World War Two Photos of Alleged Mass Murder Sites Analyzed. By Germar Rudolf (editor). During World War Two both German and Allied reconnaissance aircraft took countless air photos of places of tactical and strategic interest in Europe. These photos are prime evidence for the investigation of the Holocaust. Air photos of locations like Auschwitz, Majdanek, Treblinka, Babi Yar etc. permit an insight into what did or did not happen there. The author has unearthed many pertinent photos and has thoroughly analyzed them. This book is full of air photo reproductions and schematic drawings explaining them. According to the author, these images refute many of the atrocity claims made by witnesses in connection with events in the German sphere of influence. 5th edition; with a contribution by Carlo Mattogno. 168 pages, 8.5"×11", b&w illustrations, bibliography, index (#27).

The Leuchter Reports: Critical Edition. By Fred Leuchter, Robert Faurisson and Germar Rudolf. Between 1988 and 1991, U.S. expert on execution technologies Fred Leuchter wrote four detailed reports addressing whether the Third Reich operated homicidal gas chambers. The first report on Auschwitz and Majdanek became world famous. Based on chemical analyses and various technical arguments, Leuchter concluded that the locations investigated "could not have then been, or now be, utilized or seriously considered to function as execution gas chambers." The second report deals with gas-chamber claims for the camps Dachau, Mauthausen and Hartheim, while the third reviews design criteria and operation procedures of execution gas chambers in the U.S. The fourth report reviews Pressac's 1989 tome *Auschwitz*. 4th ed., 252 pages, b&w illustrations. (#16)

The Giant with Feet of Clay: Raul Hilberg and His Standard Work on the "Holocaust." By Jürgen Graf. Raul Hilberg's major work *The Destruction of European Jewry* is an orthodox standard work on the Holocaust. But what evidence does Hilberg provide to back his thesis that there was a German plan to exterminate Jews, carried out mainly in gas chambers? Jürgen Graf applies the methods of critical analysis to Hilberg's evidence and examines the results in light of modern historiography. The results of Graf's critical analysis are devastating for Hilberg. 2nd, corrected edition, 139 pages, b&w illustrations, bibliography, index. (#3)

Jewish Emigration from the Third Reich.
By Ingrid Weckert. Current historical writings about the Third Reich claim state it was difficult for Jews to flee from Nazi persecution. The truth is that Jewish emigration was welcomed by the German authorities. Emigration was not some kind of wild flight, but rather a lawfully determined and regulated matter. Weckert's booklet elucidates the emigration process in law and policy. She shows that German and Jewish authorities worked closely together. Jews interested in emigrating received detailed advice and offers of help from both sides. 2nd ed., 130 pages, index. (#12)

Inside the Gas Chambers: The Extermination of Mainstream Holocaust Historiography.
By Carlo Mattogno. Neither increased media propaganda or political pressure nor judicial persecution can stifle revisionism. Hence, in early 2011, the Holocaust Orthodoxy published a 400 pp. book (in German) claiming to refute "revisionist propaganda," trying again to prove "once and for all" that there were homicidal gas chambers at the camps of Dachau, Natzweiler, Sachsenhausen, Mauthausen, Ravensbrück, Neuengamme, Stutthof… you name them. Mattogno shows with his detailed analysis of this work of propaganda that mainstream Holocaust hagiography is beating around the bush rather than addressing revisionist research results. He exposes their myths, distortions and lies. 2nd ed., 280 pages, b&w illustrations, bibliography, index. (#25)

SECTION TWO:
Specific non-Auschwitz Studies

Treblinka: Extermination Camp or Transit Camp?
By Carlo Mattogno and Jürgen Graf. It is alleged that at Treblinka in East Poland between 700,000 and 3,000,000 persons were murdered in 1942 and 1943. The weapons used were said to have been stationary and/or mobile gas chambers, fast-acting or slow-acting poison gas, unslaked lime, superheated steam, electricity, diesel exhaust fumes etc. Holocaust historians alleged that bodies were piled as high as multi-storied buildings and burned without a trace, using little or no fuel at all. Graf and Mattogno have now analyzed the origins, logic and technical feasibility of the official version of Treblinka. On the basis of numerous documents they reveal Treblinka's true identity as a mere transit camp. 2nd ed., 372 pages, b&w illustrations, bibliography, index. (#8)

Belzec in Propaganda, Testimonies, Archeological Research and History.
By Carlo Mattogno. Witnesses report that between 600,000 and 3 million Jews were murdered in the Belzec camp, located in Poland. Various murder weapons are claimed to have been used: diesel gas; unslaked lime in trains; high voltage; vacuum chambers; etc. The corpses were incinerated on huge pyres without leaving a trace. For those who know the stories about Treblinka this sounds familiar. Thus the author has restricted this study to the aspects which are new compared to Treblinka. In contrast to Treblinka, forensic drillings and excavations were performed at Belzec, the results of which are critically reviewed. 142 pages, b&w illustrations, bibliography, index. (#9)

Sobibor: Holocaust Propaganda and Reality.
By Jürgen Graf, Thomas Kues and Carlo Mattogno. Between 25,000 and 2 million Jews are said to have been killed in gas chambers in the Sobibór camp in Poland. The corpses were allegedly buried in mass graves and later incinerated on pyres. This book investigates these claims and shows that they are based on the selective use of contradictory eyewitness testimony. Archeological surveys of the camp in 2000-2001 are analyzed, with fatal results for the extermination camp hypothesis. The book also documents the general National Socialist policy toward Jews, which never included a genocidal "final solution." 442 pages, b&w illustrations, bibliography, index. (#19)

The "Extermination Camps" of "Aktion Reinhardt".
By Jürgen Graf, Thomas Kues and Carlo Mattogno. In late 2011, several members of the exterminationist *Holocaust Controversies* blog posted a study online which claims to refute three of our authors' monographs on the camps Belzec, Sobibor and Treblinka (see previous three entries). This tome is their point-by-point response, which makes "mincemeat" out of the bloggers' attempt at refutation. Caution: The two volumes of this work are an intellectual overkill for most people. They are recommended only for collectors, connoisseurs and professionals. These two books require familiarity with the above-mentioned books, of which they are a comprehensive update and expansion. 2nd ed., two volumes, total of 1396 pages, illustrations, bibliography. (#28)

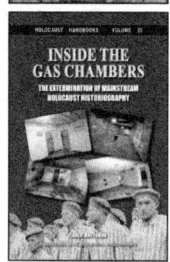

HOLOCAUST HANDBOOKS • *Free Samples* at www.HolocaustHandbooks.com

Chelmno: A Camp in History & Propaganda. By Carlo Mattogno. At Chelmno, huge masses of Jewish prisoners are said to have been rounded up and mercilessly gassed in "gas vans" or shot (claims vary from 10,000 to 1.3 million victims). Mattogno has examined reams of wartime documents and conducted on-site investigations at the Chelmno camp site and the neighboring countryside. The results challenge the conventional wisdom about Chelmno. Mattogno covers the subject from every angle, undermining the orthodox claims about the camp with an overwhelmingly effective body of evidence. Eyewitness statements, gas wagons as extermination weapons, forensics reports, coroners' reports, archaeological excavations, the crematoria, building plans, official U.S. reports, German documents, evacuation efforts—all come under Mattogno's scrutiny. Here are the uncensored facts about Chelmno, not the propaganda. 2nd ed., 188 pages, indexed, illustrated, bibliography. (#23)

The Gas Vans: A Critical Investigation. (A perfect companion to the Chelmno book.) By Santiago Alvarez and Pierre Marais. It is alleged that the Nazis used mobile gas chambers to exterminate 700,000 people. Up until 2011, no thorough monograph had appeared on the topic. Santiago Alvarez has remedied the situation. Are witness statements reliable? Are documents genuine? Where are the murder weapons? Could they have operated as claimed? Where are the corpses? In order to get to the truth of the matter, Alvarez has scrutinized all known wartime documents and photos about this topic; he has analyzed a huge amount of witness statements as published in the literature and as presented in more than 30 trials held over the decades in Germany, Poland and Israel; and he has examined the claims made in the pertinent mainstream literature. The result of his research is mind-boggling. Note: This book and Mattogno's book on Chelmno were edited in parallel to make sure they are consistent and not repetitive. 398 pages, b&w illustrations, bibliography, index. (#26)

The Einsatzgruppen in the Occupied Eastern Territories: Genesis, Responsibilities and Activities. By C. Mattogno. Before invading the Soviet Union, the German authorities set up special units meant to secure the area behind the German front. Orthodox historians claim that these unites called *Einsatzgruppen* primarily engaged in rounding up and mass-murdering Jews. This study tries to shed a critical light into this topic by reviewing all the pertinent sources as well as material traces. Ca. 850 pp., b&w illustrations, bibliography, index. (Scheduled for late 2018; #39)

Concentration Camp Majdanek. A Historical and Technical Study. By Carlo Mattogno and Jürgen Graf. At war's end, the Soviets claimed that up to two million Jews were murdered at the Majdanek Camp in seven gas chambers. Over the decades, however, the Majdanek Museum reduced the death toll three times to currently 78,000, and admitted that there were "only" two gas chambers. By exhaustively researching primary sources, the authors expertly dissect and repudiate the myth of homicidal gas chambers at that camp. They also critically investigated the legend of mass executions of Jews in tank trenches and prove them groundless. Again they have produced a standard work of methodical investigation which authentic historiography cannot ignore. 3rd ed., 358 pages, b&w illustrations, bibliography, index. (#5)

Concentration Camp Stutthof and Its Function in National Socialist Jewish Policy. By Carlo Mattogno and Jürgen Graf. Orthodox historians claim that the Stutthof Camp served as a "makeshift" extermination camp in 1944. Based mainly on archival resources, this study thoroughly debunks this view and shows that Stutthof was in fact a center for the organization of German forced labor toward the end of World War II. 4th ed., 170 pages, b&w illustrations, bibliography, index. (#4)

SECTION THREE:
Auschwitz Studies

The Making of the Auschwitz Myth: Auschwitz in British Intercepts, Polish Underground Reports and Postwar Testimonies (1941-1947). By Carlo Mattogno. Using messages sent by the Polish underground to London, SS radio messages send to and from Auschwitz that were intercepted and decrypted by the British, and a plethora of witness statements made during the war and in the immediate postwar period, the author shows how exactly the myth of mass murder in Auschwitz gas chambers was created, and how it was turned subsequently into "history" by intellectually corrupt scholars who cherry-picked claims that fit into their agenda and ignored or actively covered up literally thousands of lies of "witnesses" to make their narrative look credible. Ca. 300

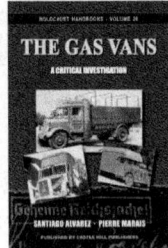

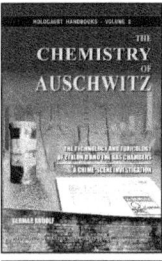

pp., b&w illustrations, bibliography, index. (Scheduled for mid-2018; #41)

The Real Case of Auschwitz: Robert van Pelt's Evidence from the Irving Trial Critically Reviewed. By Carlo Mattogno. Prof. Robert van Pelt is considered one of the best mainstream experts on Auschwitz. He became famous when appearing as an expert during the London libel trial of David Irving against Deborah Lipstadt. From it resulted a book titled *The Case for Auschwitz*, in which van Pelt laid out his case for the existence of homicidal gas chambers at that camp. This book is a scholarly response to Prof. van Pelt—and Jean-Claude Pressac, upon whose books van Pelt's study is largely based. Mattogno lists all the evidence van Pelt adduces, and shows one by one that van Pelt misrepresented and misinterpreted each single one of them. This is a book of prime political and scholarly importance to those looking for the truth about Auschwitz. 2nd ed., 758 pages, b&w illustrations, glossary, bibliography, index. (#22)

Auschwitz: Plain Facts: A Response to Jean-Claude Pressac. Edited by Germar Rudolf, with contributions by Serge Thion, Robert Faurisson and Carlo Mattogno. French pharmacist Jean-Claude Pressac tried to refute revisionist findings with the "technical" method. For this he was praised by the mainstream, and they proclaimed victory over the "revisionists." In his book, Pressac's works and claims are shown to be unscientific in nature, as he never substantiate what he claims, and historically false, because he systematically misrepresents, misinterprets and misunderstands German wartime documents. 2nd ed., 226 pages, b&w illustrations, glossary bibliography, index. (#14)

The Chemistry of Auschwitz: The Technology and Toxicology of Zyklon B and the Gas Chambers – A Crime Scene Investigation. By Germar Rudolf. While respecting the victims, whether of foul play or of circumstance, this study nonetheless tries to conduct Auschwitz research on the basis of the forensic sciences, where material traces of the crime and their interpretation reign supreme. Although it is generally agreed that no autopsy of any victim has ever been performed, most of the claimed crime scenes – the chemical slaughterhouses called gas chambers – are still accessible to forensic examination to a greater or lesser degree. This book addresses questions such as: How did these gas chambers of Auschwitz look like? How did they operate? What were they used for? In addition, the infamous Zyklon B can also be examined. What exactly hides behind this ominous name? How does it kill? And what effect has it on masonry? Does it leave traces that can be found still today? By thoroughly examining these issues, the horror of Auschwitz is meticulously dissected, and thus, for the first time, it really becomes comprehensible. 3rd ed., 442 pages, more than 120 color and almost 100 b&w illustrations, bibliography, index. (#2)

Auschwitz Lies: Legends, Lies and Prejudices on the Holocaust. By C. Mattogno and G. Rudolf. The fallacious research and alleged "refutation" of Revisionist scholars by French biochemist G. Wellers (attacking Leuchter's famous report), Polish chemist Dr. J. Markiewicz and U.S. chemist Dr. Richard Green (taking on Rudolf's chemical research), Dr. John Zimmerman (tackling Mattogno on cremation issues), Michael Shermer and Alex Grobman (trying to prove it all), as well as researchers Keren, McCarthy and Mazal (how turned cracks into architectural features), are exposed for what they are: blatant and easily exposed political lies created to ostracize dissident historians. 3rd ed., 398 pages, b&w illustrations, index. (#18)

Auschwitz: The Central Construction Office. By C. Mattogno. Based upon mostly unpublished German wartime documents, this study describes the history, organization, tasks and procedures of the one office which was responsible for the planning and construction of the Auschwitz camp complex, including the crematories which are said to have contained the "gas chambers." 2nd ed., 188 pages, b&w illustrations, glossary, index. (#13)

Garrison and Headquarters Orders of the Auschwitz Camp. By C. Mattogno. A large number of all the orders ever issued by the various commanders of the infamous Auschwitz camp have been preserved. They reveal the true nature of the camp with all its daily events. There is not a trace in these orders pointing at anything sinister going on in this camp. Quite to the contrary, many orders are in clear and insurmountable contradiction to claims that prisoners were mass murdered. This is a selection of the most pertinent of these orders together with comments putting them into their proper historical context. (Scheduled for late 2018; #34)

HOLOCAUST HANDBOOKS · *Free Samples* at www.HolocaustHandbooks.com

Special Treatment in Auschwitz: Origin and Meaning of a Term. By C. Mattogno. When appearing in German wartime documents, terms like "special treatment," "special action," and others have been interpreted as code words for mass murder. But that is not always true. This study focuses on documents about Auschwitz, showing that, while "special" had many different meanings, not a single one meant "execution." Hence the practice of deciphering an alleged "code language" by assigning homicidal meaning to harmless documents – a key component of mainstream historiography – is untenable. 2nd ed., 166 pages, b&w illustrations, bibliography, index. (#10)

Healthcare at Auschwitz. By C. Mattogno. In extension of the above study on *Special Treatment in Auschwitz*, this study proves the extent to which the German authorities at Auschwitz tried to provide appropriate health care for the inmates. In the first part of this book, the author analyzes the inmates' living conditions as well as the various sanitary and medical measures implemented to maintain or restore the inmates' health. The second part explores what happened in particular to those inmates registered at Auschwitz who were "selected" or subject to "special treatment" while disabled or sick. The comprehensive documentation presented shows clearly that everything was tried to cure these inmates, especially under the aegis of Garrison Physician Dr. Wirths. The last part of this book is dedicated to the remarkable personality of Dr. Wirths, the Auschwitz garrison physician since 1942. His reality refutes the current stereotype of SS officers. 398 pages, b&w illustrations, bibliography, index. (#33)

Debunking the Bunkers of Auschwitz: Black Propaganda vs. History. By Carlo Mattogno. The bunkers at Auschwitz, two former farmhouses just outside the camp's perimeter, are claimed to have been the first homicidal gas chambers at Auschwitz specifically equipped for this purpose. With the help of original German wartime files as well as revealing air photos taken by Allied reconnaissance aircraft in 1944, this study shows that these homicidal "bunkers" never existed, how the rumors about them evolved as black propaganda created by resistance groups in the camp, and how this propaganda was transformed into a false reality. 2nd ed., 292 pages, b&w illustrations, bibliography, index. (#11)

Auschwitz: The First Gassing. Rumor and Reality. By C. Mattogno. The first gassing in Auschwitz is claimed to have occurred on Sept. 3, 1941, in a basement room. The accounts reporting it are the archetypes for all later gassing accounts. This study analyzes all available sources about this alleged event. It shows that these sources contradict each other in location, date, victims etc, rendering it impossible to extract a consistent story. Original wartime documents inflict a final blow to this legend and prove without a shadow of a doubt that this legendary event never happened. 3rd ed., 190 pages, b&w illustrations, bibliography, index. (#20)

Auschwitz: Crematorium I and the Alleged Homicidal Gassings. By C. Mattogno. The morgue of Crematorium I in Auschwitz is said to be the first homicidal gas chamber there. This study investigates all statements by witnesses and analyzes hundreds of wartime documents to accurately write a history of that building. Where witnesses speak of gassings, they are either very vague or, if specific, contradict one another and are refuted by documented and material facts. The author also exposes the fraudulent attempts of mainstream historians to convert the witnesses' black propaganda into "truth" by means of selective quotes, omissions, and distortions. Mattogno proves that this building's morgue was never a homicidal gas chamber, nor could it have worked as such. 2nd ed., 152 pages, b&w illustrations, bibliography, index. (#21)

Auschwitz: Open Air Incinerations. By C. Mattogno. In spring and summer of 1944, 400,000 Hungarian Jews were deported to Auschwitz and allegedly murdered there in gas chambers. The Auschwitz crematoria are said to have been unable to cope with so many corpses. Therefore, every single day thousands of corpses are claimed to have been incinerated on huge pyres lit in deep trenches. The sky over Auschwitz was covered in thick smoke. This is what some witnesses want us to believe. This book examines the many testimonies regarding these incinerations and establishes whether these claims were even possible. Using air photos, physical evidence and wartime documents, the author shows that these claims are fiction. A new Appendix contains 3 papers on groundwater levels and cattle mass burnings. 2nd ed., 202 pages, b&w illustrations, bibliography, index. (#17)

HOLOCAUST HANDBOOKS

Free Samples at www.HolocaustHandbooks.com

The Cremation Furnaces of Auschwitz. By Carlo Mattogno & Franco Deana. An exhaustive study of the history and technology of cremation in general and of the cremation furnaces of Auschwitz in particular. On a vast base of technical literature, extant wartime documents and material traces, the authors can establish the true nature and capacity of the Auschwitz cremation furnaces. They show that these devices were inferior make-shift versions of what was usually produced, and that their capacity to cremate corpses was lower than normal, too. 3 vols., 1198 pages, b&w and color illustrations (vols 2 & 3), bibliography, index, glossary. (#24)

Curated Lies: The Auschwitz Museum's Misrepresentations, Distortions and Deceptions. By Carlo Mattogno. Revisionist research results have put the Polish Auschwitz Museum under pressure to answer this challenge. They've answered. This book analyzes their answer and reveals the appallingly mendacious attitude of the Auschwitz Museum authorities when presenting documents from their archives. 248 pages, b&w illustrations, bibliography, index. (#38)

Deliveries of Coke, Wood and Zyklon B to Auschwitz: Neither Proof Nor Trace for the Holocaust. By Carlo Mattogno. Researchers from the Auschwitz Museum tried to prove the reality of mass extermination by pointing to documents about deliveries of wood and coke as well as Zyklon B to the Auschwitz Camp. If put into the actual historical and technical context, however, these documents prove the exact opposite of what these orthodox researchers claim. Ca. 250 pages, b&w illustrations, bibliography, index. (Scheduled for early 2019; #40)

SECTION FOUR:
Witness Critique

Holocaust High Priest: Elie Wiesel, Night, the Memory Cult, and the Rise of Revisionism. By Warren B. Routledge. The first unauthorized biography of Wiesel exposes both his personal deceits and the whole myth of "the six million." It shows how Zionist control has allowed Wiesel and his fellow extremists to force leaders of many nations, the U.N. and even popes to genuflect before Wiesel as symbolic acts of subordination to World Jewry, while at the same time forcing school children to submit to Holocaust brainwashing. 468 pages, b&w illust., bibliography, index. (#30)

Auschwitz: Confessions and Testimonies. By Jürgen Graf. The traditional narrative of what transpired at the infamous Auschwitz Camp during WWII rests almost exclusively on witness testimony. This study critically scrutinizes the 40 most important of them by checking them for internal coherence, and by comparing them with one another as well as with other evidence such as wartime documents, air photos, forensic research results, and material traces. The result is devastating for the traditional narrative. (Scheduled for late-2018; #36)

Commandant of Auschwitz: Rudolf Höss, His Torture and His Forced Confessions. By Carlo Mattogno & Rudolf Höss. From 1940 to 1943, Rudolf Höss was the commandant of the infamous Auschwitz Camp. After the war, he was captured by the British. In the following 13 months until his execution, he made 85 depositions of various kinds in which he confessed his involvement in the "Holocaust." This study first reveals how the British tortured him to extract various "confessions." Next, all of Höss's depositions are analyzed by checking his claims for internal consistency and comparing them with established historical facts. The results are eye-opening... 402 pages, b&w illust., bibliography, index. (#35)

An Auschwitz Doctor's Eyewitness Account: The Tall Tales of Dr. Mengele's Assistant Analyzed. By Miklos Nyiszli & Carlo Mattogno. Nyiszli, a Hungarian physician, ended up at Auschwitz in 1944 as Dr. Mengele's assistant. After the war he wrote a book and several other writings describing what he claimed to have experienced. To this day some traditional historians take his accounts seriously, while others reject them as grotesque lies and exaggerations. This study presents and analyzes Nyiszli's writings and skillfully separates truth from fabulous fabrication. 484 pages, b&w illust., bibliography, index. (#37)

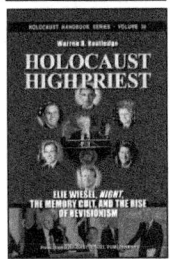

FOR CURRENT PRICES AND AVAILABILITY SEE BOOK FINDER SITES SUCH AS BOOKFINDER.COM, ADDALL.COM, BOOKFINDER4U.COM OR FINDBOOKPRICES.COM; LEARN MORE AT WWW.HOLOCAUSTHANDBOOKS.COM
PUBLISHED BY CASTLE HILL PUBLISHERS, PO BOX 243, UCKFIELD, TN22 9AW, UK

BOOKS BY AND FROM CASTLE HILL PUBLISHERS

Below please find some of the books published or distributed by Castle Hill Publishers in the United Kingdom. For our current and complete range of products visit our web store at shop.codoh.com.

Thomas Dalton, *The Holocaust: An Introduction*

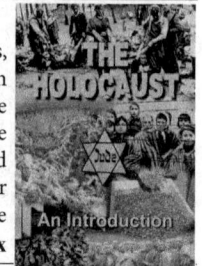

The Holocaust was perhaps the greatest crime of the 20th century. Six million Jews, we are told, died by gassing, shooting, and deprivation. But: Where did the six million figure come from? How, exactly, did the gas chambers work? Why do we have so little physical evidence from major death camps? Why haven't we found even a fraction of the six million bodies, or their ashes? Why has there been so much media suppression and governmental censorship on this topic? In a sense, the Holocaust is the greatest murder mystery in history. It is a topic of greatest importance for the present day. Let's explore the evidence, and see where it leads.

128 pp. pb, 5"×8", ill., bibl., index

Carlo Mattogno, *Auschwitz: A Three-Quarter Century of Propaganda:* Origins, Development and Decline of the "Gas Chamber" Propaganda Lie

During the war, wild rumors were circulating about Auschwitz: that the Germans were testing new war gases; that inmates were murdered in electrocution chambers, with gas showers or pneumatic hammer systems; that living people were sent on conveyor belts directly into cremation furnaces; that oils, grease and soap were made of the mass-murder victims. Nothing of it was true. When the Soviets captured Auschwitz in early 1945, they reported that 4 million inmates were killed on electrocution conveyor belts discharging their load directly into furnaces. That wasn't true either. After the war, "witnesses" and "experts" repeated these things and added more fantasies: mass murder with gas bombs, gas chambers made of canvas; carts driving living people into furnaces; that the crematoria of Auschwitz could have cremated 400 million victims... Again, none of it was true. This book gives an overview of the many rumors, myths and lies about Auschwitz which mainstream historians today reject as untrue. It then explains by which ridiculous methods some claims about Auschwitz were accepted as true and turned into "history," although they are just as untrue.

125 pp. pb, 5"×8", ill., bibl., index, b&w ill.

Wilhelm Stäglich, *Auschwitz: A Judge Looks at the Evidence*

Auschwitz is the epicenter of the Holocaust, where more people are said to have been murdered than anywhere else. At this detention camp the industrialized Nazi mass murder is said to have reached its demonic pinnacle. This narrative is based on a wide range of evidence, the most important of which was presented during two trials: the International Military Tribunal of 1945/46, and the German Auschwitz Trial of 1963-1965 in Frankfurt.

The late Wilhelm Stäglich, until the mid-1970s a German judge, has so far been the only *legal* expert to critically analyze this evidence. His research reveals the incredibly scandalous way in which the Allied victors and later the German judicial authorities bent and broke the law in order to come to politically foregone conclusions. Stäglich also exposes the shockingly superficial way in which historians are dealing with the many incongruities and discrepancies of the historical record.

3rd edition 2015, 422 pp., 6"×9", pb, b&w ill.

Gerard Menuhin: *Tell the Truth & Shame the Devil*

A prominent Jew from a famous family says the "Holocaust" is a wartime propaganda myth which has turned into an extortion racket. Far from bearing the sole guilt for starting WWII as alleged at Nuremberg (for which many of the surviving German leaders were hanged) Germany is mostly innocent in this respect and made numerous attempts to avoid and later to end the confrontation. During the 1930s Germany was confronted by a powerful Jewish-dominated world plutocracy out to destroy it... Yes, a prominent Jew says all this. Accept it or reject it, but be sure to read it and judge for yourself! The author is the son of the great American-born violinist Yehudi Menuhin, who, though from a long line of rabbinical ancestors, fiercely criticized the foreign policy of the state of Israel and its repression of the Palestinians in the Holy Land.

4th edition 2017, 432 pp. pb, 6"×9", b&w ill.

For prices and availability see www.shop.codoh.com or write to: CHP, PO Box 243, Uckfield, TN22 9AW, UK

Germar Rudolf, *Bungled: "Denying the Holocaust"* How Deborah Lipstadt Botched Her Attempt to Demonstrate the Growing Assault on Truth and Memory

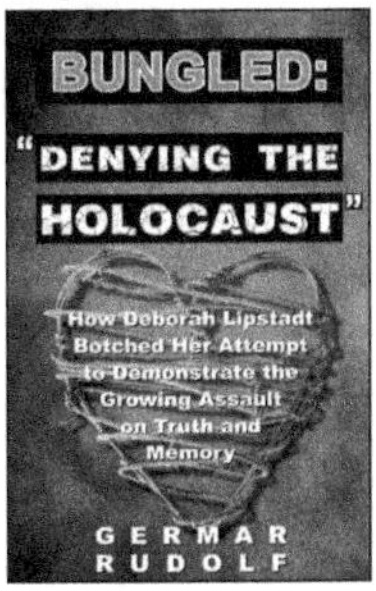

With her book *Denying the Holocaust*, Deborah Lipstadt tried to show the flawed methods and extremist motives of "Holocaust deniers." This book demonstrates that Dr. Lipstadt clearly has neither understood the principles of science and scholarship, nor has she any clue about the historical topics she is writing about. She misquotes, mistranslates, misrepresents, misinterprets, and makes a plethora of wild claims without backing them up with anything. Rather than dealing thoroughly with factual arguments, Lipstadt's book is full of *ad hominem* attacks on her opponents. It is an exercise in anti-intellectual pseudo-scientific arguments, an exhibition of ideological radicalism that rejects anything which contradicts its preset conclusions. F for FAIL

2nd ed., 224 pp., 5"×8", pb, bibl., index, b&w ill.

Carolus Magnus, *Bungled: "Denying History"*. How Michael Shermer and Alex Grobman Botched Their Attempt to Refute Those Who Say the Holocaust Never Happened

Skeptic Magazine editor Michael Shermer and Alex Grobman from the Simon Wiesenthal Center wrote a book in 2000 which they claim is "a thorough and thoughtful answer to all the claims of the Holocaust deniers." In 2009, a new "updated" edition appeared with the same ambitious goal. In the meantime, revisionists had published some 10,000 pages of archival and forensic research results. Would their updated edition indeed answer all the revisionist claims? In fact, Shermer and Grobman completely ignored the vast amount of recent scholarly studies and piled up a heap of falsifications, contortions, omissions, and fallacious interpretations of the evidence. Finally, what the authors claim to have demolished is not revisionism but a ridiculous parody of it. They ignored the known unreliability of their cherry-picked selection of evidence, utilizing unverified and incestuous sources, and obscuring the massive body of research and all the evidence that dooms their project to failure. F for FAIL

162 pp., 5"×8", pb, bibl., index, b&w ill.

Carolus Magnus, *Bungled: "Debunking Holocaust Denial Theories"*. How James and Lance Morcan Botched Their Attempt to Affirm the Historicity of the Nazi Genocide

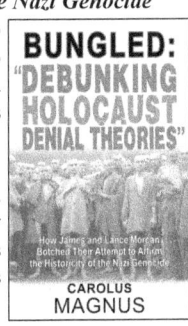

The novelists and movie-makers James and Lance Morcan have produced a book "to end [Holocaust] denial once and for all." To do this, "no stone was left unturned" to verify historical assertions by presenting "a wide array of sources" meant "to shut down the debate deniers wish to create. One by one, the various arguments Holocaust deniers use to try to discredit wartime records are carefully scrutinized and then systematically disproven." It's a lie. First, the Morcans completely ignored the vast amount of recent scholarly studies published by revisionists; they didn't even identify them. Instead, they engaged in shadowboxing, creating some imaginary, bogus "revisionist" scarecrow which they then tore to pieces. In addition, their knowledge even of their own side's source material was dismal, and the way they backed up their misleading or false claims was pitifully inadequate. F for FAIL.

144 pp., 5"×8", pb, bibl., index, b&w ill.

Joachim Hoffmann, *Stalin's War of Extermination 1941-1945*

A German government historian documents Stalin's murderous war against the German army and the German people. Based on the author's lifelong study of German and Russian military records, this book reveals the Red Army's grisly record of atrocities against soldiers and civilians, as ordered by Stalin. Since the 1920s, Stalin planned to invade Western Europe to initiate the "World Revolution." He prepared an attack which was unparalleled in history. The Germans noticed Stalin's aggressive intentions, but they underestimated the strength of the Red Army. What unfolded was the most-cruel war in history. This book shows how Stalin and his Bolshevik henchman used unimaginable violence and atrocities to break any resistance in the Red Army and to force their unwilling soldiers to fight against the Germans. The book explains how Soviet propagandists incited their soldiers to unlimited hatred against everything German, and he gives the reader a short but extremely unpleasant glimpse into what happened when these Soviet soldiers finally reached German soil in 1945: A gigantic wave of looting, arson, rape, torture, and mass murder...

428 pp. pb, 6"×9", bibl., index, b&w ill.

For prices and availability see www.shop.codoh.com or write to: CHP, PO Box 243, Uckfield, TN22 9AW, UK

Udo Walendy, *Who Started World War II:* Truth for a War-Torn World

For seven decades, mainstream historians have insisted that Germany was the main, if not the sole culprit for unleashing World War II in Europe. In the present book this myth is refuted. There is available to the public today a great number of documents on the foreign policies of the Great Powers before September 1939 as well as a wealth of literature in the form of memoirs of the persons directly involved in the decisions that led to the outbreak of World War II. Together, they made possible Walendy's present mosaic-like reconstruction of the events before the outbreak of the war in 1939. This book has been published only after an intensive study of sources, taking the greatest care to minimize speculation and inference. The present edition has been translated completely anew from the German original and has been slightly revised.

500 pp. pb, 6"×9", index, bibl., b&w ill.

Germar Rudolf: *Resistance is Obligatory!*

In 2005 Rudolf, a peaceful dissident and publisher of revisionist literature, was kidnapped by the U.S. government and deported to Germany. There the local lackey regime staged a show trial against him for his historical writings. Rudolf was not permitted to defend his historical opinions, as the German penal law prohibits this. Yet he defended himself anyway: 7 days long Rudolf held a speech in the court room, during which he proved systematically that only the revisionists are scholarly in their attitude, whereas the Holocaust orthodoxy is merely pseudo-scientific. He then explained in detail why it is everyone's obligation to resist, without violence, a government which throws peaceful dissident into dungeons. When Rudolf tried to publish his public defence speech as a book from his prison cell, the public prosecutor initiated a new criminal investigation against him. After his probation time ended in 2011, he dared publish this speech anyway...

2nd ed. 2016, 378 pp., 6"×9", pb, b&w ill.

Germar Rudolf, *Hunting Germar Rudolf:* Essays on a Modern-Day Witch Hunt

German-born revisionist activist, author and publisher Germar Rudolf describes which events made him convert from a Holocaust believer to a Holocaust skeptic, quickly rising to a leading personality within the revisionist movement. This in turn unleashed a tsunami of persecution against him: loss of his job, denied PhD exam, destruction of his family, driven into exile, slandered by the mass media, literally hunted, caught, put on a show trial where filing motions to introduce evidence is illegal under the threat of further proseuction, and finally locked up in prison for years for nothing else than his peaceful yet controversial scholarly writings. In several essays, Rudolf takes the reader on a journey through an absurd world of government and societal persecution which most of us could never even fathom actually exists....

304 pp., 6"×9", pb, bibl., index, b&w ill.

Germar Rudolf, *The Day Amazon Murdered History*

Amazon is the world's biggest book retailer. They dominate the U.S. and several foreign markets. Pursuant to the 1998 declaration of Amazon's founder Jeff Bezos to offer "the good, the bad and the ugly," customers once could buy every book that was in print and was legal to sell. However, in early 2017, a series of anonymous bomb threats against Jewish community centers occurred in the U.S., fueling a campaign by Jewish groups to coax Amazon into banning revisionist writings, false portraing them as anti-Semitic. On March 6, 2017, Amazon caved in and banned more than 100 books with dissenting viewpoints on the Holocaust. In April 2017, an Israeli Jew was arrested for having placed the fake bomb threats, a paid "service" he had offered for years. But that did not change Amazon's mind. Its stores remain closed for history books Jewish lobby groups disapprove of. This book accompanies the documentary of the same title. Both reveal how revisionist publications had become so powerfully convincing that the powers that be resorted to what looks like a dirty false-flag operation in order to get these books banned from Amazon...

128 pp. pb, 5"×8", bibl., b&w ill.

FOR CURRENT PRICES AND AVAILABILITY SEE BOOK FINDER SITES SUCH AS WWW.BOOKFINDER.COM, WWW.ADDALL.COM, WWW.BOOKFINDER4U.COM OR WWW.FINDBOOKPRICES.COM; LEARN MORE AT SHOP.CODOH.COM. PUBLISHED BY CASTLE HILL PUBLISHERS, PO BOX 243, UCKFIELD, TN22 9AW, UK